ALEXANDER HAMILTON

>>>-<<<

Jacob Ernest Cooke

Charles Scribner's Sons

New York

To
Jake

->>>->>>->>>-<<<-<<<-<<<

Copyright © 1982 Jacob Ernest Cooke

Library of Congress Cataloging in Publication Data

Cooke, Jacob Ernest, 1924–
Alexander Hamilton.

Includes bibliographical references and index.
1. Hamilton, Alexander, 1757–1804.   2. United States—
Politics and government—1783–1809.   3. Statesmen—
United States—Biography.   I. Title.
E302.6.H2C73   1982   973.4'092'4[B]   81–18223
ISBN 0–684–17344–1   AACR2

1 3 5 7 9 11 13 15 17 19 F/C 20 18 16 14 12 10 8 6 4 2

Printed in the United States of America.

Contents

Preface

Why another biography of Alexander Hamilton? Over the past 175 years his life has been chronicled time and again, but never more frequently than during the decades since World War II. In addition to the biographies that have appeared, the definitive edition of his papers in twenty-six volumes, begun in the 1950s, was completed in 1979. My own scholarly interest in Hamilton stems from participation in that project for well over a decade.

During that time and subsequently I published a good number of studies of Hamilton and the Federalist era generally, principally in the form of articles and reviews. In these, I attempted to reinterpret significant phases of the life of the man or of his time. From the outset, I hoped someday to incorporate these otherwise random pieces into a book-length reappraisal of this puzzling man, aptly described by John C. Miller, one of Hamilton's most perceptive biographers, as a "portrait in paradox." The answer to my question about the need for another biography of Hamilton is thus: Because I believe that I have something new to say.

It is not that I have unearthed hitherto unknown "facts." (In view of the thoroughness of the *Hamilton Papers,* I do not think this is likely.) It is rather that I have tried to look at familiar episodes in a different way. Whether I have succeeded, the reader must judge.

This consideration aside, I have long believed that the essential flaw of most Hamilton biographies is their failure to explain the personality of this enigmatical statesman. Biography after biography describes the seemingly contradictory or curious aspects of Hamilton's character, personal behavior, and official life. But these are usually presented as discrete episodes in narratives that pardonably enough focus on the public career and writings that earned him enduring repute as this nation's premier financier and one of America's most influential political thinkers. I also have depicted his contributions to viable nationhood and analyzed his political thought, but I have treated these as inseparable from his personal and private life.

In so doing, I have searched for the behavorial patterns that lend coherence and meaning to a life that, viewed superficially, appears to have been disjointed and riddled with contradiction. In other words, instead of treating different phases and features of Hamilton's life and career as events to be interpreted individually and in isolation, I have looked for threads that tie together and give meaning to his life as a whole. My conclusion is that behavior that is often described as aberrational or inexplicable was not atypical but typical, pieces of a puzzle that, when put together, display a clear personality profile. (Revealing examples of his presumably "singular" behavior are his well-known quarrel with General George Washington in 1782, his political warfare with Thomas Jefferson, the notorious Reynolds affair, his slashing assault on President John Adams in 1800, and his actions leading to the fatal duel with Aaron Burr in 1804.)

Any such attempt to understand Hamilton must, I am convinced, be based not on common sense or intuition (of which each writer necessarily has his own brand) but on some theoretical model of human development. In biographical writing, the only such model available is provided by psychoanalytic concepts (or dogma). My own approach is eclectic, although I have relied most heavily on Freudian theory and on the intellectually most impressive neo-Freudian of our day, Erik H. Erikson, whose distinguished psychoanalytically grounded biographies have set standards that no historian has as yet matched. However, this book on Hamilton is not intended as an exemplar of psychobiography. I merely allude to the issue here in order to indicate the concepts that implicitly inspired sections of the biography that follows. The reader who is unconcerned by such matters will, I trust, ignore them.

In sum, this biography may be read as one student's version of the career of a "great man" whose life is intrinsically interesting and who was instrumental in building, launching, and navigating a new nation that would in time fulfill his aspirations and dreams for it. As this comment implies, I have not written only for other scholars (although I hope that they will find plausible some of the reinterpretations I set forth) but also for the history-conscious reader who may be interested in the story of one of the most intriguing of this nation's Founding Fathers. It is largely for this reason that I have departed from the scholarly canon that dictates the appending of a bibliography. Bibliographies on Hamilton and his age exist in such abundance that yet another would be not only redundant but would comprise a volume in itself.

I

-≫≫-≫≫-≫≫-≪≪-≪≪-≪≪-

"My Ambition Is So Prevalent"

Well over two centuries after his birth, Alexander Hamilton's infancy, childhood, and early adolescence remain shrouded in mystery. He seldom spoke of them, and when obliged to do so (as to his children), he provided a romantically reticent, carefully edited version. The reason is clear: he was illegitimate.

Hamilton, the son of Rachael Faucett Lavien and James Hamilton, was born on the small West Indian island of Nevis.[1] If, as tradition has it, James Hamilton, a younger son of an ancient and still-prominent Scottish family, went to the West Indies to seek his fortune, his adventure was an abysmal disappointment.[2] He went from job to job, holding none long, and perhaps from woman to woman, although the record speaks only of Rachael. Her previous marriage had ended in an ugly divorce suit instituted by her estranged husband, John Michael Lavien.

Rachael had met Lavien on a visit to her sister Ann, the wife of James Lytton, a rich planter in the Danish island of St. Croix. All the assiduity of Hamilton scholars has managed to uncover little of certainty about Lavien (presumably a Danish immigrant), not even the correct spelling of the name.[3] It is clear, however, that from the outset of their marriage John and Rachael were on a collision course. The wreckage was made public after four years of marriage when Lavien swore out a complaint charging that his wife had "twice been guilty of adultery."[4] As the law demanded, Rachael was put in jail, pending a decision in the case. Before that took place, however, Lavien dropped the suit (hoping, so he later recalled, that she would reform). Once out of prison Rachael (again according to her outraged and biased husband) abandoned Lavien and her four-year-old son, Peter, and fled to "an English Island," probably Nevis. There she met, and took up residence with, James Hamilton, who was about ten years her senior. They had two children, James, Jr., born in 1753, and Alexander, who was born on January 11, 1755.[5]

At the time of Alexander's birth Rachael was still legally married to Lavien, who, for reasons unknown, had not chosen to institute divorce proceedings. This he finally did in February 1759, uncharitably charging that Rachael, "shameless, rude and ungodly," had "completely forgotten her duty and let husband and child alone." Worse yet (so three witnesses produced by Lavien averred), she had given "herself up to whoring with everyone," behavior "so well known that her own family and friends must hate her for it."[6] They presumably did not, but her son Alexander well may have.

Rachael was summoned to appear before the matrimonial court of St. Croix to answer her husband's allegations. Although the law of that day would in any event have afforded her scant protection, Rachael's failure to answer the summons assured the success of Lavien's petition. The court not only granted the divorce but also decreed that Rachael's illegitimate children surrender "all means," that is, claims to the plaintiff's possessions. Lavien might marry again (as he soon did), but in Rachael's case, "His Majesty . . . reserved the right to forbid a remarriage."[7] That right was never requested, and Rachael remained for the next six years James Hamilton's common-law wife.

One might suppose that Rachael would have avoided St. Croix, whose few inhabitants must have known of the sexual misconduct alleged against her by Lavien. Perhaps neither she nor her St. Croix acquaintances really cared, for she returned in 1765, accompanied by James and their children. Within a year or less James Hamilton walked out on her, whether because of his disdain of family responsibilities, boredom with Rachael, or dissatisfaction with life on St. Croix, we shall never know.

Alexander, who was then eleven years of age, recalled many years later that the "separation" between his father and himself "when I was very young, threw me upon the bounty of my mother's relatives, some of whom were then wealthy."[8] He no doubt wished that they were; but the fortune of the Lytton family had by then sharply shrunk, and the Hamilton children were altogether dependent upon their mother for support. She did her best to provide it by opening a small general store in Christiansted, where Alexander may have kept the accounts and thus have gained his first business experience. If so, the effect of such routine work on his future career was perforce negligible. Far more important were the young boy's formal schooling, which was meager, and his spare-time reading, the extent and nature of which can only be conjectured.

Hamilton's childhood symbolically ended in 1768. In February of that year his mother, then age thirty-nine, was stricken by what the records describe only as "a fever"; a few weeks later she was dead.[9] Rachael was buried in the Lytton family cemetery on Grange plantation. Only a handful of people stood by the grave—a few members of the Lytton family and Rachael's two sons. Aside from several female slaves left to Rachael by her mother and the small inventory of her store, Rachael's estate gave mute testimony to the sorrowful last years of a high-spirited, independent, intense, and passionate woman whose pursuit of happiness had left her twice abandoned and, in the end, all alone with her two illegitimate children. She left six silver spoons, seven silver teaspoons, one pair of sugar tongs, two chests, one bed with feather comforter and bolster, a few articles of clothing, and thirty-four books.[10] All save the books—which were bought at auction by Peter Lytton, guardian of the Hamilton boys—were promptly seized by Rachael's legitimate son, Peter Lavien. The inventory of her estate tells a story that Hamilton never related (if indeed he remembered) and that his biographers have largely overlooked. By the standards of white West Indians, Rachael was near the poverty line. Despite the thirteen silver spoons Rachael could not have set a table for guests, even had there been space for them in what must have been her single room. Nor (unless they slept on the floor) did the two boys live with her. James and perhaps also Alexander had already begun their apprenticeships. Rachael's interest, finally, lay less in silver and fine personal apparel than in books, suggesting that she might have tutored her sons, especially the younger one, whose precocity must have been evident. If she did so, Alexander either forgot or spurned acknowledgment of the debt. Indeed, in his voluminous correspondence he referred to his mother only twice, and then perfunctorily.[11]

Hamilton's reticence about his childhood and family suggests memories more painful than that of illegitimacy alone. Although he was manifestly proud of his father's Scottish forebears, he said little about his mother's relatives on St. Croix, although the Lyttons were among that island's most prominent families. Was his evasiveness the result of his awareness of Rachael's unsavory repute, perhaps of his first-hand knowledge of the embarrassing accusations preserved in St. Croix's dust-covered divorce records?

Hamilton's silence about his mother was matched by the empty formality of his infrequent references to his father. From the time the elder James Hamilton left St. Croix in 1766 until his death in 1799, only a handful of letters were exchanged between him and his younger son; and the paltry number of letters that Alexander did write show only the shallowest interest in his father's whereabouts or welfare. The father who deserted him had, after all, never subsequently offered him either a stiver for support or an apology as solace. Hamilton's indifference is thus as understandable as the fierce independence that replaced the affection that father and son must once have shared. The trust that James Hamilton betrayed would only rarely again be bestowed.

The two Hamilton orphans were left not only penniless but with no relatives who could help them. Both their uncle James, mainstay of the Lytton family, and their guardian, Peter Lytton, died in the summer of 1769, neither of them having made any provision for Rachael's children. At least Rachael's sons were housed and fed, James as an apprentice carpenter and

Alexander as a fledgling clerk. For most young men in similar circumstances the future would have been foreclosed, and ambition fruitless. That Hamilton's career was not cut to the predictable pattern was owing in part to chance but far more to the unaccountable endowment of genius. The latter was tellingly demonstrated during his brief apprenticeship.

Alexander was taken on as a clerk by the firm of Beekman and Cruger in Christiansted. The partners were transplanted New Yorkers, both members of distinguished mercantile families, whose West Indian partnership (launched in 1766) was in effect a branch office of family firms. At that time such arrangements were common among the large mercantile houses of mainland cities such as Philadelphia and New York. As was also customary, Beekman returned home a few years after the establishment of the firm. Nicholas Cruger, who married successively into two of the island's most prominent families, remained for a few years longer, operating for a short time in partnership with Cornelius Kortright (another New Yorker) but mostly on his own.

The mainstay of Cruger's business was the exchange of North American mainland products (lumber, livestock, and foodstuffs) for those of St. Croix (principally sugar, molasses, and rum). As was true of international trade generally, its successful conduct entailed shrewdness, skill, and knowledge—a familiarity with prices current on both the mainland and island markets; a mastery of the intricacies of monetary exchange; and comprehensive information on ships, shipping conditions, and customs regulations. Profitability was also premised on prudent risk-taking and, sometimes, on a willingness to evade the tangle of regulatory legislation (Danish, English, French, and Spanish) that encumbered the West Indian trade. For an able and ambitious young man, countinghouses like Cruger's provided, in sum, the equivalent of a modern college degree in business administration. Hamilton later referred to this mercantile training "as the most useful part of his education."[12] He was swiftly moved to the head of the class; within a few years he had become Cruger's deputy, directing the activities of the firm during his employer's extended absences.

For one who had started from scratch, illegitimate and an orphan, it was no mean accomplishment. Nor did Hamilton's comparative poverty and bastardy render him a pariah in Christiansted (the town numbered a mere eight hundred white people, the island itself only about two thousand). Hamilton's closest childhood friend, for example, was Edward Stevens, the son of Thomas Stevens, a prominent merchant, and he was no doubt welcomed in the households that Cruger frequented (which comprised those of the town's elite). He was also readily accepted by members of what passed as the island's intellectual community, notably by the Presbyterian minister, Hugh Knox. It was for Hamilton obviously not a carefree life but presumably a tolerantly pleasant one. Ardently ambitious and aware of his unusual talent, he consequently set his sights far beyond the idyllic setting of St. Croix, where sunlight bathed the gently sloping green hills, the yellow, orange, and raspberry building fronts, and beyond them the ocean, violet and green within the reef, shading to dark blue in the distance.

The beauty of the scenery was about all that the overwhelming majority of the island's people were entitled to enjoy. St. Croix's inhabitants were twelve to one slave, a sea of black people ruled by a few white masters whose solidarity was cemented by a common interest in continued subjugation of their slaves. Hamilton never commented on his personal reaction to the slave society in which he was reared. And as with other aspects of his youth the basis for conjecture is weak. Just as he renounced other aspects of his West Indian background, so he may also have abjured slavery. During the American Revolution, only a few years after leaving St. Croix, he advocated the enlistment of black troops and displayed an awareness of the plight and potential of American blacks that placed him at this period of his life in the vanguard of civil libertians of his day. Several years later, he would become a charter member of the New York Manumission Society.

Whatever the subsequent effects of his childhood and young adulthood on St. Croix may have been, Hamilton was eager to leave. "My ambition is so prevalent," he wrote to his friend Edward Stevens (who was then at King's College in New York), "that I contemn the grov'ling condition of a Clerk or the like, to which my Fortune, etc. condemns me and would willingly risk my life tho' not my Character to exalt my Station." Although confident that the future would provide what the present withheld, Hamilton wistfully concluded, "I wish there was a War."[13] Employing the advantage of hindsight, one is tempted to make far too much of this letter—partly, of course, because it is the only extant one of a personal nature that Hamilton wrote during his West Indian years. Actually, he was only echoing sentiments of a kind characteristic of adolescents of the time. His willingness to "risk my life though not my Character" was little more than a pious platitude; the wish for a war was merely an acknowledgment that only thus could an obscure clerk escape a seemingly stymied career.

No war was imminent, so Hamilton resolved to make himself an indispensable assistant, less by "grov'ling" than by accomplishment. His duties, the nature of the responsibilities he assumed, and the kinds of decisions he made are revealed by the firm's letterbooks, which include dozens of letters in Hamilton's flowing, rounded, clerklike handwriting. He was obliged to deal with ornery and sometimes dishonest sea captains, to gamble on market prices, to dispose of inferior products (at a loss if necessary), and, despite such difficulties, to keep the firm solvent. Small wonder that Cruger, who preferred to enjoy profits rather than to grub for them, prized his young assistant.

It is usually said (perhaps for the sake of a good transition sentence) that a hurricane blew Hamilton to the mainland. The allusion is to a newspaper article in which Hamilton described the devastating effects of a hurricane that struck St. Croix on the last night of August 1772.[14] If indeed the piece was written by Hamilton, it could have influenced only readers more impressionable than his potential patrons were. Replete with stereotyped piety, saccharinity, and stock sentiment, the essay suggested the authorship of either an amateur journalist or a gifted but unpracticed schoolboy. Similar comments would have to be made about his putative verse, depicting idyllic love in a pastoral setting, also published in the local newspaper.[15] What counts is not the quality of his verse or prose but the fact that Hamilton thus early launched what would in time earn him the reputation as one of the cleverest polemicists in American history.

Hamilton's northward trip to the American colonies was made possible largely by Nicholas Cruger, who in a display of noblesse oblige was willing to provide his talented clerk the opportunity to receive a gentleman's education. Among others who encouraged or advised Hamilton were his cousin Ann Lytton Venton, Thomas Stevens, the Reverend Hugh Knox (who may have tutored Hamilton for a few months)[16] and Cornelius Kortright. But, Cruger himself provided more than encouragement and advice. He consigned to Kortright and Company in New York City two shipments of West Indian produce (probably sugar), the proceeds to be used for Hamilton's support.[17]

In October 1772, Hamilton boarded one of the many vessels (probably a brig belonging to one of Cruger's correspondents) in Christiansted's harbor bound for Boston some fifteen hundred miles away. As the vessel sailed out of the scenic port of Christiansted, Hamilton had no regrets but rather resolved to forget. America afforded the opportunity for a new start. Unlike his father's search so many years before, Hamilton's quest would be successful.

After a voyage of about three weeks, Hamilton stepped onto one of Boston's wharves, in a harbor thronged with sailing ships. As had been arranged, the young West Indian straightaway set out for Cruger's home town, whose charms doubtless had lost nothing in the New Yorker's account.[18] Already favorably disposed, Hamilton quickly fell under the spell of what to him always would be America's first city. At the time of Hamilton's arrival, New York, the third largest city in the colonies, was confined to the lower tip of Manhattan Island. But to Hamilton, who was excited by its crowded streets, its many countinghouses, its attractive shops with their adjoining residences, New York seemed a metropolis and its cobbled streets the pathway to his own success.

The young immigrant promptly presented himself to Cornelius Kortright, to whom the funds for Hamilton's support had been entrusted. Kortright enlisted the aid of his partner, Hugh Mulligan, who made arrangements for Hamilton to stay with Mulligan's bachelor brother, Hercules, who lived above his tailor and haberdashery shop on Water Street. Fortunately for historians, Hercules Mulligan later recorded his recollections of this phase of Hamilton's career.[19]

Soon after arriving in New York, Hamilton headed for Elizabethtown (now Elizabeth), New Jersey, where he was enrolled in the preparatory school run by Francis Barber, a recent Princeton graduate. The location of the academy rather than its quality (although this may have been high) attracted Hamilton. He had been recommended by the Reverend Knox to two of Elizabethtown's leading citizens, Elias Boudinot, prominent lawyer and trustee of Princeton, and William Livingston, "the reigning Whig Presbyterian intellect of the middle colonies," who soon would become governor of New Jersey.[20] Boudinot and Livingston not only courteously received the young man but, attracted by his uncommon charm, also obligingly opened their houses to him. Hamilton apparently lodged alternately at the house of the one or the other. Although as family-conscious as members of the Jersey gentry characteristically were, Livingston and Boudinot readily accepted whatever Hamilton may have said about his personal background, if indeed the issue was raised at all. And what Elizabethtown's social leaders did not question the small town's other inhabitants took on faith, as did aristocratic visitors like John Jay, who was courting one of Livingston's daughters; William Alexander (Lord Sterling); and William Duer. Although once the capital of New Jersey, Elizabethtown consisted of only some sixty houses; those that Hamilton knew well were large frame dwellings, surrounded by spacious lawns that gave way to pleasing gardens and orchards. The town also boasted two churches, a town hall, and the Academy, a two-story wooden building. This pleasant village may well have seemed to Hamilton an American prototype, its leading citizens the archetypal Americans. Certainly it was with them, as his later career attests, that he identified.

It was fortunate for Hamilton that Barber, who was only four years older than his new pupil, was a "progressive" teacher, in the sense that he was willing to allow students to proceed at their own pace. While Hamilton's formal education was negligible, the deficiency was overmatched by his precocity. Even so, what he accomplished is remarkable. Within less than a year, he acquired a sufficient mastery of Latin and Greek (in which he had no previous training), French (of which he had only a rudimentary knowledge), and mathematics to qualify for admission to college, surely one of the speediest preparatory achievements on record. Just as remarkable as Hamilton's innate intellectual endowment was his acquired knack for winning the esteem and support of influential patrons like Livingston and Boudinot. For him, the effective exercise of that talent was essential: the fulfillment of his steadily swelling ambition depended not only on his own uncommon ability and charm but on their recognition by men able to further his career. His success in securing precisely that acknowledgment was a tribute to his astonishing facility for calling attention to his superiority without appearing to be presumptuous or brash. In sum, Hamilton's leap from the fringes of St. Croix's plantation society to the inner circle of the New Jersey and New York squirearchy required more agility than all the other accomplishments for which history has honored him.

According to Mulligan, Hamilton would have attended Princeton College had not its president turned down the young man's request that the usual rules be waived so that he might proceed at his own rate.[21] In the event, he applied to King's College in New York City, where he enrolled as a "private student" for the academic year 1773–1774, formally matriculating as a sophomore in 1774.[22] As a college closely related to the Church of England, King's was generally regarded as royalist in sympathy, a proclivity strengthened by its president Myles Cooper, an Anglican priest educated at Queen's College, Oxford. But the affiliation and political orientation of King's College presumably had scant effect on its students. Hamilton and many of his classmates were to become American revolutionaries, and in Hamilton's case the religious precepts that had been instilled by Hugh Knox and inspired by the Presbyterian piety of his Elizabethtown patrons were certainly not deepened by Cooper's stout Anglicanism. They may even have been dispelled.

If Hamilton "originally destined himself to the science of Physic," as his classmate Robert Troup recalled some four decades later, he soon changed his mind, choosing instead the liberal arts course.[23] There was nothing in the inflexibly set curriculum to baffle, much less to challenge, Hamilton. More important than his formal course of classroom instruction was his informal browsing in the King's College library, where he became acquainted with Pufendorf, Grotius, Berlamqui, Hobbes, Locke, Montesquieu, Blackstone, Plutarch, Postlethwayt, and Hume. There is no convincing evidence, however, that Hamilton's political principles derived primarily from any of these, not even Hobbes or Hume (to name the favorite candidates). His political philosophy was an amalgam of his voracious readings, the precepts of fatherly advisers, the influence of friends, personal reflection and experience, and perhaps opportunism. In other words, one cannot trace Hamilton's political philosophy to any one source, whether to a particular writer, philosophical tradition, or specific mentor or friend.

Nor can we determine precisely when Hamilton committed himself to the patriot cause or how this choice was initially manifested. There is, for example, no plausible evidence to support the family tradition that Hamilton in July 1774 delivered an impassioned address at a "great meeting in the Fields" (now City Hall Park), urging all good patriots to resist Britain's "odious oppression."[24] What we do know is that Hamilton enlisted in the New York militia in March 1776. We can reasonably infer that he had from the outset supported the American, rather than the British, side. For him, unlike most other Whigs, the outset was, of course, not 1763 but 1773, in the sense that Hamilton had been neither personally nor even vicariously involved in the decade of successive Anglo-American crises that preceded his arrival in the colonies. His knowledge of these events came principally from ardent Whigs, such as Mulligan, Boudinot, Livingston, Troup, and others whom he had met since his arrival in America—all prejudiced participants. The version of the dispute he thus heard was what would become the traditional copybook account of liberty-loving patriots pitted against a tyrannical monarchy, and it was the version of which he soon became the public advocate.

II

-»>->»->»-«<-«<-«<-

Member of
General Washington's
"Family"

Hamilton made his American debut as a journalist in December 1774 with the publication of *A Full Vindication of the Measures of Congress*.[1] *A Full Vindication* and its sequel, *The Farmer Refuted*,[2] assume importance because they afford an early and important clue to the ideas of one whose political philosophy would come to symbolize the views of an influential group of Founding Fathers, the Federalists, and (far in the future) American conservatism generally. Their significance has been overstated, however. In fact, they set forth the views of a precocious young college student who had arrived in the colonies only two years earlier and whose exposition of standard patriot ideology made no original contribution to, but instead leaned heavily on, the writings of other American Whigs. Had not Hamilton become famous, his essays—characterized by a bombastic style and satiric heavy-handedness—would merit only cursory attention.

A Full Vindication was prepared in response to an attack on the Continental Congress that had been written by Samuel Seabury, Episcopal rector at Westchester, New York. In this pamphlet, Hamilton sought to prove that "the pretensions of Parliament are contradictory to the law of nature, subversive of the British constitution, and destructive of the faith of the most solemn compacts."[3] Hamilton argued that America must in extremis resist such "pretensions" by war but preferably by steadfast adherence to the program of economic coercion adopted by the Continental Congress. That plan was, in Hamilton's view, "perfectly consonant with justice and sound policy; and will, in all human probability, secure our freedom against the assaults of our enemies."[4]

The fourteen thousand words that Hamilton spent in vindicating Congress included an exposition of the then-current natural rights and natural law

9

philosophy. As was de rigueur for American Whigs, he studded his essay with references to the "voice of natural justice" and "fundamental principles of the English constitution" and with assaults on Britain's "claim of ruling and taxing us without our consent." His essay was replete, too, with the inflammatory language that marred the less felicitous of American forays into Revolutionary polemics. Britain was guilty of "atrocious invasion of our rights" and "a wicked thirst of domination"; hers was "the lawless hand of tyranny . . . extended to ravish our liberty from us"; her design was a "system of slavery, fabricated against America." This "absolute slavery" that Hamilton insisted Britain intended to impose on her colonists would be "fatal to religion and morality . . . , debase the mind and corrupt its noblest springs of action."[5] Hamilton's article was flawed not only by such exaggeration but by leaden humor and an excessive reliance on clichés. In sum, had an impartial judge been called on to decide the debate between the Tory rector and the young patriot, the verdict would have been in favor of Seabury. Similarly, a critic attuned to ironies must be struck by Seabury's eloquent defense of political principles such as legality and order that have come to be generally regarded as particularly "Hamiltonian."

The sequel to a *Full Vindication* of Congress was *The Farmer Refuted,* an essay (two and a half times longer than its predecessor) in which Hamilton reaffirmed "the absolute non-existence of . . . parliamentary supremacy," a denial once again demonstrated by arguments "from the voice of nature, the *spirit* of the British constitution, and the charter of the colonies."[6] But there is a striking disparity in the quality of these pieces, separated in time by only two months. *The Farmer Refuted,* despite a prolixity that would mar Hamilton's later writings, is so superior to its forerunner that one is entitled to speculate that Hamilton found either a talented collaborator or an extraordinarily skillful editor.

As in his *Full Vindication,* the doctrines propounded by Hamilton were the staple fare of American Revolutionary political philosophy, but they were now not only expanded but also more convincingly defended. The political ideas that Hamilton set forth included those propounded by more skillful pamphleteers, such as John Adams and James Wilson, and some that were to be far more memorably expressed by Thomas Jefferson in the Declaration of Independence. Among the principles in the latter category that Hamilton embraced were equal rights (nature, he said, "has distributed an equality of rights to every man"); the "inherent right of all men to freedom and happiness" (the end of representative government, Hamilton went on to say, "is the happiness of the governed"); the dangers of unlimited power ("the experience of all ages makes it the height of folly to entrust any set of men with power, which is not under every possible controul"); and the right of resistance to tyranny ("when the first principles of civil society are violated, and the rights of the people are invaded . . . men may then betake themselves to the law of nature").[7] Hamilton also set forth (as did Jefferson in the Declaration) the dominion theory of government.[8]

Just as these ideas placed Hamilton squarely in the mainstream of American Revolutionary thought so also did his profession of allegiance to the king of Great Britain. The focus of the Whig attack was, after all, Parliament and not the Crown. Nevertheless, Hamilton's professed loyalty to the British sovereign seems to have been pro forma only. More arresting was his glowing description of the immense advantages the colonies would enjoy in a military showdown with England. One is obliged to suspect that in 1775 he still harbored the hope he had six years earlier shared with Edward Stevens when he had written, "I wish there was a war."

Hamilton's wish was soon granted. On April 19, 1775, on the orders of General Thomas Gage, governor of Massachusetts, a detachment of British soldiers marched out of Boston to seize a supply of rebel arms reputedly stored at nearby Concord. En route the Redcoats encountered a group of colonial militia assembled on the village green at Lexington. Some one gave an order. Shots rang out. The American empire was in rebellion. After destroying a few gun carriages at Concord, where there was again a skirmish with the Americans, the British soldiers marched back to Boston, where they soon were encircled by militiamen who had assembled there from all over New England. A month later in May 1775 the Second Continental Congress assembled in Philadelphia. Confronted with actual fighting, its emphasis shifted from conciliation with the mother country to the organization of the colonists' war effort.

Hamilton had already decided to do his part. Early every morning before classes (so a friend of the time recalled much later) he joined other volunteers who drilled in St. George's Churchyard, a short distance from King's College.[9] It is also related (again unverifiably) that he had already had his first encounter with a Revolutionary mob. This reputedly happened when he came to the rescue of the embattled president of the college. Aroused by reports that Myles Cooper was the ring leader of local Tories, a menacing mob marched on the president's house. As what Cooper called this "murderous band" rattled the "groaning gates" of the college, Hamilton "took his stand on one of the stoops, and proceeded with great animation . . . to harangue the mob on the . . . disgrace it would bring on the cause of liberty," a diversion that gave Cooper an opportunity to slip out a back entrance and to safety.[10] This depiction of Hamilton as a young David armed only with shafts of oratory calming a besieging mob is as appealing as it is unlikely—unless, that is, the mob was so tame that the speech of a young college student could sway it.

In any event, Hamilton did oppose the suppression of Toryism by mob violence (on the part of non–New Yorkers anyway). This was demonstrated when the shop of James Rivington, publisher of a Tory newspaper, was attacked by a group of patriot vigilantes from Connecticut, recruited by Isaac Sears, a leader of the New York Sons of Liberty. The incident also provided Hamilton an opportunity to renew his acquaintanceship with John Jay, who was then a New York delegate to the Continental Congress. In describing to

Jay the Rivington episode, Hamilton, in terse and eloquent phrases, also affirmed civil libertarian principles based on a jaundiced view of human nature. The two were not incompatible, of course. "In times of such commotion as the present, while the passions of men are worked up to an uncommon pitch," Hamilton wrote, "there is great danger of fatal extremes. The same state of the passions which fits the multitude, who have not a sufficient stock of reason and knowledge to guide them, for opposition to tyranny and oppression, very naturally leads them to a contempt and disregard of all authority." Although such sentiments were commonplace in Whig political thought, Hamilton did in this instance prefigure the views of his later years. But the thrust of his letter did not. His major complaint was against the interference of "populous and powerful" New England in the internal affairs of a neighboring colony, an "interposal" that would "secretly revive and increase . . . ancient animosities." If it were necessary "to repress and overawe" Tories (as Hamilton agreed it was), the task should be accomplished by congressional dispatch of "a few regiments of troops raised in . . . any other province except New England."[11] Such provincialism was as out of character as it was short-lived. In the 1790s and on into the next century New England would be the section most steadfast in support of Hamiltonian policies.

Having received a polite reply to his initial letter, Hamilton promptly wrote to Jay again. As before, his theme was the problem posed by "artful and intriguing" Tories. Suspecting that they were conniving to win control of the New York colonial legislature, Hamilton urged Jay to thwart such machinations by supporting the strongest possible Whig candidates.[12] Although it might have seemed presumptuous for a twenty-year-old college student—and a foreigner at that—to offer advice to an experienced and senior statesman, Jay did not view the matter that way.

By this time, Hamilton's involvement in America's response to the imperial crisis had crowded out more personal concerns, even his desire for a college degree. It was as well, for he did not need long years of formal study. Capable as he was of self-education, what he rather needed was an occasion for conspicuously displaying his remarkable talent. Fortunately for him, as for other young men of the time, the American Revolution provided the opportunity.

Determined to secure a military appointment, Hamilton unhesitatingly called on influential acquaintances for assistance. His Elizabethtown patron, Elias Boudinot, successfully recommended him for the post of aide de camp to William Alexander. But Hamilton turned down the offer, in hopes that he might secure a line, rather than a staff, position.[13] His acquaintance, Colonel Alexander McDougall (and perhaps also John Jay) saw to it that his wish was granted. On March 14, 1776, the New York legislature appointed Hamilton captain of a company of artillery, to be raised for the defense of the province.[14]

The beleaguered colony needed defenders. In August 1776 General Sir William Howe, heading an army of thirty-two thousand men and supported by a fleet commanded by his brother Admiral Lord Richard Howe, arrived in New York harbor. Within weeks it appeared to the dispirited New Yorkers that the British forces were invincible. At Brooklyn Heights the main American army, under General Israel Putnam, was routed and barely managed to escape capture. With a British fleet anchored in the East River and the Redcoats in a position to entrap his army on lower Manhattan, General George Washington was thus obliged to withdraw the bulk of his forces from Manhattan. During the evacuation, the American commander came close to being encircled, but once out of the city he checked Howe in the Battle of White Plains and then managed to slip away. The escape of his troops was largely offset, however, by British capture of the strong American garrison left behind to protect Fort Washington in northern Manhattan, the most stunning stroke of Howe's campaign. Outnumbered and outmaneuvered, Washington led his ragged and weary army from New York and across New Jersey toward the rolling countryside west of Philadelphia, with Lord Cornwallis hot in pursuit.

Hamilton's role in these events easily can be (and often is) exaggerated. During the Battle of Brooklyn Heights, his artillerymen remained encamped across the bay on lower Manhattan. When that post became untenable, he moved his men and equipment to Harlem Heights, which they helped to fortify. According to family legend, he then took part in the Battle of White Plains, but as a recent historian comments, "It is better that this claim cannot be supported, as the artillery on that occasion made so lamentable a showing."[15] Nor is there, finally, a scintilla of evidence that Hamilton, with courageous abandon, proposed to General Washington that Hamilton share command of a storming party to retake Fort Washington.

Hamilton did join Washington's forces in their retreat across New Jersey, however. During the cold winter of 1776–1777 he took part in the military engagements at New Brunswick, Trenton, and Princeton. The exact nature of his role is debatable, but it must have been minor. Nevertheless, it was during this period that in one way or another, he came to the attention of George Washington, most likely through the good offices of one of the young captain's acquaintances. The person who recommended Hamilton to Washington handed the obscure artillery captain the single most important opportunity of his life.

On March 1, 1777, the commanding general of the Continental army appointed Hamilton his aide de camp. Objectively viewed, the job may have been only that of a glorified secretary, but it was one that Hamilton (as his clerkship in Cruger's countinghouse had demonstrated) could turn to his personal advantage. Here was the ideal stage for the display of his unusual ability; here was the occasion for meeting, consulting, and corresponding with America's leading soldiers and statesmen. Chief among these was Washington, with whom Hamilton was now in daily communication. Hamilton made the most of the opportunity. Fortunately for him, Washington unreservedly acknowledged and characteristically rewarded diligence and talent in his subordinates.

The association between Washington and Hamilton was at the outset harmonious and would in time be one of the most creative in American history. Superficially, they had little in common. Washington, then some forty-five years old, was a native Virginian of impeccable social credentials; Hamilton a comparative youngster of twenty-two years was a West Indian immigrant. Washington was not only the foremost American of the day but was well on the way to becoming a world figure; Hamilton was merely one of the general's aides, one who was as yet unknown to most of his countrymen. Washington was patient, magnanimous, and imperturbable, even under pressure; Hamilton was impatiently ambitious and often rash, and his veneer of pride was as thin as an arriviste's is alleged to be. But despite such differences the talents of the one complemented those of the other. Their partnership in statesmanship would come with the launching of a new government more than a decade in the future, however. During the Revolution their official relationship was that of a superior officer of high rank and his subaltern.

It is customary when writing of Hamilton's accomplishments as aide de camp to magnify their importance. The fact is that many other aides (some thirty-two of them in all) served Washington ably and faithfully. Although a convincing case could be made that Hamilton was the most gifted of the group, certainly neither Washington nor his other aides (presumably Hamilton included) would have agreed that the New Yorker was the general's principal aide.[16] Had Washington and his staff been polled, that honor would perhaps have gone to Robert Hanson Harrison, familiarly known at headquarters as the "Old Secretary." Moreover, the runners-up would have included not only Hamilton but also Tench Tilghman, of whom a common acquaintance once remarked to Hamilton that "he has a penetrating intellect that flies like an arrow from a bow,"[17] and John Laurens, both talented and (for an American of that day) superbly educated. To all these especially trusted aides, and not only to Hamilton, Washington assigned important responsibilities and considerable discretion in carrying them out. Nevertheless, even among such stellar secretaries Hamilton's peculiar genius shone, and Washington, although by no means dazzled, accorded it due recognition.

By necessity Washington had to depend heavily on his secretaries. "The weight of the whole war," as Tilghman said, "may be said to lay upon his shoulders."[18] In addition to his responsibilities as commanding general, Washington was also his own secretary of war and in effect his own secretary of state, obliged to placate a grudging Congress, jealous states, and sensitive allies. His correspondence was voluminous, including not only mounds of routine letters but also reports to importunate and meddlesome congressmen, delicate negotiations with military prima donnas, diplomatic exchanges with foreign allies, and replies to letters from notable civilian correspondents. "My time is so taken up at my desk," Washington once remarked, "that I am obliged to neglect many other essential parts of my duty; it is absolutely necessary . . . for me to have persons that can think for me, as well as execute orders."[19] Hamilton could do both, and to him and a few other particularly dependable assistants Washington delegated a large number of varied tasks. Hamilton's major and most time-consuming job was letter writing. Washington did not, of course, dictate letters, nor did he always provide specific instructions to his more reliable aides. Harrison spoke for his fellow aides when he complained, "I wish to the Lord the General would give me the heads or some idea, of what he would have me write."[20] Thus, one cannot know with certainty the precise nature of Hamilton's contribution to the many letters and other documents that he prepared at the general's behest. On some occasions Washington may have given explicit directions about what to say, in other instances he may have revised his aide's draft, and in yet others he may have given Hamilton a free hand.

Among the many letters that Hamilton drafted for Washington (whether as ghost writer or amanuensis) were some of both major importance and exceptional excellence. It was Hamilton, for example, who drew up a report on the reorganization of the army, a new set of military regulations, and a plan for congressional revamping of the inspector general's office. In addition, he drafted important letters to the president of Congress, to prominent generals, and to state officials. He also wrote diplomatic dispatches. Thus, in January 1781 he drafted instructions for his friend John Laurens, envoy-designate to present the case for his country's critical need for financial aid to the French court. Because of Hamilton's fluency in French he also conducted the bulk of Washington's correspondence with foreign officers. Even so, it is necessary to insist that the letters were Washington's in the sense that they accurately and uniformly reflected his policies and ideas, not those of his aide. Hamilton's especial value lay in his ability to express in the general's own style precisely what Washington wished to say.

Hamilton was, in sum, a true alter ego. The letters he drafted for Washington's signature exemplified what Hamilton characterized as "the moderation and caution with which the General usually expresses himself,"[21] although these traits did not come naturally to Hamilton himself. In his own correspondence and conversation he was often far less temperate. For example, in a letter to Dr. William Gordon (who originated a rumor that Hamilton had publicly said that "it was high time for the people to rise, join General Washington & turn Congress out of doors") Hamilton described the New England clergyman as one "of those splenetic patriots . . . who endeavor, for sinister purposes, to instill jealousies and alarms . . . as groundless as they are impolitic and ridiculous."[22] He called General Charles Lee "either a driveler in the business of soldiership or something much worse."[23] Of Samuel Chase, a member of the Continental Congress who had sought to profit from cornering the supply of flour, he publicly asserted that "there is no strain of abhorrence, of which the human mind is capable . . . which may not be applied to him, with justice."[24]

Hamilton did more than write letters for Washington. He also compiled intelligence reports based on information from people within British occupied zones, from released prisoners, and, less frequently, from deserters. Illustrating the extent of Washington's confidence in Hamilton were the occasional military or diplomatic missions on which the New Yorker was sent. Thus, in November 1777 Hamilton was dispatched to the headquarters of General Horatio Gates, fresh from his triumph at Saratoga, to secure from that testy general troops to reinforce Washington's depleted army. Gates, irked at being given orders by a mere lieutenant colonel and also disinclined to part with any of his troops, at first balked. Deciding that deception was preferable to open defiance of the commanding general, Gates next tried to pawn off on Washington's young emissary a single, depleted unit. By a combination of tact and forthrightness, however, Hamilton prevailed, and two brigades were dispatched.

Despite Hamilton's efficient conduct of delicate quasi-diplomatic missions (as well as his important role in incidents such as Benedict Arnold's treason and in battles such as that of Monmouth Courthouse), he did not play a major part in the military history of the Revolution. He was obviously in no position to do so. Washington did not rely on his aides for advice on strategy or tactics, nor did he, in his words, even expect them to have any "military knowledge. If they can write a good letter, write quick, are methodical, and diligent, it is all I expect to find."[25] Hamilton was capable of much more than that, but his part in the war is correctly conveyed by his title—aide de camp to General Washington.

The importance of Hamilton's Revolutionary War career lies elsewhere. It was a period during which he first realized his intellectual and administrative potential. It was, more important yet, not only one of self-discovery but also of self-affirmation. He had already successfully identified himself with his adopted land—not least by speedily choosing its side in its quarrel with England. He now calculatedly cut himself loose from the moorings of his West Indian past. In so doing, he was able to cast out the incubus of bastardy and to become in the eyes of others (not least those of subsequent historians) an American aristocrat.

That transformation was made possible not only by Washington's backing but also by the support of other influential men for whom Hamilton's personal magnetism canceled out any embarrassing questioning of the family antecedents about which he was suspiciously reticent. What Hamilton wrote of a government was perhaps based on a lesson of personal experience. "If a Government appears to be confident of its own powers," he commented, "it is the surest way to inspire the same confidence in others."[26] What his admirers saw was, of course, a self-portrait, patiently and skillfully drawn and then burnished and reburnished. But eventually the man became the portrait. This imperceptible blending was the smoother because in the process of winning the praise and esteem of discriminating and respected leaders, Hamilton's estimate of himself was confirmed. Authenticated also was his status as a bona fide American. And, paradoxically, the very birthright that Hamilton lacked was a source of his ardent advocacy of American nationalism. Unlike most of his contemporaries his ties to a section or state were weak; his deepest commitment was to the new nation. It had been good to him, and his repayment was a loyalty that sometimes bordered on fanaticism. Like the proverbial convert, he was more zealous than one born into the faith.[27] In this sense, the young American, not the West Indian child, was father of the man. As if aware of the fact, Hamilton refused to dwell on an irreversible past but chose to focus instead on what he believed to be a controllable future. He was perhaps describing himself when a decade later he wrote in *The Federalist,* "There are strong minds in every walk of life that will rise superior to the disadvantages of situation, and will command the tribute due to their merit, not only from the classes to which they particularly belong, but from the society in general."[28]

The class to which Hamilton now by adoption belonged was the American gentry, although for the moment in a military setting. Hamilton excepted, the men Washington chose for his immediate staff possessed unassailable family credentials, not because Washington was consciously a snob but because a different arrangement would never have occurred to him. Certainly this was true of those who served at the same time as Hamilton and with whom he was particularly good friends. John Laurens, the son of Henry Laurens, a rich South Carolina merchant-planter and prominent member of the Continental Congress, was educated in Switzerland and at the Middle Temple in London. Richard Kidder Meade, a Virginian who was the grandson of a governor of North Carolina, had been sent to school at Harrow in England. Other such aides included Robert Hanson Harrison, member of a respected Maryland family who had practiced law in Alexandria; Tench Tilghman, grandson of William Penn's attorney general for Pennsylvania and son of a rich Philadelphian (a passive Tory who sat out the war in rural Maryland); and James McHenry, educated in Dublin and son of a prosperous Baltimore merchant.

Hamilton's most intimate associate was Laurens. Although they were both the products of slave societies, they were otherwise of such sharply different backgrounds that their almost spontaneous rapport is not easily explicable. Perhaps close friendships are not always so. In the letters that Hamilton wrote at this time, it was only in those to Laurens that he dropped his customary mask of formality. In his sparse correspondence with Laurens, conducted when the South Carolinian was absent from headquarters on various missions, he was atypically personal, warm, spontaneous, and candid. When Laurens died in 1782 during an ambush by a British foraging party, Hamilton lamented that he had lost "a friend I truly and most tenderly loved, and one of a very small number."[29] He might more accurately have said the only such friend. Of admirers and close political associates he would have many, but none with whom he would be so intimate.

To its members, Washington's staff was known as "the family." The phrase aptly describes Hamilton's reaction to life at headquarters. For at least half of his life he had lived in foster homes, first at Cruger's counting-house, then briefly at Mulligan's, next in the households of Boudinot and Livingston in Elizabethtown, and then at college. Except at King's, his position had not necessarily been that of a supplicant but certainly something resembling that of a ward. Now his adopted "family" included a half dozen or so companionable young men (most of Washington's aides were, like

Hamilton, bachelors in their twenties) with whom he was in constant and close association. At the head of the household was the paragon father substitute, as near perfect as a young man could have found—or, indeed, as America afforded.

Usually, two rooms at headquarters were allocated for the general's aides, one room for work and another where they slept. It was a spartan and strenuous schedule. "Vice is banished from . . . the General's Family," said Tilghman, perhaps by way of lament. "We never sup, but go early to bed and are early up."[30] It was an accurate description, so far as it went. What Tilghman overlooked were the varied activities that relieved the rigors of headquarters routine. Aides were occasionally given outside assignments, were called on to accompany the general on rides, and took part in the social amenities that Washington managed to preserve, although often obliged to make do with sparse provisions and cramped quarters. In winter quarters (where higher-ranking officers were often joined by their wives) there was even something of a social season. Dinner at such times was often a lively occasion (despite the commander's staid formality). One or another of his staff might act as host at the general's table, where visiting notables were frequently entertained. One guest recalled such an occasion when Hamilton "presided at the General's table." "He acquitted himself," Alexander Graydon wrote, "with an ease, propriety and vivacity, which gave me the most favorable impression of his talents and accomplishments."[31] Other visitors to headquarters (a roster of whom would comprise a Who's Who of Revolutionary America) were similarly impressed. The most important of these for Hamilton personally was General Philip Schuyler.

Schuyler, who had been elected a delegate to the Continental Congress, arrived in Philadelphia in the fall of 1779 accompanied by his wife and family. In November, the two oldest daughters, Angelica and Elizabeth, left for nearby Morristown to visit their aunt, Mrs. John Cochran, whose husband was surgeon general of the Middle Department. That army headquarters happened to be in Morristown may account for their extended visit, which lasted some five months.

The two sisters presented a striking contrast. The vivacious and coquettish Angelica was a sparkling conversationalist. Elizabeth, who was only a year younger, was reserved, rather less flirtatious, and possessed of "but few educational advantages." Elizabeth's grandson, an enthusiastic admirer, conveyed rather more than he intended when he commented that Betsy, while *"lacking the superficial grace and accomplishments* of many of her more sprightly and dashing friends, . . . must have possessed a quiet charm of her own. From all accounts she was gentle and retiring, yet full of gayety and courage, fond of domestic affairs, and probably her Mother's chief assistant."[32] In a portrait done in 1787 Elizabeth appears an attractive, but not a beautiful, young woman—dark hair, a short forehead, wide-set eyes, a long narrow nose, and somewhat thin lips. But one compensatory, even compelling, feature, inherited from her father, stands out—her dark, luminous eyes. Tench Tilghman described them as "the most . . . dark, lovely eyes that I ever saw." They "threw a beam of good temper and benevolence over her Entire Countenance."[33] But was such a countenance enough to infatuate a young man as handsome, high-spirited, energetic, and vibrant as Hamilton? Maybe he also saw in those "dark, luminous eyes" Elizabeth's social status and family fortune.

Perhaps, even so, Hamilton also settled for second best. He was, so some of his biographers insist, irresistibly drawn to Angelica. If so, he was in good company. So too, years later, would Thomas Jefferson, along with a good many London and Paris socialites, be captivated by her. But the issue—at least in the context of his courtship to Betsy—is irrelevant. Angelica was married (happily, so far as the record reveals) to John B. Church, then going under the alias of John Carter, a man "of business," one of Hamilton's friends commented, who "has riches enough . . . to make the longest life very comfortable."[34]

Hamilton wooed Elizabeth with the single-minded intensity that he usually reserved for his work. She was receptive. By March 1780, when Schuyler arrived at Washington's headquarters on business, Alexander and Betsy were engaged. There is no reason to believe that either of them ever regretted the decision. If it was not love at first sight (and for Betsy it seems to have been), it was for both of them love that swiftly developed and steadily deepened. That for Hamilton the marriage was coincidentally advantageous is also beyond doubt.

Describing to Laurens the qualities he looked for in an ideal wife, Hamilton, in an uncharacteristic moment of candor, confided, "As to fortune, the larger stock of that the better . . . as I have not much of my own and as I am very little calculated to get more either by my address or industry; it must needs be that my wife, if I get one, bring at least a sufficiency to administer to her own extravagancies."[35] Although Hamilton would in fact earn a good deal of money and Elizabeth was never a spendthrift, the Schuyler connection was a giant step toward the successful career on which Hamilton was intent. Still, viewed superficially, the match was an odd one, this union between a dashing, but poor, young officer of a lineage that he only wished to hide and a sheltered young lady who belonged to one of the richest manorial families in New York and who was also carefully attentive to her parents' status and wishes.

Just why Philip Schuyler, who characteristically displayed an almost oriental reverence for ancestors, readily approved of the engagement is even more curious. The head of a family that for four generations had played an important part in the affairs of colonial New York, Schuyler's closest associates were other members of the province's elite—the Delanceys, Livingstons, Van Rensselaers, and Van Cortlandts—many of whom were also kinsmen. In the Dutch tradition of patroonship, Schuyler was the master of large estates in the Mohawk Valley, at Cortlandt Manor, in Dutchess County, and in the Saratoga patent. He also was a successful businessman. By all accounts, he was, appropriately, the prototype of the aristocrat—tall, of a military bearing and a commanding presence, his manner austere, even haughty. It would have been both in character and the tradition of noblesse oblige had he become the patron of Washington's brilliant young aide, but to welcome him as a son-in-law was another matter. As Hamilton himself said, "I am a stranger in this country. I have no property here, no connexions."[36] Schuyler overlooked such things, and unhesitatingly and warmly welcomed as his prospective son-in-law this West Indian immigrant with no fortune and family antecedents as shadowy as his own were lustrous. On the subject of family, the New York patroon probably believed whatever Hamilton told him (and what that was we have no way of knowing). So far as Hamilton's impecuniousness was concerned, Schuyler perhaps correctly perceived that the young man's genius, charm, and drive were more than adequate compensations.

Hamilton, then a few weeks short of twenty-six, and Elizabeth, just twenty-three, were married on December 14, 1780, in the drawing room of the Schuyler house in Albany, an impressive mansion of orange brick commanding a fine view of the river and surrounded by well-tended grounds. The only friend of the groom who attended was James McHenry, Hamilton's fellow aide, who wrote a saccharine poem to commemorate the event.[37] Following a brief honeymoon in Albany, Hamilton, accompanied by his bride, reported back to duty at headquarters, then located at New Windsor, New York, where the young couple occupied temporary quarters.

III

Burgeoning Political Economist

As his marriage attests, Hamilton's career might have provided the plot of a Horatio Alger novel, except that he acquired fame unaccompanied by riches. His success, like that of an Alger hero, was the reward of calculated charm, hard work, individual study, determination, and discreet deference, but it was also owing to shrewd self-promotion. He unhesitatingly brought his ideas to the attention of leading Americans not only because of a desire to further his ambitions but because of well-placed confidence that he had sound opinions to offer. He sought, in other words, to promote his own interests by promoting the public interest. It is at least understandable if he at times confused the two.

As early as March 1777, a few weeks after his appointment to Washington's staff, Hamilton accepted the invitation of a three-man standing committee of the New York legislature (Gouverneur Morris, Robert R. Livingston, and William Allison) to share with them his observations on the activities of the army and affairs of state. He readily complied and, from March to September of the same year, submitted detailed reports and sage advice that would have done credit to a military correspondent or prominent political leader. Of particular note were his comments on the proper nature and structure of government, which prefigured the political philosophy of the Federalist statesman. From the standpoint of the advancement of his career, however, such statements of political principles were less important than the men with whom he shared them. These and other letters brought him to the attention of wealthy, aristocratic, or politically influential New Yorkers and prominent Americans elsewhere. It is a measure of their admiration of Hamilton that such Revolutionary notables should have considered him eligible for important public posts. He was, for example, recommended as congressional envoy to France to secure funds and military assistance, as adjutant general, and, by one influential admirer, as the most suitable candidate for the post of secretary of finance.[1]

Hamilton won recognition by dint of long hours of diligent labor. His official duties alone would have been work enough for most men. As Washington commented, his aides were "confined from morning til eve, hearing and answering the applications and letters," tasks that required them "to have the mind always upon the stretch, scarce ever unbent, and no hours for recreation."[2] Hamilton's mind seems always to have been as taut as a coiled spring. Certainly he permitted himself very little recreation, or what in a revealing concatenation of words he once described, in another context, as "the lethargy of voluptuous indolence."[3] His heavy workload, however, was partly of his own making. In addition to carrying out the manifold tasks assigned him by Washington he also carried on, as was said, an extensive personal correspondence, much of which took the form of thoughtful essays on public affairs that proposed innovative reforms in the American government and economy.

From the vantage point of Washington's headquarters Hamilton was able to see the war effort as a whole, not just the deficiencies of the Continental army but also the shortcomings of the Continental Congress, the problem of a union too weak and sometimes unwilling to support adequately a war for its own preservation. Thus, Hamilton's wartime experiences were the crucible in which were forged the principles and ideas whose subsequent implementation were of major historical consequence. His aideship was, in other words, his postgraduate education, during which Hamilton supplemented his practical training by a strict schedule of after-hours study.*

Hamilton's self-imposed regimen of reading broadened the knowledge he had acquired during his brief formal education, but to him learning was never for learning's sake; rather, it illuminated practical experience and was a spur to action, particularly to recommendations for the reformation of the American union. This pragmatic bent was demonstrated during his years on Washington's staff by the treatises on political economy that he cast in the form of letters to some of the nation's prominent statesmen.

Over roughly a one-year period (1780–1781) Hamilton wrote three letters that not only expressed his opinions on public policy during the Revolution

---

*The books that Hamilton read or reread during his years of military service were no doubt more numerous than his papers explicitly reveal. That he conducted a systematic program of study is suggested by the copious notes that he wrote in his Pay Book as captain of a New York company of artillery. The most plausible conjecture is that he did not begin taking these notes until the latter part of May 1777. On blank pages of his pay book Hamilton took notes on a wide variety of subjects, but particularly on Malachy Postlethwayt's *Universal Dictionary of Trade and Commerce,* Plutarch's *Lives,* and Demosthenes' *Orations.* Of these and other authors he may have read, Postlethwayt most engaged his attention, partly because Hamilton was more intent on acquiring concrete information than he was interested in theoretical speculation and partly because he found congenial the mercantilist principles that but that also adumbrated his famous state papers as secretary of the Treasury. The addressee of the first of these letters, probably written in March 1780, has never been identified, and it is possible that the letter was never sent.[5] The recipient of the second letter, dated September 3, 1780, was James Duane, a New Yorker with whom Hamilton regularly corresponded on military and public affairs.[6] It was one of the most convincing pleas for national over state sovereignty that was penned during the Revolution. The third letter, written in April 1781, was addressed to Robert Morris, who had been appointed superintendent of finance two months earlier.[7] This essay in letter form was manifestly the work of a gifted political economist.

Taken together, these letters compose a prelude announcing the major motifs of Hamilton's mature statesmanship. The themes that run through all three letters are (1) the defects of the Confederation and proposals for mending them; (2) recommendations for reforming the nation's public finance and administration; and (3) Hamilton's more abstract views of human nature and of society and polity.

"The fundamental defect" of the present system, Hamilton observed, "is a want of power in Congress." He attributed this defect to "the particular states' jealousy of all power not in their own hands," to the congressional practice of "constantly making concessions to the states, and to the insufficiency of the means at Congress'" "disposal to answer the public exigencies," an explanation that might have been subsumed in two words— state sovereignty.[8] But to Hamilton this deplorable situation was attributable not only to the assertiveness of the states but also to the pusillanimity of Congress. That body was, if its members would only recognize the fact, "vested with full power to *preserve the republic from harm.*" Elaborating on a claim that his states' rights opponents would in the future never cease to contest, Hamilton asserted that "undefined powers are discretionary powers, limited only by the object for which they were given." For the present, as he noted, that object was "the independence and freedom of America."[9]

Although Hamilton could confidently assert (in the face of the then-prevailing opinion) that the union, not the states, was sovereign, he nevertheless insisted that "the confederation itself . . . requires to be altered; it is fit for neither war nor peace." In what ways was it unfit? For one thing, it gave "to the states individually too much influence in the affairs of the army,"

---

inspired Postlethwayt's ambitious *Dictionary,* principles that were similarly set forth by Sir James Steuart and David Hume, political economists who also molded Hamilton's thought. Hamilton started his study of Postlethwayt by copying facts—for example, the geographical features of Europe and Asia, the principal productions and exports of various countries, and statistics on manufacturing, mining, and other industries. But as he progressed, he focused on more complex subjects such as money and "funds" and began to add to his notes from Postlethwayt his own ideas, some of which can be traced through his later writings. As Broadus Mitchell remarks, "The similarity [of Hamilton and Postlethwayt] in bent for promoting the public economy by a combination of limitation and liberty, or guidance by a loose reign, can scarcely be missed."[4]

whose "entire formation and control" should instead be vested in Congress.[10] For another, that body surrendered "too intirely" to the states its own rightful exercise of "the power of the purse."[11] A third flaw of the Confederation was a "want of method and energy in the administration" of national affairs, notably the lack of an efficient executive and oversight of executive departments by individuals rather than by boards.[12]

Hamilton's prescription for the congenital infirmities of the Confederation was one that he and like-minded nationalists would continue to propose until it finally was accepted almost a decade later: the immediate calling of "a convention of all the states with full authority to conclude . . . a general confederation." With what powers should it be vested? Hamilton's answer (which he would offer scores of times in as many different words) was that its powers should be "competent to the public exigencies," immediate and foreseeable.[13] The scope of these powers was indicated by the observation with which Hamilton concluded an illustrative list of them. The powers conferred, he offhandedly commented, should be extensive enough to permit "doing whatever else relates to the operations of finance, transacting every thing with foreign nations . . . &c., &c."[14] Such an assertion—in effect, a claim that the powers of the union should be conterminous with its own definition of national needs—would have astonished many prominent state officials (such as George Clinton) with whom Hamilton was then on cordial terms. It in time alienated them.

Hamilton believed that a restructured government should above all else make possible the reform of the country's faltering economy. Indeed, the centralizing drift of his model constitution was conditioned by his preoccupation with public finance. The steady depreciation of Continental currency, the crumbling state of public credit, and, in general, the Confederation's almost criminal mismanagement of the country's finances were to him the critical impediments to American military victory and viable nationhood.

"The object of principal concern," Hamilton wrote, "is the state of our currency," thus committing himself in advance to a simplified solution to the country's economic ills.[15] Nevertheless, the relentless decline in the value of Continental currency was surely the most conspicuous symptom of a deranged economy. It appeared that such currency might be worthless and the nation obliged to resort to a barter system. Unlike many of his contemporaries, however, Hamilton did not pin the blame for this situation on Congress alone. Even had that body adopted the most "provident arrangements," he conceded, it could not have arrested the currency's decline in value.[16]

The essential problem, as Hamilton astutely pointed out, was that the wealth of the nation was not sufficient to provide revenues equal to the extraordinary expenses of a wartime economy. Congress was thus "obliged, in order to keep up the supplies to go on creating artificial revenues by new emissions; and as these multiplied their value declined."[17] Although the depreciation, if viewed in this way, was not only unavoidable but also a necessary source of artificial wealth, it was imperative, Hamilton argued, to find a more satisfactory way of financing the war. Since a sound currency could be established neither by taxes nor domestic loans, the only recourse was to foreign loans. The difficult question was, How could they be most satisfactorily applied? Hamilton's answer: "convert the loan into merchandize and import it on public account" and levy a tax in kind on American farmers.[18] But these were stopgap expedients that had to be accompanied by a long-range program designed both to "accomplish the restoration of paper credit" and to "establish a permanent fund for the future exigencies of government."[19] The solution Hamilton offered was a national bank,[20] and the plan he presented foreshadowed the Bank of North America, which would soon be chartered, and the national bank that he would launch a decade later.

More generally, the policies that Hamilton proposed in 1780–1781 revealed both the weaknesses and strengths of the economic program that he would successfully recommend for the nation a decade later. His policies also demonstrated many of the fears and convictions that would premise his nationalistic program. Of central importance was anxiety that in "an empire composed of confederated states," as was the case in America, "the common sovereign will not have power sufficient to unite the different members together, and direct the common forces to the interest and happiness of the whole."[21] How, on the one hand, could this calamity be obviated and, on the other, this happy prospect be promoted? His countrymen, Hamilton answered, must "frame in time a confederacy capable of deciding the differences and compelling the obedience of the respective members."[22] Here was a belief to which he steadfastly would adhere; here also is implied a seminal idea that he would set forth in *The Federalist,* where he argued that the requisite compulsion must be by the supremacy of the law and not by force of arms.

Similarly prefigurative was his insistence that legislatures were unsuited to the administration of government. His prototype was the Continental Congress. It is "properly a deliberative corps," he wrote, "and it forgets itself when it attempts to play the executive." A legislature was by definition incapable of playing that role because "numerous as it is, constantly fluctuating," it was incapable of acting "with sufficient decision, or with system."[23] The essential corrective was a forceful and energetic executive plus independent and capable heads of administrative departments. Once such arrangements were made, Hamilton commented, "we shall blend the advantages of a monarchy and a republic in our constitution."[24] The preparation of such a proper blend was for Hamilton a lifelong preoccupation, and it prompted his critics to charge mistakenly that he was at heart a monarchist. In fact, his insistence on an energetic executive was particularly apposite to the Confederation government that strove unsuccessfully to govern the country during the American Revolution. How applicable the same prescription was to changed conditions of a later time is another matter.

Also appropriate to the fledgling nation was Hamilton's insistence that government must win the confidence of rich men, a proposition for which he has been flailed from that day to our own. Hamilton's primary concern was the establishment of an effective government. For this, an essential requirement was public confidence that would save public credit from the "irretrievable catastrophe" to which it was hastening.[25] And to Hamilton the rescue of public credit—without which neither requisite taxes nor loans were possible—was essential. "Without certain revenues," he asserted, "a government can have no power." To guarantee the first and to acquire the second, government must gain the support of those men best able to assure its financial solidarity. For example, "the only certain manner to obtain a permanent paper credit is to engage the monied interest immediately in it";[26] the only way to assure the success of a government-sponsored national bank is to link "the interests of the state in an intimate connection with those of the rich individuals belonging to it," thus also turning "the wealth and influence of both into a commercial channel for mutual benefit."[27] Neither during the Revolution nor his tenure as secretary of the Treasury did Hamilton argue that the government existed to promote the interests of the rich; in both instances he asserted that without the support of monied men an effective government and economy would be impossible.

Actually, Hamilton trusted neither monied nor any other men. Human beings, he observed, are "governed more by passion and prejudice than by an enlightened sense of their interest. A degree of illusion mixes itself in all the affairs of society."[28] The policies of government must thus be based not only on "abstract calculations" of the public interest but also on the public's perception of its own interests, taking into account that "men are . . . as much influenced by appearances as by realities."[29] This belief, one of Hamilton's pet dicta, was itself an "abstract calculation," and unfortunately, it was one that he would as Treasury secretary forget to apply to his agrarian opponents.

Hamilton's essays in letter form on political economy, his bulky personal correspondence, and his heavy work load at headquarters added up to a virtually superhuman assignment. At times Hamilton balked, taking refuge in self-pity. "I am disgusted with every thing in this world but yourself," he confided to John Laurens in January 1780. "I feel I am not fit for this terrestreal country."[30] The wellspring of such atypical pathos was not so much fatigue as it was frustration. For one as impatiently ambitious as Hamilton, continued service as a secretary was irksome. He craved an active military command. But Washington, better aware of where his aide's superior talents really lay than Hamilton himself, refused to cooperate. "I am chagrined and unhappy," Hamilton complained, "but I submit."[31] For a while he succeeded in doing so.

Acquiescence was the easier because it appeared that the war might go on for so long that in time it might afford Hamilton the type of military service he wanted. The year 1780 was one of successive setbacks for the Americans—the loss of Charleston, South Carolina, in May, for example, and General Horatio Gates's defeat by the British at Camden in August. There was, however, one harbinger of ultimate success—the arrival of the Comte de Rochambeau and French troops at Newport, Rhode Island, in May 1780. Their presence would soon oblige the British to recognize reluctantly that a popular uprising in an extensive country and especially one backed by a strong military ally could not easily be suppressed.

As the prospects of an eventual patriot victory improved, Hamilton became more and more restive. But still there was not a hint that Washington might relent and appoint him to an active command. Hamilton's growing annoyance with routine work and impatience with what he regarded as an unfairly stymied military career were increasingly difficult to suppress. His discontent erupted over a seemingly trivial incident.

Early one morning in February 1781, Washington, unexceptionably enough, told Hamilton that he needed his immediate assistance. Would it be all right, Hamilton asked, if he first delivered a letter to one of the rooms on the first floor? The general agreed. His errand swiftly accomplished, Hamilton ran into the Marquis de Lafayette, with whom he stopped to chat for a few minutes. As Hamilton bounded back up the steps, he encountered the general, whose face was flushed with anger. "Colonel Hamilton," Washington sternly admonished, "you have kept me waiting at the head of the stairs these ten minutes. I must tell you, sir, you treat me with disrespect." "I am not conscious of it, Sir," Hamilton tartly replied, "but since you have thought it necessary to tell me so, we part."[32] Washington turned away, startled no doubt by such an egregious breach of military propriety by an aide who always before had been not only amicably cooperative but also deferential. But not the type of man to bear a grudge against a valued assistant whom he liked and respected, Washington soon apologized, a singularly generous act, although one that was in character. For his part, Hamilton chose to pout, stubbornly refusing to withdraw his resignation.

Hamilton was not only unrepentant but defiant. It is customary to attribute his behavior to a temporary loss of balance. Such an explanation is too simple by far, as is demonstrated by an account of the incident that he promptly sent to Philip Schuyler. Washington was "neither remarkable for delicacy nor good temper," Hamilton charged, and he "felt no friendship for him and have professed none."[33] It was a startling revelation. Had Hamilton for four years loyally, seemingly devotedly, served a man whom he all along had held in such low esteem? Was his determination to win Washington's approval and future support so strong that he was willing thus to dissemble, even to the verge of sycophancy? What explains the inner iciness that his skillful deception had hitherto masked? The questions are germane. No other of Washington's aides expressed such sentiments; to the contrary, they consistently acclaimed Washington's virtues. Surely Washington himself was not by any objective criteria responsible for Hamilton's pique; to the contrary, he had shown Hamilton abundant trust, even affection, although understandably he had not granted his every wish. The explanation must lie elsewhere. Perhaps in this instance the West Indian lad was indeed father of the man. Having been abandoned by one father, Hamilton allowed himself to feel no deep affection for a substitute, even one as reliable as General Washington. Such a surmise perhaps explains the unaccountable as well as any other.

Schuyler gently rebuked what he implicitly construed as his son-in-law's rash and self-defeating behavior. Pitching his argument on the high ground of the public weal, Schuyler wrote, "Your quitting your station must . . . be productive of very material injuries to the public, and this consideration, exclusive of others, impells me to wish that the unhappy breach should be closed, and a mutual confidence restored." But despite Schuyler's plea that Hamilton show a bit more sympathy for "the fraility of human nature," the latter refused to retract his resignation.[34] Perhaps the problem was that he had scant understanding of his own frailities. Certainly his account of the dispute with Washington both obscured and revealed the truth. His feelings toward the general were, in other words, rather more ambivalent than he allowed. What really occurred was described by Hamilton himself, in a different context, as "a violent conflict between my friendship and my pride."[35] In Hamilton's case, pride nearly always triumphed. The quarrel was soon patched up, largely because Washington was determined that it should be, and between the two men there was never again (so far as we know) an angry exchange. But the seemingly trivial episode illuminates important features of Hamilton's personality that might otherwise remain shadowy.

If Hamilton ever regretted his churlish behavior, or even recognized it as such, he did not say so. But soon aware that continued sulkiness was self-defeating, he obligingly stayed on at headquarters to finish up a number of assignments. Perhaps, too, he reaffirmed the high estimate in which he previously had held Washington. "The blame of the unmeaning petulance of a few impatient spirits will never rest upon him," Hamilton had written in September 1779. "Whoever knows his character will be satisfied."[36]

Hamilton, in the manner of a recalcitrant son who takes parental forbearance for granted, apparently believed that it was in character for Washington to reward fractious aides. He no sooner left headquarters than he began to barrage the commanding general with renewed requests for active service. Washington was unsurprised but unrelenting, although he feared that Hamilton would attribute his refusal "to other motives" than those that actually prompted him.[37] But Hamilton was more concerned with reversing the decision than with the reasons for it. Early in July he visited headquarters to plead his case in person, and once home again, he impatiently awaited notification of the importunately sought appointment. When none came, he played the card he had kept in reserve—resignation of his commssion as lieutenant colonel. Washington's response was swift. Tench Tilghman was instructed to visit Hamilton and to assure him that if he would withdraw his resignation, he would receive as congenial an assignment as Washinton could provide. Within three weeks Hamilton's persistence was at last rewarded when he was offered the command of a battalion of light infantry.[38]

Philip Schuyler was less sympathetic to Hamilton's demands, and far more outspoken, than Washington. His son-in-law's military ardor was misplaced, Schuyler said. Why, he properly asked, should Hamilton seek to embellish an already distinguished record of military service by risking his life on the battlefield? He should rather serve in a capacity that would allow the exercise of his unique talents. Schuyler was obviously prepared to see to it that a suitable opportunity presented itself. The New York legislature, he assured his son-in-law, could be counted on to elect Hamilton a delegate to the Continental Congress.[39] As appears to have been characteristic of their friendly give-and-take relationship, Hamilton politely received Schuyler's advice and promptly spurned it.

Hamilton's opportunity to prove himself under fire came at Yorktown. Although his battalion was scheduled to take part in the assault on only one redoubt, Hamilton asked his friend Lafayette to induce Washington to give him command of the entire attacking force. Once again the general acquiesced, perhaps because he felt obliged to grant what might be Hamilton's last wish. As if intent on making it so, Hamilton was the first to leap over the British parapet to take on the Redcoats. But danger was fleeting, and the risk never great. The bayonet assault that he directed was over in minutes.

More important than Hamilton's personal role at Yorktown was the stage on which it was acted. He had taken part in the grand finale of a war victoriously concluded against seemingly insuperable odds. He had helped to christen under fire a new nation that he hoped would also be, in time, a mighty one. He was prepared to help make it so. The Revolutionary years had been his apprenticeship in statesmanship. He had been tutored in the exercise of administration, had seen the art of management as practiced by a master, and had observed the conduct of public affairs at first hand. His wartime experience, moreover, had cemented his commitment to American nationalism. It had confirmed, too, his confidence in his own superior talent and led to its recognition by those able to provide a more spacious arena for its display. "If I have talents and integrity," Hamilton had written to John Laurens in January 1780, "these are justly deemed very spurious titles in these enlightened days, when unsupported by others more solid."[40] Having already won by marriage the support of America's equivalent of an aristocratic title, it was now necessary to acquire a solid profession.

Hamilton prepared for the bar by a crash program of independent study. carried out at the Schuyler mansion in Albany. Blackstone's definitive *Commentaries on the Laws of England* was his principal source, and to facilitate the mastering of complex rules, pleas, and proceedings Hamilton drew up his own law manual, "Practical Proceedings in the Supreme Court of the State of New York," which was subsequently used as a text by other law students. He began his studies in April 1782; three months later he was admitted to the New York bar. July 1782 was for Hamilton an auspicious month, marking not only the launching of his legal practice but also his career as a public official. On the second of that month, he received from Robert Morris, superintendent of finance, an official appointment as Continental receiver of taxes for New York. Hamilton was not enthusiastic about the appointment. The pay was small, and the difficulties seemingly insurmountable. "The whole system (if it may be so called) of taxation in this State," he wrote to Morris, "is radically vicious, burthensome to the people,

and unproductive to Government . . . there seems to be little for a Continental Receiver to do."[41] What he was supposed to do was to receive the
money voluntarily appropriated by New York to help support the Confederation government; the problem was that New York, like most other states,
was disinclined to provide funds for another, seemingly foreign government.
Hamilton's four-month service as receiver was thus a predictable exercise in
frustration but one that strengthened the lesson taught him during the Revolution: the grave defects of the Confederation government could be mended
only by vesting it with the necessary powers.

How could this be done? Hamilton's familiar reply was the convening of
a constitutional convention of all the states to restructure the tottering Confederation. With Schuyler's instrumental support, he contrived to promote
that possibility by persuading the New York legislature to issue the requisite
call. The gist of the legislature's resolves, drafted by Hamilton and trans-
mitted to Congress and to the governors of the states, was that "the radical
Source of most of our Embarrassments, is the Want of sufficient Power in
Congress," a lack that should be supplied by the states' adoption of the
corrective measures "on which their immediate Safety and future Happiness
depend."[42] Although Hamilton believed the effort worth making, he presumably was not disappointed when his trial balloon promptly plummeted,
virtually unnoticed. Even in the state where it was launched, interest was
faint. Hamilton's explanation for such apathy in the face of such urgent need
prefigured a viewpoint with which his name would be inseparably connected
contemporaneously and posthumously. The government of New York exhib-
ited "the general disease which infects all our constitutions—an excess of
popularity," he explained to Robert Morris. "The inquiry constantly is what
will *please,* not what will *benefit* the people." As for his fellow citizens,
they "murmur at taxes, clamor at their rulers," and "change one incapable
man for another more incapable." Had Hamilton's supporters in the state
legislature known of this unflattering estimate, they might well never have
appointed him as a delegate to the Continental Congress.

IV

Private Respite
and Public Repute

"I am now a grave counsellor-at-law, and shall soon be a grave member of Congress," Hamilton reported to Lafayette on November 3, 1782. In a comment far more applicable to himself than to his aristocratic friend, Hamilton added, "You are condemned to run the race of ambition all your life."[1] This important milestone on the road to a public career had been handed to Hamilton in July 1782 by the New York legislature whose members were no doubt mindful of the young veteran's connection with the Schuyler family. Hamilton, who was but one of five delegates (two of whom never took their seats), did not arrive in Philadelphia, where Congress then sat, until late in November; he served as a delegate until July of the following year.

Hamilton went to the Continental Congress with concrete remedies that he repeatedly had proposed in private correspondence. His program was publicly spelled out in "The Continentalist," a series of six articles that appeared during the year or so before he was appointed to Congress.[2] Despite some minor flaws, such as occasional repetition and contradiction, the "Continentalist" essays are far superior to Hamilton's earlier pieces on political economy, though they by no means bear comparison to *The Federalist* and to his memorable Treasury Department reports.

The theme of "The Continentalist" was one that he had tirelessly harped on many times before: the major defect in the "management of our civil as well as of our military affairs" was "a want of power in Congress." This deficiency was due to "an extreme jealousy of power" that "is the attendant on all popular revolutions."[3] The solution was as simple as the problem was obvious: invest Congress with the powers essential to viable nationhood. The then-prevalent concept that Hamilton sought to refute was attachment to state sovereignty; the popular fear that he tried to dispel was the danger of an abuse of power, especially if exercised by the union. The large number of his countrymen who equated a substantial increment in the power of the central government with despotism, Hamilton insisted, misunderstood the problem. What they failed to see was that just "as too much power leads to despotism," so "too little leads to anarchy, and both eventually to the ruin of the people."[4] The issue of despotism, as his fellow Americans perceived it, was a red herring. The danger was not a despotic central government; it was rather that the members of the union "will be an overmatch for the common head."[5] What Hamilton proposed, and would repeat time and again during the debate over ratification of the Constitution, was neither an all-powerful union nor unbridled state power but divided sovereignty, an appropriate division of powers between the states and the union. Just as Congress should be "the common sovereign," so each state had "a distinct sovereignty." His position was capsulated in the comment that "the security . . . of the public liberty, must consist in such a distribution of the sovereign power, as will make it morally impossible for one part to gain an ascendancy over the others, or for the whole to unite in a scheme of usurpation."[6]

In such a distribution, with what powers should the central government be invested? According to Hamilton, they must minimally include the right to regulate trade, to appoint its own officers, to exercise custodianship of the western territories, to impose import duties, and, above all, to levy taxes, not through the agency of the states but on its own authority. Hamilton predicted an unrelievedly gloomy prospect for the American future if such rights were not affirmed: "a number of petty states, with the appearance only of union, jarring, jealous and perverse, without any determined direction, fluctuating and unhappy at home, weak and insignificant by their dissentions, in the eyes of other nations."[7]

By what means could this parade of horrible eventualities be avoided and the requisite authority bestowed on the national government? Hamilton's answer was the same as he had before proposed: the convening of a constitutional convention to rewrite the fundamental law of the land. In the concluding paragraph of the last of his "Continentalist" essays, Hamilton shared with his countrymen his own glowing vision of the American future: "There is something noble and magnificent in the perspective of a great Federal Republic, closely linked in the pursuit of a common interest, tranquil and prosperous at home, respectable abroad."[8] The Continental Congress, during Hamilton's brief tenure as a delegate, did nothing to brighten, and much to dim, such a prospect.

A gauge of the status and powerlessness of the Congress was the virtually empty chamber in which its proceedings were lackadaisically carried on. Few members bothered to show up when routine business was on the agenda; even when issues of substance were under consideration, it was difficult to round up delegates from the nine of thirteen states whose assent was required. Of the twenty-odd delegates who were in attendance at any one time, only a handful were involved enough to participate in debate and take on committee work. Among those few, Hamilton was conspicuous, as was James Madison. A striking affinity promptly developed between the dynamic New Yorker and the scholarly and resourceful Virginian, men of such seemingly dissimilar backgrounds and experiences. It was based on the shared conviction that the tottering Confederation must be strongly braced and on a mutual commitment to American nationalism. It was evidenced by their harmonious collaboration in support of these goals.

The eight-month period during which Hamilton served in Congress was in retrospect a critical one in the history of the 1780s. It was then that the central political question of the Confederation era was answered: Shall the union be granted powers adequate to govern effectively? The answer was in the negative. What were the paramount issues that Congress failed to resolve successfully? The major problem was public finance. Since requisitions on the states for funds had proved hopelessly unreliable, it was essential that some alternative system for paying the interest on, and at least a part of the principal of, the public debt be adopted. Relatedly, enough money had to be found to satisfy an unpaid and unpensioned army, reluctant to disband without some guarantee that its just claims would be met. Underpinning all else, of course, was the want of powers that would assure the efficacy of any remedial legislation.

This deficiency was tellingly demonstrated when Rhode Island refused to give its assent to Congress' proposal to levy a modest impost of 5 percent. Nationalist-minded congressmen like Hamilton might remonstrate and implore, but there was no way to coerce a fractious state. The hopelessness of correcting what Hamilton viewed as so lamentable a situation was borne in on him when the populous and powerful state of Virginia followed the lead of tiny Rhode Island and retracted its endorsement of the impost. The time was late December 1782. During the first half of the following year Congress was subjected to a series of shocks whose reverberations subsided only with the adoption of the Constitution.

At the outset, there was the gnawing fear that a satisfactory peace treaty could not be concluded. As Hamilton explained, it was as doubtful that confidence could be placed in the British negotiators (particularly in view of "the duplicity and unsteadiness" of Lord Shelburne) as it was uncertain that "the variety of interests" at stake could "be conciliated in a treaty of peace."[9] There was, more menacingly, the threat of civil disorders (some said a coup d'etat) by a disgruntled army. There was, relatedly, the failure of Congress' frantic effort to secure fixed, much less permanent, funds sufficient to satisfy its creditors, much less to fund the public debt. There was, late in the spring, the mutiny of irate soldiers of the Pennsylvania line. There was, finally, the ignominious flight of Congress, besieged by this boisterous band of mutineers, from Philadelphia to Princeton.

For well over a year following the surrender of the British army at Yorktown, it seemed that American independence was as yet unsecured. As Congress anxiously awaited news of a definitive treaty confirming that status, the Continental army remained intact, not only because of this uncertainty but also because it feared that once it had disbanded and dispersed, an un-grateful Congress would renege on its promises, whether of money, land, or half-pay. Such mistrust was not groundless. Many congressmen did appear disinclined to provide arrears of pay and pensions for soldiers whose services would, with the advent of peace, be no longer necessary and who, in view of the prevailing fear of "standing armies," should be promptly discharged. But even had Congress been disposed to honor its commitments fully, there remained the seemingly insuperable problem of paying money from an empty treasury. To the army, however, Congress itself was largely respon-sible for a situation that could be reversed by decisive, forceful action.

In January 1783 an army deputation headed by Alexander McDougall, who years earlier had been largely responsible for Hamilton's initial military appointment, arrived in Philadelphia to present the soldiers' case to Con-gress. In the ensuing debate and committee deliberations on the issue Ham-ilton played a leading role. He was, for example, chairman of a subcommittee appointed to confer with the superintendent of finance and to report on means whereby the army's demands might be met, and he was author of a grand-committee report by which Congress solemnly committed itself to the moral proposition that "the troops . . . in common with all the [public] creditors . . . have an undoubted right to expect . . . security."[10]

Such a promise was idle unless the requisite funds could be found. But where were they to come from? Since Rhode Island and Virginia had ruled out the impost, the only source available under the Articles of Confederation was a requisition on the states, based on an evaluation of lands. Such a mode was, of course, merely a refinement of the quota system by which William Pitt had unsuccessfully tried to extract money from the American colonists some fifteen years earlier. In view of the experiences of the Con-federation Congress, moreover, to call on the states for funds was to issue an invitation they were certain to refuse. But as Hamilton recognized, the system and not the refractoriness or niggardliness of the states was to blame. An adequate revenue could only be raised, he insisted, by levying uniform taxes, whose payment would be mandatory, not optional. But this superfi-cially satisfactory solution, as Hamilton also realized, raised as many ques-tions as it answered. For example, what taxes could be imposed, by what criteria, and in what amount? "The truth is," Hamilton replied, "the ability of a country to pay taxes depends on infinite combinations of physical and moral causes which can never be accommodated to any general rule—cli-mate, soil, productions, advantages for navigation, government, genius of the people, progress of arts and industry, and an endless variety of circum-stances."[11] Here, in Broadus Mitchell's phrase, "was the advanced idea" that the wealth of a country depends on its total production and resources, as well as on intangibles and on its potential.[12] Here also was prefigured a concept of national wealth that is now expressed by what we designate the gross national product.

Such larger considerations aside, what was the immediate solution to the instant problem? The states must be obliged to contribute to the union "in an equal proportion to their means by general taxes imposed under Continental authority," Hamilton answered.[13] "General taxes," yes, a majority of his fellow congressmen responded; "under Continental authority," no. So it was that in mid-February 1783 an evasive compromise was approved by which the states were asked to make surveys of the value of all lands and improvements and gather population statistics and to report to Congress by March 1, 1784. Few delegates bothered to ask by what miracle Congress could accomplish in 1784 what it was unable and unwilling to do in 1783, nor what in the meantime would happen to the army.

As to the army, most historians answer that only Washington's statesmanship prevented a mutiny, a consummation that Hamilton devoutly wished and actively promoted. The problem is that the role attributed to him is based on conjecture and inference. If one confines oneself to what he demonstrably did and literally said, one must view the matter differently.

The story of the "Newburgh affair" can be briefly told. The discontent of an already disgruntled army was fanned by anonymous addresses (in fact written by John Armstrong, Jr.) that called on the officers of the army to stand united in defiance of Congress' irresoluteness. Although the precise form such resistance ought to take was left purposely vague, the manifestly provocative addresses implied that if the war continued, the army should refuse to fight, and if peace came, it should remain intact and armed. Alarmed and dismayed at what he interpreted as a threat of mutiny, Washington decided that he must do, in effect, what Hamilton believed he should have done sooner: assume leadership and embrace the officers' cause as his own. Accordingly, on March 15, the general appeared in person before the troops assembled at army headquarters in Newburgh, New York, to discuss what measures should be adopted for a redress of grievances. In one of the most eloquent speeches of his career, Washington pleaded with the army to exercise moderateness, eschewing "any measure which viewed in the calm light of reason, will lessen the dignity and sully the glory you have hitherto maintained." Such an invocation of reason was reinforced by a more emotional appeal. It is a story often told. Midway in his speech, Washington, finding it difficult to follow the text of his address, paused and, while taking his spectacles out of his pocket, remarked: "Gentlemen, you must pardon me. I have grown gray in your service and now find myself growing blind."[14] Legend has it that the effect was miraculous. Hamilton's son, who wrote a seven-volume life of his father under the guise of *A History of the Republic,* described it this way: "Awed by the majesty [of Washington's] virtue and touched with his interest in their sufferings, every soldier's eye was filled with a generous tear . . . they forgot their wrongs, in the love of their country and of their chief."[15]

Perhaps so, but it is worth observing that neither John Armstrong, Jr., nor other army extremists had advocated an armed uprising, and despite some saber rattling, it appears unlikely that the Newburgh addresses could have spawned a coup d'etat. To assume otherwise is to attribute to one rather poorly executed broadside something of the power of the *Communist Manifesto.*

In any event, Hamilton shared Washington's relief that the army docilely heeded the advice of its commander and spurned a mutiny, if indeed that had ever been likely. Like Washington, he sympathized with the army and was indignant at congressional delay in satisfying his former comrades' just claims. "I often feel a mortification, which it would be impolitic to express, that sets my passions at variance with my reason," Hamilton confessed. But although unalterably convinced that the army's grievances were real and its demands for redress reasonable, he subordinated passion to reason. Expressing his own belief that "the claims of the army [be] urged with moderation, but with firmness," he implored Washington "*to take the direction*" of a "*complaining* and *suffering* army," and thus "to guide the torrent, and bring order, perhaps even good, out of confusion."[16] Washington did precisely that, and Hamilton's view (the conjectures of many historians to the contrary notwithstanding) was exactly as he described it. "The licentiousness of an army is to be dreaded in every government," he wrote in September 1783, "but in a republic it is more particularly to be restrained, and when directed against civil authority to be checked and punished with severity."[17]

The storm clouds that hung ominously over the new nation during the year 1783 temporarily lifted in mid-March. On the twelfth of that month news of the signing of a provisional peace treaty reached Philadelphia. Although the formal end of the war awaited the drafting and ratification of a definitive treaty, America, after seven years of fighting, was finally at peace and independent. Having long since identified himself with his adopted country, the event was to Hamilton the happy result of what had perhaps been at the outset a calculated gamble. America's future would determine his own, and he hoped that that future would provide a spacious stage for the leading role he aspired to play. For the moment, however, it appeared to him that his ambition might have to be confined to the restricted arena of a single state.

Congress' irresolute role in the army crisis and its pusillanimous position on requisitions confirmed Hamilton's conviction that state pretensions and perquisites were ineluctable barriers to the adoption of an effective, truly sovereign central government. Thus persuaded, he was imprudently forthright. To assail state sovereignty openly was to defy one of the most popular shibboleths of that day and thus to jeopardize measurably his own political future. But silence, like patience and forbearance, was foreign to Hamilton. He would never join in pacifying the states, he wrote to Governor George Clinton, a confirmed states' righter. "I would rather incur the negative inconveniences of delay than the positive mischiefs of injudicious experiments. A contrary conduct serves to destroy confidence in the government, the greatest misfortune that can befall a nation."[18]

That the surrender of national officials to a rowdy mob might be an even greater misfortune was soon demonstrated. In June 1783 a detachment of disgruntled soldiers of the Pennsylvania line marched east on Philadelphia. Surrounding the state house, in which Congress sat, they demanded as the price for lifting the siege the prompt payment of the back pay due to them.

Intimidated but unable to do the impossible, Congress called on the Executive Council of Pennsylvania to call out the state militia. Although the council would in any event have been uncooperative, Hamilton helped them to save face in the process. As the spokesman for Congress, Hamilton, his patience worn thin, abandoned the superficial civilities that had initially characterized the exchanges between Congress and council. The Pennsylvania officials, he bluntly charged, had had "a principal share" in the insult to Congress.[19] If such forthrightness was a virtue, it had all the defects of that exalted trait. The Executive Council could now disguise its intractability under a display of righteous indignation. A humiliated Congress was obliged to retreat to Princeton. A month or so later, an exasperated Hamilton returned home.

The time was not ripe for the kind of nationalist program Hamilton insistently proposed. Its consummation, as he had learned anew, awaited a constitutional revolution. It was in character that he should have believed that a handful of disinterested nationalistic statesmen (himself conspicuous among them) could have imposed a strong, powerful union on a Congress largely controlled by jealous guardians of state autonomy and on citizens whose primary loyalties were to their own localities.

Nevertheless, Hamilton's brief tenure in the Continental Congress marked an important milestone in his career. He now emerged as a public figure in his own right, both in New York and in national politics. It was for precisely such status that he had incessantly striven, and his success was a tribute not only to his determined drive but to his talent. It was also a tribute to the generous acknowledgment of his rare ability by men whose backing had helped to open doors that might otherwise have remained closed to a poor immigrant with an obscure background. It is scarcely surprising that in Hamilton's eyes such men (William Livingston, John Jay, Gouverneur Morris, Robert Morris, and Schuyler, for example) were peculiarly perceptive, broad-minded, and trustworthy, and thus particularly qualified to be guardians of the public weal. That at a later time, Hamilton exaggerated their unselfish patriotism may have been the result of a belief that his own career was in large measure owing to their disinterested support. It is at least revealing that a group often pejoratively described as the new nation's "elite" so readily opened its ranks to men like Hamilton, newcomers of accomplishment and talent.

"Every day proves the inefficiency of the present Confederation," Hamilton wrote on the eve of his departure from Congress. "It is to be hoped that when prejudice and folly have run themselves out of breath, we may return to reason and correct our errors."[20] In the meantime, Hamilton concentrated his energy on building up a law practice that would comfortably provide for his family. He left Philadelphia in mid-July and after a leisurely journey reached Albany on August 11, 1783. Awaiting him were those he loved most dearly, Eliza; his infant son, Philip; and his father-in-law, with whom he had quickly developed a close and warm friendship, the most intimate (John Laurens excepted) that he ever enjoyed with another man. It was a mutual admiration society, for Schuyler's respect for his brilliant son-in-law was boundless.

Joyous though the family reunion at the Schuyler mansion may have been, the small, quiet, Dutch village of Albany was not where Hamilton wished to stay. New York, a metropolis by contrast and always his favorite city, was where he intended to open his law office. The opportunities that that bustling center of business and commerce afforded appeared as bright in 1783 as they had a decade earlier. But for the time being Hamilton was obliged to wait, impatiently although presumably not idly. British troops still occupied the city and their commander, Sir Guy Carleton, seemed in no haste to leave. By November he could dally no longer, and the Redcoats were ordered to evacuate the city that they had occupied for seven years. With their departure, patriot exiles flocked to Manhattan, which was temporarily in shambles. Among the returning citizens were many lawyers, eager to seize the accumulated and mounting business that, owing to the flight of many Tory attorneys, awaited them. None was more eager than Hamilton, who promptly opened his law office at 57 Wall Street, where he and his family also resided. He was just as promptly a predictable success.

Hamilton was a successful lawyer in the sense that he attracted affluent clients and thus prospered. He also possessed one of the great legal minds of his day. His brilliance was unreservedly acknowledged by his contemporaries, men who by virtue of their own legal preeminence were qualified to judge. James Kent, at a later date chancellor of New York State, recalled in 1832 that among the many lawyers whom he had known during his long career "Colonel Hamilton was undisputably pre-eminent," a prominence that was due to "his profound penetration, his power of analysis, the comprehensive grasp and strength of his understanding" of the law.[21] Judge Ambrose Spencer, whose longevity afforded him an opportunity to observe two generations of America's foremost attorneys, compared Hamilton with Daniel Webster. "In power of reasoning," Ambrose concluded, "Hamilton was the equal of Webster; and more than this can be said of no man. In creative power Hamilton was infinitely Webster's superior."[22] How could one who had so little formal training in the law (Hamilton's apprenticeship was only a few months long) and whose preoccupation with public affairs left so little time for mastering its procedural intricacies have achieved such repute? Robert Troup, who knew Hamilton well, gave the answer. His fellow lawyer was not especially familiar with case law, Troup said, principally because "he had only time to read elementary books." But he "was well founded in first principles," which he applied "with wonderful facility to every question he argued."[23]

Hamilton argued many cases, some of none but narrow professional interest (similar to those that still take up the bulk of an ordinary lawyer's day-to-day practice) and a few of major public consequence (the equivalent of later important constitutional cases). His case load ran the gamut of both civil and criminal practice; he appeared in courts ranging from local ones to the state supreme court, which sat alternately in New York City and Albany.

His list of clients included common citizens as well as rich merchants and large landowners, although the latter two groups predominated.

That he could so readily attract the area's elite was owing to their recognition of his uncommon ability (to which, it will be remembered, he had called their attention during the Revolution) and to his successful participation in public affairs, most notably as a delegate to the Continental Congress. Among those who sought his services were Robert Morris, John Jay, Isaac Sears, Laurence Kortright, John Holt, and Benjamin Walker. More important yet was the business that accrued to him as son-in-law of one of New York's most influential patroons and politicians. Philip Schuyler's connections encompassed virtually the whole aristocracy of New York State. It also included the husband of Angelica Schuyler, John B. Church, who during the American Revolution had amassed a sizable fortune that he considerably enlarged after his return to England soon after the Revolution. Hamilton was not only Church's legal counsel but also his business agent, and "that alone," a recent historian comments, "would have been enough to spare Hamilton the shilling-and-pence work, that might otherwise have made up the main business of a young and inexperienced attorney."[24] Hamilton nevertheless took on "shilling-and-pence work," a part of it as legal representative of former Tories (although some of them could afford handsome fees). He handled no less than sixty such cases, many of them involving claims that arose under the anti-Loyalist statutes adopted by a vindictive state legislature.

The best known of such litigations was *Rutgers* v. *Waddington,* a case firmly entrenched in the history of American constitutional law. Years before the Revolution ended, the New York legislature had responded to the public outcry against Tories by enacting punitive legislation. The clamor was echoed by Governor George Clinton, who commented that he would "rather roast in hell to all eternity than . . . show mercy to a damned Tory."[25] Although Clinton was eager and in a position to lead the anti-Loyalist crusade, the members of the state legislature needed no prompting. In October 1779 that body approved the Confiscation Act, providing for forfeiture and sale of estates; in July 1782, the "Citation Act," relieving the debtors of Loyalists, was adopted, and in March 1783 the Trespass Act was enacted. This last measure stipulated that any citizen whose property, while within British lines, had been oocupied by any person other than its legal owner might sue such occupant for damages. A British order permitting the occupancy could not exempt the trespasser from liability.

Hamilton deplored such anti-Tory legislation, which, in his view, violated international law, the peace treaty with Great Britain, and the basic civil liberties of wartime dissidents. He also decried the resultant exodus of Tories, some twenty-nine thousand of whom left New York in 1782 alone. Months before the British evacuation of New York City, Hamilton wrote to James Duane that "we have already lost too large a number of valuable citizens."[26] Many merchants, "characters of no political importance, each of whom may carry away eight to ten thousand guineas," he observed to another correspondent, "have . . . lately applied for shipping to convey them away. Our state will feel for twenty years at least, the effects of the popular phrenzy."[27] Thus convinced, Hamilton unhesitatingly defied popular opinion and, risking his political future, accepted the case of the defendant in *Rutgers* v. *Waddington*.[28]

Elizabeth Rutgers, the plaintiff in the case, had owned and operated a brewery on the north side of Maiden Lane in New York City. A committed patriot, Mrs. Rutgers accompanied the American army that was obliged to evacuate the city, which was occupied by the Redcoats in September 1776. The brewery was seized by the British military authorities, who, after running it for about two years, authorized the commissary general to license the premises to the British merchant Joshua Waddington and a partner, who remained in possession until March 1783. Waddington incautiously remained behind after the British left New York. Once Mrs. Rutgers returned home, she lost no time in bringing suit against Waddington for redress under the Trespass Act, claiming restitution of the rental value of her property for the entire period of the British occupation.

In agreeing to represent Waddington, Hamilton was enticed not by lucrative fees (they were not in the offing) but by an opportunity to air publicly his firm opposition to the harsh anti-Loyalist legislation under which the action was brought. Hamilton realized that to defend Waddington, who was for the time being the most unpopular man in New York, was to call down upon himself the fury that American patriots felt toward an enemy that had just left the scene. He risked public outrage and possible personal retaliation not only because he believed that vital principles were at stake but also because he was aware that among the luminaries of the New York bar he was best qualified to argue the case. He was right, as the two attorneys who assisted him, Brockholst Livingston and Morgan Lewis, no doubt knew. In view of the overwhelming support that her cause elicited, Mrs. Rutgers had no trouble in finding able lawyers. Egbert Benson, the attorney general of the state, was joined by Robert Troup, John Lawrence, and William Wilcox. The case was heard on August 7, 1784, before the Mayor's Court of New York City, comprising the mayor, James Duane; the recorder, Richard Varick; and five aldermen.

Hamilton's assignment was a formidable one. The facts of the case were not in dispute, and the statute, as well as its applicability to the litigation at issue, was unequivocal. What he did was ingenious and bold. Interposing a demurrer (in effect, a plea that allows the truth of the facts alleged by the opposite party but denies their legal appositeness for a judgment), Hamilton's argument centered on two fundamental points. The first was that the actions of British authorities were consonant with international law. That is, the British commanding general, in seizing the plaintiff's property for the use of his army, had merely done what according to international law— including customs and usages of nations in wartime—he might legally do, as was also true of his licensing of the property to British merchants under the protection of their own army. Hamilton's second point was more audacious: since the Trespass Act violated the peace treaty with Great Britain (in which the two nations mutually renounced all claims for damages arising out of the war), the New York statute was null and void. Hamilton's contention startled his audience and enraged Clintonians everywhere. In a conflict between an act of the New York legislature and the treaty of peace, he argued, the treaty, as an act of Congress, must be recognized by state courts. It was, in sum, an eloquent plea for the supremacy of a national treaty (and, by implication, a national statute) over state law, a position that would become a cornerstone of American constitutional law. It was not so as yet, as counsel for Mrs. Rutgers ardently insisted. New York, Benson argued, was a sovereign state and was thus not bound by a treaty of Congress, much less by international law. A court, moreover, did not have the power to void a statute of the legislature.

On August 27, Duane, speaking for the court, handed down its decision. He probably agreed with Hamilton but for prudential reasons accepted a compromise position, which may have saved his court but satisfied neither the contending counsel nor public opinion generally. Taking refuge in technicalities, Duane, on behalf of the court, granted Mrs. Rutgers damages for only a part of the four-year period at issue, but he did not accept the power urged upon the court by Hamilton. To void the act of a legislature, Duane ruled, would be "to set the *judicial* above the legislative, which would be subversive of all government."[29] If Duane and his cohort believed that the court's straddling of the issue would placate Governor Clinton and his majority in the state legislature, they were much mistaken. The Mayor's Court and its presiding judge were censured, and the Trespass Act continued to be enforced until the end of the decade when, thanks in part to Hamilton's efforts in the state assembly, the Tories regained their rights as citizens.

The decision in *Rutgers* v. *Waddington* may have disappointed Hamilton, but as he no doubt knew, it would have been fanciful to have expected the Mayor's Court's endorsement in toto of a position that would have flagrantly ignored public opinion. Hamilton did so unhesitatingly. It was desirable, he decided, to spread before the public the argument that he had presented in Duane's courtroom.

This he did in two articles to the press, written under the pseudonym Phocion, which deceived no one interested in the identity of the author.[30] In these articles he called for strict adherence to the terms of the Anglo-American peace treaty and, more insistently, for justice and moderation in the treatment of the Tories. "Nothing is more common," he wrote, "than for a free people, in times of heat and violence, to gratify momentary passions, by letting into the government, principles and precedents which afterwards prove fatal to themselves."[31] On what rational grounds, he asked, could representatives of the people "undertake to declare whole classes of citizens disfranchised and excluded from the common rights of the society, without hearing, trial examination or proof"? To do so was contrary "to the dictates of reason and equity," an "inquisition into men's consciences," a flagrant instance of "injustice and oppression."[32] He reprobated, in sum, the punishment of Tories as a denial of due process of law, a contravention of the Confederation and state constitutions, the peace treaty, and international law. Here was the voice of the civil libertarian, a voice scarcely audible to many students of Hamilton's career.

More audible to his contemporaries—and historians—was the voice of Hamilton the nationalist. Although he was absorbed in his day-by-day law practice and in state and local affairs, the state of the union continued to be an absorbing concern. Events of the 1780s heightened Hamilton's distrust of state sovereignty and reinforced his conviction that the type of strong central government on which national salvation depended could never be achieved merely by shoring up the Articles of Confederation. "The principal defects of the confederation," as he would affirm in *The Federalist,* "do not proceed from minute or partial imperfections, but from fundamental errors in the structure of the building." These, he explained, "cannot be amended otherwise than by an alteration in the first principles and main pillars of the fabric."[33] Thus convinced, he became an expert in political seismography, carefully observing every tremor in the Confederation's structure. Although by no means confident that anything short of collapse would have to precede construction of the new, desired edifice, he nevertheless welcomed every bid for reconstruction. Most promising of all was the Annapolis Convention, to which in May 1786 the New York assembly named him a delegate.

The convention, as is well known, was the offshoot of conferences held in 1785 by deputations from Maryland and Virginia to discuss common problems such as the free use of adjoining waters and levying of uniform tariffs. Having settled their longstanding disputes over the navigation of the Potomac, the delegates decided that if two states could thus solve a local matter of common concern, then several states might similarly settle matters of national importance. The initiative was taken by the Virginia legislature, which appointed commissioners to join delegates from other states at Annapolis, Maryland, in September 1786 "for the purpose of forming such regulations of trade as may be judged necessary to promote the general interest."[34] Although such a modest proposal was a far cry from the program Hamilton advocated, he, like other nationalists, saw the convention as a possible first step on the way to far more radical reformation.

Even a baby step, it soon appeared, was by no means a certainty. During the months following his appointment as one of New York's six-man delegation, Hamilton's cautious optimism was dimmed by the manifest apathy of many states and the tardiness of others in naming delegates. To some state leaders (Governor George Clinton conspicuous among them) any such assembly, however limited its agenda, was objectionable. To many nationalists, including four of Hamilton's fellow delegates, the convention would predictably be an exercise in futility. Hamilton shared such misgivings, but believing that even an abortive beginning was preferable to inertia and perhaps also overestimating his own persuasiveness and the power of disinterested leadership, he decide to attend. Although the result can be attributed neither to Hamilton's eloquence nor instrumental leadership, the convention did fulfill his seemingly impossible dream.

On September 2 Hamilton set out on horseback for Annapolis, traveling by way of Philadelphia, which he had not visited since Congress' humiliating retreat to Princeton some three years earlier. Arriving in the Maryland capital on September 9, he probably joined the delegates who lodged at George Mann's City Tavern. Two days later the convention held its opening session in the state house. The empty seats in the senate chamber were silent testimony to the chill reception accorded Virginia's invitation to vest the Continental Congress with the modicum of power necessary to safeguard and promote national commerce. Only twelve delegates, representing merely five states were present. Among them, however, were prominent men with whom Hamilton could renew his acquaintance, such as James Madison, his congressional ally in 1782–1783, and John Dickinson, his Pennsylvania antagonist in June 1783, as well as strangers, such as Tench Coxe, an ambitious Philadelphia aristocrat and former Tory who was well on the way to becoming one of the country's foremost spokesmen for Hamilton's own brand of economic nationalism and with whom the New Yorker's career would be closely connected.

Dickinson was elected chairman, and Coxe was designated secretary of the convention, whose members "entered into a full communication of Sentiments & deliberate consideration of what would be proper to be done." They quickly agreed that with so few states represented it would be impolitic to recommend measures for a uniform commercial system. Instead, a committee was appointed to prepare an "address" to the several states. Drafted by Hamilton and adopted on September 14, it was a masterly maneuver by which ultimate success was snatched from the jaws of apparent failure. Asserting that the commercial powers of Congress could not be altered without taking other matters into consideration as well, the address recommended that the states appoint commissioners to meet in Philadelphia in 1787, there, in Hamilton's phrase, "to devise such further provisions as shall appear to them necessary to render the constitution of the Federal Government adequate to the exigencies of the Union."[35] By also sending a copy of the address to the Continental Congress, the commissioners implicitly invited that body to sign its own death warrant, an invitation that a reluctant Congress was obliged to accept.

Hamilton's biographers are seemingly irresistibly tempted to exaggerate his role in the events that led to the convening of the famous Constitutional Convention in 1787, including the part he played at the assembly in Annapolis.[36] He was indisputably a persistent and consistent proponent of a refashioned government, but it does not follow that he was more influential than other prominent nationalists, some of whom were far better known than he, or that he dominated the proceedings at Annapolis and inspired the call for what would be a bloodless coup d'etat. The report of the Annapolis Convention that he drafted incorporated the ideas of the delegates as a whole, not his own alone. It would be difficult, in sum, to sustain the argument that his contribution was more instrumental than that of other prominent convention members or even comparatively obscure delegates like Coxe. Students of Hamilton's career should be content with his own view of the matter. To him, it was accomplishment enough that he had had a hand in setting in motion plans for a convention that might scrap the Articles of Confederation, "a system . . . radically vicious and unsound."[37] But of this possibility he was anything but sanguine.

Nevertheless, to Hamilton, as to other nationalists, the central issue of the time had now at least been made clear. It was not, as some historians have claimed, primarily to fashion a government that would serve the interests of an economic elite nor to abort the growth of democracy by imposing a coercive government characterized by minority rule. "If union was to subsist at all," the quintessential problem, in the words of Andrew C. McLaughlin, a perceptive twentieth-century historian, was to devise "some scheme or plan or organization wherein there would be reasonable assurance that the states would fulfill their obligations and play their part under established articles of union and not make mockery of union by willful disregard or negligent delay."[38]

A number of prominent state leaders emphatically disagreed with this proposition. George Clinton spoke for them when he said of the report of the Annapolis Convention that "no such reform . . . was necessary; that the Confederation as it stood was equal to the purposes of the Union."[39] Such an extreme position prompted Hamilton to adopt the opposite extreme. Because of the perverse insistence of the states in "yielding to the persuasive voice of immediate interest and convenience," he insisted, "the frail and tottering edifice [of the Confederation] seems ready to fall upon our heads and to crush us beneath its ruins."[40] And to prevent such a catastrophe he persuaded himself that only a powerful, genuinely sovereign nation-state would suffice. The problem was that the overwhelming majority of his countrymen neither shared his alarm nor endorsed his particular remedy.

Whatever his countrymen may have believed, Hamilton by the mid-1780s had become one of the most influential men in New York, both in the city and in the state. His activities encompassed not only politics but also participation in fraternal and eleemosynary associations as well as economic institutions.

Hamilton saw his membership in the select and much-criticized Society of the Cincinnati as a continuation of friendships made during the Revolution and as merely a fraternal group whose members, in naming it after Cincinnatus, had proclaimed their pacifistic nature. Nevertheless, the criticism made by enemies of the society that it was "at best a comically snobbish club . . . and at worst an inner council of would-be aristocrats" was applicable to the inner Hamilton, to his covetousness of the aristocratic status to which he was not born.[41]

Hamilton's West Indian background may also have to some extent been responsible for his participation in New York's antislavery movement (moderation itself as compared to the abolitionism of a much later day). John Jay was the first president of the New York Manumission Society, of which Hamilton was counselor and an active member for the remainder of his life. This did not, however, preclude Hamilton's willingness to own slaves, a not uncommon hiatus between profession and practice during that period. Nor, if his writings be the gauge, was he genuinely disturbed by the institution of slavery. His personal relationships bear out the contention. His later antipathy to Jefferson, Madison, and other southerners was matched by his cordial relationship with William L. Smith of South Carolina and other Federalist slaveholders. In his lack of deep concern about either slavery or its concomitant racism (prevalent in the North as well as the South) he joined the overwhelming majority of his countrymen, political foes and allies alike.

Hamilton's continued interest in economic issues and institutions was demonstrated in the mid-1780s by his instrumentality in founding the Bank of New York. The initiative was not his, however. He acted at the invitation of John B. Church, then in England, and Church's business partner, Jeremiah Wadsworth, to launch a bank in New York in which they would be dominant stockholders. Hamilton was the more willing to cooperate because of a petition to the legislature by Robert R. Livingston, chancellor of the state, for the chartering of a land bank, which would, as its name implies, serve the interests of New York's agrarian group. This it proposed to do by the implementation of such policies as accepting mortgages as collateral for subscriptions to its stock and lending money on the security of acreage. Alarmed by what he viewed as a mistaken proposal, Hamilton, as he explained to Church, started "an opposition to this scheme and took occasion to point out its absurdity and inconvenience to some of the most intelligent merchants," who agreed by setting "on foot a subscription for a money-bank and called upon me to subscribe."[42] Believing that he could thus serve the interests of Church and Wadsworth and concretely express his own economic principles, Hamilton agreed.

Hamilton accordingly took the lead in organizing a "money–bank," which was to be capitalized at $500,000, consisting of a thousand shares at $500 each. The liability of stockholders was to be limited, all payments and receipts were to be only in gold or silver coin or bank notes, and the institution was to be enjoined from engaging in trade. Hamilton himself probably drafted the bank's constitution, and he definitely was the author of the petition to the legislature asking that a bank thus constituted be granted a charter. Because of legislative opposition to banks of issue—to all banks, for that mattter—the legislature procrastinated for seven years, finally granting a charter to the Bank of New York in March 1791. By that time Hamilton's interest had shifted to a far more ambitious project, the Bank of the United States, but he stuck to the conviction that the bank he had helped to launch in 1784 was a model institution, one that served not only the immediate private interests of its stockholders and the needs of New York's business and agricultural communities but also the public interest.

Hamilton's status in his adopted city was attested to by his election to the New York legislature. Since he focused his attention on national affairs, it is rather surprising that he would have sought a seat in the state assembly, particularly in view of the control of that body by stalwart Clintonians, who scarcely could be expected to give him a warm reception, much less to heed his opinions. But perhaps for the moment Hamilton despaired that any first aid could be applied to the ailing Confederation government and decided that he could help to cure the problems that in his view afflicted New York State. At the least, he might stand as the symbol of nationalism in an assembly that stood almost solidly for the doctrine of states' rights.

Hamilton's election in 1786 as an assemblyman from New York City was due both to his popularity among merchants, manufacturers, and some of the latter's satellite artisans and to the political influence wielded by Philip Schuyler. Hamilton took his seat on January 12, 1787, and since the legislature was then sitting in New York City, he was in almost constant attendance until adjournment some four months later.[43] On the day following Hamilton's appearance in the assembly chamber, Governor Clinton delivered his opening address, in the course of which he alluded (with no editorial comment of his own) to a renewed request by the Continental Congress that it be granted the authority to levy import duties. Since an amendment to the Articles of Confederation required the assent of all thirteen states, twelve of which had acquiesced, New York's endorsement was crucial. To Hamilton, the issue was the most critical one confronting the legislative session. It was also one that he had pushed vigorously since its introduction in Congress in 1781. During his tenure as a delegate to that body in 1782–1783 his efforts (ably supported by like-minded nationalists) had foundered on the rock of resistance by Rhode Island and Virginia. Now it was his own state that blocked what he considered a minimum reform of the virtually bankrupt Confederation government. Wishing to disguise its obstructionism, the legislature cooperatively acquiesced in Congress' request but then promptly rendered its agreement meaningless by insisting that the state appoint and control the proposed collectors of Continental revenue. It was precisely this demand to which Hamilton had all along objected, and he fought it now. But his eloquence in debate was wasted; he was unable to budge the Clintonians, who impatiently heard out his remarks, not even bothering to respond to his familiar, although forceful arguments. When the vote was finally taken, Hamilton and national solvency were decisively defeated.

Despite this setback (which he must have predicted) Hamilton's legislative record was not altogether barren. He was largely responsible for persuading the assembly to repeal a measure that required a legislative enactment to dissolve a marriage and to adopt an act permitting divorce on the grounds of adultery (the measure remained on New York's statute books for a century and a half). He also successfully sponsored a bill calling for the establishment of a university of the state of New York, administered by a board of regents, with superintendency over all the state's institutions of higher learning. Hamilton's legislative interests ranged widely. He valiantly tried to convince New York's lawmakers to recognize the independence of Vermont and thus to permit the latter's admission into the union. He won over the assembly but the senate balked. More important to Hamilton personally was repeal of what he still viewed as abhorrent anti-Tory legislation. He was partially successful: some of the more restrictive aspects of the Trespass Act were dropped.

Although Hamilton did not downgrade the utility of reform on the state level, it was to him of secondary importance when compared to the imperativeness of radical reform of the Confederation government. The most gratifying feature of his legislative record was thus approval of his proposal that New York send delegates to the forthcoming Constitutional Convention.

V

The Constitution:
Critic and Champion

Although Hamilton would have handily lost a legislative popularity contest, members of the New York assembly, having been impressed by his eloquence in debate and effectiveness in committee, unanimously selected him to serve at the Constitutional Convention, which assembled in Philadelphia in May 1787. While thus willing to acknowledge his talent, his fellow legislators were at the same time unwilling to give him their full confidence. His predictable support of proposals for a powerful central government was checkmated by the selection of two Clinton stalwarts, Robert Yates and John Lansing, Jr., as the other New York delegates. By this stratagem, Hamilton was not only to be kept out of mischief but also disenfranchised. A man less confident of his ability to accomplish by the force of persuasion what he could not effect by his vote might have turned down the appointment. Had Hamilton done so, his posthumous reputation might have been the beneficiary.

Hamilton and Yates set out for Philadelphia in mid-May. If their conversation was amicable, it presumably centered on the balmy spring weather and greening foliage and not on politics. The purpose of the mission of the one man was precisely contrary to that of the other. Just as Hamilton was intent on helping to "rescue" the nation from "impending anarchy,"[1] so Yates (as well as Lansing, who arrived in Philadelphia two weeks later) was determined to rescue New York from the impending threat to its sovereignty. Having arranged lodgings at the popular Indian Queen tavern on Third between Market and Chestnut streets, Hamilton took his seat in the convention on May 18.

There he sat, mostly in unaccustomed silence, for almost a month. He did not like much that he heard. In order to put the convention at the outset on a nationalist track, Edmund Randolph introduced on May 29 the Virginia, or large-state, plan of union. Prefiguring the government that was subsequently adopted, the Virginia plan provided for a national executive, a national judiciary, and a national legislature of two branches. Members of the legislature were to be apportioned according to population. The small-state rejoinder to this plan was offered by William Paterson of New Jersey. Its provision for equal representation of the states in a unicameral legislature was modeled on the Articles of Confederation, but unlike the Continental Congress, the new national assembly was to have the right to tax and to regulate commerce. As the debate on the New Jersey and Virginia plans droned on, day after warm day, it doubtless seemed to Hamilton that the delegates were merely reflecting, and not constructively dealing with, the essential problem that the convention had been called to correct: the pretensions and perquisites of the states. The debate must also have seemed to him to focus mistakenly on the structure of government rather than on the powers to be granted to it. A gauge of his exasperation was the speech that he delivered to the convention on June 18. After weeks of forbearance, he had decided that the time had come to cut through what he construed as the prevailing cant by presenting a plan so extreme, so unrealizable, that his fellow delegates would at least be nudged toward acceptance of a central government less powerful than he considered ideally desirable but still more forceful and energetic than had as yet been proposed. It would have been in character had he also decided to dazzle the assembled notables of the nation by a display of forensic pyrotechnics.

On Monday, June 18, an unusually hot day, Hamilton spoke for more than five hours.[2] His principal aim was to shatter the shibboleth of states' rights; had the convention's proceedings not been secret, he might instead have shattered his own public career. To the representatives of the several states he recommended that the states be virtually abolished. To a convention that (theoretically anyway) acted on behalf of the people, he proclaimed that "the voice of the people has been said to be the voice of God" but "it is not true in fact. The people are turbulent and ever changing; they seldom judge or determine right."[3] Before a group many of whose members only recently had fought a war to overthrow English rule, he embraced the heretical view that "in his private opinion . . . the British government was the best in the world: and . . . he doubted . . . whether anything short of it would do in America."[4] That he really had no doubts was demonstrated by the detailed plan of government that he proposed: the election of a president for life, the tenure of senators for life or during good behavior, and apppointment by the president of state governors, who also were to sit for life. The sole "democratic" feature of the plan was a lower house elected by the people and enjoying extensive powers. Such a government, as Hamilton later insisted, was "republican," in the sense of James Madison's definition of a republic as "a Government in which the scheme of representation takes place."[5] Hamilton, as he also correctly insisted, did not propose the establishment of a monarchy, in the strict sense of that word. But his program was indisputably cut to the pattern of the British system, and to seriously propose it for a nation drenched in anglophobia was foolhardy. He probably wished to make his mark as a political philosopher. He came closer to immolating himself politically.

Even so, successive generations of "democratic" historians, often more intent on damning than on understanding Hamilton's ideas, have exaggerated the importance of this one speech, interpreting it as Hamilton's political last will and testament. It was not. That the fifty-odd delegates who patiently sat through Hamilton's speech were not particularly shocked is itself revealing. Why was this? For one thing, similar ideas had been aired by other delegates, although no other had so brazenly sacrificed republican sensibilities on the altar of political principles. A second, related reason why Hamilton's proposals were so impassively greeted was their familiarity. To most educated Americans of the day, they merely expressed the traditional wisdom. Respected political philosophers had, after all, long insisted that the government of a well-ordered, effective, and just society must include a will independent of itself—that is, leaders who, because they were not dependent on public favor or popular whim, could make objective and wise decisions. In other words, just as in every free government, the will of the people should be expressed through their popularly elected representatives, so also the public good must be assured by its disinterested guardians. Hamilton's disparaging description of the people as "turbulent and ever changing" does not warrant particular emphasis. His "reservations regarding the all-embracing wisdom of the people," in John C. Miller's words, do not "necessarily stamp him as a reactionary; most of the leaders of the Revolution" shared his misgivings.[6]

What was singular was Hamilton's insistence that any new "general and national government" must be "completely sovereign," and that to this end "we must . . . annihilate the state distinctions and state operations."[7] But the belief was merely an exaggerated expression of his alarmist distrust of state sovereignty—Hamilton's political obsession. Both his extremism and the ardor of his concomitant nationalism were, in other words, reflections of his atypical career. Having spent but half of his thirty-two years in America, he lacked the intuitive understanding of its society, its political prejudices and presuppositions, that came naturally to many of his native-born countrymen. He not only lacked their loyalty to a state or region and their pragmatic approach to the problem of governmental power but he also was far more than they the prisoner of political abstractions. Nor did local attachments moderate the principal political lesson that he had learned from his wartime experiences. To him American government had appeared to be congenitally infirm, a belief reinforced by the weakness and inertia of the Confederation government during the postwar years.

But in a larger sense the question of whether Hamilton thought that the constitution then under consideration was the best possible one or whether he even liked it is a topic, as John Roche has remarked in a different context, "for spiritualists—and is irrelevant."[8] The essential point, too often overlooked, is that Hamilton did willingly work within the frame of government established by the Philadelphia convention. He did not—his critics to the contrary—attempt to subvert, but rather to interpret, the Constitution, and in the light of subsequent American history, that was surely unexceptionable. He was not only committed to working within the contours of representative government as established by the Constitution but was a "political man," not a metaphysician, whose disembodied conservatism was entombed in June 1787.[9]

The point merits emphasis. Many of the views that Hamilton set forth in his speech of June 18 were not enduring articles of his political creed, although he spent much of the rest of his life combating the notion that they were. He came to perceive, as he argued only some six months later in *The Federalist*, that indivisible sovereignty was not an essential attribute of nationhood, that, conversely, a viable federal system was possible. Hamilton's ideas, in sum, were modified by observation and reflection, and he became, as he would repeatedly insist, unreservedly attached to republican government of the kind established by the Constitutional Convention. He did not, however, shed the fear that political intrigues, foreign influence, or demagoguery might render the Constitution, in words that he much later used, "a frail and worthless fabric," an observation that has as often been misrepresented as repeated.[10] Uttered in 1802 at a time of momentary despair, the remark merely conveyed his fear that the Constitution might prove inadequate to the solution of current difficulties (which at that time he exaggerated).

Although the speech had some of the effects of a tidal wave so far as Hamilton's posthumous reputation is concerned, in 1788 it created scarcely a ripple of comment. Gouverneur Morris, a sympathetic listener, said that the address was "the most able and impressive he had ever heard." William Samuel Johnson, although impressed by its "boldness and decision," said that Hamilton "has been praised by everybody [but] has been supported by none."[11]

Hamilton had never thought that he would be. As he had said during his speech, the plan of government he proposed "went beyond the ideas of most members" (not to mention the overwhelming majority of Americans) but was nevertheless a model that should be followed as closely as possible.[12] He was aware that for the moment he could do nothing more to further that goal, the less so since the vote of the New York delegation was controlled by men determined to block any progress toward it. Thus finding himself in a "disagreeable situation," Hamilton returned home.[13] His departure was not, however, an indication of disengagement. Dismayed by the energetic campaign of Clinton and his supporters to condemn in advance the work of the convention, Hamilton countered by a slashing attack on the governor's opposition to the deliberations of a body whose proceedings, because they were secret, he could not know of. Charging that Clinton's campaign was "calculated to impress the people with an idea of evils which do not exist," Hamilton persuasively defended his fellow delegates.[14]

But although Hamilton stoutly defended them, he was for the time being unwilling to rejoin them. He returned to Philadelphia on August 13 but remained for only a few days and did not again attend the convention until September 6, only eleven days before its adjournment. Why did he thus absent himself from an assembly that had within its reach a central government at least close to that on which he long had insisted, a convention of the kind for which he had repeatedly called for a decade or more? One might surmise that, were it not so out of character, Hamilton (although not embarrassed, surely) was aware that his impolitic speech of June 18 had sharply diminished his ability to influence the convention's deliberations. Or did he perhaps despair of their outcome? Most likely, he bided his time to see if the result would be worth a struggle for ratification. Whatever its cause, his disengagement was short-lived. By the time he resumed his place in the convention on September 6, he had not only recovered his confidence in its outcome but had also come to realize the wisdom of what he would write some months later in *The Federalist:* "The truth is that the General GENIUS of a government is all that can be substantially relied upon for permanent effects. Particular provisions, though not altogether useless, have far less virtue and efficacy than are commonly ascribed to them."[15]

Hamilton was thus willing to assist in improving a plan that in June he had mistakenly derided. It was as much by way of apology as reproval that upon signing the new Constitution on September 17 he commented that "no man's ideas were more remote from the plan, than his own were known to be." With scarcely a pause his considered opinion followed. "Is it possible," he asked rhetorically, "to deliberate between anarchy and convulsion on the one side, and the chance of good to be expected from the plan on the other?"[16] George Clinton, along with a majority of New Yorkers, had no doubt about the correct answer to this question.

A good many—perhaps most—Americans did not see the issue this way. For the proposed Constitution to go into effect it was necessary to secure the ratification of nine states. That possibility had been diminished, however, not only by the opposition of a majority of the New York delegation but also by more prominent delegates like Luther Martin of Maryland, Elbridge Gerry of Massachusetts, and, most important of all, Edmund Randolph, a former governor of Virginia. What effect would Randolph's position have in the union's most populous state, whose most popular politician, Patrick Henry, also objected to the Constitution? Henry refused even to attend the Philadelphia Convention because he rightly suspected that it would propose a centralistic government that would drastically diminish state sovereignty. What would be the outcome in New York, where Clinton, spokesman of the small farmers of the upstate counties and far and away the most powerful political figure in the state, adamantly opposed a stronger central government? Clinton's position was the more crucial because the fate of the Constitution largely hinged on ratification by New York. That state's flourishing import trade and its strategic location midway between the New England and middle states made it an indispensable member of the proposed union.

Once the Continental Congress officially relayed the Constitution to the state governments, Clinton predictably threw the weight of his power and prestige into the Antifederalist scale. His authorship of a series of essays signed "Cato" (the first number appeared on September 27, and other were published intermittently over the next four months) was intentionally no secret. Nor were his staunch allies backward in proclaiming their hostility to the Constitution. Robert Yates, Hamilton's colleague at the convention, told his fellow New Yorkers that the proposed government would undermine their freedom; Melancton Smith argued that the Constitution would destroy democracy; and innumerable, now-obscure scribblers under pennames such as "Republican," "Rough Hewer," and "Plain Citizen" assailed those "aristocrats" whom they accused of attempting a monarchical coup d'etat.[17] They were, however, no match for "Publius," the pseudonym that Hamilton chose for his defense of the Constitution. Of the bulky literature spawned by the ratification controversy, *The Federalist* alone is of enduring importance.

Leadership of New York's nationalists was thrust upon Hamilton by the Clintonians, who insisted on making him their principal target. Fearful that the opposition was winning the newspaper debate by default, Hamilton decided that a public defense of the proposed Constitution was imperative. He correctly perceived that no one was better able to conduct it than he. According to tradition, he wrote the first number of *The Federalist* in his cabin on a sloop while returning to New York City from Albany, where he had spent some weeks arguing cases before the New York Supreme Court. The first Publius essay, addressed to the people of the state of New York, appeared in the *Independent Journal* on October 27, 1787.

Since Hamilton's plan called for a systematic and comprehensive clause-by-clause defense of the Constitution, he looked about for collaborators. He approached Gouverneur Morris, who during the convention had revealed an ideological affinity with Hamilton, and William Duer, a prominent Federalist and secretary of the Board of the Treasury (his reputation not yet tarnished by public knowledge of his financial chicanery). Fortunately for posterity, Morris and Duer declined. John Jay and James Madison were the most talented collaborators Hamilton could have found. Jay promptly began work, rapidly turning out four essays (numbers 2, 3, 4, and 5,) which were published early in November. But after this initial burst of energy, Jay contributed nothing more for four months, and then only one essay. An accurate title page of *The Federalist* would thus have to read "By Alexander Hamilton and James Madison, with Contributions by John Jay."

Since both Hamilton and Madison (or their partisans) laid claim to the authorship of fifteen of the eighty-five Publius essays, the issue of their respective numerical contributions sparked a century and a half of heated historical controversy. That argument is at last, it is hoped, settled on the basis of external evidence (that is, Madison's and Hamilton's alleged claims); most historians now agree that Madison wrote all the fifteen essays in question.[18] The difficulty in settling the dispute on the basis of internal evidence was owing to Hamilton's and Madison's interchangeable styles and to their remarkable ideological rapport. This affinity, along with their rare expository skill, made their literary collaboration the most constructive in American political history.

The ideas of Hamilton and Madison had no doubt diverged somewhat since 1782 when they had harmoniously striven to breathe life into the feeble Confederation government. But although close students of their careers can plausibly argue (as those of Madison in particular have done) that Madison had remained consistent while Hamilton's nationalism had become steadily more strident and extreme, the views of the two men on the proposed Constitution were virtually identical.

Madison, like Hamilton, emphasized time and again the advantages of a durable senate and an independent executive. Both men ardently advocated a strong central government. Both distrusted majority rule and proposed to structure government in such a way as to protect minority rights. Both believed in a system of checks and balances. Nor did they differ on the issue of republicanism. Both believed that only a republic was suitable for a nation of so vast a territorial extent. Both defined a republic as a government that included at least one democratic branch that would directly mirror the interests and "passions" of the people. Both, finally, believed in the protection of civil liberties—freedom of speech, of the press, of religion—and of traditional English judicial safeguards for person, liberty, and property.

Although *The Federalist* is deservedly acclaimed as a classic of American political literature, it is also preeminently a period piece. Its purpose was to provide neither an abstractly definitive treatise on federalism nor a disquisition on political philosophy. The essays were rather written to persuade the people of New York (as well as the citizens of other doubtful states) that approval of the new frame of government was in their immediate best interest. Moreover, the subject matter of *The Federalist,* its major themes, its organization, and its polemical tone were largely dictated by the charges made by critics of the Constitution. The Antifederalists, in other words, called the tune, to which the Federalists played counterpoint. The Constitution, its opponents said, would create a "consolidated" union—not a confederation of states but an all-powerful, coercive government that would undermine and eventually destroy state sovereignty. Among the more specific items in the Antifederalist bill of indictment against the Constitution were these: it gave Congress the right to levy "direct" taxes and in some instances the right of exclusive taxation, powers certain to be abused; it eliminated annual elections, the certain guarantee against legislative usurpation; it failed to prohibit "standing armies," that bugaboo of eighteenth-century American thought; it undercut the jurisdiction and prerogatives of state courts by establishing a federal judiciary; it provided for an executive who might wield virtually monarchical power; it conferred on Congress the right to make uniform commercial regulations that would be contrary to the interests of some states; and, most serious of all, it included no bill of rights guaranteeing freedom of speech, the press, and religion, trial by jury, and other traditional safeguards against tyranny.

To a refutation of these charges Hamilton and Madison devoted essay after essay. The Constitution, Publius patiently and lengthily explained (as if elucidating a simple text to inattentive school children), would not destroy the state judiciaries, deny the states the right of taxation, or abolish the state militias. Why not? The states would retain those powers not granted to the central government and in some instances exercise concurrent jurisdiction.

But the major thesis of the essays (and the one that least engages the present-day reader) dealt not with the future but with the past.

The principal theme of *The Federalist* was the manifest inability of the Confederation government to solve the urgent problems of the new nation. In essay after essay, the defects of the Articles of Confederation were painted in lurid colors and, in the process, greatly magnified. "We may with propriety, be said to have reached almost the last stage of national humiliation," Hamilton observed. "There is scarcely any thing that can wound the pride, or degrade the character of an independent nation, which we do not experience."[19] Yet Publius did properly and perceptively harp on the fundamental flaw of the Articles and point to a boldly original way of mending it. The solution, although seemingly simple, was the Constitution's single most important contribution to the theory and practice of federalism—a central government that would operate not on states (as under the Articles) but directly on individuals. Hamilton put the idea this way: "A Federal Government capable of regulating the common concerns and preserving the general tranquility . . . must carry its agency to the persons of the citizens. It must stand in need of no intermediate legislations; but itself be empowered . . . to execute its own resolutions. The majesty of the national authority must be manifested through the medium of the Courts of Justice."[20]

In other ways, too, *The Federalist* is an enduringly definitive commentary on the Constitution. What are the powers of Congress, the executive, and the Supreme Court? Why were the powers granted? Why are they necessary to the effective operation of government? Why is a tripartite division of the departments of government desirable? Why was a system of checks and balances provided for? How is the American federal system unique? How does it reconcile national authority and local autonomy? Why is judicial review an essential cement of a viable federal system? The answers given by Publius remain (in the context of American political theory and constitutional law) authoritative.

Yet one should not claim too much for *The Federalist*. Both because of its practical, immediate purpose and the haste with which it was written (Hamilton sometimes dashed off an essay in a day), the work is somewhat disjointedly organized, marred by repetition, and studded with tediously long descriptions of both ancient and modern history. Hamilton and Madison were also too caught up in contemporary problems, which they tended to view as universal and eternal. There is a static quality to their thought, largely because they failed to perceive that problems change and that altered circumstances call for different prescriptions. It would not have occurred to them, to give a single illustration, that the protection of property rights might not under all circumstances be the sine qua non of good government or that the type of "liberty" that they believed the new Constitution safeguarded might in the future need to be restrained. To the present-day reader, moreover, Publius seems to have conjured up dangers (such as a standing army and the perniciousness of faction) and sought to discredit ideas (such as annual elections as a safeguard against tyranny and the superiority of a plural over a single executive) that are no longer of consequence. For these, among other reasons, some essays seems singularly irrelevant to the problems of later eras, others appear contrived or strained, and many read rather like an attorney's one-sided plea for a defendant.

Few Americans of that day, it will be recalled, were more adept at adversary proceedings than was Hamilton. His skill was such that less attentive readers might well have failed to appreciate the full meaning of ideas that soon would be (and still are) implied by the word "Hamiltonian." *The Federalist* was, in fact, not merely Hamilton's clever defense of a public client, the Constitution, but also a comprehensive statement of his political creed. He did not, as in his June speech before the Constitutional Convention, attempt to dazzle his audience by brilliant audaciousness or startle them by championing unpopular ideas. He rather iterated, forthrightly and persuasively, political principles and prescriptions that he had many times set forth in earlier letters and essays. In other words, just as in his convention debut he had mistakenly sought by extremism to earn recognition as a political theoretician, so he now successfully asserted his claim as a political philosopher by returning to, and amplifying, ideas cast in the crucible of war and the trials of America's infant nationhood, ideas to which he would remain steadfastly committed.

The words that Hamilton most overworked were also to him synonyms for effective government. Those words were "energy" and "efficiency." "Energy of government," a representative phrase read, "is essential to the welfare and prosperity of the community."[21] On the requisite energy also depended what to Hamilton was "the true test of a good government": "its aptitude and tendency to produce a good administration."[22] An efficient administration required, in turn, "energy in the executive," which was to Hamilton "a leading character in the definition of good government."[23] In Hamilton's lexicon the antonym of "energy" was "feebleness," and just as the first was almost always linked to the word "good," the second was associated with "bad." Hamilton, in a sample passage, put it this way: "A feeble executive implies a feeble execution of the government. A feeble execution is but another phrase for a bad execution: And a government ill executed, whatever it may be in theory, must be in practice a bad government."[24]

Hamilton insisted that energy in government, expressed most effectively by an energetic executive, was the most reliable counterpoise not only to legislative supremacy and state power but also to an otherwise unruly populace. Why, he asked, "has government been instituted at all? Because the passions of men will not conform to the dictates of reason and justice, without constraint."[25] Madison expressed the same idea when he wrote, "But what is government itself but the greatest of all reflections on human nature? If men were angels, no government would be necessary."[26] Such aspersions on what later eras in our history would view as man's benign nature and limitless capabilities were, of course, unexceptionable. It is necessary to emphasize them only because historians, intent on making Hamilton the nation's symbolic antagonist of democracy, have often attributed a singularity to views that in fact were characteristic of that day. A more consequential point is that Hamilton, like Madison, did perceive the connection between democracy and anarchy, and he scarcely can be faulted for also failing to foresee that the future of American democracy would nullify his fears. In a comment that remains relevant he also posed an appropriate alternative: "The supposition of universal venality in human nature is little less an error in political reasoning than the supposition of universal rectitude."[27]

Less common in the 1780s than Hamilton's dismal view of human nature was his undisguised and bold stress on the imperativeness of governmental power. "Power" was already well on the way to being the antithesis of popular rule. It was to Hamilton, however, the ballast not only of republicanism but all viable government. "A government," he wrote, "is only another word for POLITICAL POWER AND SUPREMACY."[28] How much power? Hamilton's answer was that although "there is no rule by which we can measure the momentum of civil power, necessary," the government of the union must "possess all the means and have a right to resort to all the methods of executing the powers with which it is entrusted."[29] This idea, a cardinal principle of Hamilton's political thought, would be elaborated in his famous report on the constitutionality of the Bank of the United States. The idea would also, thanks to George Washington's acceptance of Hamilton's persuasive argument as well as Chief Justice John Marshall's endorsement of it in *McCulloch* v. *Maryland* (1819), become a fundamental principle of American constitutional law. But in 1788, such a position, although shared by many nationalists, was scarcely likely to dispel Antifederalist fears that the Constitution opened the door to a potentially mighty and coercive government. Antifederalists would have found even more objectionable Hamilton's assertion (for that time and place astonishing) that the powers confided to the national government "ought to exist without limitation: *Because it is impossible to foresee or define the extent and variety of national exigencies or the correspondent extent & variety of the means which may be necessary to satisfy them.*"[30] Had the proponents of limited government carefully read remarks such as this and recognized their anonymous author, Hamilton might not have been given the opportunity to chart the course of the new government.

But as Hamilton's critics in the 1790s would recognize, his constant trust in the curative power of national supremacy was in direct proportion to his abiding distrust of state sovereignty. "Power controuled or abridged," Hamilton wrote, "is almost always the rival and enemy of that power by which it is controuled or abridged."[31] Governor George Clinton would have applauded that remark as he pronounced an anathema on its author. Determined that his own power should be neither regulated nor diminished, Clinton's object was to outfox his Federalist opponents, particularly Hamilton, who would have liked to put the New York governorship on a par with a Dutch burgomastership. Since the governor, not Hamilton, had the power in New York, Clinton seemed certain to withhold that state's ratification of the proposed Constitution.

VI

"The Little Lion" of
Federalism

When the first issue of *The Federalist* appeared in November 1787 no state had yet ratified the Constitution. Over succeeding months, as Publius dominated issue after issue of the New York press and of newspapers elsewhere, a parade of states joined the union. Delaware was the first. Then, early in December, Pennsylvania ratified, followed by neighboring New Jersey, where the Constitution carried without a dissenting vote. In January, Georgia gave its assent, as did an overwhelmingly Federalist Connecticut. Massachusetts, Maryland, and South Carolina soon followed suit. Eight of the requisite nine states were safely in the federal fold. On June 21, four days after the convening of the New York convention, New Hampshire ratified the proposed Constitution. It was now officially adopted. The successful launching of a new government was another matter. That outcome hinged on the ratification of Virginia and New York, where opponents of the Constitution formed a solid and seemingly invincible majority. Even if Madison and his fellow Federalists in Virginia could manage to overcome such formidable odds, New York appeared an unlikely candidate for membership.

Governor George Clinton would no doubt have preferred not even to put the issue to a vote. But the Clintonian majority in the legislature, confident of their ability to preserve New York's sovereignty inviolate, obligingly scheduled elections in April for delegates to a ratifying convention to assemble two months later. For the first time in New York history every free male citizen of twenty-one years of age was to have a vote. The official records do not say what was responsible for this democratic innovation. Perhaps the Federalists went along with a measure they did not have the votes to prevent, while the governor's party counted on popular support. The Clintonians, in the event, had every right to be sanguine. Only four counties (New York, Kings, Richmond, and Westchester) chose pro-union delegates; elsewhere the Antifederalist cause was triumphant. To Federalist leaders, like Hamilton, the election foretold a woeful tale: the Constitution would go down to certain defeat by a vote of forty-six votes to nineteen if its opponents remained united, as appeared likely.

At the convention that assembled on June 17 in Poughkeepsie, a dauntless band of Federalists sought to reverse the seemingly irresistible anti-unionist tide. Chancellor Robert R. Livingston, New York's chief judicial official; John Jay, secretary for foreign affairs in the moribund Confederation; and Hamilton, who had been elected a delegate from New York City, took the lead in debate. They would have prevailed, had legal learning, diplomatic experience, and oratorical skill been the criteria for success. As it was, their very ability was something of a disadvantage among delegates who viewed distinction and superiority as a badge of aristocracy, the bugaboo of New York antifederalism. Chancellor Livingston, a tall, graceful man of "polished wit and classical taste,"[1] was the perfect symbol of the ancient aristocracy that the Clintonians distrusted. So, too, was John Jay, a New York blueblood who was married to a Livingston and whose aristocratic hauteur was only thinly veiled by his courteousness. Hamilton, actually as much the self-made man as any Clintonian, was deemed an aristocrat by dint of his association with the Schuyler family and his air of superiority.

The Antifederalists had no such illustrious team. Its captain, George Clinton, was president of the convention but rarely participated in its debates, preferring to exert his influence in off-the-floor conferences. The Antifederalist position was defended by the governor's lieutenants, local leaders such as John Lansing, Jr., Charles Tillinghast, and Melancton Smith. Smith, a delegate from Dutchess County, was "the most prominent and . . . responsible speaker on the Anti-Federal side." Chancellor James Kent, in Poughkeepsie to observe the proceedings, recalled that "there was no person to be compared to him in his powers of acute and logical discussion."[2] Such a compliment from a perceptive witness is telling testimony to the paucity of talent among the Antifederalists. Smith, who would have been ignored by history except for his few hours on the stage at Poughkeepsie, was a dogged rather than a brilliant antagonist. His frequent flat and uninspired speeches were merely replays of familiar Antifederalist themes.

Underlying the Clintonians' objections to the Constitution was their traditional distrust of a strong union and their fear that the plan proposed would undermine their own political power and perquisites in New York State. But the effectiveness and strength of their opposition was sapped by their anxiety about the likely consequences of New York's failure to ratify the Constitution. Could the state survive on its own? Would not New York find herself isolated, cut off from essential commerce with neighboring states? Would not New York City and the southern counties withdraw from the state? The answers to such questions were self-evident to many, perhaps a majority, of the Antifederalists, who would have preferred the status quo and were sin-

cerely convinced that the proposed plan of government was irremediably
defective. But the Antifederalists also knew that in the end their own self-
interest and fears would probably have to give way to the state's best
interest.

Thus circumstanced, the Antifederalists—although there were irreconcilables among them—doubtless realized that all they could hope for was to
make New York's ratification of the Constitution contingent on drastic
amendments. Certainly they were not prepared to reject it outright. This was
indicated when they acquiesced in the Federalists' insistence that debate on
the Constitution proceed clause by clause, thus protracting the convention's
proceedings. Since it was likely that by the time such a discussion ended the
requisite nine states (or perhaps more) would have approved the new government, the delay rendered New York's eventual ratification—with or without amendments—all the more inevitable.

It was this sense of inexorability that makes the formal proceedings of the
convention appear to the modern reader mere shadowboxing. They seem so
for yet another reason. The convention debates were less important than the
negotiations behind the scenes. The Federalists, aware of the chink in the
Antifederalists' armor, realized that their task was by personal appeal—or
even threats—to nudge their opponents toward a step many of them knew
they might in the end have to take.

For his part, Hamilton, although presumably aware of this situation, acted
as if his own persuasiveness and eloquence in debate could overcome Antifederalist resistance. The nickname given him by his fellow aides during the
Revolution was particularly apposite at the Poughkeepsie convention. He
was "the Little Lion" of federalism. Day after day, in address after address,
he sought to show the fallaciousness of Antifederalist anticipation of a dangerous usurpation of power under the proposed Constitution, which he pictured instead as the indispensable alternative to national shipwreck. Hamilton's
performance was one of his finest. His defense of the Constitution seemed
irresistible, his rebuttal of the opposition's charges was devastating, his language was restrained, and his manner was atypically patient and courteous.
He also successfully curbed his tendency to display intellectual audaciousness, as he mistakenly had done at the Constitutional Convention.

At Poughkeepsie, Hamilton shifted the focus of his defense of the Constitution, in order to meet his opponents on their own ground. Just as at the
Philadelphia convention his emphasis had been on the imperativeness of a
stable government and in *The Federalist* on an energetic one, so it now
centered on the "truly republican principles" of the Constitution.[3] "The
establishment of a republican government," he remarked, "is an object of
all others the nearest and dearest to my own heart"; at issue was only "the
means of accomplishing this great purpose."[4] Hamilton was neither inconsistent nor insincere. His definition of a republic was the same as it had been
at the Constitutional Convention and in *The Federalist*. "The true principle
of a republic," he again explained, "is that the people should choose whom
they please to govern them." The "great source of free government, popular

election, should be perfectly pure, and most unabounded liberty allowed."[5] But a republic should not be confounded with a "pure democracy," which, he continued to insist, had "never possessed one feature of good government": its "very character was tyranny" and its "figure deformity."[6] The opposition's argument that the form of government proposed by the Constitution was neither a democracy nor even a republic, Hamilton argued, was based on a popular misapprehension of the history and proper definition of those terms. Just as in a democracy "a single democratic assembly" was "the image and echo of the multitude," so in a republic there must be "some permanent body to correct the prejudices, check the intemperate passions, and regulate the fluctuations of a popular assembly."[7] Thus persuaded, Hamilton's defense of republicanism did not preclude a restatement of his familiar strictures on what Lincoln would later hail as government by the people and of the people (although Hamilton certainly believed that government should be *for* the people). "The people," Hamilton affirmed, "do not possess the discernment and stability necessary for systematic government."[8] That such remarks passed virtually unnoticed perhaps bespeaks a consensus among the convention delegates that might go undetected if one focused exclusively on their differences.

Nevertheless, democracy was, in a different context, the essential question at the convention. It was implicit in the Antifederalists' principal indictment of the Constitution and its proponents. Underpinning the Clintonians' attacks on specific provisions of the Constitution, there was, one senses, a more fundamental issue—their perception of an abiding antagonism between aristocrats and "the people," between the haves and the have-nots. The Antifederalists, in other words, equated federalism with aristocracy and, by implication, themselves with the common man. Although Melancton Smith and his debating team thus managed both to simplify and to becloud the actual issue, their argument was rendered at least plausible by Federalist leaders such as Robert R. Livingston. It was he, in George Dangerfield's words, "who succeeded in arousing the keenest hostility. There he stood, from his head to his toes radiant with privilege, the visible embodiment of aristocracy."[9] The resentment that Livingston and Jay aroused was based on their indisputable aristocratic status. Hamilton's inclusion among the aristocrats, however, was a case of guilt by association, both with his Federalist allies and with the Schuyler family. Hamilton might strive to give the appearance of "an amazing Republican," said one Clinton stalwart, "*but he is known.*"[10]

To Hamilton the issue of aristocracy was not only a red herring but was also bewildering. "For my part," he remarked in exasperation, "I hardly know the meaning of the word as it is applied. . . . Who are the aristocracy among us? Where do we find men elevated to a perpetual rank above their fellow citizens; and possessing powers entirely independent of them? The arguments of the gentlemen only go to prove that there are men who are rich, men who are poor, some who are wise, and others who are not—that indeed every distinguished man is an aristocrat." Hamilton's textbook definition of aristocracy is revealing. He insisted on it precisely because he genuinely did not "know the meaning of the word as . . . applied" in the convention debates.[11] He had, after all, neither experienced the life-style of an aristocrat like Livingston nor the resentment of those who had endured the hauteur of New York's patroons. In Hamilton's own experience, privilege and distinction were earned by brilliance and diligence, not conferred by birth.

The conformity of the proposed Constitution to republican principles was only one of the themes that Hamilton stressed. He also sought in speech after speech to disprove the Antifederalist argument that a strong central government would erode and finally destroy state power. "Gentlemen indulge too many unreasonable apprehensions of dangers to the state governments," ran a characteristic remark. "The state governments are essentially necessary to the form and spirit of the general system."[12] They were not only necessary but would in most areas be supreme. Hamilton repeatedly made the point in as many different words. The idea was most succinctly expressed in a speech on June 20, three days after the convention convened. "The State governments," he observed, "possess inherent advantages, which will ever give them an influence and ascendency over the national government; and will forever preclude the possibility of federal encroachments. That their liberties indeed can be subverted by the federal head, is repugnant to every rule of political calculation."[13] It was, of course, a point that he had also made in *The Federalist,* although there his implicit emphasis had been on the imperativeness of circumventing or circumscribing the inherent superiority of the state governments.

At Poughkeepsie, Hamilton was, instead, intent on dispelling the notion that the proposed government would prove to be a voracious monster that would devour the states. The fundamental safeguard against federal encroachments on the states, Hamilton pointed out, was "that division of powers, on which political liberty is founded."[14] The Constitution, he iterated, provided for a system of checks and balances, a limited government in which one branch was balanced against another and the whole checked by the states. The very structure of the proposed government, he insisted, would be a sufficient safeguard against the tyranny that the Antifederalists tirelessly anticipated. The real issue, moreover, was not tyranny versus freedom but stability versus instability: since instability "has operated most banefully in our infant republic . . . it is necessary that we . . . apply an immediate remedy." That remedy was stability, which, Hamilton said, "is essential to the government." He confidently affirmed that once stability was established, as it would be by the Constitution, "safety for the people" would be assured and "the certain tendency of the system" would "be to the public welfare."[15] Had Hamilton been a more prudential and a less forthright and candid man, he might well have here ended his case.

But it was not in character for Hamilton to sacrifice conviction to expediency. At the New York convention, as throughout the movement for constitutional reform, he insisted that an effective government needed one other ingredient: energy. And an energetic government was one vested with all the powers essential to the exigencies of the union. "When we have formed a constitution upon free principles, when we have given a proper balance to the different branches of administration, and fixed representation upon pure and equal principles," he said by way of introduction to his favorite political maxim, "we may with safety furnish it with all the powers, necessary to answer, in the most ample manner, the purposes of government. . . . Has experience taught that such a government ought not to be trusted with every thing necessary for the good of society?"[16] To this question the Antifederalists (prefiguring the position of Hamilton's political opponents over the next two decades) gave an emphatic no. Clinton and his supporters viewed as similarly heretical Hamilton's repeated assertion that under the proposed federal system the prerogatives of the states must give way to the interests of the union. "When a sacrifice of one or the other is necessary," the state "should yield, on the principle that the small good ought never to oppose the great one. . . . There must be a perpetual accommodation and sacrifice of local advantage to general expediency."[17]

Had the debate in Poughkeepsie been objectively judged and prizes awarded, Hamilton would have walked away with the trophy. But the convention was not a debating contest, and to the Antifederalists their solid majority was a sufficient answer to Hamilton's eloquence. Their own speeches were less a rebuttal to Hamilton's explanation of the provisions of the Constitution than an expression of dread about presumably predictable but unspecified acts of the proposed central government. To Hamilton their evocation of imaginary horrors was both misplaced and exasperating. Instead of conjuring up imaginary dangers, why not concentrate on present perils and place confidence in a system that "would answer the purposes of strength and safety," he asked?[18] Why harp on imaginary usurpations of the central government, an "argument of possibility and choice" that "if it proves anything, concludes against all union and government," proving only "that no powers should be entrusted to any body of men, because they may be abused"?[19] Just as Hamilton did not conceal his irritation at the Antifederalist depiction of a "danger" so "distant" as to be "beyond all rational calculations," so he could not hide his indignation at Antifederalists' attacks on his "integrity and virtue," their charges that he was "an ambitious man, a man unattached to the interests and insensible to the feelings of the people." His critics, he angrily retorted, should be obliged "to point out an instance in which he had ever deviated from the line of public or private duty."[20] According to a sympathetic newspaper reporter, Hamilton's "pathetic appeal fixed the silent sympathetic gaze of the spectators, and made them all his own."[21]

Hamilton's personal appeal may have elicited sympathy, but his political arguments did not seemingly win converts. Nor, so far as the written record reveals, did receipt on July 2 of news that Virginia had become the tenth state to ratify the Constitution. While Madison and his fellow Federalists in Richmond celebrated their triumph, Hamilton and his allies in Poughkeepsie continued their by now somewhat dispirited defense of the Constitution, clause by clause. This phase of the convention debate ended on July 7. Three days later, the Antifederalists, with John Lansing, Jr., as their spokesman, publicly unveiled the strategy that from the outset they manifestly had intended to pursue. The "plan of amendment" introduced by Lansing included "1st Explanatory, 2d Conditional, and 3d Recommendatory" amendments[22] that proposed what would, in effect, have made the Poughkeepsie gathering a second constitutional, rather than a ratifying, convention.

The answer to this Antifederalist strategy was a Federalists' proffer of a compromise: it took the form of a motion, drafted by Hamilton and introduced by Jay, that New York forthwith ratify the Constitution and at the same time recommend (not require) amendments considered "useful or expedient."[23] Perhaps Federalist leaders, confronted by a large Clintonian majority, felt obliged to be conciliatory; or perhaps they wished to provide the Antifederalists a way of saving face. But Antifederalists, confident of their solidarity, saw no need to compromise. To counter Jay's motion, Melancton Smith proposed that New York ratify the Constitution on the condition that a new convention be called to consider amendments.

In rejoinder to Smith's call for conditional assent Hamilton argued that it was both mistaken and inadmissible for the state to make its ratification of the Constitution contingent on "any restrictions or conditions whatever."[24] By now aware that no arguments of his would budge the Clintonians' unswervingly stolid obdurateness, Hamilton decided to call in an influential outside consultant. On July 19 he wrote to James Madison, then in New York City, posing a question to which Hamilton surely knew in advance the Virginian's answer. "Let me know your idea," Hamilton asked, "of the possibility of our being *received* into the Union with *the reservation* of a right to withdraw in case our amendments" are not accepted within a stipulated period.[25] There was no possibility at all, Madison predictably replied. It would be "a *conditional* ratification," and New York "could not be received on that plan."[26] The advice was unnecessary. On July 23, the day before Hamilton read Madison's letter to the convention, Melancton Smith had caved in by moving that New York ratify in the confidence that "the Amendments which shall have been proposed to the said Constitution will receive an early and mature consideration."[27] With his capitulation, other Antifederalists broke ranks, and on July 26 the Constitution was ratified by a vote of thirty to twenty-seven. By what alchemy had a majority of two to one against adoption been changed into a majority of three for unconditional ratification? Not even Hamilton would have claimed that his persuasiveness in debate or even the debates themselves were responsible. The best answer was given by Smith, who, in explaining his own switch of vote, commented that the chilling alternative to ratification would be "convulsions in the Southern part [of the state], faction and discord in the rest."[28]

Smith may have been right, but the down-staters, confident that New York would ratify, saw no need to anticipate "convulsions"; instead, they had long since begun to make plans for a celebration. Once New Hampshire ratified the Constitution on June 21, 1788, thus assuring the launching of a new national government, arrangements were put in train by jubilant citizens of New York City for a victory parade. Tradesmen and artisans busied themselves designing and painting the banners and floats. Although repeatedly postponed, the parade took place on July 23, three days before ratification by the Poughkeepsie convention. That expected event could be attributed to any number of complex and undeterminable causes, but to most merchants, mechanics, artisans, and other New Yorkers one man would be largely responsible: Hamilton. In his honor, the city's shipyard workers and carpenters hastily constructed the *Hamilton,* an almost exact replica of a regular seaworthy vessel, to be manned by thirty seamen and marines and drawn by ten horses. It was to be the leading feature of the grand spectacle.[29]

At ten o'clock on the morning of July 23, thirteen guns were fired from the *Hamilton* as a signal for the parade to commence. The miniature ship, pulled through the streets on a carriage, made "a fine appearance, sailing with flowing sheets and full sails, down Broadway, the canvass waves dashing against her sides."[30] There were also grand displays by the coopers, pump-makers, tailors, furriers, hatters, brewers, shipwrights, and virtually every other occupation in the city. Cheered on by the thousands of people who lined the streets, the elaborate procession moved down Broadway, through Great Dock Street and Queen Street. Not only the city's tradesmen but many of its prominent businessmen marched in the triumphant procession. Among them was Nicholas Cruger, who may justifiably have reflected that the best investment he ever made was in the future of the young West Indian clerk whose name was now emblazoned on banners and whose figure was carved on the prow of the *Hamilton.* What its namesake thought, sitting in Poughkeepsie, as he read the newspaper accounts of such public acclaim, we can leave to imagination. The bastardy, the near poverty, and all the other painful recollections of his St. Croix childhood stood in stark contrast to the homage now paid him as one of the architects of a new nation. Perhaps Hamilton did not think of the immense distance that he had traveled but of the distance he had yet to go before achieving the even greater fame he aspired to.

Hamilton's immediate focus, however, was on shoring up his law practice and in enjoying the company of his wife and children, from whom he had been separated for almost six weeks. Not even a ruffle disturbed his intimate, loving relationship with Eliza, whose preoccupation was the comfort and happiness of her now widely acclaimed husband. Stephen Van Rensselaer, one of her countless kinsmen, complimented her on being "so good a *housewife, housekeeper* & etc.,'' adding that her father "talks of nothing but you & the Esquire & says you and he will be models for us all."[31] Brissot de Warville, the cultivated Frenchman who was then visiting America, agreed with Philip Schuyler. Eliza was "a charming woman," Warville commented after a visit to the Hamiltons, "who joins to the graces all the candour and simplicity of an American wife."[32] Whatever de Warville may have implied by this somewhat ambiguous observation, Eliza was obliged to be a busy wife.

On her shoulders fell the management of the Hamiltons' roomy house on Wall Street and the care of four children (although there were plenty of servants around; her father would have seen to that), of whom the eldest, Philip, was six and the youngest, James Alexander, an infant. These were cheerful days for Eliza. Her husband was constantly at home (his law office was next door), and her favorite sister, Angelica Church, on a visit from England, was also often there. (Eliza would have been shocked at the view held by generations of historians that Hamilton preferred the beautiful, charming, coquettish Angelica to herself. She knew, and rightly so, that there was no basis for this surmise. Hamilton might flirt with the lovely Angelica but so also did many other visitors to her salon, both in America and in Europe.)

From his law office at 57 Wall Street Hamilton conducted a steadily increasing practice. It had to grow if he were to pay the bills entailed by a large and growing family. Fortunately for his creditors, clients flocked to the now-famous public figure. His fees were modest, however, and he earned enough only to look after current expenses. But, then, the accumulation of money meant little to him as compared to the accolades bestowed for his public service.

Now that the Constitution was ratified, Hamilton was determined to do all within his power to assure the success of the new government. But that, as he knew, could best be accomplished in an official post, and Hamilton, aware of the trust reposed in him by Washington, was confident that he would be offered an important one. In the meantime, he gave such time as he could spare from his legal practice to politics and public affairs. Characteristically, that was what to a less energetic person would have been full time.

He participated only sporadically, however, in the proceedings of the Continental Congress, to which he had been elected in January 1788.[33] There was no reason to pay close attention. As one delegate commented, those who watched over the Congress during its moribundity had nothing to do but "to adhere steadfastly to each other & to the old constitution," while remaining "very friendly to the stranger that was preparing to oust us."[34] For his part, Hamilton had never been an adherent of the "old constitution" and the word "friendly" did not adequately convey his ardent support of the new Constitution. Although Federal Hall, where the Congress met, was only a stone's throw from his residence and law office, he rarely attended. The only issue that engaged his attention was a minor one. He strove mightily, although unsuccessfully, to win a pension for his Revolutionary War comrade Baron Friedrich Wilhelm von Steuben, a perennial supplicant for public support whose applications Hamilton, as secretary of the Treasury, would continue to press.

Hamilton's justifiable indifference to the expiring Confederation government was directly proportional to his preoccupation with preparations for the launching of a new government. Like other Americans, he believed that the nation's first chief executive must be Washington, who was regarded as the indispensable man. Unlike most of his countrymen, however, Hamilton was in a position to promote the general's candidacy. He unhesitatingly did so. Washington had "no alternative, but to comply" with his countrymen's wish, Hamilton forthrightly wrote to his former commanding officer: "On your acceptance of the office of the President the success of the new government in its commencement may materially depend."[35] Already aware that only a miracle could spare him "the dreaded Dilemma of being forced to accept or refuse" the nomination, Washington finally accepted it "with more diffidence and reluctance than ever I experienced in my life."[36] He would have done so anyway, but Hamilton's blunt letter was at least marginally responsible. In acknowledging that letter Washington strongly hinted that as president he would continue to count on Hamilton's counsel. "The same manly tone of intercourse will always be more than barely welcome," Washington replied. "Indeed, it will be highly acceptable to me."[37]

Washington's election was a certainty. There was considerable doubt as to whether the voters or the members of the House of Representatives would select him, however. This was because of the cumbersome electoral procedure prescribed by the Constitution. That document stipulated that each elector cast two ballots of equal value and that the candidate winning a plurality be the chief magistrate, the second highest to be vice-president. In the event of a tie the election devolved upon the House of Representatives, an arrangement that made it possible for the voters' second choice to become the nation's president. In 1788 such an eventuality was virtually nil. What alarmed Hamilton was merely the possibility of a tie or a close vote. "It would be disagreeable," he wrote to James Madison, "to have a man treading close upon the heels of the person we wish as President."[38] The man he wanted to slow down was John Adams.

Nor was Hamilton confident that the New Englander was the most eligible vice-presidential candidate. A decade later Hamilton would reach the conclusion that Adams was not even qualified to serve as mayor of his home town in Massachusetts. In 1788, however, he questioned neither Adams' ability nor integrity. His hesitancy "with regard to Mr. Adams" rather arose "from a suggestion by a particular Gentleman that he is unfriendly in his sentiments to General Washington."[39] Hamilton's informants were correct; Adams resented not only Washington but also (as Hamilton would unhappily learn) virtually all other men who outshone or rivaled Adams. In the end, Hamilton, although "not without apprehensions,"[40] crawled to Adams' support. At the same time, the New Yorker used his already considerable influence among Federalist leaders to assure that Adams would come in as poor a second as possible.[41] Hamilton's efforts were unnecessary. His alarm was shared by other Washington admirers who had already decided to throw away enough votes on favorite sons to assure Washington a suitable triumph. The Virginian was elected unanimously, while the vote for Adams, who received a plurality, was scattered.

On April 30, 1789, Chancellor Robert R. Livingston administered the oath of office to the nation's first president. The ceremony took place on a gallery of Federal Hall in New York City, the country's temporary capital. As Washington, tall, erect, hair powdered, dressed in a suit of domestically spun brown broadcloth, wearing silver shoebuckles and a dress sword, swore to preserve, protect, and defend the Constitution of the United States, he looked down as far as the eye could see upon throngs of people who lined Wall and Broad streets. Among the spectators was Hamilton, to whom the stirring event seemed also a personal triumph. No man's ideas may in theory have been more remote from the government now inaugurated than his own, but no one had labored more tirelessly to scrap the Articles of Confederation and to build precisely the type of strong central government that his wartime commander in chief would now direct. Hamilton's satisfaction was the greater because he confidently, although unavowedly, expected to be asked to share in the direction.

In the meantime, Hamilton assumed the leadership of the New York Federalist campaign to unseat Governor George Clinton, redoubtable foe of the Constitution, and to elect congressmen committed to the success of the government. To dislodge Clinton, the hero of the small upstate farmers, Hamilton and his fellow Federalists adopted a strategy of divide and rule. To split the biennially loyal vote for the popular governor, his opponents nominated a previously stalwart Clintonian, Judge Robert Yates, who having staunchly opposed the Constitution both at the Philadelphia and the New York ratifying conventions, was now willing to shift his political allegiance and embrace the new plan of government. To make their ticket even more attractive to Antifederalists, the proconstitutionalists selected as Yates's running mate Clinton's former gubernatorial mate, Pierre Van Cortlandt, who had served as lieutenant governor of New York since 1777.

The Federalist campaign was run by Hamilton, who seemed intent on demonstrating that he was a master practitioner of the democratic brand of politics he reputedly scorned. As chairman of the New York County Correspondence Committee, he drafted political tracts for circulation elsewhere in the state; as an anonymous publicist, he assailed Clinton's record as governor and his qualifications for reelection. The focus of Hamilton's campaign was thus not Yates's eligibility but Clinton's ineligibility. Hamilton apparently could think of nothing praiseworthy to say about Yates except that he had recanted his Antifederalist heresy. "Though his opposition to the new Constitution was such as its friends cannot but disapprove," Hamilton remarked in a typically tepid endorsement, "yet since the period of its adoption, his conduct has been tempered with a degree of moderation . . . which entitle him to credit; and seem to point him out as a man likely to compose the differences of the state."[42] On the subject of Clinton's unfitness, by contrast, Hamilton could (and, had the campaign lasted longer, probably would) have written a volume. The major item in his bill of indictment was, predictably, the governor's inveterate hostility to the Constitution. Clinton's obstinate opposition was based on a "preference of partial confederacies," a "spirit of competition with the national rulers for personal pre-eminence,'' an ''impatience of the restraints of national authority,'' and ''the fear of a diminution of power and emoluments.'' If reelected governor, Clinton would thus be irresistibly tempted ''wantonly to perplex or embarrass the national Government.''[43]

On such plausible inferences, Hamilton might well have rested his case. Instead, he concluded that he must expose both the governor's manifold transgressions during his twelve-year tenure as chief magistrate and his lamentable lack of personal probity. This was the purpose of a sixteen-part series that Hamilton published in the *New York Daily Advertiser* under the signature ''H.G.''[44] He raked over Clinton's career, finding nothing but personal flaws and official faults. The governor was ''CUNNING,'' a man of ''narrow views, a prejudiced and contracted disposition, a passionate and interested temper,'' one of those ''restless and turbulent spirits'' who are ''impatient of constraint, averse to all power of superiority, which they do not themselves enjoy.''[45] What had Clinton contributed to the state he had so long governed? Hamilton's answer: *''I do not recollect a single measure of public utility since the peace, for which the state is indebted to its Chief Magistrate.''*[46] Before crediting that claim, Hamilton's readers might well have pondered how New York had managed to survive such misrule, much less to prosper under it. Hamilton himself, single-mindedly intent on stalking his political prey, neither asked such questions nor was aware of the paradox presented by his H.G. performance: How could a man who equated democracy and demagoguery practice democratic politics with such zest, demonstrating in the process the very demagoguery that he abstractly deplored? Perhaps Hamilton managed in this instance carefully to compartmentalize theory and practice. In any event, his debut as a campaign manager was unsuccessful; Clinton was reelected, as he would over the years continue to be.[47]

Although unable to unseat Clinton, Hamilton could take solace in the election of Federalist congressmen. Particularly gratifying was the designation of his father-in-law, Philip Schuyler, and Rufus King, his friend and political ally, as New York's first United States senators. The selection was not only hotly contested but was also protracted because of a legislative deadlock on the proper manner of their election.[48] At the outset, Schuyler, who was acceptable to both the assembly and the senate, seemed certain to win, but King, a Massachusetts lawyer who had changed residences as recently as 1786, was the first choice of neither body. The assembly initially nominated Schuyler and James Duane, mayor of New York City and member of the state senate. Duane's selection was owing less to his official posts, however, than to his spouse, a daughter of the lord of Livingston manor. The Livingstons confidently expected that in recognition of their prestige and political power one of their clan would be sent to the United States Senate. Unlike the assembly, the state senate was unwilling to oblige and chose instead a political lightweight, Ezra l'Hommedieu. After considerable legislative jockeying, King was accepted as a compromise candidate by both

houses. This outcome, according to scholarly tradition, was largely owing
to Hamilton, who, to his later regret, thus alienated the Livingstons.[49] Although the outcome was certainly to Hamilton's liking, Duane's defeat was
in fact attributable to the machinations of rival aspirants to the Senate seat.[50]
But, the episode bears retelling because of its effect on Hamilton's subsequent role in New York politics. The Livingstons, as we shall see, retaliated
by throwing their political weight onto the Antifederalist scale, and for this
and other reasons Schuyler at the expiration of his short term was only two
years later replaced by Aaron Burr, the candidate Hamilton would least have
preferred. It is possible that had Hamilton been a more flexible politician,
one more attuned to availability than to ability, he might have persuaded
Schuyler (who was then the Federalist boss of New York) to placate the
Livingstons rather than to preer King, who had as yet no following in the
electorate, no great personal fortune (although his wife expected to inherit
one), no network of influential kinsmen, and no national political connections.[51]

Hamilton himself had the single most advantageous connection that an
ambitious man could ask for. President Washington's respect for the ability
and acumen of his former aide was unreserved. Once inaugurated, he called
upon Hamilton for advice on the seemingly trivial but initially important
subject of presidential etiquette. Although predictably arguing that "the
dignity of the office should be supported," Hamilton practically proposed a
plan that would "steer clear of extremes." The president should "have a
levee day once a week for receiving visits," accept no invitations, extend
weekly "informal invitations to family dinners," give only occasional "formal entertainments," and allow only the most prominent public officials
direct access to him.[52] Initiating what would become almost a habit, Washington not only accepted Hamilton's recommendations but in acknowledging
them also asked "that you will permit me to entreat a continuation of them
as occasions may arise."[53] Viewed from the perspective of Hamilton's personal background the correspondence between himself and Washington was
a testimony to American democracy: where else would a parvenu, an illegitimate one at that, have been asked to prescribe the rules of etiquette for
the head of state? The rapidity of Hamilton's social and political ascent had
been dizzying. It would not have seemed so, however, to a climber who,
like Hamilton, never looked back.

Instead, Hamilton looked to the present with an eye to the future. Among
the developments that he watched with care was the record of the first session of Congress. That body deliberated lengthily and proceeded slowly, but
its accomplishments were impressive. The Judiciary Act was from the perspective of the present the single most important measure, and it may also
have seemed so to Hamilton. The appellant jurisdiction conferred on the
federal courts created by that act (as well as their implied right of judicial
review in causes arising under the Constitution, laws, and treaties of the
United States) were in precise accord with the analysis of the federal judiciary that Hamilton had made in *The Federalist*. Also consonant with his
position was the congressional decision that the president should have not

only the power to designate but also if necessary to remove his principal ministers of state. Although Hamilton viewed the incorporation of a bill of rights as a constitutional redundancy, he no doubt accepted as politically prudent adoption of the federal bill of rights. Also unexceptionable, as Hamilton must have seen the issue, was the first tariff act, which was a compromise between the advocates of a manifestly protective tariff and proponents of a tariff primarily designed to provide a reliable income for the new government. If his stance in 1789 may be inferred from his later position, Hamilton would have looked far less favorably on James Madison's proposal for discriminatory tonnage duties designed to favor nations that had made reciprocal commercial agreements with the United States (notably France) and to punish those who had imposed restrictions on American shipping (conspicuously England). Although unsuccessful, Madison's proposal raised the momentous question of whether American foreign policy should be oriented toward France or Great Britain. It was an issue on which Hamilton and Madison would in time sharply disagree and also one that would largely contribute to the development of the nation's first political parties. For the time being, however, there was no hint of a rift in the New Yorker's and Virginian's political partnership, and neither man could foresee the emergence of parties, which both of them at that time reprobated.

Hamilton may well have surmised that from a personal standpoint the most important measure of Congress's first session was the creation of executive departments and the provision for an attorney general. An act establishing the State Department became law on July 27; a measure creating the Department of War was approved early in August; and the Treasury Department was created on September 2. As attorney general (a high ranking executive officer who lacked a department) the president chose Edmund Randolph, a former governor of Virginia and an Antifederalist apostate of whom Washington was particularly fond personally. The president's predictable candidate for the War Department was Henry Knox, who had administered the corresponding office under the Confederation Congress. Washington's choice for secretary of state came as something more of a surprise. For that post, he selected another fellow Virginian, Thomas Jefferson, who was on the eve of returning home from France where his service as United States minister had earned him diplomatic distinction and Washington's esteem.

On September 11, 1789, a little over a week after the establishment of the Treasury Department, Hamilton was offered its secretaryship. Although Washington had kept his intention to himself, it was no doubt an appointment that he had from the outset of his presidency planned to make. There was no need to solicit advice or recommendations; from long and close observation the president was well aware of Hamilton's superior qualifications.[54] From personal experience he also knew something of his former aide's defects. But Washington sagely recognized that Hamilton's shortcomings were insignificant compared to his demonstrated brilliance and indisputable commitment to the public weal.

For his part, Hamilton scarcely could have been surprised by the appointment. Since his rift with the general at army headquarters in 1782, not even a hint of disagreement had disturbed their relationship. On that Hamilton had no doubt been intent. He was aware too of the implicit promise of Washington's reliance on him for advice. Although not unexpected, the appointment must, nevertheless, have been immeasurably gratifying, not only as confirmation of the national stature that he had sought with such intense determination but as an opportunity to win greater public recognition of the exceptional talent on which he quite properly prided himself. About such a private matter, propriety and prudence dictated that he be silent; so far as the written record reveals, he treated the nomination as head of the most important executive department in the new government as nonchalantly as he would have an appointment to the New York City Council.

VII

Finance Minister

"The regulation of the mere domestic police of a state appears to me to hold out slender allurements to ambition," Hamilton commented in December 1787. "Commerce, finance, negotiation and war seem to comprehend all the objects which have charms for minds governed by that passion."[1] As he had precisely that kind of a mind, the secretaryship of the Treasury afforded him an appropriate challenge. Not only was his department larger than any other but, as Hamilton remarked, "most of the important measures of every Government are connected with the Treasury."[2] The observation was particularly apposite to the government established by the Constitution. Its predecessor had foundered principally because of its failure to solve the country's financial problems. The success of Washington's administration largely hinged on its adoption of fiscal policies that would revive confidence in the fledgling nation, both at home and abroad; the success of the new administration also depended (at least to Hamilton and like-minded nationalists) on welding thirteen disparate states, each revolving in its own orbit, into one sovereign nation.

The secretary of the Treasury was in an advantageous position to help achieve this goal, for his was the only department that "had an extensive field service located in every large town and section of the country."[3] The administration of the Treasury Department could thus directly affect Americans everywhere, and as directed by Hamilton, it did. Its fiscal operations involved government stockholders (state and federal), borrowers, bankers, and investors; its customs service reached merchants, shipowners, and fishermen; its procurement policies concerned manufacturers and contractors; and its internal revenue service affected countless citizens.

The act establishing the Treasury Department had included detailed organizational arrangements. At headquarters Hamilton could in 1789 call on the assistance of five principal officers: an auditor, a register, a treasurer, a comptroller, and an assistant secretary. Of these, the first three performed tasks that were essentially clerical; only the comptroller, Oliver Wolcott, Jr., and the assistant secretary, William Duer, played even a minor role in policy-making or exercised any official discretion. Although the job of the comptroller may have been functionally more important, the assistant secretary was officially the department's second highest ranking officer. Precisely what Duer's duties were cannot be determined. Even less determinable are Hamilton's reasons for appointing him. Distantly related by marriage, the two men had been on friendly terms for many years. Duer's three years of service as secretary to the Board of Treasury under the Confederation government, moreover, ostensibly qualified him for an important post with that agency's successor. But Hamilton should have recognized that his own personal friendship for Duer and the latter's official experience were overmatched by one other vital consideration: as one of the nation's most notorious speculators, not overly scrupulous about mixing his private and the public business, Duer's most likely contribution to the Treasury Department would be to besmirch its reputation. So it turned out, and within half a year Hamilton was obliged to recognize that his assistant was committed only marginally to public service and primarily to self-enrichment. Although himself an official of exemplary probity, Hamilton was at the same time disposed to overlook the misconduct of longtime friends and disinclined to admit his own mistakes. So, he fired Duer but neither publicly exposed nor censured him. There were good reasons for doing both. But in one sense, Hamilton is not open to reproof. Had he disqualified all speculators he might have been obliged to run the Treasury Department alone.

In choosing his staff Hamilton properly perceived that he must rely on experienced assistants. The size and myriad operations of the Treasury obliged him to do so, despite his reluctance to delegate authority. By 1790 the staff at Treasury headquarters numbered over thirty clerks, as compared to the four who carried on the work of the State Department and the three who handled the business of the War Department. In addition, the personnel of the Treasury included a nationwide network of collectors, surveyors, and naval officers to supervise customs, revenue, and navigational services. Hamilton's more reckless critics charged that he used these officials as so many precinct captains, commissioned to carry out the department's corrupt policies and to promote its secretary's limitless ambition. To that accusation, however, the Treasury's voluminous records afford a conclusive rebuttal. By European standards, moreover, the department was small. Certainly Hamilton's official quarters did not even remotely resemble those of his European counterparts. Although the facts do not fit the Hamiltonian stereotype, the Treasury secretary worked under conditions of republican simplicity (although congressional niggardliness left him no choice). A Frenchman who visited the Treasury headquarters found Hamilton attired "in a long gray linen jacket," seated at a plain pine table covered with a green cloth, his files on makeshift shelves, in a room whose furnishings could not have been worth more than $10.[4]

Hamilton was too busy to notice the sparse furnishings of his office. From it, he not only closely supervised Treasury operations but also labored long hours on the reports required by law or requested by Congress. The act that established the Treasury Department provided that its head report "in person or in writing" on any subject referred to him by the House or Senate and that he also submit periodic proposals on the fiscal operations of his department.[5] The occasion of Hamilton's first major report, one of a triad that would earn him enduring fame, was prepared in compliance with a congressional mandate. On September 21, 1789, ten days after Hamilton's appointment, the House of Representatives, averring that "an adequate provision for the public credit" was a "matter of high importance to the national honor and prosperity," directed the Treasury secretary to "prepare a plan for that purpose." Since Hamilton, publicly and in private correspondence, had been harping on the subject and making just such proposals for over a decade, no assignment could have been more congenial. Nor was there any doubt about the general drift of the policies he would recommend. As Hamilton himself had commented two days after his official appointment, his "inviolable attachment to the principles which form the basis of public credit" was "well and . . . generally understood."[6] If his countrymen or members of Congress were unaware of them it was because they did not bother to check his public pronouncements—nor, for that matter, the position long taken by his fellow nationalists.

The principles underpinning Hamilton's report may have been predictable, but it remained to work out details. This was accomplished over the ensuing three months, during which time he not only read widely and pondered long but also consulted the best qualified experts he could find, among them William Bingham, the Philadelphia merchant prince; Stephen Higginson, a prominent Boston merchant; and Philip Schuyler. Hamilton also solicited the advice of Congress' single most influential member, a prominent nationalist who had been his staunchest ally during the ratification crusade and who years earlier as a fellow delegate to the Continental Congress had stoutly stood with Hamilton in an attempt to shore up the national credit. James Madison promptly obliged by recommending among other measures the levying of a direct federal land tax. On the subjects of paying in full the national and state debts, however, he said nothing, a silence Hamilton interpreted to mean that his friend saw no need to comment on the obvious. After all, Madison had unfailingly supported faithful restoration of the public credit for more than a decade. But, then, Hamilton was unaware of the pressures exerted by Madison's congressional constituency and of the Virginian's political flexibility.

In preparing his report Hamilton relied not only on his countrymen's advice but also on European precedents, as winnowed by his own experience. The record of the British Exchequer and the writings of English economists were the inspiration for his funding system. The prescriptions of John Law for the deranged state of French finances early in the eighteenth century provided some examples of what to adopt but even more of what to avoid.[7] So, too, did the record of American nationhood—particularly, the sorry state of public finance during the Revolution—and the ineffectuality of the Confederation government's faltering attempts to rescue public credit.

Instead of a respectable legacy of fiscal responsibility, the Confederation had bequeathed unpaid debts. The foreign debt, although unhonored, was at least easy to calculate. The domestic debt, by contrast, took the form not only of virtually worthless Continental currency but also a bewildering assortment of bills, promissory notes, and certificates issued by various government agencies, including the Continental loan office; commissioners for the commissaries; the quartermaster, marine, clothing, and hospital departments; and the state commissioners. On all of these, arrears of interest were due. The debts of the states were even more baffling. Hamilton's task was first to unravel this tangled mass of debt and then to propose a detailed and feasible plan for its payment. Throughout, his work was informed by one central idea: public credit must be restored by fully and faithfully honoring the fairly incurred obligations of the union. Hamilton was not timorous; he characteristically approached the problem audaciously.

On January 14, 1790, Hamilton's *Report Relative to a Provision for the Support of Public Credit* was submitted to Congress.[8] Momentarily there was not a murmur of dissent or scarcely a comment, perhaps because a close reading of the forty-thousand-word report was needed in order to digest its details, to appreciate its sweep, and to perceive its implications for the new government. Most congressmen, moreover, had expected merely modest proposals for handling the public debt, not an elaborate treatise on political economy. But gradually the general design of Hamilton's blueprint for a prosperous, strong, even preeminent, central government became clear. When it did, his report ignited an acrimonious debate that preoccupied Congress for the rest of its session.

Hamilton's report has been described and dissected (and in the process criticized or praised) scores of times. Its specific proposals, superficially unexceptionable and to all except historical specialists essentially uninteresting, need thus be only summarized. Hamilton divided the public debt—comprising accrued interest in addition to principal—into three categories: first, the foreign debt, totaling around $11.7 million; second, the domestic debt, amounting to $40.4 million; third, the debts of the states, approximately $25 million. He called for discharge of the foreign debt (plus interest) in full; payment of the face value of the principal of the domestic debt but with a reduction of stipulated interest rates (that is, a rate of 4 percent on long-term government bonds and 6 percent on short-term bonds); and assumption of state debts on the same terms as public securities but with interest payments to be postponed until January 1, 1792. To maintain the price of public securities and to manage any government surplus the Treasury secretary proposed the establishment of a sinking fund.*

To many of Hamilton's proposals there were no consequential objections. It was for example, generally accepted that national honor dictated full payment of the foreign debt and that the sinking fund was a prudent fiscal arrangement. A number of his recommendations, however, stirred up intense opposition: Although most congressmen agreed that the national debt should be paid, there was an acrimonious debate about whether to fund it at par and about the proper recipients of its predictably appreciated value. Yet more fiercely contested was Hamilton's call for the assumption of state debts. Enthusiastically greeted by states that had large debts, it was roundly denounced by states that had paid off a considerable portion of their Revolutionary obligations.

Underlying the debate on the specific provisions of Hamilton's report were divergent views on its implicit thesis and overall purpose. The essential issue was this: What direction should the nation take? The one toward which Hamilton pointed was a monolithic nationalism—a unified, centralized, strong federal government that would both reflect and serve the interests of every section and all classes, while singling out those whose support was most indispensable. To Hamilton's critics diversity was more important than unity, the preservation of the perquisites of the states more essential than the enhancement of the power of the union, the maintenance of a predominantly agrarian society and the well-being of farmers and planters preferable to a balanced economy that would pander to the interests of the mercantile and capitalistic classes.

The latter fear, the gravamen of his critics' indictment, was well founded. That Hamilton's plan was heavily weighted in favor of precisely those classes is as much beyond dispute as his purpose was, although the issue is sometimes misunderstood. He did not calculatedly encourage northern speculators unscrupulously to reap large profits on depreciated securities. He did not believe that a public debt was a public blessing and thus on principle saddle the nation with an enormous permanent debt. His primary purpose was not to serve "the rich and the well-born" or, more particularly, to enrich a small group of capitalists and speculators.

Essential to any balanced interpretation of Hamilton's fiscal policies is a correct perception of the nation's class structure. America in the eighteenth century and well on into the nineteenth was, unlike its European counter-

---

*Hamilton's expertness in finance precluded his acceptance of the then popular idea that the sinking fund provided a means of liquidating the debt by the magic of compound interest. He rather valued such a fund for its beneficial psychological effects. Systematic purchases of government stock from a sinking fund (inviolably pledged to that purpose) would, he believed, promote public confidence in the eventual retirement of the debt and thus bolster public credit.

parts, predominantly a middle-class society. The dispute sparked by Hamilton's report was, accordingly, not between a small number of very rich individuals, on the one hand, and a large number of disgruntled peasants, poor farmers, and propertyless proletarians, on the other. Rather it was, in John C. Miller's perceptive phrase, "a quarrel within the house of capitalism: There were property owners on both sides and the 'democrats' had almost as great a material stake in the country as did the 'aristocrats'."[9] It is for this reason mistaken to single out Hamilton as a particularly solicitous guardian of the rights of property, much less to depict his partisan opponents as the peculiar champions of human rights. In fact, Hamilton's insistence on the inviolability of private property was too commonplace to merit especial notice. A century earlier, John Locke had argued that government was initially instituted not only to safeguard life and liberty but also, and primarily, to protect property. And in America, to repeat Louis Hartz's impressive insight, Locke became "a massive national cliché."[10] In believing that the preservation of private property was the hallmark of liberty, the distinguishing object of civilization, Hamilton, in sum, merely expressed the consensus of his countrymen.

Nor was Hamilton's primary purpose the protection of a particular kind of property or, as has been said, the enrichment of a single class. This charge, perhaps the most common criticism of Hamilton, was succinctly expressed by John C. Miller, an otherwise friendly biographer, this way: "Hamilton's plans were conceived by a minority, designed to benefit a minority and carried into execution by a minority."[11] That minority was, of course, the moneyed interests (stockbrokers, merchants, bankers, and other capitalists) located primarily in the Northeast, and they were, in fact, the direct and immediate beneficiaries of Hamilton's program, as he intended they should be. But this was not because he wished to fill pockets already well lined but rather because he believed that winning and keeping the confidence of men with money to bestow or withhold was essential to the fiscal operations of the new government. As Hamilton had remarked at the New York ratifying convention, "Men will pursue their interests. It is as easy to change human nature, as to oppose the strong current of the selfish passions. A wise legislator will gently divert the channel, and direct it, if possible, to the public good."[12] A modern English historian, W. R. Brock, puts the same idea in a more general way: "Injustice is often done to Hamilton in supposing that he intended to use national authority simply to make" the rich even richer. "Rather, he intended to make their power, which might otherwise be against the public interest, serve a useful purpose," that is, the restoration of public credit.[13]

Similarly, it was to Hamilton unfortunate that the introduction of his program touched off a spirited speculation in the public debt that some dealers profited from and others lost by. Securities speculation itself was, of course, nothing new; it had commenced with the issuance of bonds, certificates, and other evidences of government debt during the Revolution and had continued over the succeeding years. Such securities obviously fluctuated in value with the oscillating possibility of their payment at par, partial redemption, or repudiation. Hamilton's program for funding and assumption at face value merely accelerated this longstanding practice while altering its trend. The success of his proposals was by no means certain, especially the assumption of state debts, which for many months seemed highly unlikely. Thus, speculation, particularly in the debts of the states, involved great risk, as it had all along. Those who guessed that the federal government would refuse to assume responsibility for state securities were naturally inclined to sell them; those who banked on assumption were just as eager to buy such stock. The issue, then, was not a moral one, with Hamilton cast as the patron saint of big-time buyers. It was rather the familiar story of bulls and bears. In this instance, the bulls' gamble paid off. Contrary to an implication sometimes encountered, moreover, the sum that changed hands was far too small to have brought about anything close to a redistribution of national wealth.

One can at the same time point to Hamilton's intransigent refusal to accommodate his critics by accepting any major alteration in his program. He argued as if there were only an alternative when there were, in fact, options. Although he quite properly rejected (as will be explained) recommendations that original owners as well as assignees of government stock share the profit occasioned by endorsement of his funding program, the fate of the new government did not depend on funding securities at face value. Some modification would have alienated only a few big-time stockbrokers and would have appeased a good number of Hamilton's critics, particularly Virginians and citizens of other states who had paid off or sold their government stocks. The complaints of the Treasury secretary's critics were justified. The states that had debts that were either comparatively small or largely discharged were called on to make a disproportionately great sacrifice. To ask that they do so was, moreover, contrary to Hamilton's avowed belief that attachment to the new government was directly proportional to an immediate material stake in its success. "The government of the Union, like that of each State," he had remarked in *The Federalist,* "must be able to address itself immediately to the hopes and fears of individuals; and to attract to its support, those passions which have the strongest influence upon the human heart."[14] Had he applied his own observation to his southern critics, he would have warded off much of the group and sectional mistrust that were to impede his national goals and thwart his personal ambition.

Hamilton's political blunder, in other words, was owing less to a class bias than blindness to the realities of sectionalism. One of his unique official qualifications was his comparative freedom from local or regional ties, and hence his national vision. An American first, a northerner and a New Yorker only secondarily, his nationalism was, nevertheless, not broad enough to encompass his more strident critics, especially southerners. He thus presumably discarded a precept that he had embraced only two years earlier. The person who administers a nation's finances, he had written, "should be acquainted with the general genius, habits and modes of thinking of the people at large.''[15] In forgetting that the latter included many persons who did not directly profit from his program, Hamilton himself was partly to blame that his name became an eponym for sectional and class favoritism.

It was perhaps already so to James Madison, Hamilton's most influential congressional critic; it would in time become so to Hamilton's most prominent cabinet colleague. Thomas Jefferson arrived in New York to assume his duties as secretary of state in March 1790, at a time when Hamilton's program was bogged down in Congress. If Jefferson then objected to the Treasury secretary's policies, the Virginian did not openly say so. Instead, the relationship between the two men was at the outset courteous, although certainly not cordial. Their personal backgrounds, public careers, political creeds, sharply different personalities, and contrasting manners ruled out close congeniality. Nor did either man find it easy to tolerate rivals or disagreement. Both were intent on preeminence; Jefferson was covertly ambitious, and Hamilton clearly so.

The Virginian's first doubts about the widely acclaimed merits of the Treasury secretary may have been aroused by the manifest demerits of the latter's principal assistant. By March 1790 William Duer's large-scale and reckless speculation in government stocks had rendered him a political liability. Although charitable about his friend's speculative mania, Hamilton could not condone Duer's official misbehavior. So, when in the spring of 1790 the assistant Treasury secretary tendered his resignation, Hamilton accepted it with alacrity, although charitably avoiding official or personal censure. To replace Duer, Hamilton selected Tench Coxe, a Philadelphia merchant who was also deservedly recognized as one of the nation's foremost political economists. Coxe had one other official asset. He believed as firmly in the imperativeness of funding and assumption as did Hamilton himself, and the Pennsylvanian, who was on close terms with many uncommitted or undecided congressmen, was in a good position to further the adoption of the Treasury secretary's *Report on the Public Credit*. By May 1790, when Coxe took over as assistant secretary, Hamilton needed all the help he could get.

The legislative history of Hamilton's report is an often, and sometimes inaccurately, told tale. Since payment of the foreign debt and adequate provisions for reimbursing holders of the national debt were taken for granted, the most controversial issue, as we have seen, was the assumption of state debts. But which holders of the latter were to be reimbursed, those to whom certificates had originally been issued or, as Hamilton proposed, present owners, many of whom were speculators who had bought up the debt at a nominal sum? The issue, to Hamilton's surprise, was introduced into the debate by Madison, who in mid-February recommended a plan that he insisted would do justice to the original holders of the debt and also satisfy the cupidity of assignees: Let those who had bought up government securities be paid the highest value they had reached; let the difference between this amount and par value of the stock be paid to the original holders. To Madison such discrimination was the only way to do justice to patriots who had come to the aid of a young nation in peril.*

To Hamilton and his supporters, however, Madison's recommendation for discrimination was both an unconscionable betrayal of investors who in good faith had purchased government stock and a fatal blow to the restoration of public credit. To some congressmen who might have otherwise shared the Virginian's concern, discrimination would mean an unwarranted increase in the national debt, which to them was already unacceptably swollen by Hamilton's funding scheme. The Treasury secretary's congressional allies properly pointed to another defect: even if the requisite records could be gathered, the job of distinguishing between original holders and assignees would involve the government in an administrative quagmire. Primarily for these reasons, discrimination was decisively defeated, despite an eloquent defense by Madison that a Pennsylvania congressman described as one that "would do honor to his Philanthropy & Ability before Any Assembly on Earth."[16]

The feature of Hamilton's program on which Congress now centered its attention was assumption. On this issue Congress was deadlocked until the eve of its adjournment, some six months later. It was predictably championed by states such as Massachusetts, South Carolina, and Connecticut, whose Revolutionary debts remained virtually unpaid; it was opposed by such states as Maryland, Virginia, and Georgia, whose debts had been largely extinguished. Other states with moderate or funded debts (New Hampshire, New York, New Jersey, Delaware, and Pennsylvania) were uncommitted or unpredictable. The swing state, it was widely believed, was Pennsylvania. Such a situation was an invitation to compromise, but this possibility dimmed when, on June 2, the House passed and sent to the Senate a funding bill without assumption. The Senate answered by amending the House measure to incorporate the assumption of state debts. An impasse had been reached.

The second most controversial issue confronting Congress in 1790 was the site of the nation's capital city, then located in New York City. Some congressmen wished it to remain there, others championed Baltimore, many southerners opted for a site in a wilderness near the Potomac, and Pennsylvania demanded that what was to them the country's most civilized city also be its first capital, at least temporarily. The most insistent of these claimants were, unsurprisingly, Philadelphians, who at times seemed more interested in where the government should sit than in its solvency. Their persistence was rewarded when the House, on May 31, resolved that Philadelphia be made the temporary capital. But the Senate refused to acquiesce and instead

---

*It was also dictated by personal political considerations: Since his own state had paid most of its debts, Hamilton's plan was not tailored to Virginia's needs; since Madison's longtime advocacy of the Treasury secretary's own brand of nationalism had already rendered him suspect among his Virginia constituents, his continuance in Congress measurably depended on mending his political fences at home.

awarded the prize to Baltimore. As with assumption, so with the residence issue—Congress was deadlocked.

Preoccupied with plans for reversing the House's decision on assumption, Hamilton viewed the capital controversy as something of a sideshow. While not particularly concerned whether his own city, Baltimore, Philadelphia, or the Potomac site be selected, Hamilton concluded that the issue might be the bait with which to catch the votes necessary to rescue his program. The Pennsylvanians seemed especially likely to bite. Private negotiations were promptly set in train for what became the Compromise of 1790.

According to the traditional wisdom, this compromise took the form of a bargain on the two major and seemingly irresolvable issues then before Congress—assumption and the residence. It was, so the standard version goes, negotiated by Hamilton, Madison, and Jefferson at Jefferson's house in Maiden Lane on June 20. The bargain agreed upon was this: certain features of the assumption plan that Virginians considered inequitable would be modified; Madison, while not voting for it, would not oppose the amended measure; Hamilton would round up enough votes for passage of a residence bill making Philadelphia the temporary capital and a site on the Potomac the permanent one; and Jefferson or Madison would then round up enough votes to assure the assumption of state debts. So the traditionally accepted account goes.

This familiar interpretation should be modified in a number of important particulars.[17] Although the dinner meeting at Jefferson's house took place and the agreement as usually described was made, the bargain was not, as things turned out, consummated. Neither Madison nor Jefferson was responsible for the success of assumption, and Hamilton was unable to round up a single vote for the residence measure. The Treasury secretary did not need to: the Pennsylvanians, among whom he was supposed to get the necessary votes, had committed themselves to a Potomac-Philadelphia bill sometime before Jefferson's famous dinner party. The upshot was that when the residence bill again came before Congress, it was agreed that Philadelphia should serve as the capital for a decade, at the end of which time the government would move to a permanent location on the Potomac. The promoters of Philadelphia were particularly pleased: once the capital was established in what they viewed as an irresistibly charming city, they believed it would stay.

After a wearying and wearisome debate, Congress also authorized Hamilton's funding program, including the assumption of state debts. As with the residence decision, the outcome was not due to the famous bargain concocted at Jefferson's house. It was rather owing to Hamilton's willingness to make judicious financial concessions that made assumption more palatable to its former opponents. Apportioning of the sum to be assumed and the rate of interest it would bear were to Hamilton comparatively inconsequential. What mattered was to secure acceptance of the principle that the financial obligations of the government must be honored and the public credit secured. When Congress at last acquiesced, Hamilton must have been jubilant, although he never permitted himself to display such an emotion. The first major task that he had assigned himself was now accomplished: a cornerstone had been laid on which he intended to build a sound and durable fiscal structure for the new nation.

A different kind of cornerstone might have served as well. If one confines one's conjectures to the domestic economy, it seems unlikely that the nation would have foundered had discrimination been adopted or the states obliged to pay their own debts. But Hamilton, of course, did not see things this way. To him, domestic and international affairs were inseparable. His proposals were largely based on the conviction that the United States must solidly establish its credit among European nations, bankers, and investors so that in any future crisis it might readily command foreign loans. This could be done only if America acquired an international reputation for scrupulous fidelity in discharging its financial obligations, not only foreign but also national. Nor was Hamilton sanguine that tranquillity would perpetually prevail at home. Sharing with many of his countrymen a "crisis psychology," he believed that the union must anticipate, and be prepared to deal swiftly and successfully with, inevitable internal crises. For this it might be necessary to float large domestic loans, which could be satisfactorily negotiated only if the credit of the government were unimpaired by a failure to honor past obligations. Hamilton, in sum, was looking beyond concerns of the present to exigencies of the future. American history has, in obvious ways, attested to his prescience.

For the moment, Hamilton was involved in devising plans for the large national debt obligingly created by congressional endorsement of his fiscal program. By previous American standards that debt was a staggering $80 million, a sum representing a per capita indebtedness of $20. By foreign standards, however, the debt was modest. The British national debt at this time, for example, was a mind-numbing £272 million. Nor did Hamilton believe that Congress had saddled his countrymen with a debt disproportionate to the nation's fiscal and economic capacities. Was it in any way excessive? Hamilton replied no; it could be repaid without even resorting to direct taxes. Would not a long-term debt prove a grueling national hardship? Predictable economic growth, enhanced wealth, and expanding prosperity, Hamilton believed, would render the debt inconsequential to future generations. Hamilton's vision was clear. "He perceived, as his critics did not," in John C. Miller's words, "the connection between national income and the national debt and he recognized that there was no more certain way of disposing of the debt than by stimulating the productive forces of the country."* [18]

*The mechanics of debt management (stock transfer, amortization, interest payments, and the like) were prescribed by Congress in acts that authorized (1) a $12 million loan; (2) three federal security issues (based only on the credit of the United States) for which old securities of both the assumed state and Continental debts might be exchanged; and (3) sinking-fund operations. Administration of the fiscal system thus established fell, of course, to the Treasury Department. The foreign loan was readily arranged by the Dutch banking house of Wilhelm and Jan Willink and Nicholas and

Hamilton was obliged, nevertheless, to make recommendations for interest payments on the national debt, swollen by the assumption of state debts. He proposed that such payments be met by additional duties on distilled spirits, both domestic and foreign. He did not, as was widely expected, recommend a hike in import duties on any other article, perhaps because he did not wish to alienate the nation's merchants who had rallied to the support of his program. Instead, he unwittingly antagonized the many farmers (whose support he continued to view as indispensable to the success of his program) who produced the whiskey that gushed from backcountry stills like oil from bottomless wells. Unlike the merchants, these rural distillers constituted no influential pressure group, but they cast far, far more votes. Of this, a calculating politician would have been aware. Regarding himself as a disinterested statesman, Hamilton was not so much unaware as unconcerned. He might well have pondered, however, by what miracle merchants (and not frontiersmen or southern planters) had been transformed into vestal virgins of the new republic.

Jacob Van Staphorst and Hubbard. This partnership, whose formidable title suggested solidity, became the new nation's principal international banker. For handling the transfer of old for new securities and requisite interest payments, loan commissioners responsible to the Treasury were appointed in each state. Management of the sinking fund was confided to commissioners who by and large rubber stamped the decisions of the Treasury secretary. Despite contrary professions, however, Hamilton did not use the sinking fund to pay off the debt as quickly and cheaply as possible but rather to stabilize the market price of government stock. For redemption of principal he intended to take advantage of a prospective fall in the prevailing rate of interest.

VIII

A National Bank
Is Born and Defended

Philadelphia, the temporary capital of the new republic, still bore the stamp of its founder's masterful planning. The city's commercial life was concentrated along the Delaware waterfront and nearby alleys and streets. Market Street, the main thoroughfare, was lined with two-story brick dwellings adorned with white framework and large windows. Here and on adjoining brick-paved and tree-lined streets lived the city's first families, such as the Chews, Biddles, Powells, Shippens, and Penns. Here also resided the government's senior officials. The official residence of the president was Robert Morris' imposing mansion, perhaps the most elegant in the country. John Adams maintained less pretentious, but by no means modest, quarters at Bush Hill, a handsome house about two miles from the city. Thomas Jefferson carried on the traditions of the Virginia aristocracy at his rented mansion on Market Street.

In 1790, Philadelphia, the commercial and political center of the United States, was also (to its admirers, at least) the focal point of American cultural life. Dr. Benjamin Rush, who tended to view himself as the exemplar of his city's intellectual and scientific preeminence, commented that Philadelphia's captivating cultural climate would "do more to prolong the residence of a republican Congress among us than . . . paving our streets with silver dollars."[1] And Rush, along with other Philadelphia enthusiasts, was confident that the transient governmental resident would become a permanent one.

That conviction was shared by the assistant secretary of the Treasury, to whom Hamilton delegated the task of overseeing the department's move to Philadelphia. Tench Coxe selected as Treasury headquarters his own house on Chestnut and Third streets, which he rented to the government for an annual sum of $660. For the Treasury secretary's personal residence Coxe secured Dr. Rush's house, located on South Third Street, where Hamilton was joined by his wife and their four young children (Philip, Angelica, Alexander, and James Alexander, born respectively in 1782, 1784, 1786, and 1788). If Eliza objected to the torrid Philadelphia summers or to a social scene that may not have been as attuned to her social status as New York society was, she did not say so. But, then, it was her way to acquiesce in whatever her handsome husband wished.

At the age of thirty-five, Hamilton closely resembled the dashing young aide of the Revolution. Still as slender, his bearing as erect, he stood out in any group, particularly among official colleagues such as the portly Henry Knox, the rotund John Adams, and the angular Thomas Jefferson. Hamilton's hair was of a reddish hue, and he wore it "turned back from his forehead, powdered and collected in a club behind." His forehead was smooth, his eyes bright and in color almost violet, his nose somewhat long and thin, his mouth "moderately large," his chin firm. But these features were softened by his complexion. It was, according to one acquaintance, "exceedingly fair, and varying from this only by the almost feminine rosiness of the cheeks. His might be considered, as to figure and color, an uncommonly handsome face."[2] It was complemented by his meticulous grooming and sartorial splendor. Even in a day when men's attire rivaled or outshone women's he appeared a fashion plate. He added glamour, in sum, to a sparkling social scene for which the elegant entertainment provided by the president set high standards.

The house occupied by the First Family might have been mistaken for a ducal palace. Located on the south side of Market Street near Sixth Street, the house had during the Revolution been occupied by Sir William Howe, commander of the British army. The republican president and the British general shared more in common than tenancy of the same residence. Washington's style of living was as courtly as Howe's had been. The stilted presidential levees that had been held in New York were continued, and other official entertainment remained stiffly formal. To straightlaced republicans the president's unintentionally regal manner, his liveried servants, and his "coach of state" smacked suspiciously of monarchy. So, too, did the soirees and sumptuous balls of Philadelphia's leading socialites, most particularly William Bingham, rich merchant and banker, and his wife, daughter of a Philadelphia merchant prince, Thomas Willing. This couple dazzled the newly arrived government officials by the lavishness of the parties held at their Mansion House, which was, suggestively enough, modeled on the Duke of Manchester's residence. Frequently appearing on the Binghams' guest list were the names of the secretary of the Treasury and his wife.

On a salary of $3,000 a year and with no great personal wealth to fall back on, Hamilton was unable to emulate the opulent style of the Willings and the Binghams. Nor could he match that of wealthy planters like Jefferson or rich businessmen like the secretary of war, Henry Knox. Nevertheless, Mrs. Hamilton contrived to entertain on a scale befitting the daughter of a New York patroon and the wife of a top government official, one called by some the prime minister. Perhaps she need not have bothered. According to time-established historical lore, the man once dubbed the Little Lion of Washington's military family was now lionized by the society that circled the president. In the words of a recent biographer, Hamilton "was frequently seen at the theater, assembly hall, and the card table relaxing from the cares of state. No American statesman ever combined more gracefully the hardworking administrator with the social butterfly."[3] Perhaps so, but the characterization seems incongruous. Although Hamilton's personal appearance may have somewhat resembled that of a dandy, more than an ordinary leap of imagination is required to imagine him engrossed in conventional social chitchat. To the contrary, his drawing-room conversation, if light, must have been transparently contrived, his humor heavy-handed. If his voluminous papers are a reliable gauge, Hamilton was not only essentially humorless but also a man of alarming intellectual intensity. Nor could alcohol have transformed him; by all accounts, Hamilton was conspicuously abstemious.

Whatever role he may have played in Philadelphia society, the legend persists that he was the Don Juan of Washington's official family. One of Hamilton's more recent biographers wittily expresses the familiar view this way: "In some ways, he was the greatest boon to womanhood ever to descend upon the City of Brotherly Love: when the gallant Secretary of the Treasury was among the company, it was observed that husbands were never more attentive to their wives."[4] Hamilton may perhaps have been adept at flirtation, but if either wives or jealous husbands took him seriously they were mistaken. His interest ran to women of a different social status, as was tellingly suggested by his passionate affair with Maria Reynolds, which began as early as the summer of 1791. Actually, Hamilton's official duties precluded any more than occasional attendance in what Abigail Adams described as "one continued scene of parties upon parties."[5] The complexities of international finance, intricacies of debt management, and close supervision of the Treasury's customs and other revenue services entailed long and taxing office hours.

Even more demanding was preparation of a congressionally mandated report on "the Further Provision Necessary for Establishing Public Credit."[6] To Hamilton, the indispensable prerequisite was the establishment of a national bank.* His recommendation was submitted on December 14, 1790, to

---

*Closely related to Hamilton's report recommending the creation of a national bank was his *Report on the Establishment of a Mint*, submitted to Congress on January 28, 1791. This report, which, like his major state papers, was mandated by Congress, was for Hamilton a difficult assignment, largely because it was a subject of which he had only the sketchiest knowledge. He acquired it by closely studying standard European authorities (including Sir Isaac Newton) and earlier reports on the topic by Robert Morris, Gouverneur Morris, and Thomas Jefferson. The latter's contribution was particularly important. Hamilton not only incorporated the Virginian's propo[sal] for a decimal system but also asked him to read and comment on the report. Jeffer[son] obligingly cooperated. Hamilton's report on the mint, unlike his great triad of [trea]sury reports, was not notably innovative but rather a restatement of fiscal orth[odoxy]

the Congress that had a week earlier convened for the first time in Philadelphia in its new quarters, a plain but handsomely furnished brick building located next to the state house. Hamilton's proposal for the creation of a national bank was predictable. In his letters on public affairs during the Revolution the virtual miracles that he attributed to such an institution resembled the magic that Adam Smith ascribed to the operation of natural economic laws. The views that Hamilton had expressed during the Revolution had been modified, but not substantially altered, by observation and practical experience during the 1780s. He had, for one thing, closely followed the checkered history of the Bank of North America, chartered by the Continental Congress in 1781 as a quasi-national bank but subsequently a controversial private one. He had, for another, been instrumental in launching the Bank of New York.

Hamilton had also carefully studied the history of the Bank of England, to which he, along with many other admirers, tended to attribute a kind of financial wizardry. That giant institution was in fact a model worth emulating. Although largely public in function, the Bank of England was privately owned and managed by directors who, although manifestly serving their own interest, also promoted the national interest. Through the bank's operations, British business was furnished essential financial facilities, the country was assured an adequate circulating medium, and the government was furnished with both long- and short-term loans and assistance in managing the public debt. The bank's close and prudent control of credit and currency had, in sum, provided eighteenth-century England with financial stability, promoted economic expansion and prosperity, and enhanced national wealth.

Hamilton relied not only on British practice but also on the sparse American literature on money and banking, much of which had been spawned by an attempt in 1785–1786 by the Pennsylvania legislature to repeal the charter of the Bank of North America. He acquired some useful information, for example, from James Wilson's *Considerations on the Bank of North America* and Pelatiah Webster's *Essay on Credit* but far more from Gouverneur Morris' defense of the bank.[8] More influential yet were the writings of Hamilton's assistant Treasury secretary.[9] Tench Coxe, the bank's ablest literary antagonist, had centered his objections to its recharter on the charge that it inadequately served the needs of the public and was insufficiently accountable to the state. Such an argument reinforced Hamilton's own views, and it, along with other of Coxe's ideas on banking, was incorporated into the Treasury secretary's proposal for a national bank.

The one feature of Hamilton's report that now appears singularly irrelevant and misplaced, however, was the disproportionate space devoted to the

---

He recommended a bimetallic currency at a ratio roughly the same as that employed most European countries. He also urged the minting of coins not only of large denominations but of small value as well. The latter was the most original feature of report. Small coins would assist the poor in making small purchases, he argued, ould also "enable them with more comfort to themselves to labor for less; the ges of which need no comment."[7]

Bank of North America. The reasons for this exaggerated emphasis were twofold. As the nation's first "national" bank, the Philadelphia institution was considered by Hamilton as an existent and viable precedent for the kind of bank that he had in mind. To boosters of the Bank of North America, however, it deserved to serve as something more than merely a model for a new institution: properly reconstituted, the bank chartered by the Continental Congress could be adopted by the federal Congress and rechristened the Bank of the United States. Hamilton disagreed and accordingly devoted a good part of his report to a rebuttal of the claim that there was a bank "already in being . . . which supersedes the . . . necessity of another."[10] So persuasive was his refutation that the issue did not survive the presentation of his report.

Hamilton called on Congress to charter a national bank capitalized at $10 million, one-fifth of the total to be provided by the government on its own account and the rest available to individual investors (subscribable partly in specie but chiefly in government securities). Although principally "under a *private* and not a *public* direction," the bank was based on the resources and credit of the United States and was designed to assist in its financial operations.[11] As Hamilton observed, "Public utility is more truly the object of public banks than private profit."[12] Federal funds were to be deposited in the bank, whose notes, redeemable in specie, were to constitute legal tender. It was also to facilitate the payment of taxes and import duties (for which its notes were receivable), to loan money to the United States, and generally to act as the government's fiscal agent. Underscoring the public features of the bank were stipulations that the government appoint five of its twenty-five directors and that the Treasury Department audit its books. Although Hamilton was accused of surrendering the public interest to a private institution, he in fact called for a degree of government supervision not exercised by the British government over its central banking arm, which was under unalloyed private control.

Hamilton's report on a national bank was the ablest of his memorable state papers. It was free of the prolixity that marred some of his writings. In it, he skillfully blended facts and interpretation, managing in the process to make clear, without oversimplifying, the complexities of banking and of monetary theory and practice. "If all subjects were treated in this way," commented William T. Franklin, an English admirer, "knowledge would be much more easily acquired—and Libraries might be made portable."[13]

Hamilton's plan was characteristically audacious. To an overwhelmingly agricultural country whose citizens were traditionally hostile to banks, he proclaimed that such institutions were "nurseries of national wealth."[14] To fellow citizens who for the most part viewed governmental power with suspicion, he proposed a great central bank to facilitate federal financial operations and to bolster and expand the national economy. His report was designed not only to aid but also to strengthen the new government. Implicit in his proposal were both the further subordination of the states to the union and a broad interpretation of the federal Constitution. He was convinced that the precedent thus established would be of inestimable importance in providing the national government with the flexibility essential to current and future exigencies.

The Treasury secretary's critics thought that he was strengthening the government's servitude to the business interests of the Northeast. The charge was superficially plausible. Among Hamilton's manifest goals was augmentation of the nation's active or productive capital, easier availability of credit, encouragement of private investment, and, in general, improvement of business conditions. It thus was scarcely surprising that merchants, other businessmen, and government stockholders enthusiastically approved of the proposed bank while many planters and small farmers saw nothing in it for them. There was very little. Assuming that what was good for his country was also good for all his countrymen, Hamilton saw no reason to pander to the specific needs of farmers, any more than to those of any other class. He did not, for one thing, consider his bank proposal to be special-interest legislation. For another, he was convinced that agrarian prejudices against banks and bank notes would not, in any event, yield to argument, at least not to his. He was right, but he might also have taken such prejudices into account. Had the bank he recommended included some recognition of the peculiar problems of his agrarian opponents (the acceptance of tobacco warehouse receipts as collateral for loans, for example), he might have assuaged, instead of aggravating, sectional and class antagonism.

But Hamilton was not concerned with appeasement. His overarching purpose in calling for a national bank, as in recommending the firm establishment of public credit, was to promote the best interests of all Americans; that a particular class might thereby benefit disproportionately was merely incidental. Once again, as in his first major report, he was intent on bolstering federal authority and fostering national prosperity, not with class equity or with furthering democratic goals. Once again, his own singular brand of nationalism, his identification with country rather than region, led him to overlook the realities of sectionalism and of America's manifold class interests. Once again, the ambitious stateman was an obtuse politician.

Both sectional and class interests were responsible for Congress' opposition to Hamilton's bank report. Some of his principal critics (such as James Madison and his fellow Virginian congressman, William B. Giles) were not particularly knowledgeable about banking, and others (such as James Jackson, Georgia's fiery spokesman for democracy and states' rights) were biased against all banks. Debate on the bank, however, was far less heated and much briefer than had been the dispute over funding and assumption a year earlier. A bill chartering the Bank of the United States sailed smoothly through the Senate, and in mid-February the House gave its assent after only two weeks of debate. In the latter, Hamilton's chief antagonists centered their attack not on the government's inadequate control of the bank (as might have been expected) but on the contention that only the states had the power to charter banks, which should be completely unfettered by federal supervision.

The president did not necessarily agree, but the debate in Congress made him uneasy about the measure's constitutionality. Congressional opposition may also have prompted the disquieting perception that the Constitution, in Bray Hammond's words, "had not displaced rival principles or reconciled them but had become their dialectical arena."[15] To resolve such misgivings he solicited the advice of Attorney General Edmund Randolph, who pronounced the bank unconstitutional. Still undecided, Washington turned to his secretary of state. Precisely why he did so is unclear; to any close associate, Jefferson's opinion could not have been in doubt. A constitutional fundamentalist and fiscal conservative, the secretary of state was by this time also antagonistic to Hamilton personally and deeply suspicious of his program generally. Jefferson was appalled by what he had come to view as his cabinet colleague's corrupt control of Congress and aghast at the speculative frenzy for which he believed Hamilton's policies to be responsible. Nor did the kind of institution proposed by the Treasury secretary "fit snugly into the pattern" of the Virginian's "thought or experience."[16] Jefferson accordingly set forth in his opinion on the bank a rigidly literal and strict construction of the Constitution that would have virtually strangled the national government in its infancy.

Wishing no doubt to avoid infanticide, the president sent copies of Randolph's and Jefferson's opinions to the secretary of the Treasury, implicitly requesting him to refute them. Although he was confident of Hamilton's ability to do so, Washington could not have forecast the masterfulness of the essay in constitutional law that he received in reply.[17]

Hamilton's wife, reminiscing many years later about the incident, is reported to have said that her husband dashed off his opinion in a single night. It was, in fact, the work of a full week, but as an admiring biographer remarks, "even so, this reduces the impossible to the extraordinary."[18] Hamilton, as an otherwise critical student comments, "fully recognized that this was a critical occasion. How magnificently he rose to it, the later constitutional history of his country was to show. His opinion was an extraordinarily skillful defense of his own position and a masterpiece of exposition."[19]

While demolishing Jefferson's position point by point, the major thrust of Hamilton's argument was that his antagonist's constitutional literalness would destroy "the just and indispensible authority of the United States."[20] Inherent in the very definition of government, Hamilton argued, was the proposition that every power with which it was invested was "by its nature sovereign, and includes . . . a right to employ all the *means*" not expressly precluded by the Constitution that were "requisite and fairly applicable to the attainment of the *ends* of such power."[21] Thus rejecting, almost scornfully, Jefferson's negative approach, the Treasury secretary set forth a boldly affirmative view, one that emphasized the scope rather than the limits of governmental power.

The specific question at issue was obviously the right of Congress to charter a corporation, such as the bank. Hamilton's answer: Since it is "unquestionably incident to *sovereign power* to erect corporations," it is consequently incident "to *that* of the United States, in *relation to the objects entrusted* to the management of the government."[22] As Hamilton's critics no doubt perceived, such an argument came perilously close to saying that the United States must possess the powers enjoyed by any sovereign state, including that of chartering corporations. But Hamilton swiftly drew back from that logical pitfall by affirming that the Constitution vested the government with not only express but also both implied and "resulting" powers. His argument that in constitutional jurisprudence powers may be inferred from specific provisions of the Constitution has been an axiom of American legal history ever since. What, Hamilton asked, was the test of an act's constitutionality? The "criterion is the *end*, to which the measure relates as a *mean*," he replied. "If the *end* be clearly comprehended within any of the specified powers, & if the measure have an obvious relation to that end, and is not forbidden by any particular provision of the constitution—it may safely be deemed to come within the compass of the national authority."[23] The statement left little to be said. Paraphrased by John Marshall in his historic opinion in *McCulloch* v. *Maryland*, Hamilton's succinct argument became the classic defense of a broad interpretation of the Constitution.

Although Hamilton relied on the general welfare clause, the major constitutional prop on which he constructed his defense of the bank was the clause giving Congress the power to make all laws "necessary and proper" to carry out its specified powers. "Necessary," Hamilton maintained, "often means no more than *needful, requisite, incidental, useful*, or *conducive to*. . . . The *degree* in which a measure is necessary, can never be a *test* of the *legal* right to adopt it. That must ever be a matter of opinion, and can only be a test of expediency."[24] Was this not another way of saying that the federal government could legally do anything or everything it believed requisite to the security and welfare of the nation? Hamilton chose to state the issue more circumspectly, but his critics hardly could have missed his affirmative answer, and they were appalled.

The president may or may not have perceived the drift of Hamilton's thought, but he was persuaded by the Treasury secretary's argument that the proposed bank was a constitutional exercise of the government's enumerated powers to regulate trade, collect taxes, and provide for the common defense. On February 25, 1791, Washington signed the bill chartering the Bank of the United States.

The event was a milestone in Hamilton's tenure as secretary of the Treasury. Yet another major pillar of his fiscal edifice had been set in place. Now more than ever he must have viewed himself as not only the president's trusted and virtually invincible minister of finance but also as his chief minister. His opponents had been easily overcome. Hamilton's prestige and influence among merchants and other businessmen, among many common people in the North, and among the comparatively small number of administration supporters in the South was at its height. In New York City, the picture of him executed by John Trumbull, portraitist of the nation's great, was displayed in City Hall and his alma mater awarded him an honorary degree. In upstate New York a college was given his name. In New England, Harvard College, following the precedent set earlier by Dartmouth, conferred a doctor of laws degree on him.

If Hamilton mistook such regional recognition for national popularity, he would have been more purblind than is credible. The plaudits of many northerners were matched by the enhanced hostility of his hard-core critics, particularly southerners. Perhaps they were unappeasable. It was not merely the secretary of the Treasury's program to which they objected; Hamilton himself was distrusted and disliked. As John Marshall observed, "Seldom has any minister excited in a higher or more extensive degree than Colonel Hamilton the opposite passions of love and hate," and as a recent biographer adds, "Of the two, hate sometimes seemed to be the stronger."[25] Why so? The answer lies perhaps in the symbolic role that Hamilton's critics assigned to him.

Hamilton had come to personify mounting dissatisfaction with the policies of the Washington administration generally—its insistence on the paramountcy of national authority, its presumed pandering to special-interest groups, its purported truckling to Great Britain, and its alleged aping of that nation's monarchical system. Hamilton had perhaps also become a scapegoat for what some saw as the decline of republican virtue, the thwarting of the promise of the American Revolution. Hamilton himself, persuaded of the purity of his purpose and propriety of his program, had every right to be astonished. After all, a whipping boy can scarcely be expected to understand, or for that matter to pardon, his tormentors. Yet Hamilton would not have altered his program even had he been assured of nationwide popular acclamation in exchange. He continued to believe that what was best for America was best for his critics, including southern nabobs and rural northerners and westerners.

As things turned out, Hamilton was right. The Bank of the United States did efficiently serve the national interest: it increased the active capital of the country, gave timely aid to the central government in times of financial crises, transferred government funds from one section to another, facilitated the payment of taxes, assisted in the foreign exchange operations of the Treasury, and provided a uniform circulating medium. Although Hamilton's critics continued to insist that his major purpose in creating that institution was the welfare of speculators, the federal government was thus the major beneficiary of the bank's operations. On the latter score, Hamilton himself had no doubts. Writing in August 1792, he affirmed that "the most incorrigible theorist among its [the bank's] opponents would, in one month's experience, as head of the department of Treasury, be compelled to acknowledge that it is an absolutely indispensable engine in the management of finances, and would quickly become a convert to its perfect constitutionality."[26]

Nor was Hamilton initially concerned by the feverish speculation in bank shares, a mania that his opponents viewed as a purposeful part of his sinister design to enrich speculators. Subscriptions to the new bank were postponed for four months in order to allow time for the widest possible dissemination of information about the $8 million of stock available for public purchase. The gesture need not have been made. Potential investors in remote parts of the country (as well as many southerners with money to spare) had scant interest in bank scrip. Such indifference was heavily overbalanced by the speculative appetite of eager subscribers in the urban North. Within an hour after the subscription books were opened on July 4, these ravenous investors snapped up even more than the available stock. Purchasers included not only professional and amateur speculators, well-to-do businessmen and others with idle capital, but also Harvard College, a number of states, and thirty members of Congress. As the demand far exceeded the supply, stock prices soared, affording a speculative feast.

The brisk trade in bank stock triggered frenzied speculation in the government debt. But it ended as precipitantly as it began. Rumors of a sharp depression of inflated stock prices (including a correct report that the Treasury secretary had privately commented that the true value of stock was far less than its going price) sent frightened speculators scurrying for shelter. As they dumped their securities on the market, prices fell. To preclude further decline, Hamilton authorized the use of the sinking fund for extensive purchases.* Hamilton's timely intervention not only steadied the market but within a short time brought a renewed and sharp rise in the price of bank stock, which continued to rise for six months.

Hamilton was more adept at meeting financial crises than in mending political fences. His first major setback occurred in his home state, hard on his triumph in the congressional and cabinet controversy over the Bank of the United States. Political developments in New York were of crucial importance to Hamilton. That state, plus Pennsylvania, had substantially contributed to the support essential to the adoption of his program. He could count on the virtually solid backing of New England, but that was not always enough to offset the bloc of southern votes cast against his policies. As Hamilton saw the issue, his policies were safe only so long as the support of the two important middle states was secure.

The loyalty of New York's senators, Rufus King, Hamilton's political protégé, and Philip Schuyler, his devoted father-in-law, was unswerving; and Hamilton was confident that they would either be reelected or replaced by stalwart Federalists. He was uncomfortably aware that George Clinton,

---

*Specifically, Hamilton arranged for the transfer of $150,000 from the sinking fund to William Seton, cashier of the Bank of New York, authorizing Seton to purchase the debt in the public market. "A principal object with me," Hamilton explained, "is to keep the stock from falling too low in case the embarrassments of the dealers should lead to sacrifices. . . . If there are any gentlemen who support the *funds* and others who *depress* them, I shall be pleased that your purchases may aid the former— this in great confidence."[27] It was soon apparent that these government purchases had failed to reverse the decline in stock prices, and so Hamilton authorized the expenditure of an additional $50,000 from the sinking fund. Once again, the Treasury's agent was the cashier of Hamilton's pet bank, the Bank of New York.

seemingly governor for life, remained implacably hostile to him personally as well as to the new government, which, so far as Clinton was concerned, was irredeemably tainted by the leadership of the Treasury secretary. But to counterbalance the governor's hostility, Hamilton looked to the legislature, whose Federalist majority was not only committed to his own program but also (so Hamilton confidently believed) to the reelection of Schuyler, who had drawn the short Senate term that expired in March 1791.

In January, Hamilton was jolted by the news that his father-in-law, generally regarded as one of the state's most powerful politicians, had been defeated. Hamilton was even more stunned by the identity of New York's new junior senator. "A blessed accession of strength will be added to the Senate of the U. States in the person of Col. A. Burr," one of the secretary's local political allies reported. Hamilton scarcely needed to be reminded, as his friend did, that Burr "is avowedly your Enemy, & stands pledged to his party, for a reign of vindictive declamation against your measures."[28] Burr was no dark-horse candidate. His election, carried by a solid majority in both houses, had carefully been prearranged. William Duer, still influential in New York Federalist party councils, believed that Burr's triumph was an expression of disapproval of the Treasury secretary's policies.[29] Robert Troup, Hamilton's Columbia College classmate, attributed the upset to "the bitterest opposition to the Gen'l Government."[30] James Kent, another friend of Hamilton's, believed that "Schuyler's being related to the Secretary has [had] weight" among his legislative opponents.[31] Chancellor Robert Livingston argued that Schuyler's defeat, which the chancellor helped to assure by switching to the Clintonians, was due to the public belief that the Albany patroon "leads the [New York] delegation & is supposed to be led by the Treasury," an "idea that has not been very honourable" to the people of New York nor "very promotive of their interest."[32] Clearly then, as much at issue as Schuyler's qualifications for the Senate was Hamilton's record as Treasury secretary. For that chain of reasoning Hamilton cannot fairly be blamed.

But for a different reason, Hamilton may be held measurably accountable for the outcome of the New York senatorial election. Burr's victory was due primarily not to policy considerations but to a disaffected family, for whose disgruntlement Hamilton was in large part responsible. The Livingston clan, formerly staunch Federalists, jumped to the support of Burr in order to humble Hamilton by humiliating Schuyler. Although Hamilton had not personally been responsible for the selection of Rufus King rather than a Livingston as one of the state's first United States senators, he had for unfathomable reasons refrained from using his office or his influence with the president to secure an important federal appointment for a member of this politically powerful family with whom he had been a close ally in the battle for ratification and subsequently.[33] Chancellor Livingston, for example, had his heart set on the chief justiceship, but that post went to John Jay. Nor was any other member of the manorial family offered an acceptable federal office. The pliable instrument of the Livingstons' revenge was Burr, who, as

Clinton's attorney general but at the same time a self-styled independent, might be counted on to win the support of both Clintonians and Federalists. In sum, Burr's election, as William Duer commented, was "the fruit" of Livingston's "coalition with the Governor."[34]

To Hamilton it was bitter fruit.[35] The reward for what he viewed as his disinterested statesmanship was implicit repudiation by his fellow New Yorkers. Instead of the plaudits he thought he merited, he had been handed a senator whom he already distrusted and would soon despise as a political opportunist, ambitious and unprincipled, and who openly gloated over the Treasury secretary's discomfiture. Hamilton's concern was not misplaced. A man more introspective than he might, however, have realized that he too was an opportunist, although a highly principled one, and that his own ambition matched, and perhaps exceeded, that of his antagonist.

The Encouragement of Manufactures

The *Report on Manufactures* was the last of Hamilton's great triad of reports and to many students his finest performance. "It contains both the science and the art of modern commercial development," Frederick S. Oliver, an ardent English admirer of the American financier, wrote in 1906. "In none of his measures does Hamilton show more remarkably the great force of his instinct for reality, his piercing insight into the true condition of things, his grasp upon the facts of the case."[1] Hamilton's report "contained the embryo of modern America," comments John C. Miller, the most astute of the first Treasury secretary's mid-twentieth-century biographers. "Here . . . was conceived the grand design by which the United States became the greatest industrial power in the world."[2] It was, according to Broadus Mitchell, "the broadest of Hamilton's Treasury reports, the nearest to planning for the future economy of the country. It is fiscal only incidentally, but strives to fashion prosperity and security for the new nation."[3]

Whether or not such praise is merited depends on one's standard of judgment. By contrast to the overwhelming number of subsequent American state papers, Hamilton's *Report on Manufactures* is a masterpiece; by comparison to his own finest performances, it is a less impressive achievement. Missing are the creative boldness of his *Report on the Public Credit,* the tight organization and intellectual power of his plan for a national bank, and the impressive cogency, compressed advocacy, and logical force of his opinion on the bank's constitutionality. Missing too are the conciseness and readability of the best of Hamilton's writings. It is prolix, perhaps because, as Hamilton explained, "the great copiousness of the subject . . . led to a more lengthy preliminary discussion, than was originally contemplated, or intended";[4] it is reiterative, perhaps because he persuaded himself that repetition spawns belief; it lacks organizational tautness, largely because he reintroduced subjects already comprehensively discussed. Nor is the *Report on Manufactures* characterized by the originality that distinguishes his other memorable state papers. "It contains few, if any, specific proposals that even the most enthusiastic supporters of Hamilton could maintain were original," the present-day editors of his papers observe. "In this sense, the Report is as much a product of its times as the creation of its author."[5] The first observation is the common sense of the matter; the second, although correct as far as it goes, might also apply, of course, to the writings of virtually all political economists, Hamilton's contemporaries as well as his predecessors and successors. Perhaps the problem was not that Hamilton merely mirrored the views of America's apostles of industrialization but that he too heavily relied on the works of the country's best-known advocate of a balanced economy. In the person of Tench Coxe, Hamilton, for the only time in his official career, took on a collaborator.

Nevertheless, the achievement of the secretary of the Treasury, ably aided by his assistant, was unique, impressive, influential, and enduring: unique in the sense that the *Report on Manufactures* was his generation's ablest exploration of the subject; influential in the sense that it provided the inspiration for American economists of the next generation and beyond; impressive because few American statesmen have rivaled his accomplishment; and enduring because the report is still viewed as a classic argument in support of the affirmative exercise of governmental power.

Hamilton's *Report on Manufactures,* submitted to Congress in December 1791, was two years in the making.[6] In January 1790 the House of Representatives directed him to "prepare a proper plan . . . for the encouragement and promotion of such manufactories as will tend to render the United States independent of other nations for essential, particularly for military supplies."[7] It was, obviously, a narrow mandate. In reply, Hamilton need only have recommended government encouragement, sponsorship, or erection of factories to turn out army and navy supplies and equipment—plants for manufacturing arms, naval shipyards, and the like. Calculatedly broadening the scope of Congress' order, Hamilton decided at the outset to submit a sustained argument in support of the indispensability of manufactures to a balanced national economy.

Although that belief dated back to Hamilton's earliest study of political economy, he was a late convert to the primacy of manufactures. He had, for example, said virtually nothing on the subject in *The Federalist,* where his focus had been on the superior claims of commerce. "The prosperity of commerce," he had written as recently as November 1787, "is now perceived and acknowledged, by all enlightened statesmen, to be the most useful as well as the most productive source of national wealth; and has accordingly become a primary object of their political cares."[8] Nor did Hamilton have the same close theoretical and practical knowledge of manufactures that he had of public finance. Fortunately for him, down the hall at Treasury headquarters, there was an expert. Tench Coxe had an encyclopedic knowledge of American manufactures, acquired both by extensive research and practical experience as secretary of the Pennsylvania Society for the Encouragement of Manufactures. A few days after Coxe took over as assistant secretary in May 1790, Hamilton asked him to draw up a report on the current state of the country's manufactures and recommendations for their encouragement. Drawing on both Treasury Department officials and the many well-informed proponents of American manufacturing with whom he was acquainted, Coxe promptly began to compile the requisite data. It was the basis of the report on manufactures that he handed to Hamilton a year or so later. Coxe's plan included an analysis of European experience and American exigencies, and an enumeration of those manufactures necessary for defense of the nation "or which may be deemed most essential" to its "Government & Citizens."[9] His plan was the basis of the secretary of the Treasury's report.[10]

During the torrid summer of 1791, Hamilton stuck to his desk, turning out draft after draft. He reviewed the information on local manufactures solicited from on-the-spot Treasury officials; he carefully read and incorporated much of Coxe's data on the past, present, and prospective state of the nation's manufactures, and he studied pertinent works by prominent European political economists. The result, after four drafts, was a comprehensive survey of American manufactures, a summary of their advantages and disadvantages, a plan for their encouragement, and a treatise on political economy.

Going far beyond what Congress had explicitly requested, Hamilton presented a long and cogent essay on the imperativeness of manufactures for a newly independent, overwhelmingly agricultural, and still undeveloped country. Unlike most other American economic nationalists, Hamilton did not merely infer the desirability of manufactures from their presumed instrumentality in accelerating the economic growth and national prosperity of advanced industrial countries, like Great Britain. Instead, he was intent on removing the theoretical props on which the opponents of "artificial" encouragement of manufactures (whether Physiocrats or devotees of Adam Smith) based their arguments. Assuming that mistaken economic policies were often largely the result of false assumptions, Hamilton sought to change governmental practice by discrediting the political-economic theory on which his opponents based their case for a policy of drift. His principal intellectual target was Adam Smith's *The Wealth of Nations*. Keenly aware of Smith's intellectual spell, Hamilton carried on a running debate with the distinguished Scottish philosopher.

The notion that Hamilton was Smith's disciple dies hard. The stereotyped view persists that Hamilton believed that businessmen, in the unfettered pursuit of private profit, unwittingly served the general economic welfare—an idea familiarly encapsulated in the saying that "private greed equals the public good." He is also charged, as is his presumed foreign mentor, with overlooking the fact that in following a hands-off policy a government may actually surrender control of the economy to businessmen who in reality serve only their own personal, and not any abstract national, interest. Hamilton's policies, so the argument runs, thus ministered to the needs and greed of capitalists, whom the Treasury secretary mistakenly saw as the peculiarly trustworthy guardians of the country's welfare. The insubstantiality of such an argument has already been discussed in this book in other contexts. The persistent view that Hamilton was intellectually the Scotsman's American twin needs, in sum, no refutation except a close reading of the *Report on Manufactures*.

True, Hamilton did endorse some of Smith's ideas—among several of them, the benefits of a division of labor and the use of machinery—but for the most part he set forth economic doctrines that Smith's *Wealth of Nations* was designed to topple. Mercantilism, not laissez-faire, was Hamilton's creed, if, that is, a label must be affixed to his ideas. He believed, for example, that national self-sufficiency and prosperity were the sure means for achieving national (and in time international) power, to him the desideratum of public policy. He did not, of course, offend sectional, state, and local sensibilities by explicitly acknowledging that national wealth and power were the ultimate goals of American nationhood, but no attentive reader could have ignored the implication. But intellectual tags such as "mercantilist" can be as misleading as package labels would come to be.

A nondoctrinaire statesman, Hamilton, convinced that no a priori system was suitable for all people at all times, did not subscribe to any single economic system, whether that of laissez-faire or mercantilism. He was, above all, a pragmatist, intent on putting into practice whatever ideas promised to bring the desired results.

Although his mind was brilliant, his book-learning was unimpressive; experience was his classroom, and the lessons that he tried to teach were designed to launch a program, not to win converts to any particular philosophical creed.

More specifically, Hamilton's proposals were devised in the light of his view of America's present state and his vision of its future needs. Aware that the United States, unlike countries that had reached a comparatively advanced stage of economic growth (such as Great Britain), was an overwhelmingly agrarian and largely underdeveloped country, Hamilton argued that the new nation's most urgent need was for a government that would encourage a vigorous economy based on sound credit to promote investment and on the encouragement of manufactures to foster a diversified economy. So long as the United States remained a predominantly agrarian country with a weak government, just so long would it remain a pawn in the European game of power politics. To command the respect of other nations and to enjoy prosperity the economy must be guided, not left to the workings of capricious economic law. Hamilton's purpose in the *Report on Manufactures* was to persuade his countrymen of the practical benefits of a balanced national economy. To this end, he skillfully adapted European ideas to American experience, the better to demonstrate the utility of manufactures.

The major thrust of Hamilton's argument was the essentiality of flourishing manufactures not only to the nation's security and defense but also to the growth and prosperity of its economy. What steps should be taken to encourage the requisite manufactures? Hamilton recommended, among other things, that protective duties should be levied on imported foreign articles also manufactured in the United States.[11] The imposition of such duties, Hamilton maintained, would in effect constitute a bounty for domestic producers. He also recommended withdrawal of duties levied on raw materials needed for domestic manufactures. American manufactures might be further encouraged by granting those who contrived to import machinery or industrial secrets from abroad protection equivalent to that afforded by patent law. Americans should not only borrow or clandestinely copy Europe's technological innovations but also encourage foreigners to invest capital in the United States.[12] Advantage should be taken of the Old World in yet another way: by encouraging immigration a valuable addition to the American work force would be procured.[13] But national self-reliance was more important than Europe's unwitting assistance. Internal improvements would facilitate the transportation of goods; a nationwide and accelerated circulation of bank notes would facilitate remittance of funds for the purchase of raw materials and sale of manufactured goods; the investment of public stock (created by the success of Hamilton's proposal for funding and assumption) would largely make up for the country's shortage of capital. The promotion of manufactures and thus of economic progress required above all the "incitement and patronage of government."[14]

It was to Hamilton axiomatic that if thus encouraged, manufactures would thrive, inevitably enhancing national power and prestige. Other advantages, although to him of less overarching importance, would also accrue; the division of labor, the substitution of machinery for manual labor, the establishment of new investment possibilities, the enlargement of economic opportunity, and the creation of an expanded market for American planters and farmers. His exaggerated focus on the inseparability of agricultural and industrial growth and prosperity was due to his determination to dispel the popular notion that an agrarian South and economically diversified North were inherently incompatible. To the contrary, Hamilton insisted that his program would produce a beneficial partnership between the farm and the factory and that in time South and North would come to "succour" and "befriend" each other, becoming "at length to be considered as one."[15] His opponents might well have replied that such a union was for the foreseeable future so unlikely as to border on the delusional.

More concretely, Hamilton's agrarian critics in Congress failed to see the slightest advantages for themselves in the Treasury secretary's ambitious program. They had a point. There were few advantages except in an abstract sense. Nor did Hamilton's usually reliable northern constituency unitedly endorse his report. Manufacturers in the Middle Atlantic States and New England, eager for adoption of a genuinely protective tariff, applauded, but northern merchants and shipowners, who called for an expansion rather than a possible restriction of foreign trade, were skeptical. For these and other reasons Congress refused to act on what many historians view as Hamilton's boldest and most creative state paper. The *Report on Manufactures* became for decades and decades merely a part of Hamilton's collected works. But then, in the latter part of the nineteenth century, when protectionism became the first commandment of American business, Hamilton's report was resurrected, misconstrued as principally a persuasive defense of protective tariffs, and hailed as one of the greatest performances in the history of American statesmanship. There was considerable irony involved when committed disciples of laissez-faire lauded the most memorable plan for national economic planning that our early history affords.

The Society for Establishing Useful Manufactures (SEUM) was Hamilton's attempt to concretize his report. Plans for organizing this industrial experiment predated his famous report, which included the observation that the society was being formed. Although the SEUM was made possible by the enthusiastic endorsement and official backing of the secretary of the Treasury, it was inspired by his assistant, who also furnished the blueprint for its construction. In the spring of 1791 Tench Coxe handed to his Treasury Department boss a proposed "Plan for a Manufacturing Society," which was, in effect, a pilot project for an industrial economy.[16] Hamilton readily endorsed it, no doubt because Coxe's plan reinforced his own ideas. "The more I have considered the thing," Hamilton remarked to William Duer in a letter enclosing Coxe's proposal, "the more I feel persuaded that it will equally promote the Interests of the adventurers and of the public and will have an excellent effect on the Debt."[17] Having convinced himself, Hamilton energetically sought to win converts among prominent business leaders and other potential investors. He was successful. Following a public announcement in the summer of 1791 that such a corporation was to be established, an initial stock issue of $100,000 was swiftly snapped up. Plans were soon under way for raising additional capital, devising an appropriate corporate structure, securing a suitable charter, rounding up qualified artisans for the manufacture of cotton (the SEUM's initial operation) and publicizing the profitable investment opportunity afforded by the new corporation.

To highlight the latter, Hamilton published in September 1791 the SEUM's "Prospectus," a promotional document that had already been privately circulated.[18] It was a companion piece to the *Report on Manufactures* in the sense that it also set forth the advantages America might reap from the encouragement of manufactures. But its emphasis, unlike that of the report, was on the profits to be derived from a particular corporate investment rather than the benefits to be conferred on the nation and its citizens generally. The "Prospectus" called for a seed capital of $500,000—made up of $100 shares to be subscribed either in public stock or specie—and the creation of an industrial corporation to be chartered in one of the Middle Atlantic states, preferably New Jersey.

Arrangements for launching the SEUM moved smoothly. In November 1791 the New Jersey legislature obligingly granted precisely the kind of corporate charter that Hamilton, following the recommendation in Coxe's "Plan," had called for. Overall direction of the society was entrusted to its board of directors, and the supervision of its operations, to a governor and his deputy. Its list of stockholders and especially its directors comprised a roster of the Northeast's wealthier businessmen; its first governor was the king of New York speculators, William Duer. Following some wrangling over the precise location of the SEUM headquarters, a site on the Passaic River (appropriately christened Paterson, in honor of the governor who had signed the charter act) was eventually selected. Earlier, within a month of the society's incorporation, its top jobs had been filled (largely on the basis of Coxe's recommendations to Hamilton) and shares to the value of $625,000 had been subscribed (although not fully paid in) by avid profit-seekers.[19] They were swiftly disappointed.

Operations were scarcely under way when they were curtailed by a financial panic that crippled the Northeast in the spring of 1792. Many shareholders reneged on the payments still due for their stock, several of the SEUM's directors found themselves bankrupt, and its governor wound up in debtors' prison. The corporation might have survived its governor's disgrace had its still-solvent directors been able to recover a large amount of money they had entrusted to him. They swiftly learned, as they should have known all along, the unwisdom of trusting the untrustworthy: Duer offered no accounting of the missing funds. In brief, by April 1792, the society, only six months after its incorporation, was faced with a depleted capital, discredited leadership, and mismanaged operations.

Hamilton promptly came to the rescue. But neither first aid nor managerial skill could save this now hopeless venture. It limped along for a few years, finally expiring in 1796. Its illness was congenital, and it could have been resuscitated only by a prescription for not only government patronage but also funds. But no one even suggested the propriety of federal subsidy, and no state entertained the notion of financial support. The ultimate cause of the SEUM's failure was perceptively explained by one of its severest critics. Governments must adapt "to the lights of the age," commented James Logan, and refrain from encouraging experiments "unsuitable to the ideas of the times and contrary to the opinion of the people."[20]

The "National Manufactory," as the SEUM was derisively dubbed, was a predictably dismal failure and not, as some historians insist, a grand failure. Nor was the experiment enduringly significant. It was a precedent of only passing importance; no other federally sponsored corporations were organized for well over a century and even then not along the same lines. It proved neither the superiority of laissez-faire nor the efficacy of government sponsorship, which was, after all, merely nominal. The sponsorship of the secretary of the Treasury could not, in other words, be construed as support of the federal government: his patronage was not endorsed by the president, Congress, or even his cabinet colleagues. Hamilton's dream of a powerful industrial economy would come true, but not in ways that he imagined. A model factory town had about as much effect on the accelerated growth of domestic manufactures as an experimental farm would have had on the development of American agriculture. In this case, Hamilton's dream was not customarily prescient but rather phantasmal. Paradoxically enough, however, his behavior was in character, in the sense that he acted as if his bold policies and powerful advocacy of them could accomplish for his country what ambitious self-assertion and determination had done for one American. Disappointment was inevitable. Wishing could not make the manufacturing society succeed any more than it could persuade Congress to endorse his *Report on Manufactures.*

The panic that sent Duer to prison and helped wreck the SEUM also helped make Congress less inclined to adopt innovative measures. The success of Hamilton's entire financial program seemed problematical. The setback upset Hamilton all the more because the economy had seemed to be enjoying a sustained period of growth and prosperity. The country's export and import trades were flourishing, agricultural prices booming, wages rising, land values soaring, and sufficient federal revenues coming in to meet both operating expenses and large payments of interest and principal. As he surveyed such gratifying conditions, Hamilton was uncharacteristically rhapsodic: America afforded "a spectacle of national happiness never surpassed, if ever before equalled, in the annals of human affairs."[21] Such exuberance was pardonable; just as the economy was flourishing, so too was Hamilton's own popularity. In the North his policies were generally given credit for the boom, and in the South, the center of opposition to his program, prosperity dulled the effectiveness of his critics' attacks. Now in the spring of 1792, as if some hidden law of compensation were operating, he was blamed for the sharp financial panic that then occurred.

It was a "typical stock market and financial panic."[22] Hardest hit was New York City, where its principal human catalyst was the king of that city's speculators, William Duer. Having speculated in everything in sight—western lands, manufacturing, and the like—Duer decided to restrict his appetite to federal securities (his pet gamble all along) and to stock of both the Bank of New York and that of the United States. To further his scheme, he took on a rich partner, Alexander Macomb, a New York merchant and big-time land speculator. The principal purpose of the partnership was to corner the market on certain federal bonds (specifically, those securities bearing a 6 percent interest rate) and then to unload them at inflated prices on unwary European investors. Duer's notoriety as a speculative magician served him well. Money poured in from investors eager for a quick profit. Some had only small amounts to proffer; a few, notably Walter Livingston, had bulging purses. Livingston willingly opened his, imprudently agreeing to give either notes or endorsements up to $800,000. Such a sum turned out to be too much even for a Livingston, but he did endorse Duer's notes for the then-staggering sum of $375,000.[23]

In the meantime, a rival group of speculators led by Brockholst and Edward Livingston (two of Walter's kinsmen) and Andrew Craige, a prominent Boston financier, joined forces to thwart Duer's scheme and if possible to cure permanently his gambling mania. Their plan, in simplified form, was to sell to the Duer associates bank stock and federal securities for future delivery and, in the interim, to both depress stock prices and manipulate monetary and banking operations in such a way as to cut off the bank credit on which Duer relied. They succeeded. Finding himself unable to command the money to meet his heavy and steadily mounting commitments, Duer was obliged early in March to suspend payments.[24]

His situation was rendered the more perilous by receipt of the news that the Treasury Department had instituted legal proceedings in the federal district court for New York against him for the recovery of a shortage of some $240,000 in Duer's accounts as secretary of the old Board of the Treasury. Confident that none of his friends would do to him as he did to his business partners, Duer called on Hamilton to rescue him. "For Heaven's sake," he implored, "use for once your influence to defer" prosecution. "If a Suit should be brought on the Part of the Public, under my present distressed Circumstances, My Ruin is complete."[25] Duer misjudged his man. Hamilton, who was indirectly responsible for the suit officially instituted by Oliver Wolcott, Jr., comptroller of the Treasury, had by this time decided that Duer's financial collapse was of no consequence when compared to the unsullied reputation of the Treasury Department and the continued success of his own fiscal program. He was also appalled both by the prospect of a precipitate fall in the value of government securities and the possibility that foreign investors might acquire a monopoly of them. "How vexatious," he complained, "that imprudent speculations of individuals should lead to an alienation of the national property at such under-rates." There must, he admonished, "be a line of separation between honest Men & knaves, between respectable Stockholders and dealers in the funds, and mere unprincipled Gamblers. Contempt and neglect must attend those who manifest that they have no principles but to get money."[26] No doubt the Treasury secretary had his former assistant in mind, although in correspondence with Duer he was courteous and charitable.

Hamilton's charity did not embrace collusion, however, and he firmly refused to stay legal proceedings against Duer while at the same time professing continued personal friendship. "I will not now pain you with any wise remarks," Hamilton wrote—and then proceeded to do just that. Duer must act courageously and honorably by paying what he could to "all fair creditors" and giving a preference to "Institutions of public Utility."[27] For his part, Duer had neither asked for nor wanted a lecture on private and public morality. What he wanted was an end to the Treasury Department's prosecution. But even had Hamilton done what was never remotely likely and dropped the suit, Duer still would have gone bankrupt. Only a sizable chunk of the federal government's annual budget could have saved him. As it was, on March 23, 1792, Duer wound up in prison, and his more recklessly trusting associates went into bankruptcy. "I am now secure from my Enemies," he wrote to one of them, "and feeling the Purity of my heart I defy the world."[28] His heart may have been pure, but his business schemes were manifestly nefarious and their predictable failure was largely responsible for the panic that ensued.

The panic brought in its train a decline in real estate prices, contraction of credit, and curtailment of business activity generally. Having tried to prevent Duer's misdeeds from rubbing off on the Treasury Department, its secretary decided that the time had come to shore up the crumbling price of federal securities. In a replay of the action he had taken in the late summer of 1791, Hamilton authorized sinking-fund purchases. His goal, of course, was to restore to par the value of government stock by demonstrating to wary investors the government's determination to maintain its price. All in all, successive sinking-fund purchases came to $150,000. The agent for the Treasury's rescue operation was once again William Seton, cashier of the Bank of New York. That institution's specie reserves were then dwindling dangerously low because of demands of the Manhattan branch of the Bank of the United States that the Bank of New York redeem in specie its dangerously overissued notes. Seton had implored the Treasury secretary not to draw federal funds deposited in the Bank of New York and also to exert official pressure on the Bank of the United States to prevent it from depleting the specie reserves of the smaller bank. Although it was not within Hamilton's power to influence the directors of the Bank of the United States, he did what he could: he designated Seton's institution as both the government's fiduciary agent and repository of federal revenue. Hamilton did not only rely on sinking-fund purchases by the Bank of New York but in addition called on both the city's banks to extend the time limit on outstanding loans and to substitute cooperation for ruinous competition. To restore public confidence, he also instructed Seton to announce that the United States had just successfully negotiated a large loan in Holland.

Was the Treasury secretary's use of the Bank of New York consonant with the law and the national interest? Did he display unwarranted favoritism toward a pet institution? Hamilton himself was confident that he had done nothing wrong. As he later said, no bank had received favors from him "which were not in perfect coincidence with the public interest, and in the due and proper course of events."[29] The use of the adjective "perfect" aside, Hamilton was right: what he did was legally proper and his timely intervention restored normality to the New York financial scene. More important, Hamilton's adroit handling of the panic, in Broadus Mitchell's words, meant that "at the very outset of our history . . . the resources of the national government were brought to the rescue of a locality in distress," thus forging "a precedent followed afterward on numerous occasions. Hamilton's resolute relief was the more noteworthy because at that time the obligation of the central power to render assistance to a particular place was less acknowledged than since."[30]

It is also true, however, that Hamilton failed to consider the options open to him; federal funds, for example, might have been funneled through the

New York branch of the Bank of the United States. But Hamilton acted as he did because he believed that the solvency of the Bank of New York was essential to the commercial and financial stability of one of the nation's more important business centers. There is no way to determine whether or not he was also motivated by partiality for an institution that he had been instrumental in establishing. There is no reason to believe, however, that his action was dictated by the wish to bail out Seton personally, much less to line the pockets of the Bank of New York's stockholders or to come to the aid of beleaguered speculators.

Hamilton's critics, once again especially southerners, thought otherwise. "The credit & fate of the nation seem to hang on the desperate throws & plunges of gambling scoundrels," Jefferson commented.[31] Madison's charges were yet more exaggerated. "*Who are the real friends of the Union?*" he asked. Certainly not those who coddled speculators, not those who attempted by "arbitrary interpretations and insidious precedents" to invest the federal government with virtually limitless power, not those who secretly harbored monarchical and aristocratic principles.[32] The recklessness of Madison's indictment was, perhaps, directly proportional to Hamilton's diminished popularity. Only a few months earlier, as has been said, the Treasury secretary had been generally acclaimed as the financial wizard whose policies were largely responsible for the national prosperity that was then at its crest; now he was widely attacked as the author of the speculative frenzy that had brought on economic decline. His prestige in Congress was slipping, and his policies were arraigned with increasing fervor in opposition newspapers, notably the *National Gazette*. Henry Lee summed up the situation when he sympathetically wrote from Richmond that while Hamilton was still "sometimes . . . mounted to the skys on the wings of fame," he was often "whisked into the infernal pit."[33]

Hamilton may well have thought that was where his critics belonged. But the principal lesson he learned from the short-lived panic was not the fickleness of popularity or the banefulness of speculation but rather the untrustworthiness of a few unprincipled big-time gamblers. Nor did his opponents, despite their professions, condemn speculation per se. They rather embraced it. For all the public piousness about the evils of investment in federal securities and bank stock, speculation in enterprises such as canals, turnpikes, and particularly land abated not a detectable jot. To the Americans of the 1790s, as subsequently, speculation exercised an irresistible appeal. What is curious about Hamilton's generation, then, is not its speculative mania but rather the double standard that was set: speculation in public and bank stock was somehow unethical; speculation in land was merely one of the risk enterprises of the day. And (whether to confound or to explain the paradox) for every stockjobber there were countless land speculators. For what consolation it afforded, Hamilton was at least aware of one aspect of the contradiction. "It is a strange perversion of ideas," he lamented, "that men should be deemed corrupt and criminal for becoming proprietors in the funds of their country.''[34] To his rival in the State Department the situation was neither strange nor perverse. As Jefferson saw the matter, stockjobbing was itself corrupt and the secretary of the Treasury was even more corrupt— criminally so—for countenancing and encouraging it.

X

Hamilton Versus Jefferson: A Skirmish, Not a War

The quarrel between Hamilton and Jefferson is the best known and historically the most important in American political history. At the outset, both their official association and personal relationship seemed harmonious. Perhaps this was because they saw so little of each other during the months following Jefferson's arrival in New York in March 1790 and the convening of Congress in Philadelphia, the new capital, in the following December. But viewed in retrospect, an eventual clash between two such egocentric, strong-willed, and ambitious men was inevitable. They were divided not only by political philosophy but also by divergent family backgrounds, social status, personality, and manner. Exuding the serenity and self-assurance of the aristocrat, Jefferson displayed "an air of insouciance . . . as if he were tired or half-hearted."[1] Hamilton, while acting as if he were to a New York manor born, was unable to sustain similar poise. He more characteristically displayed impatience, restlessness, and repressed energy, as if somehow denied the opportunity to fulfill his vaulting ambition for a stellar public career and deprived also of popular acclaim for his actual accomplishments.

The incompatibility of the two secretaries was heightened by the unavowed wish of each to be Washington's principal and most trusted adviser. As Jefferson must have seen the situation, his eligibility for the role was indisputable. Alone among the members of the cabinet he was already world famous, a repute that the president gladly acknowledged. It was this awareness that was largely responsible for Washington's insistence that Jefferson accept the secretaryship of state, and the latter's acquiescence may well have been due to the conviction that it was his duty to give the weight of his prestige to the new government by heading what he may well have regarded as its most important department. Once in New York, however, Jefferson must have been shocked to discover that this viewpoint was not necessarily shared by the president. Hamilton, a man considerably younger than himself and hitherto comparatively unknown, was manifestly the architect of the administration's program and Washington's principal adviser and confidant, occupying a position akin to that of prime minister. It was not a situation to Jefferson's liking, and his dislike was heightened by his personal antipathy toward the abrasive manner of a colleague whom he viewed, with aristocratic disdain, as something of an upstart.

By the same token Hamilton considered Jefferson's implied claim to official superiority as a threat to his own preeminence. Would not Washington now rely heavily on a fellow Virginia aristocrat who was also widely recognized as the superstar of the cabinet? Would not Jefferson's established repute eclipse the New Yorker's hard-earned public recognition? Would not the secterary of the Treasury's congressional leadership, based on recognition of him as spokesman for the administration, be undermined? How, in short, could Hamilton remain chief minister when, as he saw it, Jefferson coveted the same role for which the Virginian also seemed to be typecast? Outwardly self-assured, even cocky, Hamilton was inwardly wary and uneasy.

Official collision between the two stars of Washington's cabinet was the more inescapable because of the initial lack of definite lines between departments. The division of responsibility was vague and jurisdictions overlapped. Furthermore, the relationship between the president and his heads of departments was as yet not established and the need for cabinet consensus unrecognized. This lack of solidarity, as historians have long recognized, is important to keep in mind if, in the words of Henry T. Ford, one is "to understand how it was that members of the same cabinet could each feel quite free to pursue his own policy, and make use of whatever means were available to promote it,"[2] in Hamilton's case including the conduct of affairs properly within the domain of another department.

Hamilton thus unhesitatingly sought to influence the course of American foreign policy by whatever means presented themselves. This penchant was revealed in the Nootka Sound affair, a diplomatic skirmish that took place only a few months after Jefferson became secretary of state. The episode was, in the context of Hamilton's and Jefferson's colleagueship, a symbolic storm cloud, forecasting the turbulence that would soon characterize their relationship.

The controversy in question, a minor diplomatic clash between Spain and England that occurred on the faraway Pacific coast, arose in the year 1789, when the Spanish seized British vessels whose crews were attempting to establish a fur-trading base at Nootka Sound on Vancouver Island. The English ministry, eager both to humble an ancient enemy and to promote British commerce and colonization in the American Northwest, stridently protested, demanding the release of British captives, reparations, and a pledge not to molest English traders in the area. Although militarily too weak to reject summarily Britain's peremptory demands, Spain dallied, counting on the support of France. Imperiously impatient, William Pitt, Britain's prime minister, swiftly made plans to force the issue.

It appeared for a brief time that the United States might be the unwitting beneficiary of this New World clash between the Old World's colonial rivals. The iciness with which the English had greeted earlier American overtures to settle the two nation's diplomatic differences suddenly thawed. The reason was not a recurrence of Britain's maternal warmth for her former colonies but rather her fear that the United States might not only cooperate with Spain but also take advantage of the occasion to wrest long-sought-for concessions from England. America's friendship seemed to Pitt the more imperative because of his ministry's plans to order a naval siege of New Orleans, preparatory to a military campaign against Spain's other New World possessions. To many officials on both sides of the Atlantic the new look in British diplomacy presaged an Anglo-American rapprochement.

The president of the United States was not among them. By the summer of 1790 Washington was convinced that the new nation confronted not a diplomatic opportunity but a military crisis. The cause of his alarm was a report that British troops stationed in Canada were being readied for an attack on Spanish possessions in Louisiana, a report that to Washington portended a request from the Pitt ministry to march troops stationed in Canada across American territory. Washington, who had no way of knowing (as historians now do) that the British never considered making any such demand, shared his apprehension with his top advisers, asking them what answer he should give to the demand that he confidently predicted.[3]

Most accounts of the incident focus on the differences between the replies of the president's two principal secretaries. The secretary of state believed that the United States should ignore the expected demand but use it to exact diplomatic concessions from both contestants; the secretary of the Treasury argued that the United States grant the contemplated application while demanding in return that Britain yield on important issues currently in dispute between the two nations. The difference between the two secretaries, then, boiled down to this: Jefferson believed that under the cover of silence on the instant issue, diplomatic gains might be garnered, possibly from both Britain and Spain; Hamilton opted for acquiescence as the price of a diplomatic accord, possibly an opportunity to wring concessions from England, the new nation's most powerful, unyielding, and high-handed antagonist. To both men, in other words, national self-interest was the strategic purpose of American foreign policy, however divergent the tactics employed to secure it.

The Nootka Sound controversy merits attention not because it was historically consequential (the affair was settled in October 1790, when Spain, failing to gain French support, knuckled under to Britain's demands) or because it brought to the fore ideologically different approaches to American foreign policy by the secretaries of state and the Treasury (their ideas would sharply diverge only later). The affair assumes importance as an introduction to the personal and official rift between Hamilton and Jefferson, a collision that has unfortunately obscured the common goals and independent accomplishments of each. The much-touted prelude to this clash was largely orchestrated by Hamilton in collaboration with Major George Beckwith.[4]

In March 1790, at the height of the war scare between England and Spain, Beckwith was sent to New York by Lord Dorchester, the governor of Canada, pursuant to instructions from the British ministry. Acting as his government's unofficial agent, Beckwith was instructed to discern the drift of foreign-policy developments in the American capital and to do his best to assure the new nation's neutrality (or, better still, support) should Britain go to war with Spain. To accomplish indirectly what he could not do openly and officially, Beckwith contrived frequent private conferences with prominent congressmen and other influential officials. He would no doubt have preferred to exchange ideas with the secretary of state, but Jefferson was unwilling to conduct foreign relations through an informal and unaccredited diplomatic representative. In the secretary of the Treasury, however, Beckwith found a ready conversationalist, one who was cordial and seemingly candid.

Since neither precedent nor presidential directive as yet dictated that a cabinet minister confine his official activities strictly to his own department, Hamilton thought that his behavior was unexceptionable, even proper. Had the secretary of state known of Hamilton's confidential conversations with Beckwith, however, Jefferson would have viewed his colleague's behavior as an unwarranted invasion of the domain of the State Department. Certainly the Virginian's historical partisans emphatically do, charging that the Treasury secretary, "as devious as he was bold," was guilty of "duplicity," of a "clandestine maneuver" to undermine the policies of the secretary of state, and "gross misrepresentation" to the president.[5] The facts of the case dictate a rather more lenient verdict.

Hamilton's conversations with Beckwith were held at the request of the president, to whom was submitted a report of their substance, although an abridged and thus not fully accurate version. The British agent and American finance minister discussed the entire range of issues dividing the two nations. Beckwith's principal concern, as has been said, was to secure Anglo-American cooperation in the event of war between Spain and Britain. On this subject, Hamilton was purposely vague. Should such a war break out, would the United States attack Spanish possessions in America in order to acquire New Orleans, Beckwith wanted to know? Perhaps so, maybe not, Hamilton replied. Beckwith probed further. In the event of an Anglo-Spanish war could England bank on the United States as a military ally? "Wait and see," Hamilton in effect replied. How would the Americans respond to British proposals for a settlement of Anglo-American controversies and a commercial "alliance" between the two nations? Hamilton's noncommittal reply was that he did not wish to "raise or repress expectations" and could only say that the American government had "a sincere disposition to concur in obviating with candor and fairness all grounds of misunderstanding" and wished to lay a "foundation of good understanding, by establishing liberal terms of commercial intercourse."[6]

Hamilton was more forthright when the conversation turned to personalities. Of his friend Gouverneur Morris, whom Washington had sent to England on an informal mission similar to that of Beckwith's to the United States, Hamilton said that Morris' handling of delicate diplomatic exchanges left something to be desired. In his comments on the American secretary of state, the Treasury secretary was even more impolitic: the British had nothing to fear from Washington, he observed, but he was sorry to say that the same could not be said of Jefferson. Granted that a man more discreet than Hamilton would have eschewed such invidious remarks, it is also germane to add that the Treasury secretary did not tell Beckwith anything the English ministry did not already know.[7] And Hamilton also repeatedly emphasized a point that Whitehall did not overlook: the Treasury secretary spoke only for himself, not the United States government; any formal diplomatic exchanges with Britain were the province of the secretary of state.

Hamilton was, in sum, guilty not of duplicity or of censurable poaching on the State Department's preserve but of compulsive self-expression in a situation that called for silence. As it had been at the Constitutional Convention, so it was in his conversations with Beckwith, and so it would be in his talks with George Hammond, Britain's first accredited minister to the United States: Hamilton felt impelled to display his unexcelled astuteness, matchless knowledge, and superior statecraft. Had he shared the serene sense of self-assurance enjoyed by his rival in the State Department it would have been unnecessary for Hamilton to show off, even at the expense of official indiscretion.

Partly because Jefferson was as yet unaware of Hamilton's official meddlesomeness, the secretaries of state and the Treasury remained on comparatively good terms during the first ten months of their colleagueship. Soon after the convening of the Second Congress in December 1790, however, their personal forbearance and public stance of official cooperativeness was gradually replaced by mutual suspicion. It surfaced during the controversy that was provoked by Hamilton's proposal for a national bank.

The differences between the two secretaries was ostensibly confined to the legality of that institution, but Jefferson was convinced that much more than correct constitutional interpretation was at issue. "For the first time," as Merrill Peterson remarks, "Hamilton's measures began to assume the character of a system in Jefferson's mind, a system permeated with fiscalism, and from what he had seen of France and learned of Britain, fiscalism was the parent of monopoly and oppression."[8] The Virginian suspected, moreover, that the true intent of Hamilton's proposed bank was not only the enrichment of the nation's "monied interest" (particularly investors whom he derided as "stockjobbers") but also an alarming enhancement of national power.[9] Having to his own satisfaction uncovered Hamilton's nefarious objectives, Jefferson thought he detected a yet more sinister design—the existence "of a sect who believe [the British Constitution] to contain whatever is perfect in human institutions,'' a sect whose ''members . . . have, many of them, names and offices which stand high in the estimation of our countrymen.''[10] Highest of all stood the Treasury secretary, a suspicion that Jefferson was soon sharing with close friends.

As this suspicion hardened into certainty, the Virginian's list of charges against his rival grew to catalog length. The nouveaux riches created by Hamilton's policies were rapidly developing into what Jefferson scorned as ''artificial aristocrats'' (a class based as much on wealth as on birth, ''without either virtue or talents'') and displacing what he cherished as ''natural aristocrats'' (those who were endowed with exceptional talent and virtue). Hamilton's advocacy of manufacturing was, moreover, redolent of reprehensible mercantilist principles. The benefits that the Treasury secretary showered on northern businessmen were paid for by southern planters and the nation's farmers. How was this contrived? Jefferson's answer: Hamilton, an acknowledged champion of corruption as an essential component of effective government, had debauched Congress and organized a corrupt corps of Treasury officials.[11]

Jefferson's belief that the goal of Hamilton's policies, as sinister as they were devious, was the subversion of American democracy was matched by the Treasury secretary's belief that the purpose of the Virginian's personal antagonism and official obstructionism was personal preeminence and political power. In Hamilton's view, the true threat to American republicanism was not monarchism, as falsely imputed to him, but demagoguery, as personified by Jefferson. Obsessed by insatiable ambition, the secretary of state saw every opponent as a rival to be crushed. Hamilton's unswerving opinion was succinctly expressed a decade later: Jefferson, he commented in 1801, ''is crafty, not scrupulous about the means of success, not very mindful of truth.''[12]

Hamilton believed that Jefferson's policies were as misguided as his character was flawed. The enemy of sound public credit, the Virginian was determined to demolish his rival's soundly constructed financial structure. Jefferson's own economic nostrums were naive, particularly his dream of America as an Elysium of contented, prosperous, and largely self-sufficient farmers. As for the Virginian's political philosophy, it was visionary, particularly his idealized depiction of human nature, which, in Hamilton's view, was grounded in myopia induced by excessive drafts of French revolutionary doctrine. More generally, the secretary of state was the champion of French rather than American principles, an advocate of democracy or egalitarianism rather than republicanism or constitutionalism. Above all, Hamilton was persuaded that his rival's opposition to Treasury policies was actuated by personal rancor. How else, as Hamilton saw the matter, could one explain Jefferson's hostility to a responsible fiscal program designed to assure American strength and prosperity?[13]

To endorse, much less to try and justify, the position of either of the antagonists in this historical feud would be to abandon all claims to objectivity. The picture that each man sketched of the other was distorted to the point of caricature. Their mutual suspiciousness and the base motives that each attributed to the other were for the most part either groundless or greatly exaggerated, spawned by personal antagonism. The fears that each harbored about the results of the possible political triumph of the other were extravagant, if not bogus. Seen in historical perspective (a perspective that was, of course, denied to them), their personality clash did not as decisively mold the history of the first president's administration as is often alleged, although their conflicting policies and opinions on public issues often did. Even so, the important historical consideration is neither their personal enmity nor their occasional official disagreement but the complementary nature of many of their policies, the large area of their agreement on an important number of public issues and their common dedication to viable nationhood that they sought to reach by routes often divergent but sometimes the same.

American historians have not only tended to exaggerate the historical import of the Hamilton-Jefferson feud but for the sake of easy labeling have also magnified their ideological differences, in the process stretching too far the distance that separated them on the familiar political scale whose extremes are right and left or conservative and radical.

Innumerable historical studies have depicted Jefferson as the new nation's paradigmatic reformer, its most prominent (but somehow "gentle") radical, and the father of American democracy. The portrait is a good likeness if one focuses on the Virginian's glowing tributes to the virtues of the common man (or, more accurately expressed, the farmer), an expanded suffrage, and the eradication of time-sanctioned inequalities; his program for an innovative educational system; and his preference for an aristocracy of talent rather than birth or wealth. The contours of the familiar portrait change, however, if one centers on different features of Jefferson's thought and practice. In some ways the Virginian may be considered as the prototypical American conservative. Despite his insistence that a revolution every twenty years would be a good thing, Jefferson was in fact a steadfast supporter of the status quo. Wishing to hold fast to an idealized past, he saw a nation of planters and farmers, the latter tilling their own soil, turning out local manufactures, and employing only their own families, and the planters overseeing the labor of their slaves. Appalled by the prospect of ubiquitous factories, impoverished industrial workers, and urban blight, he recoiled from the budding Industrial Revolution abroad and its possible transplantation in America. The way of life he wished to preserve was that which he had known in Virginia (although about slavery his conscience was troubled). Avowedly a democrat, he was, in sum, at heart a Virginia aristocrat.

For his part, Hamilton, who is often seen as America's archetypical conservative, aristocrat, reactionary, or the like was in actuality a "portrait in paradox." Although at times professing a conservative ideology, what he wished to conserve were (by European standards) liberal principles. An avowed admirer of England's institutions and unwritten constitution, he at the same time strove to assure the success of American republicanism. The proclaimed foe of radicalism, Hamilton designed a fiscal program that, in

George Dangerfield's phrase, "must be considered the most radical of events."[15] Although expressing an abhorrence of revolution, the implications of his own program were revolutionary. Although he professed to cherish tradition, he also represented in significant ways the thrust toward modernity.

Just as Hamilton's own ideas were often paradoxical, so also the sketch that many scholars have drawn of him is a poor historical likeness. Although depicted as America's foremost advocate of aristocracy, he was actually the patron of the new nation's bourgeoisie. Frequently accused of being a closet monarchist, he manifestly labored to create a new form of government that was a challenge and affront to the monarchies of Europe. Although sometimes depicted as one who realistically rejected the notion of historical progress, his program was premised on the belief that inevitable progress followed the adoption of proper policies. Characteristically typecast as one who steadfastly took a dim view of human nature and perfectibility, his economic policies were based on the assumption that man was not only alterable but improvable. Allegedly intent on snuffing out American freedom, he was in practice a champion of civil liberties. By repute a reactionary of the Old World stripe, he was in sum, nothing more nor less than an American Whig.

To reject the stereotyped depiction of Hamilton and Jefferson and to deflate the exaggerated importance often attributed to their rivalry is to deny neither the depth of their public and political rift nor its historical consequences. For one thing, the significance subsequently attributed to the quarrel by historians has itself measurably influenced American history. For another, their official feud, despite the exaggerated importance often attributed to it, comprises an integral part of the story of Washington's presidency.

By the summer of 1792 the conflict between the two secretaries had ripened into open political warfare. Strategy and tactics had long since been prepared by their respective journalistic spokesmen. Hamilton's champion was John Fenno, whose *Gazette of the United States* Jefferson described as "a paper of pure Toryism, disseminating the doctrines of monarchy, aristocracy, and the exclusion of the influence of the people." More precisely, Fenno's one-sided presentation of the administration's views and pompously lavish praise of the president and his finance minister spilled over into sycophancy.[16] The secretary of state's mouthpiece was the *National Gazette,* established in October 1791 by Jefferson and Madison as a means of unmasking the nefarious schemes and monarchical proclivities of the secretary of the Treasury, thereby promoting allegiance to what the two Virginians viewed as the "republican cause." The editor of this nationally circulated journal was the uncrowned poet laureate of the American Revolution, Philip Freneau, who was lured to Philadelphia by Jefferson's promise of a State Department sinecure, a minor clerkship that as Jefferson said "would not interfere with any other occupation at the seat of government."[17] Freneau's unique calling was a brand of polemical journalism that, at least when Hamilton was its subject, slipped over into character assassination.

For a time, these journalistic gladiators fought out in the public arena the political contest that the two secretaries still thinly concealed behind an official facade of aloof formality. During the cold Philadelphia winter months of 1792 the facade cracked; with the onset of the spring thaw it collapsed. In March, Jefferson spoke for the first time ''of the heats and tumults of conflicting parties.''[18] Hamilton's viewpoint was succinctly expressed by his Treasury department colleague and political ally Oliver Wolcott, Jr., who observed that ''Mr. Jefferson appears to have shown rather too much of a disposition to cultivate vulgar prejudices; accordingly he will become popular in ale houses, and will do much mischief to his country by exciting apprehensions that the government will operate unfavourably.''[19]

Such expressions of distrust were mild compared to the torrents of abuse that soon followed. It was as if the adjournment of Congress in May 1792 released the swelling spite that each had contrived to dam up. Hamilton's release of his scorching resentment took the form of a long letter to Edward Carrington, a Virginia political ally who could be counted on to share with local partisans the Treasury secretary's strictures on his two most implacably hostile foes. Jefferson and Madison, Hamilton charged, were the leaders of a faction that was ''subversive of the principles of government and dangerous to the Union, peace, and happiness of the country.''[20] The personal and political enmity displayed by Madison was a puzzle that the New Yorker could solve only by imputing to Jefferson some form of hypnotic power over his younger ally. To the secretary of state Hamilton ascribed virtually satanic powers: Jefferson was the real leader of the congressional group opposed to Hamilton; he was the chief conspirator in an attempt to subvert the Treasury secretary's sound fiscal policies; he was the principal instigator of a concerted effort to sap the vitality of the national government. Was not Jefferson ''an avowed enemy of the funded debt,'' whose larger design was to destroy the national credit and its principal architect? Was not the Virginian also an exponent of commercial warfare against Britain, a policy that, if adopted, could only result in an unwarranted and disastrous war? What was really at the bottom of a program so clearly inspired by anglophobia? It was Jefferson's ''*womanish attachment to France*,'' his intoxication with all things French—religion, philosophy, science, and politics. His vision thus blurred, Jefferson could recognize neither the ''imbecilities'' of the Confederation government nor fully appreciate the Constitution, about which he continued to harbor ''many doubts and reserves.'' Nevertheless, Jefferson, although not a true believer, was willing to bend an imperfect Constitution to his own purposes. ''Mr. Jefferson aims with ardent desire at the President's chair,'' Hamilton charged, a prize he stooped to conquer by rendering government odious, promoting popular fears, and encouraging faction, even anarchy. ''I read him upon the whole thus,'' Hamilton concluded: '' 'A man of profound ambition and violent passions.' ''

While one might interpret the latter judgment as a self-revelation, this charge, as well as others that Hamilton shared with Carrington, manifestly revealed that he misinterpreted his cabinet rival. Jefferson was, as Hamilton alleged, intent on hamstringing the Treasury secretary's fiscal program, but he was even more interested in exposing what he regarded as Hamilton's attempted subversion of the State Department. Jefferson's attachment to France was warm (whether "womanish" or not), but he sincerely believed that Britain's arrogant disregard of America's commercial rights called for manly retaliation. Jefferson was, as Hamilton would always insist, intensely ambitious, but not at this time for the presidency. Nor did he wish to ride to power on the back of faction and the like but rather to block what he viewed as Hamilton's own ruthless drive for supremacy. The Virginian may have been strongly opinionated, but he was not beset by "violent passions." He was rather ostensibly a mild man but, as Hamilton would soon learn, one who moved toward his goal stealthily, outmaneuvering his antagonists by devious and subtle tactics.

In the late spring of 1792 the indirect technique that the secretary of state selected for discrediting his cabinet rival boomeranged. The maneuver was a private letter to the president in which Jefferson accused Hamilton of official high crimes and misdemeanors, revealing in the process that his personal antipathy toward the New Yorker was becoming obsessional. Hamilton, Jefferson implied, was officially corrupt, a wily schemer who sought to subvert the Constitution and overthrow the government. To what purpose? The real goal of Hamilton's measures, Jefferson warned the president, was "a change from the present republican form of government to that of a monarchy, of which the English Constitution is to be the model."[21]

The president's courteous response did not altogether obscure his sense of outrage at such preposterous charges.[22] Jefferson's fears were groundless, Washington insisted. There was no conspiracy to establish a monarchy, and if one ever were reimposed in the United States, it would most likely be the result of anarchy and discord stirred up by the country's scandalous and libelous newspapers. That Washington believed the *National Gazette* to be the principal culprit was made clear by his resentful comment that in his view, attacks on his administration were attacks on himself.

Washington greatly exaggerated the effects of newspaper scurrility. Character assassination and partisan hyperbole were becoming the journalistic mode of the day, and most readers were titillated rather than stirred to action. The keenest appetites for partisan scandal might well have been jaded by the journalistic fare—gross distortion and misrepresentation, malicious libel and partisan invective—served up by Philadelphia's rival gazettes during the summer and autumn of 1792. But Freneau and Fenno, along with other newspaper warriors, fought on and on, and newspaper subscribers read on and on. Hamilton might better have contented himself with reading. Instead, he rushed to enlist in the ranks of pseudonymous writers who filled the columns of Philadelphia's warring newspapers. Precisely what purpose did he thus hope to achieve? The enhancement of his own power and popularity? He was more likely to diminish them. To drive the secretary of state from office? He had already decided to resign. To discredit the Virginian in the eyes of his admirers? Jefferson's position as leader of an emergent opposition party would more probably be enhanced. What Hamilton thought he would accomplish is, in sum, a mystery that perhaps he himself could not have solved.

The Treasury secretary's newspaper crusade was begun late in July 1792. In a diversionary tactic his first shots were aimed at Philip Freneau: "The editor of the 'National Gazette' receives a salary from government. *Quere*— whether this salary is paid him for *translations*, or for *publications . . .* to oppose the measures of government, and, by false insinuations, to disturb the public peace?"[23] Freneau pleaded innocent. Hamilton, renewing the charge, cast his net wider: This journalist qua government clerk was merely the pawn of the secretary of state. Jefferson had hatched this collusive scheme in order to impugn the official integrity of the Treasury secretary and to discredit the administration that the Virginian ostensibly supported. How could Jefferson "reconcile it to his own personal integrity and the principles of probity to hold an office under [the government] and employ the means of official influence in that opposition?"[24] The answer was implicit in his depiction of the Virginian as a political trimmer who had been equivocal about the merits of the Constitution under which he accepted office and who had actively opposed the measures of a republican Congress that he professed to respect.

Such charges were only the initial blasts in a war that Hamilton seemed determined to protract indefinitely. Under one pen name or another (Catullus, Fact, Amicus, Scourge, Metellus) he pressed his attack on the secretary of state, becoming in the process increasingly shrill.[25] Jefferson was an "intriguing incidenary" whose tenets tended to promote "*national disunion, national insignificance, public disorder and discredit,*" the "interested ambitious and intriguing head of a party," the "instigator of distraction" and perpetrator of "the most wanton and flagitious acts that ever stained the annals of a civilized nation." Beneath his sphinxlike stance Jefferson was also wily, a master of deceit.[26] Here was one explanation of Hamilton's self-defeating behavior—Jefferson's inscrutability, "the difficulty," in Dumas Malone's words, of "getting at him and grappling with him."[27] It was as if the Treasury secretary were goaded beyond endurance by his rival's aloofness, his Olympian silence, or perhaps Hamilton persuaded himself that the salvos of his pen would blast Jefferson from his mountaintop retreat in Virginia.

But Hamilton's performance cannot be attributed merely to angry resentment of an elusive antagonist. His behavior was typical. Jefferson's antagonism in 1792 was no more to be silently borne than General Washington's rebuke in 1783. Hamilton's insistence on publicly exposing his cabinet colleague's misdeeds was, moreover, of a piece with his exposé of George Clinton's political sins in 1789. Such forthrightness was not a virtue, as Hamilton no doubt believed it to be; nor was it, as he thought, volitional. But viewing political antagonism to himself as an affront actuated by personal malice, he characteristically convinced himself that he could by the force of his superior intellect and polemical skill overcome all opposition.

Thus convinced, he no doubt considered the public exposure of his opponents as a civic duty. It was, in fact, a reflection of an unresolved inner conflict. His assumed American identity and assurance of his countrymen's acclaim were not secure enough to withstand assaults. The very ferocity with which he fought off public challengers suggests that something more than official rivalry was at stake. His insecurity, paradoxically enough, was the source both of his rashness and seeming arrogance, traits that repelled not only many of his contemporaries but subsequent historians as well.

XI

Anglophiles Versus Francophiles

Far from being repelled, Washington's respect and admiration for his obstreperous finance minister, toward whom he had always exercised an almost parental indulgence, was undiminished. But he was deeply troubled by Hamilton's venomous brawling in Philadelphia newspapers and Jefferson's vicious sniping in private correspondence. Hoping to arrange a truce between the two feuding secretaries, he wrote virtually the same letter to each, asking not that they agree but that they exercise mutual forbearance and charity. "Differences in political opinions," the president's letter to Hamilton read, were not only "unavoidable" but perhaps also "necessary." But, as he added in his letter to Jefferson, such "internal dissensions," were "harrowing" and were "tearing" apart the unity essential to a vital administration.[1] Washington had every reason to remonstrate. A man of iron self-control, his own composure was outwardly unruffled by official disagreement or personal abuse; to engage in counterattacks, public or private, would have been unthinkable to him. In calling for "liberal allowances . . . instead of wounding suspicions, and irritating charges," he was implicitly pleading with his prickly secretaries to display something of his own self-restraint and equanimity.[2] He might as well have asked them to be born again.

Although both errant ministers nodded "assent to the patriarch's wisdom," neither "showed a disposition to reform."[3] Hamilton agreed that such official discord was disruptive and piously expressed a hope for peace. Otherwise, he said, the president must replace his warring ministers, meaning, of course, that Jefferson must mend his ways or go. For his own part, Hamilton was willing to call a halt to the cabinet warfare, as soon, that is, as he finished his public defense of Treasury Department policies and his official probity against the "uniform opposition from Mr. Jefferson" and his followers. The secretary of state was even more recalcitrant.[4] How could he be expected to compromise with evil? Hamilton's system "flowed from principles adverse to liberty, and was calculated to undermine and demolish the republic." Had he not all along been immoderately patient in the face of extraordinary provocation? Whatever he may have expressed privately, he had not publicly denounced what he regarded as Hamilton's corrupt control of Congress and his gratuitous attempts to subvert the secretary of state's control of his own department and conduct of foreign affairs, what Jefferson called "my system." In fine, Hamilton invariably was the aggressor, the Virginian's own motives were consistently pure, his official behavior beyond reproach. He now wished to withdraw from the relentless war that the secretary of the Treasury had declared and, to that end, would soon quit public office. In the meantime, he told the president that he contemplated retirement "with the longing of a wave worn mariner, who at length has the land in view."[5]

Jefferson's imagery was revealing, suggesting as it did that he had courageously sought to steer the new nation on a true course only to find himself battered by the storm of Hamilton's merciless assault. Jefferson had indeed been buffeted, but he overlooked the fact that he had helped to raise the storm, not only because of his steadfast commitment to principle but also because of distaste at having to battle an antagonist whom he would have preferred to dismiss as unworthy of notice. "I will not suffer my retirement to be clouded," he haughtily exclaimed, "by the slanders of a man whose history, from the moment history can stoop to notice him, is a tissue of machinations against the liberty of the country which has not only received and given him bread, but heaped honors on his head."[6] Perhaps Hamilton had all along sensed this aristocratic hauteur, his rival's scorn, disdain of a poor West Indian emigré of uncertain family connections, contempt for an upstart who acted as if he were Washington's prime minister and maybe heir apparent. Perhaps, too, the New York arriviste perceived a contradiction of which the Virginia gentlemen was unaware: how could Jefferson reconcile such snobbish disparagement of the self-made man and his simultaneous praise of the superior virtues of the common man?

Presumably Jefferson entertained no questions of this kind. Nor would it have been in character for Washington to ponder such paradoxes. He was, instead, disturbed by practical concerns and political considerations—fear that the feud between his two chief ministers might prove irreconcilable and the consequent prospect that party strife would increase. He was even more troubled by the possibility that the rift in his official family might oblige him to reconsider his firm decision to retire at the end of his first term. That decision had been made early in his first administration, and wishing above all else "to return to the walks of private life," he balked at reversing it.[7] Pressure to do so crowded in from every quarter, from both the North and the South, from private citizens, and from official colleagues. Among the latter, none were more importunate than the rival prima donnas of his cabinet, who suspended their acrimonious disagreement on everything else political to urge the president to stand for reelection. Jefferson's motivation was transparent: no person other than Washington ("the only man in the United States who possessed the confidence of the whole") could be counted on to resist the Treasury secretary's ruthless drive for power.[8] The reason for Hamilton's insistence was also obvious: with Washington at the helm, the Treasury secretary was confident that his own influence on national affairs would remain undiminished.

For Hamilton the election year had begun some six months earlier when his longtime friend John Jay had unsuccessfully contested George Clinton's seeming life-tenure as governor. Alarmed by reports that some influential New York Federalists were pushing the candidacy of Aaron Burr, Hamilton moved swiftly to cut down this shrewd and pliable politician, whom he profoundly distrusted and by now also considered both a deadly contender for leadership of the Federalist party in New York and a potential rival in the national arena. In order to abort Burr's political aspirations, Hamilton prevailed upon Jay to leave his safe berth as chief justice and to gamble on unseating New York's favorite politician.

Although happily assuming the role of governor-maker, Hamilton would have preferred to operate behind the scenes. But as the son-in-law of Philip Schuyler, New York's ostensible Federalist chieftain, and, next to the president, the nation's most prominent Federalist spokesman, the secretary of the Treasury's policies and politics were bound to be aired. They were not only publicly debated but, as the acrimonious campaign wore on, also seemed to be its central issue, eclipsing that of the respective eligibility of Clinton and Jay for the governor's chair. On the latter issue, the opinion of the electorate was unclear. Jay initially appeared to have won by the slender margin of 400 votes, but Republican canvassers, claiming electoral irregularities in three of the state's counties, refused to accept the voters' verdict. After a great deal of unseemly partisan maneuvering, the board of canvassers, voting along strict party lines, rejected the disputed votes of the counties in question, acclaimed Clinton the victor by 108 votes, burned the disputed ballots, and thus robbed Jay of both his rightful victory and legal redress. To Federalist extremists who urged that the Clintonians' theft be thwarted by "Conventions" and, if necessary, "the Bayonett," Hamilton counseled moderation. "I do not feel it right or expedient," he cautioned, "to attempt to reverse the decision by any means not known to the Constitution or Laws. The precedent may suit us today; but tomorrow we may rue its abuse."[9] Under similar circumstances a decade later Hamilton would try to establish just such a precedent, revealing that consistency was not his strong suit.

In at least one instance, however, Hamilton was steadfast. His support of Washington—whether due to self-interest or concern for the national welfare—never faltered. But neither Hamilton's pleas nor those of many other prominent Americans had any effect on the president's unwillingness to announce his candidacy for a second term. Over the months following his return to Philadelphia from Mount Vernon in October 1792, Washington continued to remain mute. No rival candidate presented himself, and there was not even a whisper that one would. Aware that he was in a field of one, Washington no doubt knew that the electorate would take his silence for assent. And they did, predictably according him a unanimous vote. His running mate, John Adams, was also returned to office, although by a vote of only seventy-seven, against fifty for his opponents.

Adams' reelection had from the outset been uncertain. Persuaded that the vice-president was as politically vulnerable as his chief was invincible, critics of the Washington administration decided to show their strength by unseating the New Englander. For this purpose they chose the nation's most successful gubernatorial vote-getter, George Clinton. New York's veteran political warrior readily accepted the challenge, presumably unbothered by the inconsistency of seeking high office under a government that only four years earlier he had denounced as tyrannical. Hamilton was not greatly disturbed by the candidacy of his longtime enemy. His response was merely to affirm his unreserved support of Adams, about whom he in fact had strong reservations. That Hamilton was unruffled by Clinton's candidacy was probably the result of his awareness that the governor's principles easily bent to the winds of political change. It was quite otherwise with the rumor, passed on in mid-September by Rufus King, that Aaron Burr "is industrious in his canvass" for the vice-presidency.[10] While almost persuaded that Burr's maneuvers were nothing "more than a diversion in favor of Mr. Clinton," Hamilton decided to take precautionary countermeasures.[11] These took the form of letters to a few influential political allies to whom he harshly denounced Burr as one who was "for or against nothing but as it suits his interest or ambition," an "embryo-Caesar," a "bold, enterprising, and intriguing" opportunist bent on becoming "the head of the popular party" and thereby climbing "to the highest honors of the State." To Hamilton it was "a religious duty to oppose his career."[12]

What Hamilton interpreted as a religious duty was in fact a private obsession. His perception of duty was, moreover, not singular but consistent. By way of illustration one need go no further than the mudslinging newspaper campaign he was at the very time carrying on against Jefferson. The charges hurled at the latter and at Burr were similar, although the vocabulary may have varied. Both the New Yorker and the Virginian were dangerously ambitious men "determined to climb to the highest honors" of the state and the nation, respectively. Both were deadly intriguers whose object was "to play a game of confusion." That game was designed in both instances to obscure their stealthy rise to the leadership of a popular party, thus to seize supreme political power. With some retouching of the features, the picture was, of course, a self-portrait. Hamilton himself was manifestly ambitious, although he believed that his own was of a more laudable kind. He too wished to achieve the "highest honors," but presumably aware that he could not reach the pinnacle of the presidency, he instead craved fame and glory. Hamilton also aspired to political leadership, although, as he saw it, of a party based on the principle of responsible stewardship for the national weal by contrast to a "popular party," always to him the instrument of merely personal aggrandizement and eventual despotism. In sum, what Hamilton scorned in others were the traits that he was incapable of acknowledging as his own.

Hamilton's recognition of Jefferson's implacable hostility was well placed, however. During his long vacation at Monticello from July to October 1792 the Virginian had nursed his grudge against his rival in the Treasury Department, and after his return to Philadelphia he dropped the pretense of forbearing silence and moved to the offensive, although from behind the scenes. One indication of his altered behavior was his waspish treatment of Hamilton at cabinet meetings. More revealing yet was his leadership of the campaign of Virginia Republicans to drive Hamilton from the government. The tactic decided upon was an official investigation of the Treasury secretary's alleged mishandling of the nation's finances. To lead their anti-Hamilton congressional crusade, Jefferson and Madison called on a fellow Virginian, William B. Giles, a tenacious legislative fighter but graceless orator who had made Hamilton-baiting the hallmark of his congressional career.

On January 23, 1793, Giles introduced five resolutions designed to convict Hamilton of illegal handling of the public debt. A beefy, ruddy-faced man whose slovenly appearance accurately mirrored his grasp of finance, Giles accused the Treasury secretary of allocating funds borrowed to discharge the foreign debt to purchase or to pay interest charges on the domestic debt. This juggling of funds, Giles charged, was in violation of congressional statutes adopted in August 1790 that had authorized two loans, one specifically designed for paying foreign obligations and the other for meeting payments at home. Hamilton was also accused, among other crimes, of failing to account satisfactorily for approximately $1.5 million of government funds. During the weeks following, Giles worked up yet more damaging charges that bore the imprint of a pen far more skillful than his own. The ghost-writer was the secretary of state, who, avoiding the legal complexities at issue, bluntly assailed not only Hamilton's official probity but also his personal integrity.[13] The Treasury secretary had knowingly violated both the law and the Constitution. He had also neglected "an essential duty of his office" by failing to inform Congress of his fiscal operations. Compounding his offenses, he had insulted that body by submitting misleading reports. He had committed "an indecorum to this House" by questioning its motives in investigating him. He had, more gravely yet, acted in flagrant disregard of "the public interest."[14]

To rebut his critics' accusations of malfeasance, dereliction of duty, and high-handed obstructionist tactics, Hamilton inundated Congress with lengthy reports, replete with relevant documents and statistics. A gargantuan amount of labor was required, but within a month he and his associates had compiled what amounted to a fiscal history of the United States since the inauguration of the new government. The loans negotiated under the authority of the acts of 1790, he asserted, had been legally proper, had been acceptable to the Dutch bankers through whom American loans abroad were negotiated, and had afforded the Treasury flexibility in handling the public debt. His official conduct in these as well as in other instances, Hamilton insisted, "was regular," was "within the discretion of the department," and was "the most eligible."[15] Most congressmen agreed, as attested by the decisive vote by which he was exonerated of official misconduct.

To Jefferson such a verdict was a miscarriage of justice but explicable: Since two-thirds of the members of the House consisted of jobbers and speculators in government stock, they could hardly be expected to censure their purportedly corrupt Treasury Department benefactor. Jefferson was wrong, but he stubbornly stuck to the conviction that had a fair trial been possible, Hamilton would have been found guilty and driven from office in disgrace. Had the Virginian detested Hamilton less obsessively and studied finance more closely, he would have known better than to challenge his rival on the latter's own ground. Instead, at Jefferson's prompting, his congressional allies, like Giles, unabashedly aired their ignorance of a subject of which Hamilton had a masterful command. Even had they been aware of their intellectual deficiency, they would not have been concerned. The secretary of state and his followers realized that they had suffered a setback rather than a rout and needed only to regroup in order to fight another day. For the moment, other issues overrode their concern with Hamilton's alleged official misconduct. As a North Carolina congressman commented, "The affairs of France have absorbed the attack on the Treasury department."[16]

The battle between Washington's rival secretaries had all along been based not only on seemingly irreconcilable differences on domestic policy but also on the proper orientation of American foreign policy. Should the new nation seek a rapprochement with its former mother country or adhere firmly to its Revolutionary War ally? Hamilton opted for England, Jefferson for France, and each equated his preference with the national interest, which both ideally viewed as isolation from the affairs of Europe and America's unhampered control of its own destiny. As Hamilton, in a remark that well might have been penned by Jefferson, had commented in *The Federalist*, "We may hope ere long to become the Arbiter of Europe in America; and to be able to incline the balance of European competitions in this part of the world as our interest may dictate."[17] Progress toward such a lofty goal was obstructed by the outbreak of revolution in France, a cataclysmic development that also became a central issue in the Hamilton-Jefferson feud, which henceforth focused as much on international as on domestic policies.

To Jefferson, the French Revolution was a replay of the American revolutionary scenario: a battle against royal absolutism and aristocratic privilege was another chapter in the story of man's struggle for justice, freedom, and equality. Hamilton emphatically disagreed. To him, the upheaval in France bore no relation to the American Revolution. The latter had been a struggle for self-determination, a defense of established rights, a crusade for the protection and expansion of American liberty; the French Revolution, by contrast, was a social upheaval that sought to uproot not so much royal tyranny as all tradition, the still viable along with the lamentably despotic. "I am glad to believe," he wrote, "there is no real resemblance between what was the cause of America and what is the cause of France—that the difference is no less great than that between Liberty and Licentiousness."[18] By "licentiousness" Hamilton meant atheism, anarchy, and the eventual emergence of demagoguery.

Neither Jefferson nor Hamilton understood the French Revolution for what it really was—a struggle by the bourgeoisie to remove the shackles of feudalism and to secure control of the state for its own benefit. Hamilton confused the bourgeoisie and the sansculottes; Jefferson equated the French aristocracy and the American bourgeoisie. Both men projected domestic political and class divisions onto the foreign scene and then reinterpreted American issues in the light of the mistaken projection. They thus managed, as Louis Hartz has commented, to misunderstand the uniqueness of American political issues and conflict.[19]

Nevertheless, the general war that engulfed Europe in 1793 not only intensified the conflict between Hamilton and Jefferson but also, as Jefferson said, "kindled and brought forward the two parties."[20] To Hamilton and his fellow Federalists, Britain was the bastion of constitutional government and America's natural ally; to Jefferson and his Republican followers, the French were following the freedom trail blazed by the United States in 1776 and thus deserved the encouragement of all liberty-loving Americans. Such exaggerated attitudes flowed from unexamined ideological rather than factual premises, in the sense that the partisan debate suggested the lack of any clear notion of the kind of foreign policy that would best serve the national interest or any precise idea of what that interest was.

Washington's perception of the problem was clear, however. Studiedly impartial, he believed that the war in Europe posed a grave threat to the new nation's independence, which must be safeguarded by a policy of neutrality. But in view of the Franco-American Revolutionary War treaties, how could such a policy be pursued? By the terms of those treaties the United States had promised to come to the aid of France should that nation become involved in a war; her prizes (but not those of her enemies) might be brought into the United States' ports, and her West Indian possessions were guaranteed. Was not the sacrifice of national honor the price of reneging on commitments made to America's Revolutionary War ally? Was not England's enmity—or even war with England—the inevitable consequence of meeting treaty obligations to France? Was not a quarrel with Britain in any event certain if that country high-handedly interfered with American commerce on the high seas, as seemed highly likely? Washington sought to avoid the risk of a naval confrontation with England and the danger of diplomatic retaliation by France, by eschewing a formal suspension of the French alliance while informally disregarding its stipulations. This was the implicit intent of his famous Proclamation of Neutrality issued in April 1793, in which he announced his determination to pursue "a conduct friendly and impartial toward the belligerent powers" and enjoined his countrymen against aiding either combatant.[21]

Both Jefferson and Hamilton also favored neutrality, but they disagreed on the means of achieving it. To Jefferson, the proclamation was premature. The belligerents should be obliged to bid for American neutrality, the asking price: "The *broadest* neutral *privileges*."[22] Since this had not been done, the president had issued a proclamation not of neutrality but partiality; it was a watery concoction that would dilute the cause of freedom that France represented. For his part, Hamilton not only endorsed the president's proclamation but also was instrumental in its promulgation. At the same time, however, he wished for a provisional suspension of the French treaties and adoption of a policy of nonrecognition toward the French republic.[23]

Still, Hamilton believed that the Proclamation of Neutrality was vastly preferable to what he viewed as the Republicans' inexcusable partiality for France. Thus convinced, he came to the administration's defense in a series of newspaper articles under the somewhat misleading pseudonym of "Pacificus."[24] The themes of Hamilton's essay were the wisdom of the proclamation, the president's constitutional authority to issue it, and the baselessness of the Jeffersonian claim that American foreign policy should be dictated by the debt of gratitude due to France for its aid during the American Revolution. Although Hamilton characteristically attributed sinister motives to his adversaries (a "spirit of acrimony and invective," an "opposition to government . . . pursued with persevering industry"), his partisanship did not in this instance either blunt his intellect or blur his statesmanlike vision.[25] His performance as Pacificus was masterful.

The opposition argument on which Hamilton focused was the contention that the United States owed France a debt of enduring gratitude. He scornfully rejected a notion that to him was based sheerly on sentimentality and a wrongheaded reading of universal, including American, history and, in the process, set forth a persuasive argument that national interest should be the lodestar of American foreign policy. Although by no means original with Hamilton, the contention has seldom been more convincingly presented. "It may be affirmed as a general principle," Hamilton wrote, "that the predominant motive of good offices from one nation to another is the advantage of Nations, which perform them." A nation is seldom justified in indulging "the emotions of generosity and benevolence." While denying that he advocated "a policy absolutely selfish . . . in nations," Hamilton nevertheless maintained "that a policy regulated by their own interest is and ought to be their prevailing policy."[26]

As Pacificus, Hamilton was not only the advocate of realpolitik but also the proponent of presidential power. His bold assertion of the nature and extent of power conferred on the nation's chief magistrate by Article II of the Constitution would have startled its authors as much as it in fact shocked Jefferson and his followers. Nevertheless, Hamilton's view of presidential power has served as a model for strong chief executives, particularly in wartime, from his day to our own. Article II of the Constitution did not prescribe the limits of executive power, he argued; that article was a general grant of powers and those therein enumerated were merely the principal ones conferred, illustrative of those that were implied. In Hamilton's formulation, in other words, executive power became virtually conterminous with national exigencies, not only domestic but foreign as well.

Such an assertion flabbergasted knowledgeable students of the Constitution and appalled the Treasury secretary's personal and official antagonists, none more so than the secretary of state. "For God's sake, my dear Sir," Jefferson wrote to Madison, "take up your pen, select the most striking heresies and cut him to pieces in face of the public."[27] Although justifiably alarmed that he himself might be slashed to bits in verbal swordplay with the agile and adroit New Yorker, Madison, donning the mask of "Helvidius," reluctantly agreed to the match.[28] Hamilton's "vicious" claim that the president possessed inherent powers to unilaterally make treaties and wars, Madison charged, was an attempt to transform the royal prerogatives of King George III into presidential prerogatives of George Washington. The right to decide whether the United States should go to war, Madison strenuously insisted, resided exclusively in Congress and that unqualified right could not in any way be curbed by presidential diplomacy, much less annulled by executive action created by what Hamilton had described as "an antecedent state of things that might render war inevitable." Madison no doubt expressed the true intent of the Constitution's authors and the commonly accepted belief of most of his countrymen. But the Virginian shied away from what was manifestly the essential question, presumably because he could not satisfactorily answer it. If control of foreign affairs was Congress' exclusive domain, how could the nation's diplomacy be efficiently or successfully conducted? Hamilton was not only aware of Madison's evasiveness but also presciently insisted that the inevitable risk of unavoidable and indispensable presidential diplomatic ascendancy was possibly a war, whether quasi or full, de facto or de jure, undeclared or implicitly endorsed, popular or unpopular.

Although heatedly contested at the time, Hamilton's prescription of presidential power became an incalculably important precedent. His immediate purpose, however, was to persuade his countrymen that the United States should disengage itself from entangling alliances and thus avoid involvement in France's quarrels and Europe's wars. And he insisted that neutrality as proclaimed by the president was the best way to avoid "the mischiefs and perils" that would result from a strict and unnecessary commitment to Franco-American treaty obligations.[29]

Closely related to the proclamation of neutrality, which Hamilton masterfully defended, was the related problem of receiving the new minister of the French republic, Citizen Edmond Genêt. Aware that Genêt would insist that America honor its treaty obligations and do whatever else it could to aid an embattled sister republic, the Washington administration was squarely confronted with the difficulty of maintaining the nation's neutrality in the face of its diplomatic vulnerability. Genêt, "brash, egoistic, extravagant in his

ambition,'' was certain that he could make the United States into ''an out-
post of French revolutionary sentiment and also of recrudescent French imperialism.''[30] A great number of Americans, blithely unaware of the
Frenchman's unneutral expectations, warmly welcomed Genêt as the symbol
of a steadfast ally and beleaguered sister republic. Enthusiastically greeted
on his leisurely tour from Charleston, South Carolina, to the nation's capital,
his arrival in Philadelphia on May 16, 1793, was greeted by the salvo of
cannon and the ringing of bells. The president's treatment of the French
emissary was in sharp contrast: Washington's icy manner would have frozen
the enthusiasm of all but the most insensitive of diplomats. Genêt was singularly obtuse. Disregarding the president's cautionary signal, the advice of
friendly disposed Republicans, and the laws of the United States, Genêt
stuck to the belief that the Americans need only hear his clarion call to rally
around the standard of the French Revolution. Thus self-deceived, he pursued policies suggesting that the United States was France's satrapy rather
than that nation's sovereign ally. He organized expeditions against Florida
and Louisiana, outfitted and armed privateers, directed that their prizes be
returned to American ports, and organized ''Democratic Societies'' to pop-
ularize the notion that the survival of American republicanism hinged on the
success of French arms.

In the face of Genêt's flagrant abuse of his ministerial post, the secretary
of state was astonishingly indulgent. Having convinced himself that the emissary of America's close republican ally could do no wrong, Jefferson insisted on giving Genêt the benefit of every doubt. But the doubts soon
became irrepressible, and by early August, Jefferson, having decided that
the French minister was a ''madman,'' confided to Madison that Genêt ''will
sink the Republican interest if they do not abandon him.''[31] The secretary of
state accordingly joined his cabinet colleagues in approving the president's
decision to demand Genêt's recall.

Hamilton had favored such a measure virtually from the moment the
French minister had set foot in Philadelphia. Had he been a more astute
politician, he might rather have relished Genêt's rash behavior. But failing
to share Jefferson's awareness that Genêt, if left alone, might ''sink the
Republican interest,'' Hamilton acted instead as if the survival of the United
States hinged on the repudiation of one flamboyant and irresponsible envoy.
The way by which he chose to make his point was to correct the purblind
partiality of the State Department chief and his zealous followers by the
same method that he had employed two months earlier to discredit opposition
to the Proclamation of Neutrality. A newspaper crusade such as that conducted by Pacificus would, he believed, prompt an irresistible popular demand for the Frenchman's recall. While Hamilton ostensibly had little faith
in the discretion and discernment of the people, he unhesitatingly banked on
their open-minded receptivity to his appeal to reason.

Although much of the material that Hamilton included in his ''No Jacobin'' articles, published in New York and Philadelphia journals in August
1793, would have been better suited to a casebook in admiralty law than to

a newspaper column, his essential argument was simple enough. Its focus was Genêt's reprehensible behavior. The French minister had denigrated the American people and insulted their president by threatening to appeal over Washington's head to the nation's voters. What was the purpose of this affront, as well as of Genêt's patently illegal violations of American neutrality? His purpose, Hamilton replied, was "to drag us into the war, with the humiliation of being plunged into it without even being consulted." It was impossible, the Treasury secretary charged, to think of "conduct less friendly or less respectful than this." It was "a novelty reserved for the present day, to display the height of arrogance on one side and the depth of humiliation on the other."[32]

It was, as things turned out, not the United States but Genêt who suffered humiliation. The official disgrace of this brash diplomat came when his superiors in France, bowing to Washington's firm insistence, ordered him home. Genêt himself was bothered less by the indignity of a reprimand than by fear that he might lose his head. Instead of returning to France, he quietly settled down in rural New York, eventually marrying a daughter of the governor of that state. Hamilton no doubt viewed such a close connection with George Clinton as punishment enough for any crime.

In any event, the former French minister, as Hamilton saw the matter, deserved a lighter sentence than the American secretary of state, who had for months condoned the Frenchman's flagrantly unneutral behavior. Hamilton's reaction to Genêt's dismissal was thus mild compared to his satisfaction at the news that his chief rival planned to quit the State Department. The Virginian submittted his resignation on July 31 (to become effective at the end of December 1793) and left for Monticello a month later. Since he did not return to the capital until November, his September departure marked all but the end of his official relationship with Hamilton, the one individual whom Jefferson detested above all others.

Before the Virginian returned to the capital in November, the worst yellow fever plague in recent memory had struck Philadelphia, claiming thousands of victims. The Treasury secretary came close to being counted among them. First detected in mid-August in the congested area along the waterfront, the epidemic spread rapidly. Once the Philadelphia College of Physicians confirmed that "the malignant fever now prevails," panic gripped the city.[33] Thousands of Philadelphians fled to nearby towns or to the country, and those too poor to flee endured the city's hot, infested, and fetid air, in daily dread that the deadly fever might strike. "The distress . . . among all classes of people," Dr. Benjamin Rush reported, "was nearly equal to that which was produced by the great plague in London in the years 1664–1665."[34] The mortality record told the grisly tale: at least four thousand and perhaps as many as six thousand people died.

Hamilton was stricken on September 6 and for a few days seemed unlikely to recover. That he survived may largely have been the result of the treatment prescribed by his boyhood friend Dr. Edward Stevens, who kept a constant vigil by Hamilton's bedside. Medical opinion on treatment varied greatly. The dominant school, aggressively led by Dr. Rush, tried to draw out the infection by purging and bleeding; another, of which Stevens was the representative, sought to build up the patient's resistance by rest and by other remedies that Stevens described as "cordial, stimulating, and tonic"— a full diet, cold baths, a mild opiate, and moderate doses of other soothing medicine.[35] Whether Stevens' treatment was responsible or not, Hamilton's rapid recovery was in sharp contrast to the deaths of thousands who were purged and bled. Within less than a week after he contracted the fever, Hamilton was no longer in danger and, although still enfeebled, began to make plans to escape the humid, mosquito-infested air for the cooler, cleaner air of upstate New York, there to rejoin his five children, who had been hastily sent from Philadelphia to stay with their grandparents. Accompanied by Eliza, who was also recuperating from an attack of the fever, Hamilton traveled by slow stages to Albany, confident that once ensconced in the Schuyler mansion and surrounded by his solicitous family his convalescence would be swift.

It rather appeared that he might be obliged to return to Philadelphia. When he reached the outskirts of Albany on September 21, he learned that the town's mayor and council, alarmed that Philadelphia émigrés might be infected by the disease, had imposed stringent measures to prevent their entry. The secretary of the Treasury was accorded preferential treatment, however. Once the Hamilton entourage was given a clean bill of health by Albany physicians, the council permitted the Hamiltons and their staff to enter the city. Public reaction was swift and shrill. "The fears of the citizens," Albany's mayor explained, were "beyond conception, from the Idea that the Carriages & baggage of Coll. Hamilton and Servants may contain Infection, & possibly Spread the disorder."[36] The town council responded by enjoining Philip Schuyler to conform strictly to promises that he had previously made: the clothing worn by Hamilton and his wife would be destroyed, their baggage would be jettisoned, and they would travel "in an open Chair without servants" to the Schuyler mansion, which was to be quarantined. Although annoyed by what he viewed as official harassment that violated his "rights of citizenship," Hamilton was, for once, too feeble to argue.[37]

Once his strength began to return, Hamilton, irked by enforced idleness, insisted on returning to Philadelphia. Having arranged to take up residence at Robert Morris' country house on the Schuylkill, he and Eliza arrived on October 23. By then a merciful frost had arrived, blanketing the capital in joyous optimism that the plague would soon be over. It was, but Hamilton might as well have remained at the Schuylers. For the next month, he was recurrently ill, probably because of the lingering effects of the fever. Nevertheless, he managed to catch up on urgent official business, to attend some cabinet meetings on the pressing issue of American neutrality, and to draw up recommendations for the president's opening speech to the Congress, scheduled to convene on December 3.[38]

Washington's address, based largely on Hamilton's draft, was upstaged by the secretary of state's long-awaited report on the privileges and restrictions imposed by other nations on American commerce. That report had been requested by Congress in February 1791, but Jefferson had repeatedly postponed its submission. The time was, he decided, now propitious. Not only was his tenure at the State Department drawing to a close, but foreign dispatches enhanced the possibility of public approbation and congressional approval.

The British government was determined to cut off the flourishing American trade with the French Caribbean ports made possible by the decision of France (announced soon after the outbreak of war in February 1793) to throw open her previously jealously guarded West Indian trade to the United States. Britain's determination took the form of a number of orders-in-council that cavalierly ignored neutral rights. That of June 8, 1793, against which Jefferson had lodged a vigorous protest before he left Philadelphia in September, directed His Majesty's naval commanders to seize and confiscate any cargo of corn, flour, or meal bound for France in a neutral vessel. By November, it was apparent that Britain, far from heeding Jefferson's demand for revocation of the objectionable order, intended to accelerate her spoliations of American commerce. This would be borne out two months later when news arrived that an even more restrictive order had been adopted on November 6, 1793. Jefferson needed no such confirmation of Britain's relentlessly high-handed disregard of America's neutral rights. On December 16, 1793, he presented Congress with his long-delayed account of the burdens imposed on United States commerce by foreign countries.[39] The villain in the story told by Jefferson was England, with whom the bulk of the new nation's trade was carried on.

The secretary of state's report was not only a defense of his insistence on the desirability of Franco-American friendship and commercial reciprocity but also an implicit assault on Hamilton's alleged subservience to Britain's economic rapacity. Jefferson's thesis was the just claims of the nation's commerce to particular solicitude; the most arresting feature of his report was its insistence on the encouragement of manufactures as a means toward achieving a balanced national economy. Such advocacy scarcely dovetails with Jefferson's repute as America's foremost exponent of agrarianism. It is also at odds with the stereotyped view of the irreconcilably divergent economic views of the Virginian and his rival in the Treasury Department. What is the difference between Jefferson the advocate of "tariff duties on the protective principle" and Hamilton the arch protectionist?[40] What separates Jefferson the proponent of manufactures and Hamilton the prophet of industrialization? A recent historian has offered a perceptive answer. Both men "employed the resources of government to promote development," Stuart Bruchey observes, and both "bespoke the interests and wishes of a nation anxious to root its political independence in the soil of economic growth."[41]

Neither Jefferson nor Hamilton acknowledged agreement on such important principles. They focused instead on their sharply different positions on American commercial policy. Jefferson insisted on the adoption of strong "countervailing" measures to coerce England into acceptance of the principle of "reciprocity"; Hamilton argued that national interest, prosperity, and growth hinged on placating Britain, America's best customer and principal supplier. Who was right? It is impossible for a historian to decide, although many have tried. Jefferson's program was not for a long time put into practice; the successful implementation of Hamilton's ideas does not mean that other policies would have failed. To both Hamilton and Jefferson, it should be added, such a judgment would have been scornfully dismissed as an evasion of the fundamental issue. Jefferson went home to Monticello, leaving Madison and Tench Coxe (Hamilton's official assistant but the Virginian's supporter) and other allies to fight for the triumph of the only proper commercial policy—his own. Hamilton stayed on as Treasury secretary, striving to assure the success of his policies, the only ones in his view that would assure a flourishing foreign commerce and, relatedly, national prosperity.

XII

Washington's Prime Minister

If Hamilton believed that Jefferson's retirement would diminish congressional opposition to Treasury policies, he was swiftly disabused. As Madison observed, the secretary of the Treasury's "trial is not over."[1] That it dragged on was largely because of Madison, who was determined to find some way to discredit "this collossus who stood astride the path" by which the Jeffersonians "hoped to bring about a revolutionary change in the government to what they considered a more democratic system."[2] The attack on Hamilton was launched some two weeks after the submission of Jefferson's report on American commerce.

On January 3, 1794, Madison introduced in the House resolutions reflecting that report's anti-British bias and its principal recommendations. The thrust of Madison's resolutions was the substitution of the principle of commercial reciprocity and the adoption of retaliatory legislation against England for the alleged pro-British policies of the administration. Among other proposals Madison called for an increase in tonnage rates for nations (like England) that had spurned treaty arrangements with the United States and a decrease for those (like France) that had agreed to commercial treaties, countervailing measures against nations that imposed restrictions on American shipping, and retaliatory penalties on goods imported from any country that seized United States vessels or cargoes.[3]

What Madison in effect proposed was an American navigational system based squarely on the British model and on mercantilist principles. Since critics of the Treasury secretary scathingly denounced his presumed allegiance to these very ideas, Madison's program was another instance of the ideological confusion that characterized the partisan controversy of the time. The adoption of such principles by Hamilton's opponents was also ironical, in the sense that the recommended retaliation against Great Britain would ostensibly aid northern merchants who opposed Madison's resolutions and damage southern planters (by way of enhanced prices for manufactured goods and steeper transportation charges) who endorsed the Virginian's program. Neither the ideological confusion nor irony of the situation concerned the secretary of the Treasury, who focused instead on the essential difference between the overarching purpose of his commercial policy and that advocated by the Jeffersonians: a rapprochement with England or stronger ties with France? Hamilton did not need to ponder the question. But in the absence of any congressional mandate for a report, what form would his answer take?

It took two forms: a public appeal in his characteristic mode of newspaper articles (this time signed "Americanus") and an address to Congress, ghostwritten for delivery by William Loughton Smith of South Carolina.[4] The speech, which has been described by a recent pro-Hamilton scholar as exemplifying "reasoning" that "made Jefferson's promptings seem superficial," was the more stellar performance.[5] Supporting his argument with statistics supplied by his staff at Treasury headquarters, Hamilton's address contended that Great Britain, despite its restrictive navigation acts, actually favored American commerce more than France, which although seemingly friendly, was in no position to enhance the trade of the United States. Not only was Great Britain the latter's best customer, but it also (as Jefferson had conceded in his report on commerce) supplied three-fourths of United States imports. Jefferson had not, however, conceded what to Hamilton's spokesman was a similarly vital consideration: British credit was "an essential nutriment" of American economic growth in the sense that it freed the new nation's meager store of capital for essential investment at home.[6]

In view of these facts, what purpose would commercial retaliation serve, Smith asked? England, a powerful and proud nation engaged in a war that she regarded as a struggle for survival, was unlikely to bow to pressure by an economically underdeveloped, militarily weak nation. Instead of risking ruinous commercial warfare with its principal customer, the United States should focus on internal development, preserving its robust prosperity, expanding and diversifying its economic activity, thus conserving its strength until the day when it might confidently challenge a mighty foreign power. It was a constructive program. But the partisanship fanned by the debate on Madison's proposals rendered dispassion a rare commodity. From the perspective of a later time, it appears that both the effort to retaliate against the former mother country or to side with its former Revolutionary War ally were more likely to further divide the United States than to coerce England or to placate France. But if congressional debates can be used as the gauge, many Americans were firmly convinced in the early months of 1794 that the nation's future hinged on the comparative treatment meted out by France and England to American fish, tobacco, timber, and ships.

In any event, not even an orator as uncommonly skillful as Smith was able to pass off Hamilton's words as his own. "I am at no loss to ascribe Smith's speech to its true father," Jefferson confided to Madison, who presumably did not need to be told. "Every tittle of it is Hamilton's except the introduction."[7] Having performed a similar service for congressman William B. Giles a year earlier, Jefferson qualified as an expert in the detection of ghost-writers.

With or without literary assistance, Giles was eager to renew a crusade to drive from office the master of financial malfeasance who presided at the Treasury Department. Hamilton himself provided the opportunity. Persuaded that the bill of official health Congress had given him in the spring of 1793 should be cleaner yet, the Treasury secretary asked the Congress that convened in December of the same year to resume its investigation of his conduct. Delighted to oblige, Giles drew up a number of resolutions dealing with virtually every aspect of Treasury Department affairs, from bookkeeping to sinking-fund operations, which were turned over to a committee of fifteen for investigation and report. The committee, as Hamilton saw the situation, was stacked—a majority of its members, he commented, were "either my political enemies or inclined against me."[8] In a replay of the scenario of the preceding year, the investigation centered on the Treasury secretary's management of funds borrowed in Holland on the authority of statutes enacted in August 1790.* Once again, Hamilton was called on to furnish reports that constituted in effect an account of operations of the Treasury Department from its inception; once again, his masterful defense would have obliged even the most scrupulous financial auditors to accord him an unqualified exoneration.

An overwhelming majority of Congress was in fact willing to do just that, but Hamilton's hard-core opponents, led by the indefatigable Giles, were neither convinced nor willing to be convinced. Starting from the premise that Hamilton was both unconscionable and ruthlessly ambitious, they jumped to the proposition that he would not scruple to engage in criminal acts to further his goals, and then confidently concluded that he was guilty as charged of official misconduct. And so they doggedly protracted the secretary's trial long after his acquittal became a certainty. The virtual guarantee

---

*A new issue figured prominently in the revived investigation of 1794. This was a charge leveled against Hamilton by a former clerk in the Treasury Department, Andrew G. Fraunces, who had been dismissed for drunkenness and incompetence. Fraunces, who then became a small-time stockbroker, managed to obtain some Board of Treasury warrants, issued in the 1780s and probably already redeemed, which he presented for payment. Upon investigation, Hamilton concluded that Fraunces' claim was fraudulent and accordingly turned it down. The latter sought revenge by publicly charging the Treasury secretary with a catalog of crimes, most notably that Hamilton had joined William Duer in illegal stock speculation. Fraunces also contrived to have his accusations brought before the House of Representatives. A committee of the latter rejected the charges and resolved instead that in this episode Hamilton had "acted a meritorious part toward the public."[9]

of exoneration would have been enough for any public servant capable of recognizing the manifest implacability harbored by Giles and his band of congressional allies. But it was not enough for Hamilton. As customarily, he interpreted official criticism, however ill-founded and malicious, as an impugnation of his personal integrity that must be publicly challenged, lest his silence pass for assent. Thus obsessed, he felt himself obliged to force his unappeasable critics to acknowledge his innocence. In his determination to reconcile the irreconcilables, Hamilton for once pushed the president too hard.

At issue was Washington's approval of the Treasury secretary's allocation of money presumably earmarked exclusively for discharge of the foreign debt to meet payments on the domestic debt. The congressional committee charged with investigating Treasury Department operations, detecting what its members sensed might be the weakest link in Hamilton's strong defense, insisted that the Treasury secretary provide documentary evidence of Washington's approval. Although Hamilton denied that the committee had the authority to examine the relationship between the president and the head of a department, the importunities of his congressional inquisitors finally impelled him to ask the president for a firm statement that would oblige the committee to drop the issue. "I cannot charge my memory with all the particulars which have passed between us, relative to the disposition of the money borrowed," Washington replied. "Your letters, however, and my answers . . . speak for themselves, and stand in need of no explanation. As to verbal communications, I am satisfied, that many were made by you to me on this subject; and from my general recollection of the course of proceedings, I do not doubt, that it was substantially as you have stated it . . . [and] that I have approved of the measures, which you, from time to time proposed to me for disposing of the Loans, upon the condition that what was to be done by you, should be agreeable to the Laws."[10] Obviously, this was as far as the president was either prepared or could be expected to go, presumably because he did not recall whether or in precisely what manner he had sanctioned every aspect of Hamilton's fiscal stewardship. And the president had in fact gone far enough to satisfy the Treasury secretary's congressional interrogators. To Hamilton, however, the president had been unacceptably evasive and should either "render the main fact unambiguous or . . . record the doubt."[11] Hamilton for the moment presumably forgot who was chief magistrate and who chief minister. He also overlooked the obvious fact that Washington's delegation to him of extensive powers whose exercise was usually endorsed provided no justification for demanding the president's unalloyed approval. Justified or not, official carte blanche was precisely what the secretary of the Treasury asked for. "The situation is indeed an unpleasant one," Hamilton wrote. "Having conducted an important piece of public business in a spirit of confidence dictated by an unqualified reliance, on the one hand, upon the rectitude, candour, and delicacy of the person under whom I was acting, on the other, by a persuasion that the experience of years had secured to me a reciprocal sentiment . . . and by the belief likewise that however particular instances might be forgotten, the general course of proceeding in so important an affair could not but be remembered—I did not look for a difficulty like that which now seems to press me.''[12] Washington was obviously not convinced that Hamilton was being borne down by unpredicted and unsupportable difficulties, but he no doubt endorsed his minister's comment that the "situation" was "indeed an unpleasant one." The president's characteristic reaction was Olympian silence, perhaps prompted by recollection of Colonel Hamilton's churlish reaction to a minor rebuke from General Washington some ten years earlier. The president also sagely realized what Hamilton tended to overlook. There was nothing for the nation's two top officials to quarrel about: Hamilton's full vindication by a Congress that had initially seemed intent on at least a minor reprimand was also a triumph for the fiscal accomplishments of Washington's administration.

Instead of probing microscopically the details of Treasury Department operations, Congress might better have looked into the desirability of national preparedness. As Congress' anti-Hamilton phalanx droned on and on, daily adducing new "evidence" (or shrill accusations that served in its place) of Hamilton's misdeeds, British ship captains, armed with the sweepingly inclusive order-in-council of November 1793, daily stepped up their seizure of American vessels. News of these wholesale captures reached Philadelphia at the height of the debate over Madison's commercial propositions, affording dramatic support of the Virginian's accusation of Britain's high-handed assaults on American commerce. Had consistency or logic been the hallmarks of congressional behavior, Britain's spoliations would have assured the success of Madison's retaliatory program. Instead, this renewed example of England's contempt for America's neutral rights channeled Republican energies during the winter months of 1794 into "a flood of legislation aimed at war,''[13] unchecked even by repeal of the objectionable order-in-council of the previous November and the diminution of the indiscriminate condemnation of American vessels by British admiralty courts in the West Indies. Assertion of the principle of commercial reciprocity and enactment of retaliatory trade measures seemed a shamefully pallid response to Britain's imperious assumption that it might treat a newly independent nation just as it had decades before treated its American colonies. To most congressmen, as to other Americans, such an affront must not go unchallenged: the time had come for yet another successful chastisement of imperial presumption. And for the first time in a long while Congress was united.

On March 26, a one-month embargo (later extended) on all foreign shipping was imposed, followed by an unsuccessful effort to sequester debts due from American to British citizens. These punitive measures were accompanied by a Federalist-sponsored program of national preparedness calling for harbor fortification, an increase in the army, and the building of warships. To most Republicans, however, such preparations were unnecessary: a good cause, a stout militia, and a united nation could do again in the 1790s what brave Americans engaged in a worthy cause had accomplished in the 1770s.

To this fanciful proposition few Federalists subscribed, certainly not Hamilton. Although he readily acknowledged that Great Britain had displayed "strong tokens of deep-rooted hatred, and hostility toward this country" and believed the injuries inflicted on the United States by Great Britain must be redressed, Hamilton rejected the Republicans' advocacy of countervailing measures at the risk of war and recommended to his fellow Federalists a policy of negotiations backed up by military preparedness.[14] The time was ripe for neither military strut nor unilateral retaliatory measures but for diplomacy. Successful negotiations, Hamilton insisted, were the only sensible alternative to a ruinous war. The president agreed, and could he have had his wish, the American negotiator would have been his most trusted cabinet adviser. But Hamilton's presumed anglophilism, allegedly extending even to monarchism; his controversial position in American politics; and the resultant storm that his designation would raise precluded the New Yorker's nomination. After canvassing other qualified envoys—John Adams, Chief Justice John Jay, and Jefferson among them—Washington acted on Hamilton's convincing argument that "Mr. Jay is the only man in whose qualifications for success there would be thorough confidence."[15]

Hamilton might also have added that Jay was among the few men who could be confidently counted on to carry out Hamilton's own ideas. Although supervision of such a diplomatic mission was manifestly the responsibility of the State Department, the secretary of the Treasury predictably assumed control. He furnished the president (at the latter's request) a memorandum on the nature, purpose, and conduct of Jay's mission; he unhesitatingly submitted his ideas on the forthcoming negotiations to Edmund Randolph, who was Jefferson's replacement as secretary of state and may well have shared his predecessor's indignation at Hamilton's presumptuous management of a fellow cabinet member's department. Nevertheless, the instructions drawn up by Randolph were modeled closely on the advice of Hamilton. There were limits to the secretary of state's willingness to accept the Treasury secretary's direction of foreign affairs, however, and Randolph insisted on inserting into Jay's instructions certain significant provisions to which Hamilton objected. The differences centered largely on Hamilton's insistence that American demands be restricted to those that England reasonably could be expected to meet and that the United States acquiesce in points on which Britain could under no circumstances be expected to make concessions. Hamilton particularly objected to that part of Jay's instructions directing the latter to sound out the ministers of Denmark, Sweden, and Russia on the possibility of American cooperation with the Armed Neutrality, an agreement between Sweden and Denmark to withstand England's violation of the rights of neutrals, an issue that must be stressed because of the historical controversy that it subsequently spawned and even now prompts.[16]

But in the main Jay's instructions faithfully mirrored Hamilton's ideas, especially his insistence that those instructions be largely discretionary rather than narrowly prescriptive. The American envoy was directed to persuade England to perform the unexecuted parts of the Anglo-American peace treaty of 1783 (particularly Britain's evacuation of the Northwest posts and compensation for slaves carried off by its army in 1783), to secure indemnification for the capture and condemnation of American vessels, and to win acceptance of an Anglo-American commercial treaty. The instructions also included two obligatory provisions: Jay was to sign no treaty that either conflicted with American engagements to France or failed to give American ships entry to ports of the British West Indies.

The moderateness and conciliatoriness of Jay's instructions reflected Hamilton's keen perception of American weakness as contrasted to British strength. This viewpoint he presumably conveyed to Jay in a number of conversations (since the chief justice had already agreed, he must surely have been a receptive listener) held during the brief period following the latter's appointment as minster plenipotentiary on April 19 and his departure shortly thereafter.*

No doubt Hamilton would have been pleased by his own appointment to a diplomatic post for which he believed himself to be superbly qualified and would have welcomed a respite from a cabinet post of which he was beginning to tire. But such disappointment was assuaged by satisfaction that he was largely responsible for the mission itself, the selection of the man to conduct it, and the instructions that the chief justice carried. As Nathan Schachner comments, Hamilton was "never more triumphant than at this moment of seeming defeat for his private aspirations. . . . He was at the peak of his career."[17] His principal rival had been driven from the official arena, and Jefferson's successor at the State Department seemed unable (or unwilling) to check the Treasury secretary's dogged determination to direct American foreign policy. Other cabinet members—particularly Secretary of War Henry Knox—not only acquiesced in Hamilton's views but seemed amiably disposed to allow the Treasury chief to think for them. Not even the president, certainly no man's rubber stamp, made any effort to rein in a powerful assistant with whose policies he agreed. Outside the administration, Hamilton was also at the pinnacle of his personal prestige and power. To the most influential of his own party's leaders, Hamilton was the paragon of Federalism. Thus circumstanced, he was not especially troubled by awareness that the Republican opposition continued to view him as public enemy number one and that he enjoyed no particular popularity among the rank and file of his own party. Short of occupying the executive's chair himself (which only in the most abandoned flights of fancy could he have expected to fill), Hamilton had reached the top. Perhaps awareness of his powerful position caused

---

*Hamilton was determined not only that the chief justice be given appropriate official instructions and sound advice but that he also be provided with the requisite data on the history of Anglo-American commerce. As Jay's teacher, Hamilton chose Tench Coxe, always a willing tutor in economic history. During the week preceding Jay's scheduled departure on May 10, Coxe sent the envoy-designate report after lengthy report in which he set forth detailed data on Anglo-American trade.[18]

him to forget momentarily that Washington was head of his own administration and Randolph was spokesman for the State Department.

Such a lapse would at least explain why Hamilton acted, once again, as if his ministerial portfolio included not only the Treasury Department but the State Department as well. That he should at the president's request play a role in the conduct of foreign affairs (as in the preparation of Jay's instructions) was unexceptionable. The propriety of reenacting the scenario he had played with Major George Beckwith in the summer of 1790 by privately conferring with the British minister, George Hammond, on the condition and prospects of Anglo-American relations (including Jay's negotiations in England) was another matter and, to most historians, highly dubious behavior.[19] The gravamen of the charge against Hamilton was a conference in which he assured Hammond that the United States had decided not to cooperate with the armed neutrality that Sweden and Denmark had concerted in 1794 to resist Britain's disregard of neutral rights. The English minister lost no time in relaying these glad tidings to his superior in London, Lord Grenville. Grenville, relieved of the fear that the United States would, as rumored, join other nations in resisting Britain's maritime practices, promptly insisted on much stricter conditions than he had led Jay to expect that Britain would exact. Historians who unqualifiedly accept such a version of this diplomatic tale have understandably censured Hamilton harshly. The sentence was recently pronounced by Richard B. Morris, a distinguished American historian: by depriving "the American envoy of a major weapon which could conceivably have brought the British to terms," Hamilton behaved in an "unconscionable manner." He adds, "It is difficult even today at a time so remote from these negotiations to justify Hamilton's conduct on any ground. With all due charity, Hamilton, although a man of overpowering talent, was a difficult if not treacherous collaborator."[20]

Such an interpretation of Hamilton's behavior both distorts what he in fact said to the British minister and the effects of his comments on the Jay-Grenville negotiations. Neither Hammond nor Grenville deceived themselves that Hamilton spoke authoritatively on foreign affairs for the Washington administration. As Hammond had also long since learned, Hamilton, far from being always or fully candid, was capable of bending, concealing, or distorting facts in the service of what he perceived to be America's national interest.

Moreover, Hamilton was in no position to speak for Jay who "does not seem to have . . . wielded a threat throughout the entire negotiations" and who so far as we can tell did not even view American membership in the armed neutrality as his diplomatic trump card. Nor did the British foreign secretary. Although Grenville "attached some importance to the project," he "realized that Sweden and Denmark were not capable of carrying on a naval war against Great Britain" and "could exert little influence on the Baltic" without the aid of Britain's allies.[21] In sum, although the British foreign secretary instructed Hammond to observe carefully developments in the United States and to try to prevent American cooperation with European neutrals, there is no reason to believe that the threat of American membership in a league of armed neutrality would have obliged Grenville to make significant concessions to the American envoy.[22] Nor did the Treasury secretary in the course of his conversations with the British minister renounce America's recourse to war in the face of continued British maritime assaults and diplomatic obdurateness. Contrarily, Hamilton not only accepted the chance that such a war might occur but also refused in that event to rule out the possibility that the United States might informally join England's other enemies (including members of the armed neutrality) or implement the Franco-American alliance.[23]

Yet even if one concedes that Hamilton's conversations with Hammond had no appreciable effect on the Jay-Grenville negotiations, it may still plausibly be argued that Hamilton was not only indiscreet but that he also employed a double standard of official conduct. When Jefferson opposed Treasury Department policies, Hamilton angrily insisted that it was the duty of a cabinet member to suppress private reservations and to support measures approved by the president. In making known his objections to United States cooperation in an armed neutrality, Hamilton was thus engaging in behavior of a type that he had scorned when practiced by Jefferson. The issue is essentially irrelevant, however. The historian should not mirror but reflect on the behavior of Washington's rival cabinet members, endorsing neither the resentment of Jeffersonians at Hamilton's imperious manner and gratuitous meddling nor Hamilton's own self-serving defense of his conduct. Instead, the historian should eschew the double standards set by participants in this now distant and puzzlingly passionate debate, recognizing that partisanship distorted their vision and warped their judgment.

In any event, the diplomatic agreement that was reached in London in the summer and fall of 1794, the most famous peacetime treaty in American history, was the work not of the secretary of the Treasury but of the American envoy John Jay,[24] on whom contemporaneously fell the praise (faint though it was) and the blame (which soon became a national chorus, ever mounting in volume). Jay understandably believed that in view of the disadvantages under which he labored, he had sacrificed no more than was indispensable and had secured all the concessions possible. The representative of a young, economically undeveloped, militarily unprepared nation that as yet weighed lightly in the European balance of power, Jay had confronted a world power that was comparatively mature industrially, well-armed, and indisputably mistress of the seas. Just as Jay, ever aware that he was negotiating from a position of weakness, was in no "position to demand from Britain most or all of what his government sought with regard to the frontier, trade, and neutral rights," so Lord Grenville, aware not only of British strength but of the essentiality of English trade and credit to American fiscal and economic stability, believed that "war between the United States and Great Britain would be inconvenient for England but fatal to America."[25]

In view of this situation and since there is, in Marcus Cunliffe's phrase, "no tenderness in international diplomacy," Jay won rather more concessions than a knowledgeable diplomatic realist would have expected.[26] Britain promised to give up the posts in the Northwest by June 1796, to pay for the spoliations upon American commerce, and to sign a commercial treaty granting the United States certain trading privileges with India and narrowly limited commerce with the British West Indies. In return, Jay renounced maritime principles that the United States hitherto had stoutly supported (in effect, the familiar insistence of neutral nations on freedom of the seas) and accepted instead Great Britain's interpretation of international law. More specifically, Jay acquiesced in Britain's definition of contraband of war, its contention that provisions could not under all circumstances be carried to enemy ports in neutral ships, her insistence that trade with enemy colonies prohibited in time of peace was also illegal in time of war, and her demand that America not open its ports to the ships and privateers of England's enemies. As Jay and Grenville viewed their handiwork, moreover, the treaty was as important for the machinery it established for setting long-standing disputes as for what it formally stipulated. Joint commissions were to be set up for the arbitrament of the amount of compensation for spoliations, the claims of British creditors against American citizens, and the fixing of the northwestern boundary between the United States and Canada.

To a good many Americans, however, the true measure of Jay's treaty was not its provisions but its omissions and shortcomings. The oversights that aroused the greatest furor were the absence of any offer of compensation for slaves freed by the British in 1783 and silence on the issue of impressment of bona fide United States sailors by the English navy; the shortcomings most often lamented were Britain's refusal to grant the United States an unrestricted, rather than a partial, privilege of trading with the British West Indies and the stipulation that American ships would not carry molasses, sugar, coffee, cocoa, and cotton to any other part of the world.

The prevalence of such beliefs among Republicans suggests that for them to judge the treaty a success Jay would have been obliged to have won Britain's surrender on every substantive issue. To the Jeffersonians, in sum, diplomatic success seemed to mean the capitulation of one's rival rather than compromises between negotiating parties.

To Hamilton, as well as to most Federalists, Jay had gained about as much as Grenville and the British cabinet's careful appraisal of American power made them willing to concede. The proper goal of United States foreign policy, Hamilton believed, was conciliation, even if bought at the cost of an imperfect treaty, not confrontation, which might lead to a war the nation was poorly prepared to fight. America's primary need was not so much a particularly favorable treaty nor even an advantageous foreign alliance but time—a long period of peace to develop America's resources, to diversify and expand its growing economy, to create a great common market, to cement a still shaky union, and in these ways to establish a powerful nation capable of challenging the war machines and naval strength of Europe's foremost powers. In sum, although the specific provisions of Jay's Treaty conceded to the United States far less than Hamilton had hoped for,[27] he agreed with Jay's comment to Secretary of State Randolph that "I have no reason to believe that one more favorable to us is attainable."[28]

XIII

Insurrection and Imperium:
Resignation and Reflection

"There is really My Dear Sir a crisis in the affairs of the Country which demands the most mature considerations of its best and wisest friends," Hamilton wrote to John Jay on September 3, 1794.[1] The crisis, Hamilton might have added, was domestic as well as foreign. While Jay was seeking to wrest from England respect for America's sovereign status and recognition of its rights as a neutral, the Washington administration was attempting to assure the supremacy of federal law against defiantly delinquent taxpayers. At issue was the excise on distilled spirits levied by Congress in March 1791 at the insistence of Hamilton and despite the resistance of many westerners and southerners. Opponents of the measure centered on the greater ease and efficiency of state collection of taxes on widely scattered stills, often located in remote rural areas, and on the gratuitous accretion of national power entailed by the establishment of federal internal revenue officers. They could succeed, commented Senator William Maclay, by "nothing short of a permanent military force," adding in a thinly veiled allusion to Hamilton "that this, for aught I knew, might be acceptable to some characters."[2]

Neither congressional opposition nor subsequent popular resistance to this species of taxation took Hamilton by surprise nor moderated his position. In *The Federalist* he had commented that "the genius of the people will ill brook the inquisitive and preemptory spirit of excise laws."[3] But in the same essays, he had conceded that it probably would be necessary for the proposed government to bear with popular discontent: since justice dictated that the states "contribute to the public treasury in ratio to their abilities" and since some states necessarily would pay an undue share of duties on imports, "it is necessary that recourse be had to excises; the proper objects of which are particular kinds of manufactures.''[4] As secretary of the Treasury, Hamilton insisted that the manufactures most eligible for direct taxation were distilled spirits, manifestly the most superfluous of luxuries. Such a tax, he argued, would not only improve public health and morals by reducing the consumption of alcoholic beverages but would also provide revenue essential for the discharge of payments due on the public debt. That federal preemption might stymie state utilization of such a valuable tax source must surely also have occurred to him. Hamilton got his way, as he so often did during the first years of his secretaryship, with passage of the excise law of March 1791.*

Although the excise law was sporadically resisted in several parts of the country, the seat of opposition was in the four western counties of Pennsylvania. Here—or so the stereotyped view goes—was the very incarnation of frontier democracy, here an individualistic people dedicated to freedom, as willing to resist the ''tyranny'' of the Federalists in the 1790s as that of the English in the 1770s. In both cases tyranny was equated with taxes, a popular comparison of which the Treasury secretary was no doubt aware.

Nor was Hamilton surprised when opposition to the excise in Pennsylvania's western survey erupted into violence. As he well knew, opposition to excise taxes long antedated adoption of the Constitution and had been kindled anew by the tax imposed in March 1791. Hostility was initially expressed by public protest meetings and remonstrances, but in September 1791 it spilled over into violence when the collector for Washington and Allegheny counties was tarred and feathered, a treatment also meted out to a federal official sent to serve summonses on the perpetrators of the offense.

Avoiding a tough law-and-order position, Hamilton opted for a pacification program, including legislative mending of flaws discovered during the first year of the law's operation. He consonantly proposed alterations, and Congress promptly adopted them in May 1792. Duties on imported spirits were raised, the tax on domestic spirits was slightly lowered, procedures were simplified, and concessions were made to small country distillers, the tax law's most vociferous opponents.

Having made what he considered to be conciliatory gestures that should have mollified even a citizenry ''little accustomed to taxes,'' Hamilton believed that opposition to the law would abate and gradually disappear.[8] What he failed to perceive was that the only policy acceptable to hard-line oppo-

---

*For the collection of the whiskey tax that statute authorized an internal revenue service, a nationwide organization of revenue officials, consisting of a supervisor for each district (or state),[5] one or more inspectors for each ''survey'' (as subdivisions of the district were called),[6] and such additional officers as the supervisors should consider necessary. It also stipulated the rates to be imposed (ranging according to strength and material from twenty to forty cents per gallon on imported spirits and from nine to thirty cents per gallon on domestic spirits), prescribed the manner of collection in such a way as to prevent arbitrary action by revenue officers (trial by jury was mandatory and indiscriminate search and seizures were prohibited), and provided safeguards for importers and dealers.[7]

nents of the excise law was not its reform but its repeal. Even before disgruntled distillers had time to ponder the possibly ameliorative effects of the amended act (if indeed they knew about it), active resistance was resumed. In Pittsburgh a mass meeting, attended by at least four members of the state assembly, loudly reaffirmed its unappeasable antagonism to the excise and proposed countermeasures that would, in the words of Inspector John Neville, give a *"mortal stab to the Business"* of tax collection.[9] Neville's prediction was borne out by subsequent events. In late August 1792, opponents of the excise, angered by the opening of an inspection office in a house rented from one Captain William Faulkner, drew a knife on the captain and "threatened to scalp him, tar & feather him, and finally to reduce his House to ashes." Faulkner, who obviously preferred to relinquish the paltry rent he received rather than to put his assailants' threats to the test, promptly published a newspaper notice that his house would no longer be used as an inspection office. Unable to find any other landlord willing to risk the fury of local vigilantes, Inspector Neville was obliged to report to Treasury headquarters that he would have to desist from further attempts to fulfill the law.[10]

After carefully studying the reports, Hamilton intructed Tench Coxe, commissioner of the revenue, to dispatch George Clymer, supervisor for Pennsylvania, to the scene of the disturbance to investigate, initiate legal proceedings against the principal offenders, and convince the people of the survey that the federal government would not long remain "a passive spectator of such perservering and contemptuous resistance to its laws."[11] If objectivity and conciliatoriness were prerequisites for such a mission, Clymer was the wrong choice. An intractable law-and-order advocate, he predictably found a situation that reinforced his preconception that the western survey was not only plagued by "bad temper" and an "infatuation" with lawlessness but also dominated by "Unprincipled men."[12] Since the secretary of the Treasury shared such preconceptions, he neither needed nor waited for Clymer's report.

Even before the supervisor's investigation was fully under way, Hamilton had decided on the necessity of a presidential proclamation "stating the criminality of such proceedings and warning all persons to abstain from them, as the laws will be strictly enforced against all offenders."[13] By September 7, Hamilton (once again assuming the role of prime minister) had prepared the draft of a proclamation admonishing all persons to "refrain and desist from all unlawful combinations and proceedings" that might obstruct the operation of federal laws.[14] A week later the document was signed by Washington, whose name, for once, worked no magic. A month following the presidential proclamation Coxe reported to Hamilton that the "prejudices and opposition" of the western malcontents "are such as almost entirely to defeat the execution of the revenue laws."[15] Nevertheless, neither the defiant distillers nor vigilant Treasury officials were spoiling for a fight, and from the late fall of 1792 until the spring of 1794 a truce prevailed.

It was fragile, however, and both its prevalence and duration were largely due to the pacification program pursued by Treasury Department officials, including repeated efforts of the commissioner of the revenue, backed by Hamilton, to modify the more unpopular features of the law.[16] Governmental forbearance might well have succeeded in reconciling all but the most extreme antitax men had the issue been the whiskey tax per se. As things were, the excise symbolized the dissatisfaction of western Pennsylvanians with federal policy generally. The Washington administration was lambasted for not securing unhampered navigation of the Mississippi River, for laggardness in forcing the British to relinquish posts in the Northwest, and for Jay's appointment to iron out the difficulties with England (indicative, it was charged, of the government's unpardonable partiality for the former mother country). In a larger sense, these frontier dissidents may, as a mid-nineteenth-century historian observed, have been "at war with all restraints of government."[17]

The whiskey excise was, nevertheless, the issue on which the disaffected citizens of Pennsylvania's westernmost counties focused and the one that finally brought a confrontation between irate taxpayers and federal troops. The president, Hamilton, and other federal officials genuinely wished to assuage the angrily recalcitrant taxpayers and would no doubt have continued to tolerate protests and demonstrations against the law, perhaps even what a much later generation would call passive resistance. Violent resistance to duly enacted federal laws was another matter, however, and it was this that led Washington, consonant with the advice of his principal ministers—particularly Hamilton—to decide on a military showdown.

Beginning in the spring of 1794, reports of occasional violence had begun trickling into Treasury headquarters: in March, irate distillers threatened John Neville, inspector of the survey, with retaliation by the local militia if he did not resign his office; in May and June attacks were made on the property of two distillers who insisted on complying with the law; in July, revenue offices in Westmoreland and Washington counties were besieged and mail packets en route from the west to Philadelphia were seized.[18] Perhaps such comparatively minor incidents would have been ignored had on-the-scene federal officials been less inclined to magnify virtually every individual misdemeanor into a major riot, for it was the accounts of these officials and their immediate superiors on which the commissioner of the revenue relied for his reports to the Treasury secretary on the state of affairs in Pennsylvania's fourth survey. Far from being impartial, the revenue agents stationed there along with their boss, Inspector John Neville, and the supervisor for Pennsylvania, George Clymer, tended to see a conspiracy under every still.[19]

It is also possible, however, that the presence of open-minded, conciliatory revenue agents would have made no difference. Irreconcilable distillers in Pennsylvania's westernmost survey were determined to flout the law, and the Washington administration took the position succinctly expressed on another occasion by Hamilton: "A LAW by the very meaning of the term includes supremacy. It is a rule which those to whom it is prescribed are bound to observe.''[20] By July 1794 neither side seemed willing to any longer countenance forbearance: each accused the other of having adopted an uncompromisable change of policy. At Treasury headquarters, the change seemed to be from sporadic outbursts of violence to a comprehensive campaign calculated to shut down operation of the federal revenue service in the fourth survey, by force if necessary. To antitax forces in western Pennsylvania, the change appeared to be the federal government's abandonment of a policy of moderation for one of repression and reprisal.

Both parties to the dispute may have exaggerated the attitudes and intentions of the other, but one fact was indisputable: violence in the fourth survey was on the rise. In mid-July a United States marshal was sent to the area to deliver subpoenas to a number of distillers who had refused to pay the tax. Accompanied by Inspector Neville, the marshal delivered most of the writs without incident. One intractable distiller, William Miller by name, not only refused to accept the summons but also called to his aid a group of neighbors, who fired on the federal officials and chased them out of the survey. A few days later a body of armed insurgents set fire to the house of the area's chief revenue officer, General Neville. Emboldened by such open defiance of federal process servers and tax gatherers, leaders of the antitax movement stepped up their protests. Noisy mass meetings were conducted, and the extremists among the tax resistants even called for a rendezvous of the militia of the state's western counties to arrange an assault on Fort Pitt, the one federal citadel in the region, and an attack on Pittsburgh, the area's center of anti-insurgency. As such incidents increased, so did Hamilton's determination to quell resistance to his own department's subordinates and to federal law. The decision would obviously be up to the president, but the Treasury secretary was confident that as so often in the past his advice would prevail.

Hamilton's confidence was well placed. On August 2, Washington met with his cabinet, the attorney general, and Pennsylvania's Governor Thomas Mifflin, accompanied by two other high officials of the commonwealth, to settle on measures to deal with what seemed to be an imminent insurrection. Among the participants there was no consensus.[21] Although Pennsylvania officials unanimously agreed that the seriousness of the situation had been exaggerated and that federal military intervention was unwarranted, the president's cabinet was divided. Hamilton outspokenly "insisted upon the propriety of an immediate resort to Military force," a position that Knox, who almost always assented to Hamilton's views, could be counted on to endorse, that Bradford appeared to favor, but that Randolph manifestly opposed.[22] Confronted by such division and inconclusive debate, Washington followed his familiar practice of requesting the conferees to submit written opinions. In writing, as in speaking, Hamilton called for the use of troops to quell what he unhesitatingly termed treason. The secretary of war, while advising that certain preparatory steps be taken first, predictably agreed. So too did the attorney general. "Insurgency was high treason," William Bradford argued, "a capital crime, punishable by death," and the insurrection in the west must be squelched by military force. The secretary of state and Governor Mifflin disagreed, Randolph for prudential reasons and the governor on the grounds that if military intervention should become necessary (which was unlikely), it should be by Pennsylvania alone.[23]

As a knowledgeable contemporary remarked, "With the President the whole business rests."[24] Aware that even as the cabinet deliberated, some five thousand dissidents, many of them armed, were assembling at Braddock's Field, Washington's decision was prompt. The western counties, he informed Hamilton on August 21, were engaged in "open rebellion," which must be suppressed.[25] Similarly convinced, the president had some weeks before issued a proclamation commanding the insurgents to disperse and exhorting all inhabitants of the area to "prevent and suppress dangerous proceedings."[26] Having thus made the administration's position clear, he now awaited the results of negotiations by commissioners whom he had earlier appointed to offer the malcontents amnesty for past offenses in exchange for a promise to acquiesce in the execution of federal laws. After several interviews with the insurgents, the United States commissioners reported on August 30, 1794, "that we have still much reason to apprehend, that the authority of the laws will not be *universally* and perfectly restored, without military coercion."[27] The report was one of those important events, of which none was alone decisive, that were inexorably drawing the administration into the armed confrontation it by now considered unavoidable and that the insurgents, who seem to have viewed the government's threats as mere bluster, did nothing to avert.

On August 24, Washington conferred with Hamilton and Randolph, asking "shall orders issue for the immediate convening of the whole or any part of the Militia?"[28] Upon receiving an affirmative answer, the president instructed Hamilton, who was then doubling as secretary of war for Henry Knox, who was in Maine on personal business, to order the governors of Pennsylvania and neighboring states to call out their respective militias, and on September 9, Washington approved orders, prepared by Hamilton, for a general rendezvous of these troops at Carlisle.[29]

Washington, convinced that his own participation would render the military expedition somewhat more palatable, personally assumed command of the expected fifteen thousand militiamen, a military force that administration critics considered extravagantly large. Hamilton also decided to go along. Although he had no difficulty in explaining his decision, Hamilton's presence only enhanced the unpopularity of the campaign and strengthened the resolve of defiant distillers, whose steadfastness was beginning to waver, although neither the president nor the Treasury secretary acknowledged the fact. Hamilton rationalized his request to accompany the troops by the argument that since measures of his own department were the "ostensible" cause of the insurrection, it could not "but have good effect" for him to share in the "danger of his fellow citizens."[30] He no doubt genuinely believed that the militia would encounter danger, although we now know that armed resistance to the federal soldiers, much less anything remotely resembling an armed rebellion, was extremely remote. Hamilton also justified his decision by the conviction that at stake were such fundamental questions as these: "Shall the majority govern or be governed? Shall the nation rule, or be ruled? Shall the general will prevail, or the will of a faction? Shall there be government, or no government?"[31] The alternatives Hamilton proposed were exaggerated: the continued vitality of the nation, much less its survival, was not gravely jeopardized by a localized taxpayers' strike. Nor did resistance to the whiskey excise set what Hamilton called "an example fatal in its tendency to everything that is dear and valuable in political society."[32]

Such historical second-guessing is gratuitous, however, in the sense that it wrenches Hamilton's ideas out of their historical context: the situation at the time could reasonably have been construed as he interpreted it, his alarm was real, and his convictions were genuine. Nor did Hamilton, as is often charged, advocate military suppression of defiant frontiersmen in order to enhance not only his own popularity but also that of the Federalist party. He steadfastly believed, as he had commented years earlier, that "in politics as in religion, it is equally absurd to aim at making proselytes by fire and sword. Heresies in either can rarely be cured by persecution."[33] Nevertheless, the advantage of hindsight obliges one to recognize that Hamilton was prompted by some motives that were unavowed, presumably because he was unaware of them. The craving for active military duty that had soured his relationship with General Washington many years earlier had been suppressed, not abandoned. It surfaced with the opportunity to join the president on what Hamilton viewed as the most important military expedition in the new nation's history. However viewed, the presence of the secretary of the Treasury at the side of the nation's commander in chief on a military campaign against his own countrymen reinforced his critics' belief that he was a would-be Caesar, an incipient tyrant as unwilling to tolerate opposition as he was eager to stifle dissent by military force.

At 10:00 A.M. on September 30, the president, with Hamilton on his left, rode out of Philadelphia to join the troops beginning to assemble at Carlisle.[34] From there, Washington and his entourage journeyed westward to Fort Cumberland and then to Bedford, where all the militia would soon rendezvous. Having bestowed on the expedition the prestige of his personal presence, Washington returned to Philadelphia, where Congress was scheduled to convene early in November. As he stepped into his carriage on the morning of October 21, "his most personal, particular goodbye was said to Hamilton," who was left behind to assist in the successful execution of the expedition.[35] Hamilton was no doubt delighted, but the advantages to be gained by his remaining with the army were lost on virtually everyone except himself and the president. As his replacement as commander of the federal troops, Washington designated Governor Henry Lee of Virginia, whose instructions were prepared by Hamilton. The latter would no doubt have been given Lee's job had not the president been politically too astute to have made such a predictably unpopular appointment. As he may have realized, he did not need to. It was the secretary of the Treasury, as a contemporary critic said, who "gave the supreme direction to the measures that were pursued" by the western expeditionary force; his was the "paramount influence" during the army's four-week march to Washington, Pennsylvania, the cradle of the insurrection, and then to Pittsburgh.[36] Hamilton's role was made the easier by the fact that there was no armed resistance to the federal troops, not even a skirmish.

The militia did serve, however, as a visible reminder of the administration's determination to uphold the supremacy of federal laws, and the presence of federal troops dissuaded even the extremists of the antitax movement from further resistance to the excise. Nevertheless, Hamilton insisted on the arrest of the leaders of the abortive insurrection, a policy that appeared to his critics as harsh and vindictive. The secretary of the Treasury emphatically disagreed. "I hope there will be found characters fit for examples," he explained to a sympathetic president, "and who can be made so."[37] Although the task was not an easy one, Hamilton managed to ferret out such characters and declared that "all possible means are using to obtain evidence" and "accomplices will be turned against the others."[38] By mid-November hundreds of alleged insurgents had been interrogated, and 150 of them had been imprisoned, awaiting trial in Pittsburgh.

Hamilton was at his most imperious. De facto commander of the western expedition, he enjoyed (with the president's covert blessing) virtually supreme power, which, to his critics, he egregiously abused. Such accusations did not in the least bother him. Nor did he—as he busily accumulated evidence of treason, interrogated rebel suspects, and made mass arrests—ponder whether he was, in fact, dealing with unrepentant rebels, dangerous insurrectionaries, contrite rioters, or mere lawbreakers. He was, however, unalterably convinced of both the necessity of the western expedition and its success.

By November 17, the troops were in readiness for the long march home, and two days later Hamilton himself set out for Philadelphia. What had he accomplished by accompanying the army and by remaining with it for some four weeks following the president's return to the capital? What tangible results compensated for the added abuse heaped on him by his political opponents and their journalistic allies? Hamilton himself answered such questions this way: "It is long since I have learnt to hold popular opinion of no value," he explained to Washington. "I hope to derive from the esteem of the discerning and in internal consciousness of zealous endeavors for the public good the reward of those endeavors."[39] That he should thus have equated his own official policies and behavior with the public good was too typical to warrant comment and that he would easily earn the plaudits o[f] many fellow Federalists was certain. That he cared far more for public [ac]claim than he was willing to concede is also clear, despite his disingen[uous] disavowal of any such concern.

His ostensible disdain of public opinion was the easier becaus[e] determination to leave public office. On December 1, three days return to Philadelphia, Hamilton informed the president and the Speaker of the House of his intention to resign on January 31, 1795.[40] During the interim, he handled the bulky paper work that had accumulated during his long absence and made preparations for his official departure. He was also prodded into conducting an increasingly rancorous correspondence with his revenue commissioner, Tench Coxe, who, perceiving that his long-cherished expectation of succeeding his boss as secretary of the Treasury would not be realized, attempted to make Hamilton's final weeks in office as trying as possible. Coxe was successful in the sense that a large part of Hamilton's final two months in office was taken up in answering the Philadelphian's copious complaints and serious charges. But Coxe was wrong in believing that by discrediting his boss he could win Washington's endorsement for his own candidacy for the Treasury secretaryship.[41] Contrarily, the president's trust in Hamilton's superior ability and integrity was unshakable, and it was the latter's advice that would determine the designation of his successor. Having long since lost all confidence in Coxe (whom Hamilton viewed as a political apostate who was also dangerously devious), Hamilton's choice was Oliver Wolcott, Jr., the comptroller of the Treasury who was not only a conscientious civil servant but also a stalwart Federalist. Hamilton's judgment was sound. The Connecticut Yankee turned out to be an uncommonly able, although not an outstandingly distinguished, secretary of the Treasury. But, then, the New Yorker's act was a hard one to follow.

Hamilton's accomplishments were remarkable enough to earn for him posthumous repute as the most distinguished head of the Treasury Department in our history. For his own contemporaries, Hamilton spelled out his achievements in his last major official report, one of "the more significant and neglected of Hamilton's state papers."[42] Hamilton's "Valedictory Report" was an account of both his management of the country's finances and policies that should be pursued after his retirement.[43] It also included an incisive essay on the vitalness of public credit to viable nationhood.[44]

The first section of Hamilton's three-part report was a fiscal history of the new nation launched by the Constitution. It was thus a recounting of the policies he had proposed, an accounting of his own stewardship, and a record of his accomplishments. The report's second section set forth ten "propositions, which appear necessary . . . to complete our system of public credit."[45] Recalling that his critics had on several occasions charged him with unnecessarily obfuscating subjects that were already complex, Hamilton "took pains . . . to explain luminously each measure."[46] His major emphasis was on a proposition that not only startled his contemporary critics but that also plays hob with the familiar depiction of Hamilton as the proponent of the notion "that a public debt is a public blessing." "*The progressive accumulation of debt,*" Hamilton commented, "*must ultimately endanger Government.*" To remove such a dire possibility Hamilton recommended the national debt be extinguished by using existing sources of revenue providing additional revenue for the sinking fund, which must, he urged, be "inviolably applied" to the payment of the public debt

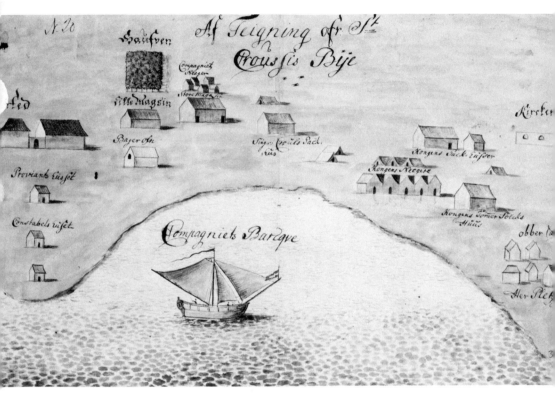

St. Croix's Town. Watercolor, ca. 1740. Rachel Faucett, Hamilton's mother, met her first husband, John Michael Lavien, on the Danish island of St. Croix in the 1740s. She was briefly imprisoned there, pending decision on a complaint filed by her husband charging her with adultery. Once out of prison, she abandoned Lavien and her four-year-old son, Peter, and fled to "an English island," probably Nevis, where she met James Hamilton. *Courtesy State Archives, Copenhagen*

Alexander Hamilton. Oil painting, P. T. Weaver, ca. 1799. Hamilton's journey to the American colonies in 1772 was made possible largely by Nicholas Cruger, his employer in St. Croix. He arrived first in Boston, then traveled to New York three weeks later, where funds for his support had been entrusted to Cornelius Kortright. He soon headed for Elizabethtown, New Jersey, to attend preparatory school. In Elizabethtown he was introduced to two of New Jersey's leading citizens, Elias Boudinot and William Livingston. *Courtesy the Museum of the City of New York*

Elizabeth Hamilton. Portrait, Ralph Early. Daughter of General Philip and Catherine Schuyler, Elizabeth met Hamilton in the fall of 1779 in Morristown, New Jersey, where he was serving as aide-de-camp to General Washington. They were married in the Schuyler mansion in Albany, New York, in December 1780. *Courtesy the Museum of the City of New York*

Alexander Hamilton. Oil painting, P. T. Weaver, ca. 1799. Hamilton's journey to the American colonies in 1772 was made possible largely by Nicholas Cruger, his employer in St. Croix. He arrived first in Boston, then traveled to New York three weeks later, where funds for his support had been entrusted to Cornelius Kortright. He soon headed for Elizabethtown, New Jersey, to attend preparatory school. In Elizabethtown he was introduced to two of New Jersey's leading citizens, Elias Boudinot and William Livingston. *Courtesy the Museum of the City of New York*

Elizabeth Hamilton. Portrait, Ralph Early. Daughter of General Philip and Catherine Schuyler, Elizabeth met Hamilton in the fall of 1779 in Morristown, New Jersey, where he was serving as aide-de-camp to General Washington. They were married in the Schuyler mansion in Albany, New York, in December 1780. *Courtesy the Museum of the City of New York*

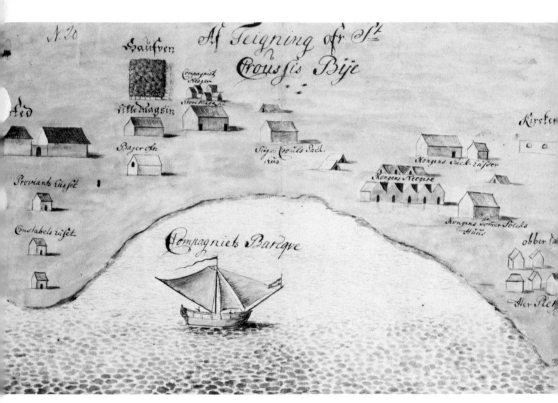

St. Croix's Town. Watercolor, ca. 1740. Rachel Faucett, Hamilton's mother, met her first husband, John Michael Lavien, on the Danish island of St. Croix in the 1740s. She was briefly imprisoned there, pending decision on a complaint filed by her husband charging her with adultery. Once out of prison, she abandoned Lavien and her four-year-old son, Peter, and fled to ''an English island,'' probably Nevis, where she met James Hamilton. *Courtesy State Archives, Copenhagen*

The Schuyler House in Albany. Watercolor, Philip Hooker, 1818, drawn on a real estate prospectus when the property was up for sale. Alexander and Elizabeth Hamilton lived with General and Mrs. Schuyler in this impressive mansion for a good part of 1782 and 1783. In 1783, the Hamiltons settled on Wall Street in New York City. *Courtesy the New-York Historical Society*

General Philip John Schuyler. Portrait, John Trumbull. Soldier, statesman, and landowner, General Schuyler had connections encompassing virtually the whole aristocracy of New York State. He unhesitatingly and warmly welcomed Hamilton, with no fortune and shadowy antecedents, into his family as his son-in-law and greatly influenced Hamilton's career. *Courtesy the New-York Historical Society*

Lt. Col. John Laurens. Etching, E. B. Hall. The son of Henry Laurens, a rich South Carolina merchant-planter and prominent member of the Continental Congress, John Laurens was Hamilton's most intimate associate. In the letters Hamilton wrote to Laurens while they were both aides to General Washington, Hamilton dropped the formality customary in his other correspondence. *Courtesy the New York Public Library*

George Washington. Crayon drawing, C. B. J. F. de Saint-Mémin; said to be the last portrait done from life. Hamilton became Washington's aide-de-camp on March 1, 1777. To its members, Washington's staff was known as "the family." Washington's association with Hamilton was at the outset harmonious and became in time one of the most creative in American history. *Courtesy the New York Public Library*

The State House in Philadelphia. Engraving, Charles Willson Peale, 1787. After a drawing by James Trenchard. The Continental Congress was meeting in Philadelphia when Hamilton arrived as a New York delegate in November 1782. The State House was surrounded in June 1783 by disgruntled soldiers of the Pennsylvania Line demanding back pay. A humiliated Congress, still temporizing on the demands, was obliged to retreat to Princeton. A month or so later, Hamilton resigned and returned to New York. *Courtesy the New York Public Library*

James Madison. Portrait, James Sharpless, ca. 1796. In an effort to win New York's ratification of the Constitution in 1787, Hamilton and Madison formed a literary collaboration that is perhaps the most constructive in American political history. *The Federalist,* eighty-five essays (only four of which were written by John Jay) published under the name "Publius," was instrumental in securing ratification. *Courtesy the Independence National Historical Park Collection*

Thomas Jefferson. Portrait, John Trumbull. The quarrel between Jefferson (first secretary of state) and Hamilton (first secretary of the Treasury) is the best known and historically important in American political history. A clash between two such egocentric, strong willed, ambitious men was inevitable and was heightened by the unavowed wish of each to be Washington's principal and most trusted adviser. *Courtesy the Metropolitan Museum of Art. All rights reserved*

John Adams. Engraving from original portrait by Gilbert Stuart. Hamilton's confidence in president-elect Adams's sound judgment and probity was not reciprocated by Adams. During the 1796 presidential campaign, Adams initially refused to credit gossip that Hamilton was plotting to elect Thomas Pinckney president and to relegate Adams to the vice-presidency. But as rumors multiplied, so Adams's confidence in Hamilton's integrity dwindled. *Courtesy the New-York Historical Society*

The Grange, 1895. By 1801, Hamilton had purchased about thirty acres of land in Harlem, then some eight miles north of the center of New York City, that extended from a wooded height to the Hudson River. Designed by John McComb, the two-story house built on the site was christened The Grange, the name both of the ancestral Hamilton estate in Ayrshire and the St. Croix plantation of the Lytton family, his early guardians. *Courtesy the Museum of the City of New York, the J. Clarence Davies Collection*

Aaron Burr. Portrait, John Vanderlyn, 1809. Called a man "of irregular and insatiable ambition" by Hamilton, Burr sought revenge for Hamilton's years of public and private invective against him. Shortly after dawn on July 11, 1804, in Weehawken, New Jersey, Burr mortally wounded Hamilton in a duel with pistols. Hamilton died the following day. *Courtesy the New-York Historical Society*

Alexander Hamilton. Portrait, John Trumbull. This portrait was painted in 1806, two years after Hamilton's death. *Courtesy the Museum of Fine Arts, Boston, bequest of Robert C. Winthrop. Copyright © 1980. All rights reserved, Museum of Fine Arts, Boston*

within a determinate period. Nor should any new debt be created without the simultaneous provision of means of redemption. Hamilton confidently predicted that if his recommendations were followed, the national debt would be discharged in thirty years. Hamilton, in sum, presented "a grand design for extinguishing the entire debt."[47] Here, his critics charged, was the ultimate irony—a proposal by the man who was responsible for the creation and perpetuation of the public debt that the latter would be a national curse and therefore must be extinguished. To Hamilton's opponents the situation may have been ironical, but it also placed them in a predicament. As Fisher Ames, one of Hamilton's warmest partisans, explained, the Republicans had "trained their men to bawl for a reduction of the debt; and now it is proposed and urged, they are grovelled, for still they would oppose."[48]

The theme of the final section of Hamilton's report was a refutation of the notions that the government had "the right of taxing the public funds" or "of sequestering them in time of war." Although he convincingly rebutted such beliefs, the conclusion of his report was more memorable as a masterful essay on the imperativeness of sound public credit. The latter "might be emphatically called the invigorating principle," he wrote. "No well informed man can cast a retrospective eye over the progress of the United States, from their infancy to the present period, without being convinced" that the establishment of public credit had played "a principal agency in that increase of national and individual welfare, since the establishment of the present Government which is so generally felt and acknowledged though the causes of it are not as generally understood."[49] This was, obviously, another way of saying that to Hamilton himself was due all honor and glory for enhancing the nation's economic growth and promoting its prosperity. It was an immodest claim but nonetheless a valid one.

The prominent niche that Hamilton occupies in the gallery of famous Americans is primarily owing to his achievements as the new nation's first secretary of the Treasury. It is as idle to speculate about his historical repute had he not held that office as it is futile to conjecture whether the history of that era would have been the same or different had another man held that office. What Justice Oliver W. Holmes once said of John Marshall applies equally well to Hamilton: "A great man represents . . . a strategic point in the campaign of history, and part of his greatness consists of his being there."[50]

Hamilton's exceptional accomplishment was to define the infant nation's problems and to propose immediate and long-range programs to solve them. Most of Hamilton's policies were neither unique nor unfamiliar, but Hamilton provided the requisitely creative inspiration and energetic eagerness. "It is a rare occurrence under popular government," Frederick Oliver, one of Hamilton's most astute biographers, commented in 1906, "for a young statesman to hold the predominant power, for the polity of a nation to be moulded by the thoughts of a fresh and eager mind, and executed by the vigour of a spirit not yet tamed to an immoderate reverence for obstacles. For where the people hold the ultimate control, a patient dexterity, with which no man was ever born, has in the long game of politics an undue advantage. Youth, with a wise instinct, abstains as a rule from conspicuous activity in serious matters until it has acquired the craft which is the necessary complement of its force."[51] That Hamilton was precisely this kind of young statesman was largely attributable to his status as an atypical rather than archetypal American of that day. Acquired rather than inherited, his commitment to American nationalism was unrestrained by provincial attachments. Hamilton's career as secretary of the Treasury was the fruition of the continental vision that from the outset had marked his attachment to his adopted country. The national exigencies of the post-Revolutionary years required precisely that type of prescience. Hamilton was thus not only in the right place at the right time but was also uniquely the right man.

As secretary of the Treasury, Hamilton's primary concern and major accomplishment, as has repeatedly been said, was the secure establishment of public credit. The latter, as he reaffirmed on the eve of his retirement, "is not only one of the main pillars of the public safety—it is among the principal engines of useful interprise and internal improvement."[52] Hamilton's program, as Bray Hammond observed, "combined magnitude and comprehensiveness, on the one hand, with, on the other, meticulousness in detail and a thorough understanding of all he was talking about."[53] If genius, as Lord Acton once observed, "deserves to be judged by its own best performance," then any appraisal of Hamilton should be based on his major state papers.

Hamilton was one of America's most farsighted statesmen, and (although the judgment is at odds with the traditional historical account) his program was for his day revolutionary. "In one sense," George Dangerfield, a prominent historian of our day, has explained, "the American Revolution was not complete until the government set up by the Constitution of 1787 established its credit abroad" by adoption of Hamilton's fiscal policies.[54] Thus viewed, Hamilton's program was one of the most constructive achievements in America's early national history.

Hamilton's contributions to the history of the new republic were not confined to his official reports. His accomplishments were manifold, among them these: he helped to assure the supremacy of the national government by making the Constitution, in Bray Hammond's words, "a plenary charter for a national government to which the states would be ineluctably subordinated[55]"; he established high standards for public administration and in fact was, as Leonard White concludes, "the greatest administrative genius of his generation in America, and one of the greatest administrators of all time[56]"; he was the most prominent of the young nation's proponents of a carefully planned and centrally managed economy, of what might appropriately be termed "state capitalism."[57]

To point only to Hamilton's innovative ideas and accomplishments is not to imply that his program was perfect or his official career flawless. Supremely confident of the correctness of his policies, Hamilton never considered that alternative ones might be feasible, as, in fact, they often were.

Serenely certain of his own superior ability, he seems on occasion to have believed that exemplary administration was the hallmark of good government rather than its structure or goals. Convinced that whatever course he pursued was invariably the right one, he quite naturally concluded that it merited public endorsement. When this did not happen he adopted a stance of indifference to, or even disdain of, public opinion. Actually, he cherished popularity but often did not know how to win it, thus, by way of compensation, sometimes coming perilously close to accepting the notion that the measure of the merits of his policies was their unpopularity.

Why was public acclaim denied Hamilton? His failure to win the people's affection may have been due to the very nature of his program. The restoration of public credit and thus viable nationhood were not issues (funding, assumption, revenue measures, international monetary arrangements, and the like) that captured the popular imagination. Nor were his policies inspired by any unifying moral (as distinguished from national) purpose that might have earned him the approbation of the common man. He spoke for them, not to them.[58] Hamilton did not, despite his occasional disclaimers to the contrary, disdain public opinion. What he cherished above all else was a "love of fame, the ruling passion of the noblest minds."[59] And he was aware that such recognition must often be posthumously bestowed.

Nevertheless, in Hamilton's own lifetime his achievements were acknowledged by many notable Americans, by none more appreciatively than Washington. Shortly after Hamilton's resignation on January 31, 1795, he received from the president what Broadus Mitchell has described as "the top testimonial in American history."[60] The president wrote, "In every relation, which you have borne to me, I have found that my confidence in your talents, exertions, and integrity, has been well placed. I the more freely render this testimony of my approbation, because I speak from opportunities of information which cannot deceive me, and which Furnish satisfactory proof of your title to public regard."[61] Such praise no doubt strengthened Hamilton's conviction that "the esteem of the discerning" outweighed by far the plaudits of the people.[62] For the moment neither counted as much as his relinquishment of public service and a return to private life. But he could, no more than his great rival, Thomas Jefferson, divorce himself from affairs of state. Nor could Hamilton refrain from doing unofficially what he for five years had officially done: he was soon advising the president, his cabinet, and Federalist congressmen on virtually the whole range of national problems.

XIV

Legal Luminary
and
Gray Eminence

Upon resigning as secretary of the Treasury, Hamilton did not intend to substitute unofficial advice for formal administrative decisions. "Having contributed to place [the finances] of the nation on a good footing," he wrote to Angelica Church, "I go to take a little care of my own: which need my care not a little."[1] His more implacable opponents refused to believe that a man as corrupt as they considered Hamilton to be had not diverted to his own account some of the millions of dollars in public funds that he had handled as secretary of the Treasury. Actually, the New Yorker's financial situation, as his friend Brockholst Livingston commented, "had been greatly injured, if not entirely ruined by that gentleman's attention to public business."[2] Hamilton agreed. His debts probably exceeded his assets, he said, and should he die his family would be dependent on "the benevolence of others."[3] According to Robert Troup, his college classmate, Hamilton's financial condition was even worse than the latter knew. Urging Hamilton to join him in large-scale land speculation, Troup commented that otherwise, as he had often said, "your friends would be obliged to bury you at their expence."[4] But Hamilton had neither the necessary funds nor any desire to take part in land speculation, that era's economic extravaganza.[5]

Hamilton aspired not to riches but merely to an income sufficient to support comfortably his growing family. By 1795 there were five Hamilton children, the oldest of whom, Philip, was thirteen, and the youngest, John Church, two and a half, and there would presumably be more. That his family had been kept well above the poverty line and that as Treasury secretary he had contrived to maintain a style of living at least not embarrassing to a high government official was almost certainly owing to the financial assistance of his father-in-law, Philip Schuyler. But from the outset of his marriage Hamilton had been determined to make his own way, and although grateful for Schuyler's generosity (most of which was no doubt surreptitiously provided through Elizabeth Hamilton), Hamilton was made uneasy by financial dependence of any kind or degree. That he had accepted any assistance at all was only because the irresistible appeal of high public office outweighed most other considerations. As a private citizen, he was in a position to renew his resolve to be altogether financially independent. His legal expertness made that possible.

Hamilton did not immediately reopen his law office, however. He and his family left Philadelphia in mid-February and traveled at a leisurely pace to New York City, where they stayed for about two weeks. On February 27, that city's chamber of commerce staged an elaborate banquet "in Testimony of their Esteem" for Hamilton. Attended by more than two hundred prominent citizens, the event, as described by the local press, was characterized by "great decorum as well as conviviality" and the guests expressed peculiar satisfaction in this opportunity, of demonstrating their respect for a man who, by discharging the duties of an important office, "has deserved well of his country."[6] Early in March, the Hamilton family arrived at the Schuyler mansion, where they planned to remain, so Hamilton wrote to Angelica Church, "till June, when we become stationary at New York, where I resume the practice of law."[7] For Hamilton to take such a long vacation seems oddly out of character, but he stuck to his plans and remained in Albany for three months. He even atypically permitted himself the luxury of a week-long sight-seeing tour. Accompanied by Henry Glen, an acquaintance from Schenectady, Hamilton leisurely traveled to Cooperstown, where he visited the grand seignior of that village, Judge William Cooper. Soon after his return from this excursion, Hamilton left for New York City, and by the beginning of June, having rented a house at 63 Pine Street that served both as living quarters and law office, he had resumed his law practice.

It was not long before Hamilton became the most prominent, if not the most prosperous, lawyer in New York. His clients included, in the words of his grandson, "nearly every one of wealth and influence in New York."[8] Among that number were Walter Livingston, William Bayard, Herman Le Roy, James McEvers, Benjamin Walker, and James Watson. The attorneys with whom he was associated in important litigation constituted the luminaries of the New York bar, including Troup, Richard Harison, Brockholst Livingston, and Burr. Although Hamilton's fees were modest, his income steadily mounted, rising to three or four times the paltry salary of $3,000 a year that he had struggled to get along on as secretary of the Treasury.

Hamilton's practice was not limited to New York alone; it extended also to wealthy litigants from other states, both individuals and partnerships. What we would call his "corporate practice" was particularly lucrative. He was regularly retained by the Bank of New York. He represented the Yazoo claimants to millions of acres of land in Georgia, and large-scale land companies, such as the Holland Land Company (formed in 1796 by a consortium of Dutch banking firms), that owned vast tracts of land in western New York and Pennsylvania. The bulk of his civil practice, however, involved maritime litigation, which owing to British and especially French depredations on United States commerce crowded court dockets during these years. He served as counsel for individual shipowners, but his major client was the United Insurance Company, whose business was large enough to have kept a lawyer less industrious and able than Hamilton busy full time.

Hamilton's single most important admiralty case was *Le Guen v. Gouverneur and Kemble,* in which he, along with Burr and Richard Harison, represented the plaintiff. The suit, which involved the sale and export to Europe of large quantities of cotton and indigo by Gouverneur and Kemble as agents for Le Guen, dragged on in court after court for some five years. In the end, Hamilton won for Le Guen a judgment of approximately $120,000, probably the largest award up until that time in a personal damage suit. A grateful Le Guen wanted to pay Hamilton a fee commensurate with the size of the judgment, but the latter would accept no more than $1,500. (Burr unhesitatingly asked for a fee several times larger.)[9]

Upon the resumption of his law practice, Hamilton had intended to confine his activities to state courts (where litigation was more profitable and challenging) and to forgo appearances before the United States Supreme Court. In one signal instance he relented, however, and accepted the invitation of Attorney General William Bradford to represent the government in the landmark case of *Hylton v. United States.*[10] At issue was the constitutionality of the carriage tax, which was among the excise measures proposed by Hamilton and adopted by Congress in 1794. The precise legal question was whether the carriage tax fell within the category of "direct" taxes that, according to the Constitution, must be apportioned among the states according to their population. To resolve the question, Treasury secretary Oliver Wolcott, Jr., decided to institute proceedings leading to a decision by the federal courts. Amicable litigation based on a statement of fictitious facts was arranged and reached the Supreme Court on appeal. Hamilton's three-hour argument, heard by a packed gallery, was so convincing that even those "in the habit of reviling him" were overcome by "his eloquence, candour and law knowledge."[11] The New Yorker contended that the carriage tax was an excise and not among the direct taxes covered by the constitutional stipulation in question. It must accordingly merely be uniform throughout the United States and was valid without apportionment among the several states.[12] The Court endorsed Hamilton's argument in a ruling that stood unchallenged until almost a century later, when the Court, in a startling departure from precedent, overruled it in holding an income tax unconstitutional. Hamilton's opinion was eventually validated by the Sixteenth Amendment to the Constitution, however.

"I hear that you have renounced every thing but your profession," William Bradford wrote to Hamilton in July 1795. "But it is in vain to kick against the pricks—You were made for a Statesman, & politics will never be out of your head."[13] Bradford was right. Public affairs continued to be

Hamilton's overarching absorption, and predictably, he could not refrain from active participation.

The issue that preoccupied Hamilton in the year 1795 was Jay's Treaty. Having played an instrumental role in the negotiations, he was now prepared to do all that he could to assure ratification of the document that Jay and Grenville had signed in November 1794. The treaty reached the secretary of state in March 1795, two months after Hamilton's official resignation. President Washington called an emergency meeting of the Senate, to which, once it convened on June 8, he submitted Jay's handiwork without any opinion of his own. After two weeks of debate conducted in secret session, the Senate, by a vote of twenty to ten (precisely equal to the two-thirds majority required by the Constitution), advised him to ratify the treaty on condition that the clause restricting American trade with the British West Indies be suspended, pending further negotiations. It was left unclear whether the president should reopen negotiations before signing the treaty or ratify it and negotiate subsequently, but he opted for the latter course and finally signed the document in mid-August.

Weeks before that time, the provisions of the treaty were leaked by its opponents to Philadelphia newspaper editors who, as a Massachusetts congressman commented, were eager "to expose it . . . for the purpose of finding fault."[14] It was an understatement. The sharp criticism and scorn heaped on the treaty by Republican editors sparked a popular furor that had not been matched since the violent days of Tory witch-hunts during the Revolution. Demonstrators surrounded the house of the British minister in Philadelphia, Jay was assailed as a traitor, and Hamilton was stoned by an angry mob in New York.[15] There were antitreaty demonstrations not only in Philadelphia and New York but also in cities and towns throughout the country. Although both the critics and proponents of the treaty pitched their arguments on the high ground of principle, the controversy was essentially partisan: Federalists stoutly defended the treaty against the shrill attacks of Republicans.

The protracted fight over Jay's Treaty was an important milestone in American political history. The conclusion reached in the 1950s by Joseph Charles is by now an historical maxim: "In its political effects, [the treaty was] the most important measure . . . between the institution of Hamilton's financial program and the election of 1800."[16] Not only did the treaty controversy signify the maturity of the country's first political parties, but it also occasioned fundamental shifts in partisan loyalties. An influential number of prominent public figures who had steadfastly supported the Washington administration—among them, John Dickinson, John Langdon of New Hampshire, Charles Pinckney of South Carolina—now openly embraced the Republican opposition.[17]

If one views Jay's Treaty in the perspective that the passage of time presumably lends to historical controversies, one wonders how this peacetime treaty dealing with matters such as the rights accorded to neutrals under international law, the size of United States vessels to be admitted to British

West Indian ports, or the procedures for the adjudication of boundary and spoliation claims could have provided the catalyst for the maturation of the nation's first party system. The explanation perhaps lies in the popular perception of injured national pride: the belief that the realization of national identity and autonomy demanded that the foremost power of the Old World unreservedly acknowledge the full sovereignty of a new nation whose maritime and neutral rights (as well as other claims that were at issue in Jay's Treaty) were not open to negotiation. For these and for manifestly partisan reasons, most Republicans, ignoring diplomatic and military realities, considered confrontation better than a compromise based on concessions, even minor ones. To a few hard-liners, war itself was preferable to a settlement as imperfect as the one Jay had accepted. Such extremists ("A numerous party among us," Hamilton said) were "steadily endeavoring to make the United States a party in the present European war, by advocating all those measures which would broaden the breach between us and Great Britain and by resisting all those which would tend to close it."[18]

Nevertheless, had there been a public referendum on the issue, Jay's Treaty would no doubt have been roundly rejected. But the decision was up to the Senate, and that body, acting in secret session, advised the president to conditionally ratify it. Washington complied, but the partisan storm raised by the treaty did not abate. It changed direction, however. Mass meetings, effigy hangings, and the like were replaced by verbal battles that dominated the nation's newspapers. Dozens of scribblers scathingly denounced Jay's Treaty in tediously long articles that led one treaty-weary observer to remark that the document had more critics than readers.[19] Its closest reader and stoutest champion was "Camillus," the pen name that Hamilton and Rufus King chose for the numerous and lengthy essays in which they dissected and defended virtually every aspect of every article of the treaty, producing in the process what a recent diplomatic historian had described as "a Federalist manifesto on foreign policy."[20] Of the thirty-eight essays (which beginning on July 22, 1795, appeared in the *New York Argus* and were widely reprinted elsewhere), King prepared the ten numbers that centered on the maritime and commercial articles of the treaty[21] and Hamilton wrote the rest. A third New Yorker served as behind-the-scenes editor and consultant. John Jay, surely the nation's foremost authority on his own work, readily provided advice on virtually every essay.[22] According all due acknowledgment to King's collaboration and Jay's consultation, however, the voice of Camillus was primarily Hamilton's.[23]

As did other Federalist publicists, Hamilton predictably and cleverly glided over the shortcomings and extolled the advantages of a treaty that was widely denounced as inconsistent with America's national interests and a violation of its treaty commitments to France. Denying such allegations, he examined the several clauses of the treaty not only to refute the objections that had been raised against them but also to demonstrate that they represented the maximum concessions that Britain was willing to make. Hamilton insisted that there was no point in harping on which party to the peace treaty of 1783 was guiltier of breach of promise. Not only was the question point-less but, from the United States' standpoint, embarrassing: the initial and principal infringements, Hamilton disingenuously argued, had been by the Americans. But for the most part, Hamilton tried to avoid the attribution of blame to one side or the other, depicting it as essentially irrelevant. His performance was instead a skillful juggling act, balancing England's cessions against American concessions. Britain's refusal to yield on the issue of im-pressment (a complex problem not readily solved, Hamilton argued) was balanced by its willingness to hand over the western posts, which were of inestimable importance to the United States. America's agreement that its citizens pay the debts they owed to English creditors (an indisputable, ines-capable, and just obligation, Hamilton said) was balanced by Britain's prom-ise to make reparations to the Americans for spoliations (a suitable remedy for a justified United States complaint). On only one substantive point did Hamilton assail Great Britain: its refusal to grant Americans more generous access to England's West Indian ports was, he argued, myopic, and the Senate had exercised sound judgment in withholding its assent to that stip-ulation of the treaty. Despite his strenuous attempt to counterpoise British capitulations against American cessions, Hamilton concluded that the En-glish had surrendered more than the Americans. Nor did the treaty, in his view, violate the Franco-American alliance or any other American interna-tional commitment. Far from deserving obloquy, John Jay merited praise for negotiating a settlement that served his country's national interest.

Although some of Hamilton's arguments were strained and his logic oc-casionally tortured, Hamilton understood more clearly than most of his con-temporaries the fundamental issue: The United States should, above all, avoid a war that might sap its ever-increasing vitality and prosperity and stifle its accelerating economic growth. Peace, not war, should be the desid-eratum of American foreign policy.

Hamilton's performance as Camillus has generally been regarded as one of his finest, second only to his accomplishment as Publius in 1787–1788.[24] His most astute English biographer, Frederick S. Oliver, overstated the fa-miliar view: There is in Hamilton's essays "a noble spirit of vigorous wis-dom. . . . Even in his onslaught upon the factions and mischief-makers he is magnanimous. . . . Looking beyond the persons of his opponents, he pours out a measureless scorn upon government by weak men and vague words; upon the policy of drift, which possesses neither the courage to fore-see results nor the energy to prepare for them."[25] Undeniably so, but equally applicable is Oliver's unintentional admission that such high praise should be subject to qualification: "Camillus is a tremendously long document. . . . The process of conquest by exhaustion is carried so far that one marvels at the heroic qualities of the generation that was wooed in such a fashion."[26] Camillus was not only a "tremendously long document" but also a prolix and at times tediously legalistic one. Oliver's attribution of "heroic quali-ties" to Hamilton's readers is, moreover, as misplaced as his belief that they were successfully "wooed." Hamilton's defense of Jay's Treaty had no discernible effect on official policy or on public opinion. If Washington carefully read all of the virtually book-length essays by Camillus (and since he was anything but an avid reader, it is doubtful), his decision to ratify the treaty was due less to Hamilton's learned essays than to the New Yorker's personal letters on the subject.[27] Certainly Camillus did nothing to allay the determination of Republican leaders to abort implementation of the treaty.

The overall strategy adopted by the antitreaty forces was refusal by the House of Representatives to appropriate funds to carry out the treaty's provisions. Their initial maneuver was a motion introduced by Edward Livingston of New York on March 2, 1796, requesting the president to submit to the House copies of Jay's instructions and all related correspondence. After three weeks of debate—"a verbal spectacle that called forth the talents and pretensions of dozens of Congressmen on both sides of the aisle"[28]—the motion was adopted. Forecasting such an outcome, Washington, convinced that such a request was unconstitutional, sought confirmation of his belief by consulting top-ranking government officials and, through the good offices of Secretary of the Treasury Oliver Wolcott, the country's top Federalist, Hamilton.[29]

Presidential acquiescence, the New Yorker replied, "cannot fail to start a new and unpleasant game" that would prove "fatal to the negotiating power of the government." At the same time, Hamilton expressed anxiety that "a too preemptory and unqualified refusal might be liable to just criticism" and recommended "much careful thought on the subject."[30] Hamilton followed his own prescription and, after pondering the issue for more than a week, came up with a list of thirteen reasons why the "usurpation" of the House should be resisted by the executive branch.[31]

On the eve of Congress' predictable approval of Livingston's motion, Washington appealed personally and confidentially to his former finance minister for advice.[32] Hamilton's reply reinforced the decision Washington had already made. "I entertain a final opinion," Hamilton wrote, "that it will be best . . . to resist in totality" the congressional request.[33] And so the president, courteously but emphatically, did: "A just regard to the Constitution and to the duty of my Office," Washington's terse message to the House concluded, "forbids a compliance with your request."[34] Would the House Republicans, conscious of Washington's heroic standing among his countrymen, acquiesce? Most Federalists would have agreed with the enthusiastic yes voiced by New Hampshire's William Plumer, who explained that "the incomparable answer of our great Chieftain . . . is very popular with the sovereign people" and has greatly "increased his fame."[35] But Republican congressmen were not dazzled by Washington's charisma. Challenging the president's contention that the Constitution did not require assent of the House to validate a treaty, Republican leaders countered with the claim that the House had the "Constitutional right and duty . . . to deliberate on the expediency" of the execution of any treaty.[36] The Constitutional issue, although significant, was largely an abstract one, however. The more immediate question was whether the House could refuse to make the requisite appropriation for implementing the treaty (a sum amounting to about $80,000), an issue that throughout the month of April preoccupied Congress, the chief executive, the press, presumably the public, and certainly party leaders. Among the last, Hamilton was the most conspicuous, and it was he who mapped out Federalist strategy.

To many disheartened Federalists the situation called for magic rather than strategy. Not only did the Republicans comprise a majority of the House, but as every roll call indicated, they were solidly united. Unless this firm majority could be broken, the appropriation necessary to carry into effect the treaty would be turned down. Hamilton's strategy was to deluge the House with protreaty petitions. "We must seize and carry along with us the public opinion," he wrote Rufus King, Federalist floor leader in the Senate. If the House refused to heed the popular clamor, other forms of pressure must be applied, among them, a public remonstrance by the president, protests by merchants in Philadelphia and elsewhere, and the decision of the Senate "to hold fast and consent to no adjournment" until the House approved the appropriation. "Great evils may result," Hamilton admonished, "unless good men play their cards well, and with promptitude and decision. . . . The glory of the President, the safety of the Constitution, the greatest interests depend upon it."[37]

Hamilton's alarm was shared by many other Federalists, particularly in New England, where a campaign to muster public opinion in support of the treaty, including a flood of petitions to Congress, was well under way even before the New Yorker had proposed such a course of action to King. "The New England States have been ready to rise in mass against the House of Representatives," Madison lamented. "Republicanism is perfectly overwhelmed."[38] In New England, yes, but not yet, as Madison well knew, in the House of Representatives, where opponents of the treaty appeared to be firmly united, as day after day they continued to lambast the treaty as an abject surrender to Great Britain, an inexcusable impugning of America's national integrity. Unless Republican ranks were broken, the treaty seemed doomed. Could this be accomplished by the protreaty campaign, headed by Hamilton and other Federalist leaders?

The first Republican defection took place on April 19 when Samuel Smith of Maryland announced that he would acquiesce in the views of his constituents, tellingly expressed in their petitions to Congress, and vote for a treaty that he still detested. Additional defections indicated that the once seemingly impregnable Republican majority was crumbling. The time had come for the Federalists to bring out their most brilliant spokesman, the eloquent orator from Massachusetts, Fisher Ames. On April 28, Ames, dressed in dark clothes, frail, looking manifestly ill, rose to speak. "Mr. Chairman," he said, "I entertain the hope, perhaps a rash one, that my strength will hold me out to speak a few minutes."[39] Using no notes, Ames's blaze of oratory lasted for an hour and a half. It was a spectacular performance, described with some exaggeration by the Speaker of the House as a display of forensic pyrotechnics "never exceeded in [this] House."[40] Ames's speech, a recent

Hamilton biographer writes, "was Camillus compressed, but with an added eloquence that none but he could have supplied."[41] Ames's oratorical skill may have swayed a wavering Republican or two, but most of the ten who switched their votes on the following day were more likely prompted by public opinion as manifested by the tidal wave of protreaty petitions or perhaps by weariness with what by now was becoming a frayed subject. The crucial vote took place on April 29, the day following Ames's speech. The result was a tie—forty-nine in favor of the appropriation, forty-nine against. The decision was up to the chairman of the Committee of the Whole, to which the subject had been handed over. Frederick Muhlenberg of Pennsylvania, nominally a Republican, sided with the Federalists to break the tie. "The late turn of the treaty question makes us all very happy," Hamilton understatedly commented.[42] Personally, he had every reason for self-congratulations. The treaty might as appropriately have been labeled Hamilton's as Jay's. It was Hamilton who was responsible for its inception, the designation of an American envoy, the instructions that the minister carried, and it was he who had taken the lead in public defense of the treaty and had masterminded the successful campaign to overcome the House's initial refusal to make the requisite appropriations.

The protracted dispute over the Constitutional rights of the House in the treaty-making process reinforced Washington's determination to resign at the end of his second term. Four years earlier he had been similarly inclined but had bowed to popular clamor and the insistence of both his official family and prominent citizens in every section of the country that his continuance in office was essential to assure "such a tone and firmness to the Government as would secure it against danger."[43] Now, in the final years of his second term, Washington was unswervingly certain that "ease and retirement" were "indispensably necessary" to him.[44] He was also convinced that despite hostility toward some policies of his own administration "a great change has been wrought in the public mind," particularly the widespread recognition of the correctness of Federalist foreign policy.[45] Thus convinced, his major concerns were the form and timing of the announcement of his retirement. His first inclination was to use a modified version of a valedictory message that James Madison, at the president's behest, had drawn up in September 1792, some months before the election of that year. Madison had tailored his work to fit the heroic mold of the foremost American of his day, a legendary figure even to his contemporaries. The Virginia congressman thus eschewed any discussion of the specific controversial issues that divided the administration, Congress, and the people at large. He chose instead to justify Washington's wish to relinquish public office and to focus on commonly cherished national sentiments, such as the perfection of the Constitution and the necessity of preserving the union.

Rereading in 1796 what his fellow Virginian had written four years earlier, Washington concluded that Madison's work had with one exception withstood the test of time: it needed only to be updated in order to take into account the "considerable changes" that had subsequently taken place both at home and abroad.''[46] The president himself undertook this assignment, penning a terse appraisal that he tacked unto Madison's draft. The most important part of Washington's contribution was a discussion of diplomatic policy, a demonstration of the extent to which foreign affairs had dominated his second administration. The president's supplement to Madison's original address was cast in the form of a list of what he called "wishes." The term was something of a misnomer for what was in fact a "collection of diverse thoughts and ideas" that were "neither closely integrated nor systematically organized,''[47] a recapitulation of the personal indignities he had endured as chief magistrate, the lamentable party divisions and other domestic difficulties he had encountered, and, to repeat, the centrality of foreign-policy problems that he had wrestled with during his second administration. Apropos of the latter subject, Washington described the dangers to be confronted, the pitfalls to be avoided, and the proper policies to be followed. Among the dangers Washington warned against was foreign influence in American domestic affairs. The pitfalls he pointed to included avoidance of both political connections with other nations and acceptance of the notion that in international relations nations are guided principally by altruistic motives. The most important policies to be followed were fidelity to treaty commitments, pride in America's distinctive nationality, adherence to a policy of genuine neutrality, and preservation of the union. The final paragraphs of Washington's addendum were an indignant rejoinder to critics who during the later years of his presidency had attacked his administration and heaped abuse on him personally. Washington here revealed that despite his stance of imperviousness to criticism he was almost as thin-skinned as his former finance minister, although certainly far more capable of suppressing his resentment.

However great or small their personal affinity, Washington unfailingly relied on Hamilton for official advice. He now called on the New Yorker to revise the rough draft of his valedictory address (Madison's original version, a few paragraphs now deleted, plus Washington's addendum, along with a brief introduction that the president also had provided). Hamilton was asked not only to edit the document but also, if he considered it necessary, "to throw the whole into a different form." Should Hamilton select the latter alternative, he was nevertheless to send along an edited or amended version of the document as submitted to him, for which Washington forthrightly expressed a decided preference.[48]

Intent that the president's farewell address bear the imprint of his own, and not Madison's, ideas, Hamilton's strategy was shrewd. Instead of submitting an edited version of the Madison-Washington essay along with his own draft of a farewell address, Hamilton, taking advantage of Washington's authorization to "throw the whole into a different form," gave all the time he could spare from mid-May until the end of July to the composition of his own version of the president's address. The description that Elizabeth Hamilton, writing decades later, gave of her husband's literary labors has been repeated by virtually every Hamilton biographer from that day to this. "The address was written," Mrs. Hamilton recalled, "principally at such times as his Office was seldom frequented by his clients and visitors, and during the absence of his students to avoid interruption; at which times he was in the habit of calling me to sit with him, that he might read to me as he wrote, in order, as he said, to discover how it sounded upon the ear, and making the remark, 'My dear Eliza, you must be to me what Molière's old nurse was to him.' ''[49]

Hamilton sent what he labeled his "Original Major Draft" to the president on July 30. In an accompanying letter, the New Yorker wrote that he had already begun to comply with the request that he also provide an amended version of the Madison-Washington address.[50] Having demonstrated his cooperativeness, Hamilton followed up with an opinion on the acceptance of which by the president he confidently counted (relying no doubt on the record of their long official relationship). "The more I have considered the matter," Hamilton confessed, "the less eligible this plan has appeared to me. There seems to be a certain awkwardness in the thing. . . . Besides that, I think that there are some ideas which will not wear well in the former address."[51] Nevertheless, Hamilton dutifully drew up a revised version of the material Washington had sent him some two months earlier (labeling it a "Draft for Incorporating"), which he forwarded to Philadelphia on August 10.[52] The New Yorker's private prediction was accurate: by this time the president was convinced of the superiority of Hamilton's "Original Major Draft," and it was this document that became the most famous presidential valedictory in American history.

It would, however, be mistaken to attribute authorship of the farewell address exclusively to Hamilton. In preparing his "Original Major Draft," he neither started de novo nor presented only his own ideas. He could not have done so even had he wished to. Although Washington did not consider himself a particularly talented literary craftsman, he was, as Hamilton recognized, a man of "strong penetration" and "sound judgment"[53] who readily issued under his signature a skillfully executed exposition of his ideas but who would never have palmed off as his own sentiments with which he in the slightest disagreed. Accordingly, the address written by Hamilton, although bearing the imprint of his particular genius and including a good many ideas uniquely his, incorporated not only in substance but also in form much of Madison's and most of Washington's drafts. A close student of the farewell address has estimated that somewhat more than one-half of Hamilton's own version directly quoted from, or paraphrased the Madison-Washington essay, while the rest was largely the New Yorker's own work.[54] Even so, Hamilton, although pleased at the prospect of thus enshrining many of his own favorite political principles, was careful to include none that were at variance with Washington's.

How then should one interpret Hamilton's role in the preparation of this deservedly famous state paper? Hamilton's skillful amplification of ideas expressed in Washington's draft and stress on principles that he believed should be the lodestars of American foreign policy transformed what otherwise would have been a memorable state paper into a "political testament" of enduring importance. So it was with Hamilton's particular mode of admonishing Americans against permanently entangling alliances with other nations, his insistent focus on the national interest as the desideratum in international relations (to him the "great rule of conduct" for American foreign policy), his heightened emphasis on the inevitability of the practice of power politics among sovereign states, and, more generally, his recognition, in Felix Gilbert's words, of the "basic issue of American foreign policy: The Tension between Idealism and Realism."[55]

XV

Period of Peril:
Public and Personal

Washington's farewell address, Fisher Ames predicted in September 1796, would "serve as a signal, like dropping a hat, for party racers to start."[1] The presidential campaign was given a boost, but the word "racers" did not properly describe the two leading contenders. Thomas Jefferson, the informal, tacit "nominee" of Republican leaders, was an unwilling candidate who revealed his reluctance to run by sitting out the campaign at Monticello. John Adams, heir presumptive to Washington, was an acknowledged aspirant but a passive participant. He too stayed at home. The campaign of each candidate was perforce run by party leaders in the various states. Their conduct of a contest between two recognized rival parties whose nominees set forth different views on major issues of the day (or, in later parlance, ran on different platforms) indicated that the first American party system had reached maturity. It was also becoming increasingly representative of the people and responsive to their wishes. The number of states in the union had by this time increased to sixteen. In eight of these, presidential electors were now selected by popular vote, and in the remaining eight, where the legislatures still chose electors, the campaign was clearly between two well-organized parties and their acknowledged chieftains.

The great issue in the campaign of 1796 was American foreign policy—whether to cement the French alliance by voting for Jefferson (even at the risk of war with Britain) or to endorse an Anglo-American rapprochement by voting for Adams (even at the price of a war with France). In other words, the election was largely a national referendum on Jay's Treaty, only narrowly approved by Congress and still anathematized by stalwart Republicans. But the proper orientation of American foreign policy was too abstract to be emotively effective, and Jay's Treaty was, after all, a fait accompli. So it happened that Republican leaders (spearheaded by Tench Coxe, one of the party's principal strategists) subtly shifted the party dialogue to more emotionally freighted issues: majority rule versus aristocracy, symbolized by French republicanism versus English monarchism.[2]

Nevertheless, the outcome of the election, as party leaders recognized, would be determined as much by geography as by ideology. New England seemed safely in Adams' camp, most of the South was solidly Jeffersonian, and so the election appeared to hinge on the Middle Atlantic states, particularly Pennsylvania, which was widely regarded as the swing state. Here in this pluralistic society, characterized by an ethnic mix and religious diversity, party lines were more rigid and statewide political organizations more efficient than elsewhere; here was the state whose vote, as Jefferson once remarked, "can generally turn the balance."[3] That the balance would be turned in the Virginian's favor was rendered likely by a Republican campaign that was masterminded by two of the nation's more adroit behind-the-scenes political manipulators—John Beckley, clerk of the House of Representatives, and Tench Coxe, once Hamilton's assistant in the Treasury Department, quondam Federalist, and now one of Jefferson's most influential political lieutenants. Beckley and Coxe deluged the state with campaign material, swamped it with stump speakers, and, in the event, managed to put Pennsylvania in the Republican column, although victory in that state alone would not assure Jefferson's election.

But what Beckley and Coxe could not unaided do, Federalist leaders unwittingly came close to accomplishing. The latter, alarmed by Adams' much-touted independence and stubbornness, his lack of popularity in the South, and his feeble support of Hamilton's fiscal policies, cast around for a way to deprive the New Englander of the presidency and to maneuver his running mate, Thomas Pinckney of South Carolina, into that office. The strategy agreed on was manipulation of the cumbersome electoral procedure prescribed by the Constitution, which, as described previously, provided that each elector cast two ballots of equal value, the candidate winning a plurality to be declared president, the second-highest vote-getter to be designated vice-president. This awkward arrangement presented neither problems nor opportunities for the Republicans, who were generally agreed that Aaron Burr be elected vice-president. According to the generally accepted version of the episode, however, northern Federalists, led by Hamilton, perceived that this Constitutional loophole might be stretched wide enough to allow Pinckney to crawl through to first place. The opportunity was provided by the fact that although the Federalist candidates appeared to enjoy equal strength north of the Potomac, Pinckney was more popular than Adams in the South and West. The strategy appeared simple: if it could be contrived that Pinckney receive one more electoral vote than Adams, while both did better than Jefferson, Pinckney would be the nation's second president.

What in the view of these Federalist schemers—Hamilton allegedly chief among them—were Pinckney's superior presidential assets? A member of the numerous and prominent South Carolina Pinckney clan, Thomas had earned national acclaim for negotiating a treaty with Spain that had broadened trade between the two nations and opened the Mississippi River to American vessels. But it was not Pinckney's diplomacy that appealed to Hamilton and like-minded Federalists but rather his presumed receptiveness to their advice if he were elected president.

Hamilton's role in such electoral chicanery has almost universally been exaggerated or misunderstood. His object was not so much to contrive Pinckney's elevation to the presidency as it was to deprive Jefferson of that office. To achieve the latter, Hamilton used all the influence he could wield to assure that Federalist electors vote equally for Adams and Pinckney. It was not that he admired, respected, or even liked John Adams but rather that he came to realize, after flirting with other possibilities, that the New Englander could not safely be jettisoned.*

In May 1796, before it was fully recognized that party unity depended on Adams' candidacy, Hamilton and Rufus King discussed the eligibility of alternative candidates. King suggested to Hamilton the farfetched notion of running Patrick Henry as the Federalist candidate.[5] But Hamilton, certain that Henry, now sixty years of age and scarred by decades of political strife, would refuse, came up with a better idea. "I am entirely of opinion," he wrote to King, "that P. H. declining Mr. P—— ought to be our man. It is even an idea of which I am fond in various lights. Indeed on later reflection, I rather wish to be rid of P. H. that we may be at liberty to take up Pinck-

---

*This was Hamilton's own version of his role, one that he carefully explained in his notorious *Letter . . . Concerning the Public Conduct and Character of John Adams,* which was published during the presidential campaign of 1800. In order to set the record straight, Hamilton's version deserves to be quoted in full: "Well-informed men knew that the event of the Election was extremely problematical; and, while the friends of Mr. JEFFERSON predicted his success with sanguine confidence, his opposers feared that he might have at least an equal chance with any Federal Candidate. To exclude him, was deemed, by the Federalists, a primary object. Those of them who possessed the best means of judging, were of opinion that it was far less important, whether Mr. ADAMS or Mr. PINCKNEY was the successful Candidate, than that Mr. JEFFERSON should not be the person; and on this principle, it was understood among them, that the two first mentioned gentlemen should be equally supported; leaving to casual accessions of votes in favor of the one or the other, to turn the scale between them. In this plan I united with good faith; in the resolution, to which I scrupulously adhered, of giving to each Candidate an equal support. This was done, wherever my influence extended."

At the same time, Hamilton conceded (as is stated in the text above) that "it is true that a faithful execution of this plan would have given Mr. PINCKNEY a somewhat better chance than Mr. ADAMS; nor shall it be concealed, that an issue favorable to the former would not have been disagreeable to me; as indeed I declared at the time, in the circle of my confidential friends. My position was, that if chance should decide in favor of Mr. PINCKNEY, it probably would not be a misfortune; since he, to every essential qualification for the office, added a temper far more discreet and conciliatory than that of Mr. ADAMS."[4]

ney.''[6] As the inevitability of Adams' candidacy was borne in on Hamilton, however, he dropped the notion of putting forth any other nominee. From May until November 4, 1796, he did not again openly propose the possibility of contriving Pinckney's election as president, although, as he publicly conceded four years later, ''it is true'' that faithful adherence to the policy of supporting Adams and Pinckney equally ''would have given Mr. PINCKNEY a somewhat better chance than Mr. ADAMS,'' an outcome that ''would not have been disagreeable to me.''[7] Nevertheless, Hamilton unswervingly insisted that ''all personal and partial considerations must be discarded, and everything must give way to the great object of excluding Jefferson.'' Commenting on the rumor that some New England electors might withhold votes from Pinckney to assure that Adams secure first place, Hamilton remarked that ''should this happen, it will be, in my opinion, a most unfortunate policy. . . . Pinckney has the chance of some votes southward and westward, which Adams has not. This will render our prospect in the main point, the exclusion of Jefferson, far better.''[8] A month later, Hamilton tersely expressed similar sentiments: ''My chief fear is that the attachment of our Eastern Friends to Mr. Adams may prevent their voting for *Pinckney* likewise,'' he commented to Jeremiah Wadsworth, ''& that some irregularity or accident may deprive us of *Adams* & let in Jefferson. . . . Tis therefore a plain policy to support Mr. Pinckney equally with Mr. Adams.''[9]

In sum, it may be that some notable Federalists contrived to again consign Adams to the vice-presidency and to choose Pinckney as Washington's successor, but Hamilton was not among them. Indeed, it is highly unlikely that there was any such systematic plot at all save in the perfervid imagination of some Republican leaders and Adams' more extreme partisans in New England. Stephen Higginson, prominent Bostonian and a stalwart supporter of Adams, explained the mistaken beliefs of the latter group to Hamilton:

> *The blind or devoted partisans of Mr. Adams . . . seem to be alarmed at the danger he was in of failing; & they have the folly to say, that this danger was incured wholly by the arrangement of pushing him & Pinckney together. They go farther & say, that this arrangement was intended to bring in Pinckney & exclude him. . . . At the head of this Junto, as they call it, they place you & Mr. Jay; & they attribute the design to him & you of excluding Mr. A: from the Chair, which the arrangement was intended to effect. . . . These Sentiments, however foolish & impudent They may appear, are dealt out freely . . . & it is believed that mr. A: himself entertains them.*[10]

Whatever the suspicions harbored by Adams and his more ardent New England partisans, it was, in the event, unnecessary for the Federalists to stoop in order to conquer. Pierre Adet, the meddlesome French minister to the United States, handed them victory on a diplomatic platter. On October 27, 1796, Adet informed Secretary of State Timothy Pickering of an *arrêt* issued some four months earlier by the French Directory stating that France "will treat the flag of neutrals in the same manner as they shall suffer it to be treated by the English."[11] In his menacing letter of explanation, the French minister minced no words—the action of his government was in retaliation for America's unpardonable partiality toward England, a favoritism exemplified by Jay's Treaty. That the purpose of Adet's bluntness was not so much to intimidate Pickering as to impress American voters was suggested by the simultaneous publication of the Frenchman's letter in the Philadelphia *Aurora,* an act that was in flagrant disregard of diplomatic protocol. Its purpose was made clearer yet by the appearance of Adet's diatribe in other leading Republican newspapers four days before the voters of Pennsylvania were to select presidential electors.

Federalists were outraged both by Adet's diplomatic gaucherie and his open interference in domestic politics, none more so than the secretary of state. Pickering promptly drew up an acrimonious answer to Adet's threats that was approved by the president and handed both to the French minister and to the newspapers on November 3. Although obliged to act swiftly, Washington was not certain that he had decided wisely. He would have preferred to have deferred an opinion until receipt of a reply to a letter that he had written to Hamilton (who was requested to consult John Jay also) the day before publication of Pickering's indignant rejoinder. While uncertain as to how the affair in general should be managed, Washington was particularly bothered by the propriety of a public airing of his administration's diplomatic correspondence. "May not the dignity of the Government be committed," he anxiously asked Hamilton, "by a Newspaper dispute with the Minister of a foreign Nation and an apparent appeal to the people?" To what extent, moreover, should Washington's personal conduct reflect the official position of the American government toward the French minister? What, Washington asked, if Adet should attend, as was his wont, the president's weekly levee: "Should he be received with the same cordiality as usual, or with coolness"?[12] To the president's first question, Hamilton's answer ("that no immediate publication of the reply which may be given ought to be made")[13] had already been superseded by the appearance of Pickering's rejoinder in Philadelphia newspapers, [14] although the New Yorker's related comment that "did I not know how guarded you will yourself be, I should be afraid of Mr. Pickerings *warmth*" reinforced the president's own doubts about the propriety of publishing official correspondence. Hamilton's related advice on American foreign policy also coincided with Washington's views. "We must if possible avoid rupture with France," Hamilton counseled, thus putting forth a position exactly contrary to that historians usually ascribe to him. To Washington's second question Hamilton suggested that Adet's conduct "ought not to pass *unnoticed*" by the president. "The true rule on this point would be to receive the Minister at your levies with a *dignified reserve,* holding an *exact medium* between an *offensive coldness* and *cordiality.* The *point* is a nice one to be hit, but no one will know better how to do it than the President."[15]

The exchange of letters was a telling demonstration of the close relationship, the mutual respect, confidence, and warmth, that had developed between Washington and Hamilton during their five-year official collaboration. Hamilton's feelings may (as his critics insist) have been tinctured by self-interest just as Washington's (as even the Virginian might himself have conceded) were colored by his need for a gifted and trusted confidant. But these things do not measurably diminish the constructiveness of their collaboration in statecraft, which was one of the most remarkable in American history. The relationship between the Virginia aristocrat and the New York arriviste also attested to the personal affection that Washington, so often depicted as reserved and aloof, could readily give and the respect and fondness that Hamilton, so frequently caricatured as coldly and arrogantly self-serving, could on occasion bestow. To put the matter in a different context (and admittedly into a twentieth-century one), Washington was perfectly typecast as the father that Hamilton's psychological wholeness required. Not all men are as lucky as was Hamilton in finding such a man. In other personal relationships, however, Hamilton would find no such satisfactory solution to deep-seated psychological problems, as his affair with Maria Reynolds would tellingly reveal. The public revelation of this unseemly sexual intrigue was in the near future. For the moment, Hamilton was still preoccupied by the presidential election of 1796.

In the crucial state of Pennsylvania, voters were to select electors on November 4. Elections in other states, however, were scheduled for different days over many succeeding weeks, and the outcome of the election was not expected until late in January. Long before that date, however, it seemed certain that the next president would be John Adams. But who would come in second? Although acknowledging the strong liklihood of his own triumph, Adams reported on December 20 that "it is supposed to be certain that Mr. Jefferson cannot be President and a narrow squeak it is, as the boys say, whether he or Pinckney shall be Daddy Vice."[16] When the electoral vote was finally counted, it was Adams who narrowly squeaked through, while the margin between the two vice-presidential contenders was not so thin as the president-elect predicted. The electoral vote was Adams seventy-one, Jefferson sixty-nine, Pinckney fifty-nine, and Aaron Burr thirty, with the remaining votes scattered among minor candidates. States in the North (except for Pennsylvania, where a smashing Republican victory came close to giving Jefferson the election) voted overwhelmingly for Adams; states in the South (save for Maryland and South Carolina, which were divided) went solidly for Jefferson. The vice-presidential vote was neither sectional in character nor close; Burr received full party support only in Pennsylvania, Kentucky, and Tennessee, and the second votes of the seventy-one Federalist electors were widely scattered. A number of Federalists from New England deserted Pinckney, thus reducing the South Carolinian's vote not only far below Adams' but also below Jefferson's. If the presumed Federalist intrigue to flout the will of the voters by elevating Pinckney to the presidency ever went beyond the talking stage (which, as was said, is doubtful), it backfired.

Not only was the South Carolinian roundly defeated but the bête noire of the Federalists would be the next vice-president. Hamilton, for one, may have found the prospect glum, but he was not surprised. He long since had perceived that "by the throwing away of votes in New England lest Pinckney should outrun Adams, it is not unlikely that Jefferson will be *Vice President*."[17]

While Republicans could take pride in their impressive show of popular strength, the Federalists, still divided, were apprehensive not only about future election prospects but also by Jefferson's presence in the new administration. Commenting on the purportedly widespread belief that Adams and Jefferson would harmoniously forge "a united and vigorous administration," Hamilton commented that "sceptics like me quietly look forward to the event—willing to hope but not prepared to believe. If Mr. Adams has *Vanity* 'tis plain a plot has been laid to take hold of it. We trust his real good sense and integrity will be a sufficient shield."[18]

Hamilton's confidence in the president-elect's sound judgment and probity was not reciprocated by Adams. During the presidential campaign, Adams had initially refused to credit gossip that the New Yorker was plotting to elect Pinckney president and to relegate Adams to the vice-presidency and another fours years of what the New Englander viewed as an official prison sentence. But as the rumors multiplied so Adams' confidence in the New Yorker's integrity dwindled. That confidence was finally demolished by Abigail Adams, whose opinions Adams tended to view as commandments or at least higher truths. Of Hamilton's alleged campaign intrigues, Abigail reminded her husband that she had often cautioned him that the New Yorker was as "ambitious as Julius Caesar, a subtle intriguer. . . . I have ever kept my eye upon him."[19] Thus warned, Adams himself took a closer look, discovering exactly what he had been told he would find. Hamilton was a "proud-spirited, conceited, aspiring mortal, . . . with as debauched morals as old Franklin." Conceding that Hamilton possessed "talents," Adams boasted that "I dread none of them. I shall take no notice of his puppyhood but . . . maintain the same conduct toward him that I always did—that is, to keep him at a distance."[20]

As Adams swiftly would learn, it was no easy task to keep Hamilton at a distance. The discovery did nothing to weaken the president's resolve, but instead turned distrust into detestation. Although usually a quick learner, Hamilton was in this instance somewhat slow in perceiving Adams' implacable animosity, and when he did, he chose not to placate Adams but to undermine and outmaneuver him. In the process, Hamilton overlooked the fact that the man he tended to scorn as a rival easily bested was, as chief magistrate, the nation's most powerful political figure. But had he been aware of that fact, Hamilton would no doubt have acted the same role. He was incapable of remaining silent on issues that in his view involved the national interest, whether these problems concerned fiscal, foreign, or any other affairs of state. Nor could he refrain from candidly giving his opinion on such affairs when asked to do so by the principal ministers of Adams' cabinet. He no more questioned the indispensability and correctness of such advice than he did its propriety. He also never doubted that at a time of national crisis he would be called on to play an active part in solving the country's problems.

These things would be demonstrated during Adams' ill-starred administration. At its outset, however, it appeared that the public surfacing of Hamilton's personal problems might consign him to political oblivion. The problem at issue in 1797 was Hamilton's own publication of the details of his amorous adventures with Maria Reynolds, a public confession that provided powerful ammunition for his political detractors.

Hamilton began this celebrated affair with Maria Reynolds in the summer of 1791. According to his own account,[21] Mrs. Reynolds called at his home on South Third Street in Philadelphia and introduced herself as a fellow New Yorker, a native of Dutchess County and related, closely or by marriage, to some of that area's most notable families.[22] Having thus established her social credentials, Maria, her manner easily conjecturable, told Hamilton a hard-luck story about being deserted by her husband and asked the Treasury secretary to lend her a small sum so that she might return home. Obviously enticed by the strong scent of seduction, Hamilton replied that "her situation was a *very interesting one*—that I was disposed to afford her assistance . . . , but this at the moment not being convenient," he would call on her that evening. When, as promised, he arrived at her house on Market Street, Maria, no coy seductress, led him right away to her bedroom. Hamilton handed over the money, and in his words, "some conversation ensued from which it was quickly apparent that other than pecuniary consolation would be acceptable."[23]

Following that evening's *affaire*, Hamilton manifestly found Maria an enchantress whose sexual spell kept him in thralldom, for he continued the liaison long after an iota of discretion would have warned him of its danger. In December 1791, James Reynolds, Maria's allegedly estranged husband, appeared on the scene, as had apparently from the outset been arranged. Unlike his wife, Reynolds could claim no connection with the New York squirearchy. Nor could he point to any personal accomplishments: his principal preoccupation seems to have been the avoidance of an occupation by chicanery or fraud. For a few days Reynolds amateurishly acted the role of outraged husband. "Sir," he wrote to Hamilton on December 15,

> *you took the advantage [of] a poor Broken harted woman. instead of being a Friend. you have acted the part of the most Cruelist man in existence. You have made a whole family miserable. She ses there is no other man that she Care for in this world. now Sir you have bin the Case of Cooling her affections for me. She was a woman. I should as suspect [as] an angel from heven. and one where all my happiness was depending. . . . But now I am determined to have satisfaction. It shant be onely one family thats miserable.*[24]

Undeceived by such saccharine professions of endangered marital bliss, Hamilton sensed immediately what kind of satisfaction Reynolds was after. Four days after his first letter to Hamilton, Reynolds conceded that his concern was not Maria's marital fidelity but blackmail: "God knowes I love the woman and wish every blessing may attend her," Reynolds piously wrote. But "I Dont think I can be Reconsiled to live with her. when I know I hant her love. . . . give me the Sum Of thousand dollars," he bluntly concluded, "and I will leve the town . . . and leve her to Yourself."[25] So long as Hamilton continued to pay for the privilege, Reynolds might well have added. Hamilton accepted the invitation to resume his visits to Maria and handed over the money.[26] Predictably, he was obligated to continue to pay: first $400, then $100, then $40. Although Reynolds was obviously willing to cut prices, Hamilton nevertheless found it increasingly difficult to support two households, a difficulty that finally outweighed his sexual obsession. In August 1792 he accordingly wrenched himself from Maria in order to free himself from Reynolds' greedy clutches. As his lust abated, Hamilton no doubt congratulated himself on being safely rid of an expensive pimp and his promiscuous wife. He should have known better.

Hamilton had been given a respite, not a release. In November 1792, James Reynolds again showed up, not in Hamilton's office but in a Philadelphia prison. This time around Reynolds' offense was not blackmail but subornation of perjury and an attempt to defraud the government. Reynolds' partner in crime was Jacob Clingman, who was in line as Maria's next lover, if not already so; the victim was one John Delabar, who was persuaded to commit perjury so that Reynolds and Clingman could pose as executives of the estate of a claimant against the United States. The attempted fraud was brought to the attention of the comptroller of the Treasury, Oliver Wolcott Jr., who immediately initiated suits against the three conspirators. Clingman promptly solicited the influence of Pennsylvania congressman Frederick A. C. Muhlenberg, former speaker of the House, for whom Clingman had once served as a clerk. The bait that Clingman held out for his own extrication was Reynolds' disclosure that he and the secretary of the Treasury had been partners in illegal speculation, an accusation that Clingman buttressed by handing over documentary evidence supplied by Reynolds as proof of the secretary of the Treasury's criminality. Its possible political repercussions prompted Muhlenberg to share the accusation with two Republican congressmen from Virginia—Senator James Monroe and Representative Abraham B. Venable. The two Virginians wasted no time in verifying Clingman's story. On December 12, within hours after Muhlenberg repeated the allegation, Monroe and Venable sought out Reynolds, who was still in prison and who affirmed the accuracy of the accusations that he had made.[27] On the evening of the same day, the Virginia detectives called on Maria Reynolds, who corroborated the story that she and her husband obviously had carefully rehearsed. The results of these interviews, plus a close examination of the incriminating documents that Reynolds had revealed, convinced the congressmen that not even a man as wily as they believed the secretary of the Treasury to be could wiggle out of the tight spot he now was in.[28]

On December 15, 1792, the three investigators called on Hamilton and explained that "information had been given them of an improper pecuniary connection between Mr. Reynolds" and the Treasury secretary and that "they had contemplated the laying the matter before the President, but before they did this, they thought it right" to give Hamilton "an opportunity of explanation."[29] It was agreed that the evening of the same day would be an appropriate time. At that meeting (also attended, at Hamilton's request, by Wolcott) Hamilton confessed to his unofficial interrogators that "my real crime" was not "improper pecuniary speculations" with Reynolds, but "an amorous connection with his wife, for a considerable time with his privity and connivance . . . with the design to extort money from me."[30] In substantiation of his statement, Hamilton handed over to the three congressmen a number of letters between him and Mr. and Mrs. Reynolds and the husband's receipts for blackmail. Satisfied that the secretary of the Treasury was guilty of adultery and not fraud, the three men assured him (so Hamilton believed) that his secret was safe and that the episode was ended. For double assurance Hamilton requested, and was accorded, permission to make copies of the incriminating documents that he had handed over to the congressmen. Monroe's retention of the originals did not trouble Hamilton, who accepted the then virtually unquestioned view that the word of a gentleman was a pledge of his honor. On that score Hamilton read Monroe correctly, despite the charges that the New Yorker would make five years later. After the meeting on the evening of December 15, 1792, Monroe, so he later recalled, "sealed up his copy of the papers mentioned and sent or delivered them to his Friend in Virginia."[31] What Hamilton failed to realize, however, was that the door to public exposure had been left ajar when the conferees had called in John Beckley, clerk of the House of Representatives and an inveterate Hamilton baiter, to make copies of the incriminating documents. For the next five and a half years Hamilton presumably heard neither a whisper about the affair nor a word about the Reynoldses. Actually, Maria had instituted proceedings in May 1793 for a divorce from Reynolds, charging that he had committed adultery. The divorce was granted about two years later, and Maria married Clingman. (In 1798, the couple were living in Virginia but subsequently moved to England. James Reynolds, like his wife, "returned to the obscurity from which he had emerged.")[32] With the passage of time Hamilton no doubt grew ever more confident that the Reynolds episode was over, the incriminating documents permanently locked up. Wishing that it were so, he perhaps conveniently forgot that a number of keys were still out, two of them in the possession of people whom he by now distrusted and who intensely disliked him—Monroe and Beckley. But, then, Monroe was for a good part of the time out of the country, serving as American minister to France, and Hamilton had no way of knowing that Beckley not only detested him personally and considered him officially corrupt but was also the most tireless purveyor of official gossip in Philadelphia.[33]

In the spring of 1797 the secret that Hamilton complacently believed to be safely hidden became public property. It was revealed by James T. Callender, one of the most unscrupulous editors of a period characterized by unprecedented journalistic scurrility. A native of Scotland, Callender had escaped to the United States following his indictment for authorship of an allegedly seditious pamphlet. In the comparatively relaxed legal climate of his adopted country, Callender specialized, without government interference, in libel rather than sedition, proving himself a master at character assassination. Hamilton was the first big target.

The attack was made in Callender's *History of the United States for 1796 . . . ,* published in July 1797.[34] The lead story in this grab bag of scandal was the charge that the former Treasury secretary was guilty of illegal speculative ventures with James Reynolds. As proof, Callender printed the documents that had been featured in the December 1792 meeting between Hamilton and his three congressional interrogators. Scorning Hamilton's "voluntary acknowledgment of seduction" as merely a shield for his speculation in public funds, Callender charged that Hamilton, alarmed that the Reynoldses might tell all, had "packed them off."[35]

From whom had Callender secured these documents that James Monroe averred had been deposited with a friend in Virginia? From Jefferson, who was Monroe's close friend and political patron and who was also on cordial terms with Callender? From Monroe, of whose guilt Hamilton himself was, as we shall see, certain? From John Beckley, who, having been recently dismissed as clerk of the House, was vengeful toward his Federalist opponents, especially Hamilton? Beckley would no doubt have considered the publication of documents incriminating such a public enemy as a public service, and most historians now agree that he appears to be the most likely source of the damaging documents that Callender gleefully presented to the public.[36]

And it was Beckley who disclosed the Hamilton-Reynolds documents, but he did not hand them over to Callender. The Virginian rather shared them with his close political ally in Pennsylvania, Tench Coxe, formerly Hamilton's chief assistant in the Treasury Department and by the mid-1790s the New Yorker's fierce enemy. In October 1796, at a time when Beckley and Coxe were managing the Republican campaign in Pennsylvania, the Virginian wrote to his political co-captain the following cryptic note: "Enclosed are Hamilton's precious confessions. Be pleased to preserve every scrap; they are *truly* original and *authenticated* by himself."[37] In view of the phrase "precious confessions," what could the enclosure have been if not the Reynolds material that Beckley had made copies of in December 1792? The supposition that it was Coxe, not Beckley, who handed over the damaging material to Callender is strengthened by the latter's emphatic denial that the quondam clerk of the House was the culprit. In the preface to his scandal sheet disguised as an annual history, Callender himself called attention to the rumor "that Mr. John Beckley is the author of this volume" and asserted that "he did not frame a single sentence of it." Such an accusation was prima facie absurd, said Callender, if only on the grounds that Beckley "is unacquainted with my handwriting, and I could not be sure to distinguish his."[38] Although there was no need to say so, Callender was familiar with the handwriting of Coxe, with whom he occasionally corresponded. This fact obviously does not prove that Coxe supplied Callender with copies of the Reynolds documents, any more than Callender's denial of Beckley's agency was necessarily the truth; but when combined with other circumstantial evidence, such as Coxe's penchant for settling scores with political enemies by anonymously publishing documentary evidence of their official and private misdeeds, the Philadelphian seems the most likely culprit. At least, this is as plausible a solution as is possible to this frequently recounted mystery story, whose conclusion can never be known with certainty.[39]

Such a solution never occurred to Hamilton, who was, in any event, far less interested in identifying the purveyor of the damaging documents than in securing from Muhlenberg, Venable, and Monroe an unequivocal statement of their unaltered belief in the absolute truthfulness of the story he had told them on the evening of December 15, 1792. To Hamilton, such an emphatic reaffirmation was the more imperative because of the publication of two documents that he had not before seen. One was a memorandum by Monroe, Muhlenberg, and Venable, dated December 16, 1792, that read: "We left him under an impression our suspicions were removed."[40] The second was a note in which Monroe described a meeting between himself and Clingman in which the latter had reaffirmed his conviction that Mrs. Reynolds was "innocent and that the defense [by Hamilton] was an imposition."[41] To Hamilton, the fact that Monroe had registered neither agreement nor disagreement with Clingman's exculpation of the Reynoldses and indictment of himself was particularly disturbing. It was essential, Hamilton decided, to get a full exoneration from Monroe—a denial both that he had left Hamilton "under an *impression*" that the Virginian's doubts were removed and that he endorsed Clingman's remarks.

The dispute resolved into one between Hamilton and Monroe alone largely because of the alacrity with which Muhlenberg and Venable satisfactorily reaffirmed their acceptance of the explanation that Hamilton had given in December 1792. Hamilton was the more disposed to pronounce Monroe guilty because of his ever-growing dislike both of the Virginian's political beliefs and associates and his conduct as United States minister plenipotentiary to France, where, as Hamilton saw the matter, Monroe had ministered to the needs of his own political allies at home and misrepresented the Washington administration. Hamilton relentlessly pursued the Virginian, cross-examining him with a pertinacity similar to that of a vengeful prosecuting attorney intent on a conviction. Conference between Monroe and Hamilton followed conference, a seemingly interminable exchange of letters ensued, and the two were at one point a hair's breadth from a duel, as Hamilton continued to ask for more than Monroe would concede and the Virginian came close to giving Hamilton what he demanded, then equivocated, then backtracked, and so on.[42]

Nevertheless, Monroe was willing to issue a statement that, while not precisely what Hamilton desired, would have included a clear presumption that the former Treasury secretary was innocent of the charges of official corruption leveled against him by Reynolds and exposed by Callender. Such a statement, combined with the exonerating affidavits supplied by Muhlenberg and Venable, would have been sufficient to clear Hamilton's name before any reasonably fair audience.

Why, then, not publish these documents, and let the matter rest? Why publicly air his personal infidelity by answering libelous charges that only those already implacably antagonistic to him would credit? What could be accomplished by a public confession of adultery other than to serve the public gratuitously a platter of delectable gossip? Hamilton was undeterred by such questions, if indeed he asked them. Obsessed with maintaining a public image of probity and also goaded by Monroe's refusal to give him the precise kind of bill of clean moral health that he demanded, he instead rashly decided to put his case before the public. This he did in the Reynolds pamphlet, published on August 25, 1797. The ninety-five page confession of adultery designed to prove himself innocent of fraud was a best seller, but predictably, it embarrassed his political allies, failed to convince those inclined to doubt his honesty, and provided additional ammunition for his political enemies. Noah Webster's judgment was sound: "What shall we say," Webster wrote some years later, "of a man who has borne some of the highest civil and military employments, who could deliberately . . . publish a history of his private intrigues, debase himself of charges which no man believed; to vindicate an integrity which a legislative act had pronounced unimpeachable?"[43]

What shall one say? Hamilton was neither the first nor the last public figure in American history to have a mistress; he is, so far as this writer knows, the only one to publish a detailed account of his affair. At that time in America, as in Europe, liaisons such as Hamilton's were no bar to political success, although circumspection and decorum were expected. Hamilton himself fulfilled such expectations until he was publicly accused of conspiring with a swindler like James Reynolds to mulct a government that, as secretary of the Treasury, he had faithfully served. Once the charge of malfeasance in office was made against him, the jettisoning of discretion seemed to Hamilton a small price to pay for salvaging his official integrity. Nor did he calculate the cost in humiliation and pain that his family, particularly his wife, would have to pay. All must be sacrificed to preserve untarnished his self-image as a selfless, dedicated, and incorruptible public servant. The self-portrait was surely a good likeness, but one is nevertheless left with the tantalizing question of why his sense of private worth, in this and other instances, so largely depended on the reflected image of public esteem.

The Reynolds affair raises yet other teasing questions. At issue in such a context is not so much why Hamilton published a full confession of his adultery but its symbolic meaning (more precisely, its psychical etiology), a problem that is not satisfactorily solved by merely pointing to the obvious, although appropriate, biosexual explanation—Maria's sensual appeal or sexual adeptness and Hamilton's merely human response. The affair rather raises tantalizing questions of a different sort: Why was Hamilton so readily lured into, and why did he compulsively continue for so long, an affair that was likely to be made public and thus besmirch his public reputation? Why was he willing to risk grievously wounding and even alienating his family? Any but the most enthralled admirer would soon have recognized that Maria's promiscuity was public knowledge and that she also was her husband's ally in blackmail. What, then, was the nature of the spell that Maria cast over him? Why did he find this particular promiscuous woman sexually irresistible? To say that she merely happened to be available is scarcely a sufficient answer. So, too, were many prostitutes, of whom Philadelphia had its fair share, as well as amorously inclined but discreet women in Hamilton's own social circle. Nor is it enough to point to what is implied by Hamilton's alleged sexual banter at social gatherings. Nor is the issue resolved by repeating the related allegation that he was oversexed and an inveterate philanderer. The charge was most bluntly made by John Adams: Hamilton's relentless ambition, the second president commented, derived from a "superabundance of secretions" that he "could not find whores enough to draw off."[44]

What calls for explanation, to repeat, is not Hamilton's behavior per se but the nature of, and reasons for, his choice of this particular partner. It can perhaps best be supplied by psychological conjecture. The conclusion seems irresistible that Hamilton was unconsciously acting out unresolved conflicts of his early life. Of whom was Maria a symbol? Even one who only begrudgingly acknowledges the application of psychoanalytical theory in biographical writing might unhesitatingly reply: Rachael Lavien. In view of his youthful attachment to his mother and his inescapable awareness of the charges of promiscuity leveled against her, could he have escaped the spell of an attractive woman, such as Maria, who in significant ways mirrored Rachael's conduct? Such speculation may be merely fanciful, but it serves as well as any other to unravel what is, in the end, an insoluble mystery. And it is pardonable for yet another reason: the Reynolds affair was one of those rare events in Hamilton's life when what was essentially a private affair intersected with, and directly affected, his public career.

For the moment, Hamilton's future in public life depended not only on a public lapse of memory about the Reynolds episode but on John Adams' appraisal not so much of Hamilton's sexual irregularities but of the latter's political usefulness and experience in statecraft. To the few people aware of the new president's deeply hued antagonism toward Hamilton, the result of such an appraisal was clear. Fortunately for him, the New Yorker was not among that small group.

XVI

Statesman in Retirement

On March 4, 1797, John Adams, wearing a new suit of pearl-colored broadcloth, was sworn in as the second president of the United States. "He assumed on this occasion," the English minister to the United States observed, "what compared with the usual simplicity of his appearance, might be looked upon as a degree of state."[1] Seated beside Adams on the elevated dais in Congress Hall were his presidential predecessor and the vice-president-elect, Thomas Jefferson. The latter, although seemingly composed, was doubtless wary of serving as the second highest official in a government controlled by a party that he only recently had contested at the polls and that he still distrusted. Washington, while outwardly as composed, even impassive, as usual, was inwardly delighted to be relinquishing an office that he had never really wanted.

Adams was on this occasion an unusually adept mind reader. His inauguration, the new president wrote, was "a solemn scene . . . made affecting to me by the presence of the General, whose countenance was as serene and unclouded as the day. He seemed to enjoy a triumph over me. Methought I heard him say, 'Ay, I am fairly out and you fairly in! See, which of us will be happiest.' "[2] Any knowledgeable student of the nation's unresolved problems or astute judge of Adams' capacity to handle them could readily have supplied the answer: the prospects for harmony at home and a respite from troubles abroad were glum. Although Adams aspired to statesmanship, he lacked the qualities essential even for presidential effectiveness—particularly the requisite managerial skill, emotional balance, impartiality, finesse, patience, and composure. More conspicuous for the envy and grudges he harbored than for his recognition of personal or party loyalty, Adams also found it difficult to acknowledge the possibility of disinterested public service by those who balked or rivaled him, a group that included a good many prominent Americans, most notably the nation's first secretary of the Treasury.

Hamilton, as has been said, was unaware of the new president's enmity, presumably because he knew of nothing he had done to warrant it. During Washington's administration the official relationship of the two men had been usually unruffled, although unaccompanied by any hint of personal affinity or cordiality. Their differences in background, experience, temperament, and aspirations, while markedly different, could be surmounted, as Hamilton's relationship with Washington readily revealed. Hamilton accordingly saw no reason why he should refrain from what he construed as the friendly gesture of offering Adams the same kind of counsel that he had frequently provided Washington, both when requested to do so and without invitation. Even should the new president prove unreceptive, Hamilton believed that he might with propriety still give guidance to members of Adams' cabinet, particularly if they asked for it.

The new chief executive and his ministers needed all the sound advice they could get. Following the ratification of Jay's Treaty, Franco-American relations had dangerously deteriorated. French leaders, unalterably convinced that the treaty signaled not only an Anglo-American detente but also an informal alliance, responded by a diplomatic counteroffensive. The newly established Directory was all the more willing to clip the wings of the fledgling nation because of France's recent military victories, among them the subjugation of Holland and the success of Napoleon's first Italian campaign.

Reaction thus followed swiftly. A first step was taken in the summer of 1796 when France suspended diplomatic relations with the United States and announced the recall of its minister, Pierre Adet. Instead of being ordered home, however, Adet was left in Philadelphia to report on American developments and to act as agent provocateur. His first assignment (executed clumsily and ineffectually) was, as we have seen, to manipulate the election of 1796 in such a way as to drive the Federalists from office, replacing them with a party friendly to France. That such political intrigue damaged more than it helped the Republicans did not deter the Directory from continuing on its ill-fated course. Its intervention in American politics had, in any event, been secondary to its assault on United States commerce. Under the authority of a series of decrees against neutral trade, French privateers, beginning in July 1796, captured every American vessel they could find that was bound to or from ports in the British empire. French prize courts obligingly condemned virtually every capture. Such an all-out maritime assault seemed likely to sweep United States ships from the high seas. By June 1797, a year after the Directory's initial decree against neutral commerce, over three hundred American vessels had been seized and, in many instances, their crews subjected to unmitigated cruelty. Nor could the United States rely on normal diplomatic channels for remonstrances.

Late in 1796, Charles C. Pinckney had been dispatched as American minister to France to replace James Monroe, whose openly pro-French position and criticism of his own government had made his diplomatic mission, in John Adams' words, "a school for scandal against his country" and "its government."[3] The Directory accorded Monroe a grand farewell party and promptly informed the new American envoy "that France would not receive another American minister until her grievances were redressed."[4] Upon receiving notice a few weeks later that he was liable to arrest if he remained in France, Pinckney left for Amsterdam, where he awaited instructions from home. One of the new president's first major tasks was to find a way out of this diplomatic imbroglio.

Although Adams would never have acknowledged the affinity, he and Hamilton shared almost identical views on how to weather the diplomatic storm then battering the new nation. In the winter of 1796–1797 and on through the spring of the latter year, Hamilton played almost perfectly the role of sage statesman in retirement. His abrasively aggressive imputation of nefarious motives to those who opposed him was replaced by an atypical display of impartiality. His program for resolving the crisis in Franco-American relations was essentially the same as the one he had recommended in 1794 for settling America's quarrel with England. Just as he had then insisted that United States policy toward Great Britain should be one of reconciliation rather than confrontation, he now argued that the United States should cultivate friendly relations with France. As he had explained to Washington on the eve of the president's retirement, "We seem to be where we were with G Britain when Mr. Jay was sent there—and I cannot discern but that the Spirit of the Policy, then pursued with regard to England will be the proper one in respect to France *viz* a solemn and final appeal to the Justice and interest of France, & if this will not do, measures of self defence. Any thing is better than absolute humiliation."[5] Hamilton's conciliatory stance represented not only a moderation of his previously strident denunciation of the French Revolution and all its works but also a rejection of the views of a prominent wing of the Federalist party whose views he had previously shared. To Federalist extremists such as William L. Smith, who in a letter to Hamilton had advocated an immediate declaration of war against France rather than protracted and predictably futile attempts at pacification, the New Yorker sharply retorted, "We seem now to feel & reason as the *Jacobins* did when Great Britain insulted and injured us, though certainly we have at least as much need of a temperate conduct now as we had then. I only say, God grant, that the public interest may not be sacrificed at the shrine of irritation & mistaken pride."[6]

Although Hamilton's admirers agreed with Oliver Wolcott's exaggerated statement that Hamilton's "influence upon the friends of government" was so great that the New Yorker had only to express an opinion on an issue and "so the thing must and will be,"[7] decisions on foreign affairs were obviously up to the president, not Hamilton. And advice from the latter was to Adams as much an affront as the very mention of the New Yorker's name was an irritant. The president's attitude was revealed soon after his inauguration in a conversation with Uriah Tracy, Federalist senator from Connecticut. Unaware that one of the nation's most prominent Federalists had been anathematized by his party's chieftain, Tracy shared with Adams a letter he had received from New York. In this letter, Hamilton (so he later recalled) had proposed "the immediate appointment of three commissioners of whom Mr. Jefferson or Mr. Madison to be one, to make another attempt to negotiate." Hamilton went further, so Adams recollected years after the event, and also recommended "a whole system of instruction for the conduct of the President, the Senate, and the House of Representatives." Frostily acknowledging Tracy's good intentions in relaying the New Yorker's advice, the president suppressed his volcanic anger. "I . . . really thought" that Hamilton "was in a delirium . . . thus to prescribe" administration policy without being consulted, Adams recorded years after he left office. "I despised and detested the letter too much to take a copy of it."[8]

Adams' disdain of Hamilton's letter was matched by his contempt for its author, to whom he apparently imputed protean power. "That letter, though it had no influence with me," the New Englander wrote, "had so much with both Houses of Congress, as to lay the foundation of the overthrow of the federal party, and of the revolution that followed four years afterwards."[9] Adams conveniently overlooked the fact that the New Yorker was at the time recommending policies that coincided exactly with the president's own: Hamilton, like Adams, believed that the best way out of the impasse in Franco-American relations was to take the diplomatic initiative. On the eve of his inauguration, the president had unsuccessfully sought to win Jefferson's consent to serve as American emissary and had then requested the vice-president to ascertain if Madison would accept appointment as a member of a diplomatic mission. That Madison was not given an opportunity to decline such a commission (which he surely would have done) was because of the reaction of Adams' cabinet, whose members threatened to resign en masse if the Virginian were named. Adams deferred to the partisan prejudices of what might be termed his secondhand cabinet.

Instead of conducting a talent hunt of his own, Adams had chosen to retain the members of Washington's cabinet—Timothy Pickering as secretary of state, Oliver Wolcott, Jr., as secretary of the Treasury, James McHenry as secretary of war, and Charles Lee as attorney general. Since they had ably served Washington, Adams was certain of their official competence; since they were manifestly stalwart Federalists, he foresaw no disagreement over public policy; since they expressed their willingness to remain in office, he had no reason to doubt their loyalty. "Pickering and all his colleagues are as much attached to me as I desire," the president-elect wrote to Elbridge Gerry in February 1797. "I have no jealousies from that quarter."[10] Adams would in time issue a blistering recantation that has long been accorded scholarly acquiescence: virtually all historians agree that Adams' department heads neither merited the president's trust nor heeded his directions but listened instead to Hamilton, the high priest of Federalism, who dictated their opinions from his New York law office. Like so many other stereotyped interpretations, however, this one should be qualified. That Hamilton had enjoyed Washington's unalloyed confidence and friendship during the two years following the New Yorker's official retirement did indeed lead him to believe that his counsel would continue to be appreciated. He thus unhesitatingly, and perhaps without pondering the reaction of a new and prickly chief executive, offered his advice to high-ranking government officials who often asked for, and gratefully acknowledged, it. Among these were the principal members of Adams' cabinet, Pickering, Wolcott, and McHenry, who as in the past often solicited, and were guided by, the opinions of their longtime friend. But the frequency, nature, extent, and effect of the New Yorker's influence has been greatly magnified.

Because Adams granted his cabinet members wide discretion in the management of their departments, accepting most of their decisions without question, and because of the president's prolonged absences from the capital, the department heads were necessarily obliged to act not merely as executors of policy but also as policy-makers. In exercising that responsibility they turned for advice to other leading Federalists, among them Hamilton. The response of Adams' cabinet members to Hamilton's advice differed, however: Pickering, staunchly independent and supremely confident of his own ability, felt as free to reject as to follow Hamilton's counsel, which, in point of fact, was only infrequently proffered. Wolcott, also an independent man and one who was unquestionably capable of running his department without tutelage from New York, was more receptive to the views of his predecessor. But Hamilton was only one of the Federalist leaders with whom Wolcott corresponded and who also gave him advice. The Connecticut Yankee accepted or rejected proposed policies (Hamilton's as well as those recommended by others) as his own judgment dictated. The one cabinet official who needed, asked for, and unquestionably followed instructions from New York was James McHenry. But the situation was due not to Hamilton's quest for power but to McHenry's administrative incompetence. The secretary of war, as Hamilton confided to Washington, "is wholly insufficient for his place, with the additional misfortune of not having himself the least suspicion of the fact!"

Whatever the extent of Hamilton's influence on Adams' cabinet, there was (historical traditionalism to the contrary) no serious rift between the latter and the president until the winter of 1799, when Adams, on his own initiative and without consultation with his department heads, adopted a new departure in American foreign policy.[11] Until that time, Adams and his cabinet worked together harmoniously, largely because for the most part they agreed on the broad outlines of government policy, particularly on the conduct of diplomacy. And during Adams' administration foreign affairs overshadowed all else.

In view of the menacing attitude of the French expressed both by the summary dismissal of Pinckney and continued depredations on American commerce, Adams issued in late March a proclamation calling a special session of Congress to convene on May 15, 1797. In his opening address the president decried the Directory's distinction between the people of America and their government and affirmed his intention of preserving national honor while at the same time pursuing a just settlement of the Franco-American dispute.[12] To that end, Adams nominated, and the Senate confirmed, a three-man diplomatic mission, consisting of Pinckney, John Marshall, and Elbridge Gerry. While thus seeking a rapprochement, Adams also recommended to Congress proposals for strengthening America's defense. Congress grudgingly obliged by authorizing a small loan and a slight tax increase, appropriating a paltry sum for fortifications and passing an act for the completion of three frigates—the *Constitution,* the *President,* and the *United States.*

The reluctance of the Federalist majority in Congress to endorse the program of their party's president had been foreshadowed by the chilly reception the House had accorded Adams' proposal that the United States take the initiative in reaching a rapprochement with France. Hamilton was on the president's side: "I like very well the course of Executive Conduct in regard to the Controversy with France . . . but I confess I have not been well satisfied with the answer reported in the House," the New Yorker wrote to Wolcott on June 6. "It contained too many hard expressions; and *hard words* are very rarely useful in public proceedings. . . . *Real firmness* is good for every thing—*strut* is good for nothing."[13] Over the months following, Hamilton's absorption in public issues gave way to his engrossment in personal affairs as he strove from July 1797 and on into the succeeding year to clear himself of James Reynolds' charges of official misconduct and to unmask the slanderer who had publicized the accusations. By the time this absorption abated, the diplomatic mission appointed by Adams to reach a Franco-American accord had failed and the two nations hovered on the brink of war.

From the time of their arrival in Paris, the American envoys were obliged to confront the remote possibility of success. As if intent on pushing the United States into war, Talleyrand, who had for some years been an exile in America and was now French foreign minister, instructed his agents—the notorious X, Y, and Z—to demand of the United States envoys an apology for President Adams' criticism of France in his May 1797 address to Congress, a "douceur for the pocket" of 12 million livres, and a large loan.[14] Two of the Americans, Marshall and Pinckney, accurately averred that they were unauthorized to accede to any of these demands and, convinced that France was in any event unwilling to negotiate with the United States, demanded their passports. Gerry, presumptuously assuming that, instructions or not, he might contrive to avoid a war, remained in Paris some four months longer, until Talleyrand's gibes and insults forced him to leave.

When the XYZ dispatches reached Philadelphia in March 1798, the president and his advisers were incensed by what they viewed as an unmitigated insult to the independence of the United States and an invitation to war. An overwhelming majority of Americans agreed, and the Federalists found themselves more popular than they had been since the first year of Washington's administration. Messages of support poured into the office of the president, who, presumably in a state of shock over the rude reception accorded his peace mission, dashed off bellicose replies that dismayed even some of his fellow Federalists, among them Hamilton, who described such presidential pronouncements as "intemperate & revolutionary."[15]

Hamilton, while criticizing Adams' rashness, fell into the same pattern in a series of articles entitled "The Stand," which were published in March and April 1798.[16] Even his most admiring modern biographer concedes that "the excited rhetoric" of these pieces "is not so convincing as at calmer moments Hamilton knew how to be."[17] The moderation that he had displayed a year earlier was now gone, the mantle of statesman replaced by the garb of demagogue. France "was the most flagitious, despotic, and vindictive government that ever disgraced the annals of mankind," he exaggeratedly exhorted, "a volcano of atheism, depravity, and absurdity." How could his countrymen calmly view "the disgusting specticle of the French Revolution"? How could they tolerate in their midst a "high priest of this sect" (Jefferson, of course), who was "of so seditious, so prostitute a character" as to look forward to becoming "the proconsul of a despotic Directory over the United States, degraded to the condition of a province"?[18] Here was a startling replay of Hamilton's pseudonymous defamation of the secretary of state in 1792. Had his steadfast belief that one of Jefferson's most dedicated adherents, James Monroe, was responsible for public exposure of Reynolds' malicious charges led imperceptibly to a renewal of the conviction that Virginia's most prominent Republican was the nation's most deadly enemy? More likely, Hamilton on this occasion unthinkingly donned once again the well-worn garb of partisan gladiator. But not for long. He soon resumed (perhaps unwittingly) the role of gray eminence, which he had played during the previous year. It all suggested that Hamilton was capable of acting not one but many parts, the self-casting depending largely on fluctuating moods that he himself could not have explained.

While Hamilton was writing his intemperate attack on France, he was, somewhat contradictorily, also proposing to Timothy Pickering and other influential government officials a comparatively moderate program based on his conviction that the price of peace was preparation for war. Since France's refusal to receive America's ministers was clearly "a virtual denial of our Independence that must if necessary be defended," Hamilton counseled, the United States must "take vigorous and comprehensive measures of defense." At the same time, the administration must be flexible, "leaving still the door to accommodation open and not proceeding to final rupture."[19] The preparedness program prescribed by Hamilton largely prefigured the measures that Congress would adopt—permission for American merchant vessels "to arm and capture those which may attack them," completion of previously authorized frigates and the building of "a considerable number of sloops of war," the augmentation of the regular army and the raising of a provisional one, and an increase in revenue to pay for these measures.[20] Hamilton's advocacy of such a program was not new. He had proposed a similar one in the spring of 1794 when war with England seemed imminent. "We ought to be in a respectable military posture," the secretary of the Treasury had then advised the nation's commander in chief, "because war

may come upon us, whether we choose it or not and because to be in a
condition to defend ourselves . . . will be the best method of securing our
peace.'' In sum, underpinning Hamilton's program in 1798, as in 1794, was
his belief that national ''safety can only be found in uniting energy with
moderation.''[21]

President Adams' reaction to the XYZ affair was energetic enough but
immoderate. Believing that France had deliberately and inexcusably humiliated a nation that he as president had sworn to preserve, protect, and defend, Adams was hostilely intransigent.[22] ''I will never send another minister
to France,'' he said in June 1798, ''without assurances that he will be received, respected, and honored as the representative of a great, free, powerful and independent nation.''[23] Aware that the likelihood of such assurances
was remote, Adams convinced himself that since a declaration of war was
inevitable, a large-scale program of military preparedness must be immediately launched. So it was that, despite his later denial of any responsibility
for the war measures adopted by Congress in the spring and summer of
1798, he was no passive onlooker but warmly endorsed them, although his
ardor would soon be dampened and then dispelled.[24]

The members of the Fifth Congress, which adjourned on July 16, had not
needed to be spurred on by the president. Buoyed by the enthusiastic support
accorded them by the country at large, Federalist congressmen used their
commanding majority to put through a preparedness program, including the
establishment of a department of the navy, an appropriation for purchasing
arms and ammunition, an augmentation of the regular army, and authorization for the president to raise a provisional army. Congress thus not only
took steps to prepare the country for armed conflict but also rendered war
the more likely by allowing merchant vessels of the United States to defend
themselves against French depredations, suspending commercial intercourse
between the United States and France and the latter's dependencies, and
declaring the Franco-American treaties void. By the time Congress adjourned in mid-July 1798, it had stopped just short of a formal declaration
of war. Although there predictably was pro forma partisan opposition, most
Americans approved of this national defense program, the levying of requisite taxes excepted.

More controversial were the measures adopted to safeguard the country
against subversion and to punish disloyalty. From that day to this, the Alien
and Sedition Acts have been exhibit number one in historians' indictment of
the Federalists. Of the three alien laws adopted, the Alien Enemies Act of
July 6, 1798, was perhaps most open to challenge on constitutional grounds.
It provided that whenever a proclamation by the president announcing war
or predatory invasion was issued, alien enemies should be liable to apprehension and removal; the president was authorized ''to direct the conduct to
be observed, on the part of the United States, towards the aliens who shall
become liable.'' The notorious Sedition Act of July 14, 1798, appeared to
be an even more egregious invasion of civil liberties. It was aimed at unlawful combination or conspiracy whose aim was to oppose the measures of

government or impede their implementation. Among other sweeping prohibitions, the act stipulated punishment of anyone who published scandalous and malicious writings against the government, either house of Congress, or the president with intent to defame them or to bring them "into contempt or disrepute."[25]

Hamilton applauded Congress' adoption of measures to prepare the country for war by shoring up its defenses, although he would have preferred a more ambitious program. He did not, however, fully approve or unreservedly censure either the measure that authorized the deportation of aliens or the act that stifled dissent under the guise of punishing sedition. On Hamilton's reaction to this legislation far too much ink has been spilled both by his historical advocates, determined to make him a civil libertarian, and his adversaries, eager to prove that his real motive was to equate partisan opposition with sedition. In fact, Hamilton wrote no more than two brief paragraphs on the issue. Apropos of "An Act respecting Alien Enemies," he inquired of Timothy Pickering a month before formal enactment of that measure:

> *If an Alien Bill passes I should like to know what policy in execution is likely to govern the Executive. My opinion is that while the mass ought to be obliged to leave the Country—the provisions in favour of Merchants ought to be observed & there ought to be* guarded *exceptions of characters whose situations would expose them too much if sent away & whose demeanor among us has been unexceptionable. There are a few such. Let us not be cruel or violent.*[26]

The admirable sentiment expressed in the final sentence of this paragraph excepted, Hamilton clearly was not opposed to the deportation of aliens so long as a few seemingly necessary exceptions were made. Of the Sedition Act, usually regarded as a far graver violation of individual liberties than the alien laws, Hamilton's only known statement was made to Oliver Wolcott, Jr. "There are provisions in [the Sedition] Bill," he wrote,

> *which according to a cursory view appear to me highly exceptionable & such as more than any thing else may endanger civil War. . . . I hope sincerely the thing may not be hurried through.* Let us not establish a tyranny. Energy is a very different thing from violence. *If we make no false step we shall be essentially united; but if we push things to an extreme we shall then give to faction* body *& solidarity.*

Since one cannot know to precisely which provisions of the sedition bill Hamilton objected, one cannot determine what he believed to be either the permissible latitude or necessary limitations on free speech. Nor without knowing how he defined "tyranny" can one know precisely what Hamilton meant by the seemingly libertarian phrase "let us not establish a tyranny."[27] The only conclusion that one can confidently draw is that had Hamilton strenuously objected to the Sedition Act, he would no doubt have written considerably more on the subject than he did; on issues that greatly concerned him he was, after all, more often than not prolix.

Neither Hamilton's own approval or disapproval of the Alien and Sedition Acts nor their uniqueness and worthiness of censure is as incontrovertible and as consequential as is usually assumed. The essential issues have nowhere been more perceptively put than in Page Smith's observation that criticism of the Federalist sponsors of those measures should be tempered by the consideration that a hundred and fifty years after their passage, the United States "long instructed in the ways of freedom, powerful, and united . . . gave way . . . to panic fears, enacting legislation in the name of 'internal security' that later historians may well judge far more harshly than the Alien and Sedition Acts. Those unhappy measures were neither unconstitutional nor, strictly interpreted, inimical to the freedom of the press. They were simply impolitic."[28]

At this time, however, Hamilton's primary concern was neither loyalty to the union nor its subversion but military preparedness. The aspect of that program in which he had the greatest personal interest was the augmentation of the regular army, recruitment of a provisional one, and the authorization given the president to nominate a commander of the United States Army and a "suitable number of major-generals." One of these was to be inspector general, a post that Hamilton was confident he would fill.

That Washington would head the expanded army was never in doubt. On July 2 he was duly nominated by the president as lieutenant general, the nation's first, and his appointment as "Commander in Chief of all the armies raised, or to be raised, in the United States" was confirmed by the Senate on the following day.[29] As predictable as Washington's appointment was his conditional acceptance: he would not assume active command unless "it becomes indispensable by the urgency of circumstances."[30] Although Washington thus intended to serve as an armchair general, the president and his Federalist allies believed that the wonder-working powers of the Virginian's name were necessary for popular acceptance of the nation's newly adopted military program, not to mention the success of American arms should war break out. Adams underscored his own belief in Washington's indispensability by directing Secretary of War James McHenry to personally deliver the Virginian's commission. Adams also instructed McHenry to ascertain the general's opinion of the state of military affairs and requirements, including his recommendations for major appointments to the army's general staff. "Particularly, I wish to have his opinion of the man most suitable for Inspector General, and Adjutant General, and Quarter-Master General," Adams instructed McHenry. "His opinion on all subjects must have great weight."[31] Washington readily obliged, and McHenry returned from Mount Vernon with the former president's nominees for the major generalships in the following order: "Alexander Hamilton, Inspector General, with rank of

Major General. Henry Knox, Major General. Charles C. Pinckney, Major General.''[32] As Washington's most reliable biographer comments, ''The decision had not been easy, but now that it was determined, Washington assumed it would stand.''[33]

Adams, momentarily suppressing his disdain of Hamilton, apparently agreed that Washington's decision must prevail: the Virginian's candidates for the three major generals, in the order in which he had listed them, were promptly submitted to the Senate, which confirmed the appointments on July 19. That decision, if undisturbed, bestowed on Hamilton de facto command of the army, so he and his supporters (most notably Washington and the secretaries of war, state, and the Treasury) believed.

As soon as Congress adjourned, the president, as was his custom, hastened to Quincy, Massachusetts, bolstered by the belief that the party he headed was not only united but as widely popular as the fierce partisanship of that politically passionate age allowed.[34] Once home, his high spirits were dampened by a grave illness that struck Abigail. They would not in any event have lasted long. Ease and complacency were not in character; enemies (real and imaginary), troubles, and anxiety were. Despite his preoccupation with his wife's illness, he soon began to think about his political enemies and then to reflect on the military appointments that only a short time earlier he had almost offhandedly acquiesced in. Had he then undergone, he must have wondered, a psychical version of the physical incapacity that Abigail was now undergoing? How could he rationally have proposed that Hamilton, whom he not only distrusted but also detested, be given command of the United States Army? How could he undo his lamentable rashness? An answer came quickly. The order in which he had submitted the names of the major generals to Congress was merely fortuitous and implied no precedence. The comparative rank of the principal appointees accordingly must be determined by the date of their Revolutionary War commissions. No doubt congratulating himself on such a shrewd decision, the president wasted no time in relaying to the secretary of war his emphatic opinion that ''General Knox is legally entitled to rank next to General Washington, and no other arrangement will give satisfaction.''[35] McHenry, smugly satisfied that supreme military command had been conferred on his own alter ego and political hero, was stunned. Smothering his anger and dismay, however, the Marylander (having first conferred with his cabinet colleagues) politely reminded Adams that Hamilton's precedence in rank had ''proceeded originally and exclusively from General Washington'' and that Knox, however much disgruntled, should reconcile himself to serving under Hamilton.[36]

The implication that the president must defer to the wishes of his predecessor and his own military appointee infuriated Adams. ''There has been too much intrigue in this business,'' he angrily replied. ''If I shall ultimately be the dupe of it, I am much mistaken in myself.''[37] The secretary of war quite properly construed such an imputation and rude rebuke as an indirect request that he resign, which he promptly offered to do.[38] But Adams, revealing that he was as temperamental, mercurial, and capricious as Hamilton would later accuse him of being, startled his cabinet subordinate by affirming that McHenry's "conduct through the whole business . . . had been candid."[39] The president's expression of confidence did not encompass an endorsement of McHenry's redoubtable championship of Hamilton's military claim. Instead, Adams renewed his determination that the rank of the newly designated major generals should be consonant with the dates of their commissions during the Revolution.

To the cabinet triumvirate that stalwartly supported Hamilton's claim to superior rank, Adams' resolve could be reversed. To accomplish this, they adopted a two-pronged approach. Pickering and McHenry undertook to convince Washington to insist that the president acknowledge the right of the army's senior commander to designate the relative rank of his subordinates.[40] Wolcott, the cabinet member whose views Adams most valued, was to write to Quincy, again setting forth the argument that Hamilton merited the preference accorded him by Washington.[41] The denouement of the scenario was precisely what Adams' principal cabinet members hoped for. On September 25, 1798, Washington wrote to the president, insisting politely but with atypical sternness that the military arrangement he had originally proposed be respected; on October 9, Adams replied that "I some time ago Signed the three Commissions and dated them on the Same day, in hopes . . . that an amicable Adjustment or Acquiescence might take place among the Gentlemen themselves. But if . . . Controversies should arise, they will of course be submitted to you as Commander in Chief" for resolution.[42]

Although generations of historians have contended otherwise, the meddling of the cabinet trio had no effect on the outcome of the imbroglio over the relative rank of the army's senior officers. As Adams' letter of October 9 reveals, he had already reconciled himself to the futility of pitting the powers of the presidency against the popularity of Washington and was accordingly prepared to acquiesce in the terms set forth in Washington's forthright letter. For his part, the Virginian had independently decided—long before the receipt of the entreaties of members of the president's cabinet—that his second in command must be Hamilton. Nevertheless, Adams complied only grudgingly, inwardly raging at being compelled to promote over the heads of generals he believed to be more-deserving candidates "the most restless, impatient, artful, indefatigable and unprincipled intriguer in the United States, if not in the world, to be second in command."[43]

This seemingly trivial dispute had unfortunate results that were to reverberate throughout the remainder of Adams' administration. His enmity toward Hamilton was enhanced, and the possibility that the president would work cooperatively with the inspector general of the army and its de facto commander was reduced almost to the vanishing point. But a question of national and international import remained: How could an augmented (presumably necessary) army be recruited, equipped, and trained if the constitutionally designated commander in chief of the army and his principal military subordinate were at logger-heads? The answer was obvious: It could not, although Hamilton, his spirits buoyed at achieving the type of post he had always yearned for and unaware too of the relentlessness of the New Englander's malice toward him, could not foresee Adams' readiness to obstruct any organization that might further the New Yorker's ambition or repute.

The outcome of what appeared to be a minor squabble over military rank had yet other consequences. The incident planted in the president's mind reservations about the loyalty of his principal cabinet advisers, doubts that would in time turn into certainty that they served not him but the interests of the army's inspector general. The situation was ironical. Once persuaded, Adams girded for battle with officials he could at any time have dismissed with a stroke of his pen. The irony deepens when one considers that the final victim of Adams' suspiciousness and spite would be not Pickering, McHenry, Wolcott, or Hamilton but the president's own party.

XVII

Inspector General of the Army: Ambition Fulfilled and Frustrated

Hamilton now had the military status he thought himself entitled to and the martial opportunity he had dreamed of. What would he make of the position and the possibilities it afforded? The likelihood of success was from the outset greatly diminished by the obvious difficulties that must be surmounted. He could not, as he was soon compelled to concede, count on the president's cooperation nor, as he from the outset knew, the effectiveness of the secretary of war. How, then, was he to raise and equip a competent fighting force? The army existed mostly on paper, and its augmentation depended on overcoming not only the impediments already referred to but also popular opposition to a "standing" army, by which was then meant the very type of regular, well-equipped permanent force that Hamilton wished to establish.

The expanded military force that Hamilton was to command consisted of the additional twelve regiments of infantry and six troops of dragoons, totaling some 12,500 officers and men (known as the New Army, to distinguish it from the miniscule regular one that already existed) authorized in July 1798 by a war-conscious Congress that had also provided some months earlier for a "provisional" army of 10,000 troops. In March of the following year the potential size of the army was once again enlarged by a federal statute providing for an "Eventual Army" (also "provisional" in the sense that the president might organize and mobilize it only in the event of war or imminent invasion of the country). Of the additional troops thus made possible no attempt was made to raise any but the New Army, and it never came close to the authorized maximum of 12,500 men, though even that number would have been a mere bagatelle compared to the armies of European powers.[1]

The story of the laggard recruiting and faltering administration of this military force (in the event, unnecessary and soon disbanded) would not bear the retelling did it not implicitly reveal much about the largely undeveloped state of the economy of the new nation as well as the sectional and partisan divisiveness that rendered the last years of the 1790s an uncommonly intense "Age of Passion."[2] Even in a biography of Hamilton, inspector general and de facto commander of the proposed army, the subject merits emphasis only because of its effects on Hamilton personally and the insistence of many historians that this phase of his career conclusively demonstrated his Napoleonic ambitions.

Hamilton's two years as inspector general were the most frustrating of his public life. The type of army that he headed and the nature of his responsibilities rendered his inspector-generalship an inevitable official failure and a harsh personal disappointment. As one of his subordinate officers appropriately commented, Hamilton's "military talents . . . were confined in their execution to too small a compass."[3] "Most that he was called on to do," echoes a recent biographer, "was petty, unworthy of his powers."[4]

From the outset, Hamilton's attempt to raise a formidable army on the weak and shaky foundation that he inherited presented difficulties that the most experienced and brilliant commander could not have surmounted. Supplies and equipment of all kinds were scarce.[5] Recruiting was sluggish.[6] Many of the volunteers who signed up were as unaccustomed to discipline as they were averse to formal training. But while discipline and adequate training might in time have been successfully imposed, there seemed no way to step up recruiting.

A major hurdle was that officers had to be appointed (about four hundred were required for the new regiments) before enlistment could proceed. John Adams, obviously intent that the recruiting of an army to serve under General Hamilton proceed at a snail's pace, contrived as best he could to delay the selection of officers.[7] To McHenry's proposals and entreaties "the President remained aloof and unhelpful," and when a list of officer candidates finally was proposed, Adams first directed that the nominees be approved by cabinet members and congressional party leaders and then devised other stratagems to delay the delivery of commissions.[8] The army's top commanders, Hamilton included, abetted his procrastination by insisting that appointees must have a clean bill of political health, which for the most part meant that they be Federalists in good standing.[9]

Once the enlistment of noncommissioned soldiers finally commenced in April and May 1799 the number of volunteers exceeded the predictions of the army's senior staff, whose expectations had no doubt been lowered by the tardy selection of junior officers. Even so, the new regiments were far from filled and seemed unlikely ever to be. It was improper to speak of an army, Washington appropriately reminded Hamilton in March 1799, but "more properly of an embryo one, for I do not perceive . . . that we are likely to move beyond this."[10]

Even had there been an abundant crop of recruits, other impediments would have hampered the establishment of an effective military force. A major human handicap was the cabinet member directly responsible for army administration, James McHenry, whose official ineptitude hampered the efficient exercise of Hamilton's military responsibilities. Even before organization of the army was under way, Hamilton had shared his misgivings about McHenry's administrative competence with Washington. In view of his first-hand knowledge of the administrative inefficiency of his longtime friend, Hamilton strongly doubted that augmentation of the army could "make any tolerable progress" under McHenry's direction.[11] Washington, although characteristically reluctant to acknowledge the shortcomings of a former loyal official subordinate, agreed, candidly conceding that McHenry's talents were "unequal to great exertions or deep resources."[12] But as the former president well knew but refrained from saying, Hamilton's own energy and capabilities were great enough for himself and McHenry too, and predictably, the inspector general also doubled, when necessary, as secretary of war. Hamilton unobtrusively tutored McHenry on the proper procedures and policies to be pursued, gently chided him for mistakes or procrastination, drafted legislation that Congress ordered the secretary to propose, and on occasion ghost-wrote the general orders that the War Department was supposed to draw up for the guidance of the army's general staff, the inspector general included.

Although Hamilton may at times have felt put upon, he was for the most part able to shove aside misgivings about the meaningfulness of his own labors. Nevertheless, neither the importance nor demands of the inspector-generalship justified the energy and time that Hamilton put into it. If he often managed to think otherwise, the self-deception was due to his insistence on overseeing trivia that he might easily have delegated to subordinate officers, despite the lack of experienced or qualified ones, and a minuscule personal staff.[13] To relate a few of many hundreds of possible examples of the petty details that Hamilton, when asked, insisted on handling is sufficient to convey this tedious official tale: he arranged for the transmission of authorized but undelivered commissions; he prescribed discipline for ordinary soldiers (in one instance a lowly surgeon's mate); he decided what degree of illness warranted a medical discharge (one correspondent asked about swollen glands); he gave opinions on what rations to allow (in one case for a young civilian who was the voluntary assistant of an army lieutenant); and he obligingly responded to complaints about the details of army uniforms (one indignant correspondent asked why yellow rather than white buttons should be used on artillerymen's jackets).[14] Hamilton also directed every detail of the floundering recruiting service (including extensive editorial revision of its *Rules and Regulations*)[15] and made a strenuous effort to attract every possible rookie, able-bodied or not, by attempting to resuscitate the seemingly lifeless subordinate officials responsible for filling the ranks. In addition, he personally oversaw such routine matters as exercise for the troops while in camp or in the field, the use of trained military police for garrisons, proper instruction in the manual of arms, and even "regulations respecting salutes."[16]

Hamilton's absorption in minor military matters by no means precluded the effective handling of substantive ones, and when the opportunity presented itself, he reenacted his stellar performance as secretary of the Treasury by inaugurating innovative programs of enduring importance: he devised detailed plans for a United States military academy (which would be organized two years later), took the preliminary steps that in time led to the formation of a naval academy, and arranged for the organization of a hospital department as well as other branches of the military service.[17]

Despite the demands (in part self-imposed) of the inspector-generalship, Hamilton found time to keep his law practice alive (he had to if his family was to be housed and clothed) and to act as gray eminence for the Federalist majority in Congress. His backstage direction of public affairs, if generally known, was for the most part not considered censurable, contemporaneously or subsequently.

It was quite otherwise with the alleged use that he intended to make of the army. This presumed purpose is the principal basis of the conspiracy theory that most historians have relied on to indict Hamilton's official conduct during this brief phase of his career. On the domestic scene, Hamilton is said to have contrived to use the army to quell partisan dissent (notably in Virginia). On the foreign front, the inspector general is accused of conspiring with the Spanish-American adventurer Francisco de Miranda to seize a South American empire that would slake his imperialistic thirst, his yearning to emulate the exploits of Caesar in ancient times and the contemporary military adventures of Napoleon. To expose the fallacies, factual and logical, of the conjectures that support such accusations should be the task of a leisurely monograph and can only be cursorily dealt with here.

That Hamilton secretly and ardently wished for a war with France that would win him military glory appears to be cemented onto the pages of American history books. John Adams expressed it this way: All of Hamilton's machinations as inspector general were "for the very purpose of ensuring a war with France, and enabling him to mount his hobby horse, the command of an army of fifty thousand men."[18] Just as Adams' judgment was warped by his detestation of Hamilton, so the familiar historical indictment that the New Yorker "was loud for war" is, as Broadus Mitchell remarks, "baseless."[19] The policies that Hamilton in fact followed from the spring of 1798 on called for building up the military strength of the country in order to force France to negotiate and, if that desirable outcome failed, to assure the young nation's ability to wage war successfully. His consistently held opinion was expressed in a letter that he wrote to Lafayette in January 1799: the repeated assurances of the United States that it wished to settle the dispute "amicably" were "sincere," and France could actualize those wishes merely "by reparation to our merchants for past injury, and the stipulation of justice in the future."[20]

What of the charge that Hamilton intended to use the army for the military suppression of partisan opposition at home?[21] Such an accusation substitutes the imputation of covert schemes that cannot be reliably documented for Hamilton's repeatedly avowed reasons for the augmentation of the army and explanation of the conditions under which it might be called into action. The facts are that he, along with many of his fellow Federalists (and apolitical countrymen as well), were alarmed by the threats that Talleyrand and his agents had made to the United States' envoys; by the likelihood that Great Britain's seemingly imminent defeat would leave the United States at the mercy of a vengeful Directory (whose members had strongly hinted that the fate of Venice might well befall the United States); by the possibility of a French-inspired insurrection of southern blacks; and, finally, by the threat of an armed uprising of French partisans in the United States should war with France break out. The real issue was put succinctly and perceptively many decades ago by Samuel Eliot Morison, who wrote that the indictment "that the regular and provisional armies were designed primarily to suppress democracy, and not to protect the country against France, is not supported by the slightest evidence."[22] As Hamilton saw the issue, the program of national preparedness that he directed was, in sum, not to suppress domestic opponents but to impress European opponents.

Even had Hamilton and like-minded Federalists really wished to use military force to stamp out democracy, the army at their disposal was woefully inadequate to any such grandiose plans. Its strength would have been taxed even by the effort to suppress a minor insurrection; the most it could have effectively done was to quell a large-scale riot such as that led by John Fries in several counties in eastern Pennsylvania in 1799, which was, in fact, put down by the Pennsylvania militia assisted by a few army regulars. The army that Hamilton headed may have been impressive on paper, but it was in fact primarily composed of inadequately equipped and poorly trained recent recruits and a small number of even those. At its peak strength in the fall of 1799, fifteen months after passage of the act establishing the New Army, not even half (considerably less than five thousand men) of the troops authorized had been recruited. As a mid-nineteenth-century historian observed, such was "the bugbear of the democracy" of that time, "the instrument by which a revolution was to have been accomplished . . . friends of liberty crushed . . . a throne erected. For whom?"[23] To Republican extremists of that day, as well as to many later historians, the answer was clear: Alexander Hamilton.

The principal evidence usually offered for Hamilton's desire to crush his partisan opponents by military force was his alleged proposal to dispatch troops to quell Virginia's resistance to federal authority. That Hamilton genuinely believed that the Virginians were arming themselves for this purpose is indisputable. The conviction was not the fancy of his own disordered imagination but was shared by other Federalists, among them prominent

Virginians. News of Virginia's presumed preparation for war against the United States had reached Hamilton from a number of sources. Such rumors were lent the more credence by remarks made by Virginia Federalists during the debate over the famous Virginia resolutions in late December 1798.[24] General Henry Lee, for example, charged that the militant majority of the Virginia legislature "struck him as recommending resistance." George K. Taylor, another Virginia Federalist, concurred; the consequences of measures adopted by that body, he maintained, might be "a resort to arms, civil war, and carnage, and probable dismemberment of the Union."[25] The laws to which these on-the-spot Federalist alarmists pointed were measures reorganizing the militia, levying additional taxes, and authorizing the governor of the state to procure arms. The Virginians were not, in fact, arming themselves to contest the authority of the United States, much less to conduct a war against it. The military measures, initiated much earlier, were rather intended to restore the long-neglected defenses of that commonwealth by strengthening and provisioning its militia.[26] But Hamilton fully shared the belief that Virginia was contemplating armed resistance to federal power, largely because he was already firmly convinced that the Republicans of a state that had given the nation such perverse obstructionists as William B. Giles, James Madison, and Thomas Jefferson were capable not only of disruptive political behavior but also the destruction of national authority.

The retaliatory measures that Hamilton proposed were disproportionately severe. In a letter that for the most part dealt with the appropriate reaction of the federal government to the Virginia and Kentucky Resolutions, Hamilton wrote to Congressman Theodore Sedgwick, "When a clever force has been collected let them be drawn toward Virginia for which there is an obvious pretext—& then let measures be taken to act upon the laws & put Virginia to the test of resistance." Taken out of context this sentence may seem to suggest that Hamilton was recommending a military invasion of Virginia in order to stamp out Republican dissent there. Actually, the purpose of his proposal, as Hamilton explained to Sedgwick, was to "give time for the fervor of the moment to subside, for reason to resume the reins, and by dividing its enemies . . . enable the Government to triumph with ease."[27] Should that not happen, Hamilton was indeed recommending a show of force to put down overt disobedience to the laws of the union,[28] as had been done in western Pennsylvania in 1794 and would shortly be done in the eastern part of the same state.

In any event, could Hamilton have had his way he would have conquered contiguous Spanish territory, not the commonwealth of Virginia. The possibility of such a foreign military adventure was enticingly dangled before him by Francisco de Miranda, who importunately sought the support of prominent Americans in furthering his long-cherished scheme of liberating Latin America. Rufus King, United States minister to England, was warmly receptive, confident that such a project would enhance the "Destinies of the New World" by laying "deep and firm the foundations of lasting accord between its rising Empires."[29] Although King described his enthusiastic endorsement of the plan to Hamilton, who shared his friend's reaction, the American diplomat, aware that the inspector general was in this instance powerless, centered his attention on those who manifestly did have the authority to further Miranda's plans—the secretary of state and the president.[30] The chilly response of Pickering and Adams put an end to King's aggressive support of Latin America's aspiring liberator but not to the envoy's daydreams.[31]

For his part, official propriety required that Hamilton keep his opinions to himself. But restraint was never his strong suit, and his longing for the United States' expansion glittered between the lines of his letters to Miranda, in which he gratuitously expressed his approval of the Latin American's plans while properly proclaiming that he could not participate in them "unless patronized by the Government of this country."[32] As one historian of the subject has astutely observed, "at the heart and center" of Hamilton's wishful thinking "lay Louisiana and Florida."[33] Nor was his aspiration for American dominion in the New World prompted merely by the events of 1798. A decade earlier he had written in *The Federalist,* "Our situation invites and our interest prompts us, to aim at an ascendant in the system of American affairs."[34] Many of Hamilton's fellow citizens, Federalists and Jeffersonians alike, agreed. That Thomas Jefferson, the nation's foremost Republican, should a scant four years later realize Hamilton's dream is ironical: The Virginian was crowned with laurel for accomplishing a design that earned Hamilton notoriety as an incipient imperialist, the would-be Napoleon of the New World.

The double standard applied by historians to Jefferson and Hamilton on this issue is no doubt a result of the third president's acquisition by diplomacy of what the New Yorker wistfully thought could be acquired only by conquest. Despite his ultimate success, Adams' conduct of American diplomacy, as Hamilton saw the matter, rendered the annexation of foreign territory impossible.

The difference between Adams and Hamilton on the management of Franco-American relations has been persistently, even perversely, misunderstood.[35] Neither Adams nor Hamilton could readily accept their country's passivity in the face of insult and outrage by a foreign nation. Both men, as has been said, endorsed the Federalist program enacted in the summer of 1798 to shore up the nation's defenses; both leaders believed that whether the result would be war or peace was up to France, which, confronted by a militarily strong and united America, might choose to negotiate. Should peace overtures thus be the happy outcome of America's military preparations, both men expected the United States to respond affirmatively, amicably, and with alacrity. Neither the president nor Hamilton believed that the decision to put the nation on a war footing must inexorably lead to a choice between a declaration of war, advocated by a minority of Federalists, or appeasement, advocated by many Republicans. Although neither man acknowledged the affinity, they shared the hope that successful diplomatic negotiations would be enhanced by a posture of military strength. Hamilton spoke for them both when he expressed the belief that since "peace or war will not always be left to our option," the country should be in a position as fully to exploit the one as to wage the second.[36] Hamilton and Adams differed not on diplomatic strategy but on tactics. This seemingly narrow disagreement broadened, steadily widening the personal and official antagonism of one for the other. Their controversy over the conduct of Franco-American relations exploded only a few months after Hamilton was appointed inspector general.

On February 18, 1799, Adams, without previously consulting his cabinet, members of Congress, or prominent Federalist leaders, tersely announced to the Senate the nomination of "William Vans Murray American minister resident at the Hague, to be minister plenipotentiary of the United States to the French Republic."[37] For once, the hackneyed word "bombshell" was appropriately descriptive. The president's fellow Federalists, cabinet members, congressmen, and party regulars everywhere were stunned. Theodore Sedgwick denounced the nomination as "the wild and irregular start of a vain, jealous, and half frantic mind"; Timothy Pickering sorrowfully observed that "we have all been shocked and grieved."[38] Such hyperbole and astonishment were largely due to the widely held opinion that Adams still remained steadfastly committed to the policy that he had proclaimed in June 1798 in the wake of the XYZ affair. "I will never send another minister to France," Adams had emphatically averred, "without assurances that he will be received, respected, and honored as the representative of a great, free, powerful and independent nation."[39]

It presumably did not occur to Adams that strong and skillful presidential leadership might be necessary to assure public acceptance, as well as the success, of such a major shift in American policy. Focusing exclusively on the indubitably correct idea that the conduct of the country's foreign policy resided in the president, Adams overlooked the equally incontrovertible consideration that to disregard the opinions of leaders of his own party in his cabinet, in Congress, and in the states was politically obtuse. Opposition by prominent Federalists only strengthened the president's resolve that his policy—both its substance and the manner of it execution—was the only true course to follow and his only concession was to yield to pressure from Federalist congressmen that he name a three-man commission instead of a single envoy. Even so, had Adams been bent on dividing his party, he scarcely could have acted more effectively. As Page Smith has said, "A measure which he had hoped would isolate the extremists threatened seriously to demoralize his own party."[40]

Procedural consideration aside, why did Adams unilaterally decide to reopen negotiations? Over preceding months news of the Directory's conciliatory mood had reached him from a number of independent sources. But the decisive reason for his diplomatic about-face was receipt of what Adams regarded as "authentic, regular, official, diplomatic assurances" from Talleyrand, the French foreign minister.[41] Although Hamilton was not altogether certain that either the noun or the adjectives were appropriate, he did not, as

Adams later charged, connive with "all his confidential friends" to undermine the president's decision.[42] When he first heard of Adams' appointment of a new mission, Hamilton had written that "as it has happened, my present impression is that the measure must go into effect."[43] While not opposed to negotiations per se, the New Yorker was critical of the manner in which the president initiated them. In view of the treatment accorded both Pinckney and the XYZ envoys, Hamilton believed that the French should have been required to send an envoy to the United States "with adequate powers and instructions," a concession that in his view the Directory would have made.[44] Since the president obviously had rejected such an approach, Hamilton offered an alternative: Adams "might secretly and confidentially have nominated one or more of our ministers actually abroad for the purpose of treating with France; with *eventual* instructions predicated upon appearances of . . . peace."[45]

Hamilton's misgivings about the propriety of Adams' diplomatic procedures were shared by other Federalists in and out of Congress. But Federalist senators (in an implicit but reluctant acknowledgment of presidential initiative in the conduct of foreign affairs) joined their colleagues in approving the peace mission. Soon thereafter, Congress adjourned and Adams, as he invariably did, hastened home to Quincy. Some seven months elapsed before the American commissioners sailed for France, a delay that Adams would later attribute to the stubborn procrastination of Secretary of State Timothy Pickering and to the "insidious and dark intrigues" of Hamilton.[46] Actually, the postponement was caused by Adams himself, who continued to insist that the Directory give unequivocal and formal "assurances" that the American envoys would be received and treated with respect. Four months elapsed before the requisite pledge (which William Vans Murray had been instructed to acquire) reached Philadelphia and was forwarded to the president, who then directed the secretary of state to draft diplomatic instructions "as promptly as possible."[47] This was done, but news having reached the Department of State of "a very portentous scene," perhaps "another explosion," in France, Pickering recommended to the president that the mission be temporarily suspended.[48] Adams agreed, but also decided that in view of such a delicate diplomatic situation his on-the-spot oversight was desirable.

Arriving in Trenton, New Jersey (the temporary capital), on October 10, the president swiftly convinced himself that his presence was not merely desirable but imperative, not so much to direct the deliberation of his cabinet as to abort what he wrongly construed as an official conspiracy. The ring leader, he believed, was Hamilton, who, Adams was angrily startled to discover, was also in Trenton. Hamilton's arrival was, in fact, fortuitous; he was there, in company with General James Wilkinson, to confer with the secretary of war on plans for the western army. In Adams' view, however, the alleged reason for Hamilton's presence was merely a camouflage for the New Yorker's stealthy scheme to usurp presidential powers. "I transiently asked one of the heads of departments," Adams would recall, whether Hamilton had hurried to the capital "to persuade me to countermand the mission." Since the president had in advance convinced himself of the answer, his question was not only "transient" but also irrelevant. "Unsuspicious as I was, I could not resist the evidence of my senses [that] Hamilton unasked, had volunteered his influence," Adams self-righteously asserted, thus affirming the suspiciousness that he had just disavowed. "I know of no business he had at Trenton. Indeed I know, that in strict propriety, he had no right to come to Trenton at all without my leave."[49] (Presumably the secretary of war was for the moment viewed merely as a figurehead.) Whatever doubts Adams may have still harbored about dispatching the peace mission in the face of reports of renewed turmoil in France were now promptly dispelled.

On the evening of October 15 the chief executive met with his cabinet to review the instruction already prepared for the commissioners but "he was silent," Oliver Wolcott observed, "on the question whether the mission ought to proceed."[50] That such secretiveness was due to sullen resoluteness and not to indecisiveness became clear on the following morning. Upon arriving at his office, the secretary of state was startled to find a curt message from the president ordering Pickering to deliver immediately "the instructions, as corrected last evening" and to order the envoys to sail for France no later than November 1.[51] Pickering, who was neither sharply intuitive (else he would have been forewarned) nor readily submissive to official authority, was dumbfounded by what he construed as both undue interference in his own department and Adams' precipitate and capricious behavior. Hamilton, who was as stunned as the secretary of state, echoed Pickering's strained argument that the dispatch of the mission was likely to jeopardize America's hard-earned and precarious détente with England.[52] Oliver Wolcott's argument in opposition to Adams' hasty decision was more pertinent and also prophetic. "The effects . . . appear to be incapable of mitigation," the Treasury secretary observed. "It is certain that the federal party will be paralyzed . . . the President will gain no new supporters; his former friends will be in disgrace with the public, and the administration of John Adams, so much extolled, will end by the transfer of the powers of government to the rival party."[53] The prediction was correct, although the causality was far more complex than Wolcott realized.

Whatever the political effects of Adams' decision, its diplomatic results belied the dire predictions of Hamilton and other notable Federalists, as Hamilton himself (once he regained his balance) recognized early on. While continuing to deplore Adams' decision, Hamilton also reconciled himself to the coldly consoling belief that "America, if she attains to greatness, must *creep* to it. Well be it so. Slow and sure is no bad maxim. Snails are a wise generation."[54] It was also as well that the army commander was able to take the proverbial long view. Since the Directory had resolved to reach a negotiated settlement in order to remove the irritant of a quasi-war with its Revolutionary War ally, the American envoys had little difficulty in arriving at a settlement that vindicated Adams' decision, one that the president himself described "as the most disinterested, prudent and successful . . . in my whole life.''[55] The Convention of 1800 (which comported with neither the American expectations nor the envoys' instructions) did not avert a war, for France had already decided not to fight one; it did not for long soothe, much less settle, the differences between France and the United States, as their stormy relations during Jefferson's administration would attest. But it briefly restored amicable Franco-American relations and also postponed for a decade American involvement in a foreign war, which when it came (ironically, one is entitled to argue) was with England rather than France.[56] More germane to the subject of this book is the effect of the Franco-American accord on Hamilton: it ended his lifelong dream of a distinguished military career.

Months before the signing of the Mortefontaine Convention in September 1800, the pygmy army that Hamilton's detractors insisted on viewing as the mighty wave that the inspector general, an incipient Caesar, intended to ride to conquest was virtually defunct. Its imminent extinction was foreseeable once Adams substituted diplomatic negotiations for military preparations, whose success had from the outset been rendered unlikely by the feebleness of his encouragement. In this instance the president merely mirrored the overwhelming public repudiation of the stockpiling of arms and buildup of any army.

Even such insubstantial support for a national preparedness program as still flickered (principally on the part of New England war hawks, who were still a congressional force to be reckoned with) had already diminished in December 1799 with the death of Washington. Among a nation of grief-stricken citizens none felt the loss more painfully and personally than Hamilton. As he wrote to Martha Washington, ''From a calamity which is common to a mourning nation, who can expect to be exempt? Perhaps it is even a privilege to have a claim to a larger portion of it than others.'' Hamilton's sorrow was no doubt genuine, but it was also strongly alloyed by self-interest. Shifting attention almost imperceptibly from expressions of heartache at Washington's death to its possibly damaging effect on his own career, Hamilton's letter to the general's widow continued, ''I may without propriety, allude to the numerous and distinguished marks of confidence and friendship of which you yourself have been a witness,'' and then with considerable impropriety, ''but I cannot say in how many ways the continuance of that confidence and friendship was necessary to me in future relations.''[57] Reading Hamilton's sympathy letter literally—as was her wont—Martha Washington was no doubt pleased by an expression of shared sorrow by the general's longtime principal adviser. But to a reader rather more attuned to nuances of meaning, Hamilton's tinsel sentiments were remarkably revelatory of both himself and the true wellspring of his close relationship with Washington. ''He was,'' Hamilton himself forthrightly conceded, ''an Aegis very essential to me.''[58]

No protector, not even an eighteenth-century Zeus, could have saved the forlorn army that limped to expiration under its now dispirited commander. The auxiliary army, which, according to its critics, was to allow the inspector general to overrun the country and to conquer continents, had by now

dwindled to four regiments stationed on the frontier and a couple of squad-
rons of cavalry and artillery. What might have appeared to an Old World
military expert to be the irreducible was in the winter of 1800 shrunk yet
further by a congressional measure authorizing the president to discharge
before June 15 all the New Army except for an inconsequential remnant of
staff officers, artillery and engineers, and dragoons.

The disbandment was easily accomplished one day before the deadline.
In a brief farewell address, in the form of general orders, to the remnant of
troops that he had commanded, Hamilton wrote that ''the zeal with which
they came forward in defence of their country . . . does great honor to their
patriotism and spirit.'' No doubt so, but Hamilton was engaging in wishful
thinking when he asserted that the soldiers, who had enlisted reluctantly
(most of them for the wages) and reacted indifferently to military training,
had ''exemplified how speedily American soldiers can be prepared to meet
the enemies of their country.''[59] As Hamilton for the last time closed the
door of his headquarters at 36 Greenwich Street and headed homeward, he
also closed the door to the successful military career he had dreamed of
since childhood. If in imagination he later looked back on his experience as
inspector general and dreamed of what might have been, he did not say so.

It would be charitable to hope that he never did. His tenure as inspector
general was an anticlimactic ending to what had been a brilliant, and still
seemed to be a promising, career. His well-wishers (and perhaps Hamilton
himself) could reflect that this military episode had been mercifully brief: he
did not assume active service until November 1798; it ended twenty months
later, during which period (especially the latter part) he was on leave or
comparatively inactive.

Following the disbandment of the auxiliary army, Hamilton set out on a
tour of the New England states, ostensibly to review for the last time the
troops stationed there but actually to confer with that section's Federalist
leaders. His conversations centered no doubt on how to ditch John Adams
and to elect a more effective president, one more sympathetic to the canons
of Federalism and no doubt to Hamilton personally.

XVIII

"His Character Is Radically Deficient in Discretion"

Just as Congress' dismantlement of the army and Adams' envoys' successful negotiation of a peace treaty with France dispelled Hamilton's dreams of martial glory, so the election of 1800 aborted his political ambition. But for that neither congressmen nor any other government officials were responsible. The New Yorker himself wrote the disappointing finale to his distinguished public career. Could Hamilton have borne his disdain of Adams in silence and, outwardly at least, supported the New Englander's presidential campaign, things might have turned out differently. Not that he could have assured Adams' reelection; that was subject to circumstances (chance included) over which neither he nor the president had control. But he might at least have basked in the admiration of his many partisans and remained a respected and powerful leader of the party that he had been instrumental in forging. But for that to have happened Hamilton would have had to have been politically and personally "born again," or at least to have undergone drastic psychological surgery. Any such transformation was, of course, impossible, and so he followed the familiar path of self-defeating assertiveness and compulsive self-aggrandizement that served no purpose but that of assuaging an irreducibly inflated pride.

The major difficulty was Hamilton's irreversible resentment of what he viewed as Adams' misguided foreign policy, stubborn resistance to an effective program of national military preparedness, and manifest scorn of Hamilton personally. On the latter score, the New Yorker was indisputably correct, and he returned the president's antipathy in full measure. Jumbling such personal considerations with the exigencies of public affairs, Hamilton was convinced that Adams' record as president was one of unmitigated blunders, revealing immeasurable ineptitude. Although such an assessment was scarcely disinterested and surely distorted, the president had (almost willfully it seemed) divided his own party and thus jeopardized the Federalists' chances in the presidential election of 1800.

Adams' estrangement from prominent members of his own party had been sparked by his conduct of foreign affairs in 1799 and 1800, which James McHenry wrote to Washington, would "become an apple of discord to the federalists that may so operate upon the ensuing election of President, as to put in jeopardy the fruits of all their past labours, by consigning to men, devoted to French innovations and democratizing principles, the reins of government. It is this dreaded consequence which afflicts, and calls for all the widsom of, the federalists."[1] Hamilton emphatically agreed, and in the context of politics at that juncture, he was (apropos of McHenry's last sentence anyway) no doubt right. It is plausible to contend retrospectively that had the president been less precipitate and consulted with his official family and other party leaders, the political consequences might have been less dangerous. A policy of cooperation rather than confrontation, in other words, could possibly have unified the Federalists behind a policy of preparedness for war accompanied by willingness to negotiate.

Nevertheless, the rift within the top echelons of the party was not generally known, and the Federalists continued to enjoy considerable popularity among the electorate, as reflected by their commanding majority in Congress. In the election of members to the Sixth Congress (scheduled to convene on December 2, 1799) the party had triumphed not only in New England but in the South as well, making impressive gains in North Carolina and Virginia. Although events justified Hamilton's gloomy belief that "no real or desirable change had been wrought" in many of the states that went Federalist, such an outcome was not preordained.[2] It was, in fact, to be in part determined by Hamilton, largely because he resisted, as the campaign progressed, what seemingly could not be avoided: the selection of Adams as the Federalist standard-bearer. As presidential incumbent and the choice of most party leaders in New England and the South, Adams was far and away the most eligible of Federalist candidates, his selection inescapable unless the party wished to forfeit the election. In sum, the country at large (unlike Adams' cabinet and many top Federalists in Congress) endorsed the president's twin policies of negotiation and token defense. Those whom he had antagonized had no choice but to crawl to his support. Initially, Hamilton was among them.

Support of Adams appeared, to Federalist extremists and moderates alike, the more imperative because of the seemingly clear political alternative: Thomas Jefferson's election as president. To those Federalists who viewed Jefferson (variously or all-encompassingly) as a fanatic Jacobin, an ultrarevolutionary, a zealous atheist, or dangerous anarchist, Adams appeared by contrast the bulwark of republican virtue and the champion of constitutionalism, his alleged defects almost undetectable blemishes. Although the Virginian (as was his wont) did not publicly promote his candidacy, his position as front-runner in the Republican race was indisputable, even beyond contest. He had seen to that.

As vice-president, Jefferson, the acknowledged leader of the opposition to an administration of which he was the second-highest-ranking official, had been confronted with a conflict of interest (at least by the standards of a later date). But if he saw the issue in this light, awareness of it troubled him only fleetingly, if at all. Adams, at the outset of his administration, had made amiable overtures to the Virginian. They were not returned, however, and the second president himself conceded that "party violence soon rendered" such cooperation "impracticable, or, at least useless; and this party violence was excited by Hamilton more than any other man."[3] The distorted reasoning that made Hamilton the culprit for partisan developments that Jefferson bore the greater responsibility for did not disturb Adams, who early on in his presidency came to attribute demonic powers to the inspector general he had been obliged to appoint. Sharing Adams' phobia about Hamilton (but few other of the president's ideas and policies), Jefferson was the more willing to lead opponents to a Federalist government, particularly one that included Hamilton as active military commander, and to work energetically, albeit covertly, to enhance his own eligibility as Adams' successor. To the student who attempts to unravel the complexities of Hamilton's career, the arresting question is neither the Virginian's political agility and deviousness nor the New Englander's partisan ineptness but the New Yorker's central position in a contest between the ostensible principal protagonists. A ready answer is that Hamilton (shoved by Adams) put himself onto center stage. In any event, the election of 1800 has a historical significance that overshadows the contemporaneous role of its leading players.

Although that election was not, as Jefferson remarked years later, as genuine a revolution as that of 1776, its importance is attested to by the lavish attention given to it by most historians of the country's formative years. Like the elections of 1828, 1840, and 1860 (to confine oneself to the nineteenth century), it continues to be interpreted as one of that small number of quadrennial watersheds in American party history for two major reasons: it ushered in a new era in the nation's political history, marked first by the decline of the Federalist party and then by the crumbling of the first party sytem, on whose ruins would rise a second; and it served, in retrospect, to legitimize the idea of partisan opposition, to demonstrate that the democratic way to unseat an unpopular government is not to revolt but to replace it. The triumph of the Republicans in 1800 was, in sum, an epochal development in the nation's politics in the sense that it was an alembic for the political processes of American democracy.

The first critical test of party strength was provided by the New York election in April 1800. That election was for state officials, but in New York, as in several other states, the legislature chose the presidential electors. The results of the legislative race and consequently the bestowal of the Empire State's twelve electoral votes hinged on the outcome in New York City. There, Aaron Burr, aware of the high stakes, put together a ticket comprised of a galaxy of Revolutionary War heroes and engineered a vigorous campaign—the indexing of voters, their assiduous cultivation, and the like—that prefigured the democratic techniques of a later day. His personal indefatigability and political tactics were successful. "The New York election," a Republican stalwart gloated on May 8, has resulted "in the complete triumph of the republican interest. . . . I consider by this measure, that Mr. Jefferson's election for the President is secured."[4]

Hamilton no doubt agreed but concluded that what had seemingly been secured might be unfastened. He was perhaps less troubled by a popular verdict that he deplored than by its having been largely contrived by the man he unalterably believed to be his own and the nation's (characteristically he scrambled the two) most dangerous enemy—Aaron Burr. In his frantic effort to abort the victory and political preferment of his archrival, Hamilton thrust aside scruples about thwarting the public will. The result has been described by one of his otherwise most friendly biographers as "a desperate and degrading proposal."[5] The slender opportunity that Hamilton sought to grasp was to contrive the casting of New York's electoral vote by the Federalist-dominated lame-duck legislature before the recently elected Republican-controlled assembly could convene. The plan took the form of a letter to Governor John Jay proposing that Jay promptly call the expiring legislature into special session and request that it adopt a measure transferring the power of choosing electors from the legislature to the people, who would vote by districts. This way at least some Federalist presidential electors might be chosen. Although Hamilton somewhat feebly contended that this plan was technically "legal and constitutional," he was blithely unconcerned about its ethicality. "In times like this in which we live," he confided to Jay, "it will not do to be overscrupulous. It is easy to sacrifice the substantial interests of society by a strict adherence to ordinary rules." What was the compelling end to which the prevailing standards must be sacrificed? It was to prevent Jefferson, "an *atheist* in Religion and a *fanatic* in politics from getting possession of the helm of state."[6] Hamilton's role as defender of Christianity (to which his commitment had previously been merely pro forma) was no more convincing than was his assumption that one must fight a fanatic with fanaticism. Indeed, to set forth such a plan entailed some convenient amnesia. Apropos of Federalist attempts to overrule the legislature's fraudulent election of George Clinton in 1792, Hamilton had observed that "I do not feel it right or expedient to attempt to reverse the decision by any means not known to the Constitution or laws. The precedent may suit us today; but tomorrow we may rue its abuse."[7] Jay sided with Hamilton the statesman of 1792 rather than Hamilton the political zealot of 1800. The governor did not respond to his friend's letter but instead wrote at the bottom of it, "Proposing a measure for party purposes, which I think it would not become me to adopt."[8]

For his part, Hamilton appeared increasingly willing to adopt any measure at all that served party (as well as personal) purposes. Such readiness was not atypical, as evidenced by his scorching and rash newspaper assault on

Jefferson in 1792 and his scathing attacks on Burr's eligibility for the vice-presidency during the election of the same year. Now, he was confronted with the political ascendancy of the two men he had long considered his most implacable enemies (largely no doubt because they had impugned his integrity and ignored his intellectual prowess). To attack detractors whose opposition he might more prudently have endured silently was by now an involuntary reflex. Any remote possibility of behavioral change was negated by a third enemy, who, if his scorn of Hamilton be the gauge, was the most implacable of them all.

John Adams, whose quality of hatred was unstrained, reserved his most unflagging enmity for Hamilton. The resentment set afire by the imbroglio over the rank of major generals for the New Army in August and September 1798 burned hotter and hotter as Adams convinced himself that the principal author of his presidential problems was the wily, unscrupulous rogue who commanded the army and, in Adams' view, also commanded the president's cabinet. Beginning in the spring of 1800, Adams declared war on Hamilton and his alleged conspiratorial allies among the president's official family, thus further alienating the New Yorker and his supporters and deepening the fissures among the Federalists. Since his first term was, after all, drawing to a close, Adams' timing was odd. Perhaps he believed, not altogether mistakenly, that the Hamiltonian wing of the party would do more to wreck than to enhance his chances of another four years in office. Perhaps he was more intent on demonstrating that he was master in his own presidential house than on assuring another term there. In any event, the measures Adams now adopted could be construed as an attempt to antagonize Hamilton and his associates further. One such act was the pardoning of John Fries, who had been convicted of treason for his leadership of an alleged insurrection (actually it was only a riot) in northeastern Pennsylvania in the early spring of 1799.[9] Another act that could have been interpreted as an indirect strike at Hamilton was Adams' approval of two statutes, the first ending enlistments in the New Army and the second disbanding it.[10]

While these actions may possibly have been spawned by conviction rather than personal malice, the president's next step was clearly an open challenge to Hamilton. Having long endured subordinates who, he was now certain, took their orders from Hamilton rather than him, Adams decided early in May 1800 to dismiss the more flagrant offenders. "Their presence," a modern scholar writes, "did nothing for Adams' disposition. He lived in a kind of continual rage, like a diminutive volcano that might erupt at any moment."[11] The first to go was Secretary of War James McHenry, who had been obliged (in the absence of strong presidential leadership) to seek Hamilton's counsel not because of official disloyalty but, as we have seen, because of official incompetence. Having requested McHenry to consult him on departmental business, the president burst into a torrent of abuse, furiously lashing out at McHenry, Federalist critics of Adams' administration, and especially Hamilton. The Marylander, visibly shaken at such an unprovoked tirade, promptly resigned.[12] Four days later, on May 10, the president, in the midst of an unseemly temper tantrum by which even he later was embarrassed, requested the resignation of his secretary of state, who, despite Adams' contrary conviction, was emphatically not Hamilton's lackey; when Pickering refused, Adams curtly informed him that "you are hereby discharged."[13] Why, just as the presidential campaign was getting under way and party unity might have appeared to be of paramount importance, did Adams fire cabinet members who were also prominent party leaders for offenses that, so he said, they had been guilty of from the beginning of his administration? Perhaps as Hamilton, Pickering, and other Federalists charged, the results of the election in New York convinced him that he no longer had to appease either the Federalists of that state or their leader and expected by sacrificing the Hamiltonian members of his administration to pick up support elsewhere. If so, the prediction was not borne out. Instead, Adams demonstrated that he was as incapable of serving as mediator between competing factions of his own party as he was unwilling to moderate that contest.

Nevertheless, Adams' presidential incumbency plus his manifest popularity among New Englanders and southerners all but assured him top place on the Federalist ticket. This was confirmed early in May when Federalist congressmen, assembling on the second floor of Congress Hall in Philadelphia, endorsed Adams and chose as his running mate Charles Cotesworth Pinckney, the popular South Carolinian who had recently served as one of Adams' peace commissioners to France and as Hamilton's fellow general in the augmented army. The caucus also exacted a pledge that all Federalist electors would vote equally for Adams and his running mate. Also assembling in Congress Hall during the same month, the Republican congressional caucus took the same pledge on behalf of their nominees. As had never been in doubt, Jefferson was promptly and without dissent selected for top place on the ticket. The choice of a running mate presented something more of a problem, but in view of the recent party triumph in New York, it was agreed that the nominee must come from that state. Burr's instrumentality in electing a Republican legislature made him (rather than the leader of any other group in the faction-ridden politics of the Empire State) the most eligible candidate. That Jefferson had justifiable misgivings about the suitability—and especially the character—of his running mate was either unknown or overlooked.

The Republicans were irrepressibly optimistic that victory was within their reach. Enthusiastically united behind a popular chieftain who remained isolated but not incommunicado on his Virginia mountaintop, they could view with satisfaction the acrimonious squabble between John Adams and other Federalist leaders. As Theodore Roosevelt once observed, Adams' party included "many men nearly equal in strong will and great intellectual power" whose "ambitions and theories clashed; . . . while in the other party there was a single leader, Jefferson, supported by a host of sharp political workers."[14] To the latter it appeared certain that with New York already safely in the Republican fold, success at the polls would be assured if the electoral vote of Pennsylvania could be united with that of the southern and western states.

The valid basis for such optimism was not lost on Hamilton, though he was also aware that the balance of political forces was rather closer than the Republicans cared to concede. Such awareness led him initially to suppress his disdain of Adams and to endorse the decision of his party's caucus that Federalist electors throw away no votes but uniformly support Adams and Pinckney equally. Such a course, Hamilton advised Theodore Sedgwick, Speaker of the House, "is the only thing that can save us from the fangs of *Jefferson*. It is therefore essential that the Federalists should not separate without coming to a distinct and solemn concert to pursue this course *bona fide*."[15]

Hamilton's conviction was short-lived; the "fangs of Jefferson" soon seemed rather less dangerous than the fatal flaws of John Adams. In the course of a trip through New England in June, Hamilton openly expressed his preference for Pinckney over Adams, and soon after that he was contriving to manipulate the electoral college in order to assure his preference.[16] In view of the masterful campaign tactics and strategy of the Republicans, machinations of this kind were more likely to prove fatal to both Federalists than to secure Pinckney's election.

Such a likelihood would have been transparent to a politician less preoccupied by his own private obsessions and public ambition than Hamilton was. Given the strength of the Federalists in New England and the nationwide support they had won only a year before, the Federalist party was still a viable national organization, capable of overcoming the disadvantages by which it appeared to be hamstrung in the spring and early summer of 1800. If Adams could carry South Carolina, as seemed possible, and pick up some votes in Pennsylvania, which appeared likely, he could win reelection even in face of his defeat in New York. Nor did the rift within the Federalist party necessarily jeopardize its chances if Adams, forgoing his tendency to battle his own party leaders, adopted a stance of temperamental moderation and partisan conciliatoriness. Had he tried, he might even have curbed Hamilton's meddlesome rashness, though that would no doubt have entailed the working of a minor miracle.

Although the party contest had really begun soon after Adams was sworn in as president on March 4, 1797, the campaign reached its height during the summer and on into the late fall of 1800. The election in each state took place at different times, stretching from early summer until December (in the event, some results were not known until the end of that month). As Federalist campaign strategists interpreted the electoral map, the states of New Hampshire, Vermont, Connecticut, Massachusetts, and Delaware could be counted on to cast unanimous votes for Adams and Pinckney. The outcome in New Jersey was considered somewhat less certain, but it was put in the Federalist column by most party leaders. Their principal challenge was to pick up the requisite number of votes in states where the outcome was conceded to be doubtful (that is, those in which the electoral vote would be split between the two parties). The most crucial of these were Pennsylvania, North Carolina, and South Carolina, where a substantial vote for Adams and Pinckney might assure a Federalist victory. Republican campaign strategists (virtually certain that unanimous votes for Jefferson and Burr in Virginia, Kentucky, Tennessee, Georgia, and New York would offset the Federalist stronghold in New England) concurred in the opposition's assessment of doubtful states, although the Jeffersonians centered their attention on Pennsylvania and South Carolina.

Jefferson himself ostensibly confined his attention to the lovely vista spread out before him at Monticello, to the rural life that he always cherished, and, characteristically, to reading and personal letter-writing. That he could stand aloof from the fierce contest then being fought on his behalf was because of the flock of efficient political lieutenants scattered throughout the states. It was better that way. The relationship between Jefferson and his countrymen reminds one of Jakob Burckhardt's comment about "the mysterious coincidence between the egoism of the individual and the communal will."[17] Jefferson was by temperament and intellectual endowment better equipped to provide his party with ideas than to direct its organization, better suited to serve as a lofty symbol of democracy than to join the ranks of rough-and-tumble campaigners. On them he could confidently rely not only to spread the Jeffersonian political gospel but to counter, by means fair or foul, the opposing views and personal assaults of the Federalists. His trust was well placed, as attested by the effective leadership of political subalterns such as his good friend Edmund Pendleton in Virginia, John Langdon in New Hampshire, Gideon Granger in Connecticut, Burr in New York, Governor Thomas McKean and Tench Coxe in Pennsylvania, and his longtime political confidant and worshipful disciple John Beckley, who was, in all but name, national coordinator of his fellow Virginian's campaign. Jefferson could rely too on the brilliant, if scurrilous, invective of newspaper editors like William Duane, editor of the Philadelphia *Aurora* (a national newspaper insofar as the country can be said to have had any and thus a significant clue to the issues of the election), whose pages were given over to calumny and character assassination, particularly of John Adams.

Billingsgate aside, Duane and his fellow Republican campaigners had a seemingly bottomless bag of issues from which to draw. The "Spirit of 1776" (which Jefferson himself never ceased talking about) was evoked; Jay's Treaty was trotted out to show the anglophilism of the Federalists; the alien law was attacked; the Sedition Act was scored; and the familiar alarm was rung to warn of the axiomatic dangers of a "standing army." Nor was the ever-popular bread-and-butter issue of taxes overlooked; in a shrewd and effective concatenation of ideas, publicists linked high taxes and British influence, and relief from taxation and friendship with France. But none of these issues were the central ones of the Jeffersonians' campaign. These were succinctly set forth by Tench Coxe, gray eminence of both the Republican campaign and covert coeditor of the influential *Aurora*. The quintessential themes that Coxe and others incessantly harped on (in a replay of the

1796 presidential campaign) were "aristocratical plots," "contempt of Republican principles," "British influence," and "monarchical doctrines," slogans made to order for a people already saturated in anglophobia. Although these slogans were a well-blended potpourri, one particular ingredient dominated. Repeatedly and tediously, Republican partisans hammered at the issue that to them symbolically subsumed all others: monarchism, foreign and domestic, symbolized by British influence and personified by John Adams.[18]

Ironically, the target of the Republican smear campaign used the same issue, directing it against his principal antagonist in his own party. Prompted by his resentment of Hamilton, Adams had begun as early as the winter of 1800 to talk angrily of a British faction within the United States, clearly implying that it included not only the New Yorker, its chief, but also the dissident members of his own cabinet.[19] The charge would surface again at the peak of the campaign with results that were, from the Federalist standpoint, lamentable and in the end disastrous.

In the meantime, party leaders who were willing to work for Adams' reelection (and many, including not only Hamilton but also Fisher Ames, George Cabot, John Lowell, Francis Dana, and the president's Secretary of the Treasury Oliver Wolcott, Jr., were not) waged a campaign as muddy as that run by the opposition. Convinced that the country must be rescued from the perils of Jacobinism, Jefferson was depicted as a Francophile who, as president, would pursue a course prefigured by French revolutionaries. "Murder, robbery, rape, adultery, and incest will be openly taught and practiced," so one perfervid traducer commented, and "the air will be rent with the cries of distress, the soil will be soaked with blood and the nation black with crimes."[20] Yet more pernicious was the Virginian's alleged atheism, a charge that was monotonously intoned during the campaign. Both the press and the pulpit hurled anathemas on Jefferson the infidel. The issue was hyperbolically and succinctly expressed by the *Gazette of the United States:*

THE GRAND QUESTION STATED
At the present moment the only question to be
asked by every American, laying his hand on his
heart, is "Shall I continue in allegiance to
GOD—AND A RELIGIOUS PRESIDENT:
or impiously declare for
JEFFERSON—AND NO GOD!!!"[21]

As Dumas Malone commented, "Exaggeration is to be expected in a political campaign, but the invocation of God in behalf of the Federalists is a striking example of the conjunction of self-righteousness with arrogance."[22]

Hamilton did not invoke God, but his stance of self-righteousness and arrogance was unmatched by his Federalist cohorts. There was a difference between them, however. The New Yorker seemed more intent on convicting his own party's chief of official high crimes and misdemeanors than in demonstrating Jefferson's unfitness for the chief magistracy. It would have been clear to any but the most purblind Federalist partisan that the New Yorker's animus for his own party's choice rendered him less an effective partisan leader than a political liability. Hamilton and Adams joined hands to reinforce such a conviction.

Late in July a rumor reached Hamilton that the president had denounced him as the leader of a "damned faction" of "British partisans," a group of men who were "more inimical to the country than the worst Democrats or Jacobins."[23] Such shrill abuse of a prominent member of his own party (even one whom he despised and whose endorsement he scorned) suggests, at the least, some derangement of an ordinarily rational, though highly suspicious, mind.[24] Hamilton's prompt rebuke suggests that he had also lost his emotional balance, or at least all sense of political decorum. Describing the reports that he had heard of Adams' charges, Hamilton imperiously demanded an explanation: "I must, sir, take it for granted," he wrote the president on August 1, "that you cannot have made such assertions or insinuations without being willing to avow them, and to assign the reasons to a party who may conceive himself injured by them."[25] Such insolence shocked even one who viewed the New Yorker as a "Creole bastard," a "lecher and schemer with the cunning of a serpent." Adams predictably "exploded into a fine, shaking rage. Of course he would not reply to the would-be Caesar, but the letter rankled nevertheless."[26]

The New York lawyer's peremptory demands on the nation's chief executive were merely a foretaste of things that would rankle even more. Hamilton's response to a rebuke was never paralysis of the will; an attack was rather a spur to action. Its form was virtually inevitable. As Allan Nevins once said of Hamilton, his "fingers whenever he was in a tight place always itched for the pen"[27]—not only when he was cornered but also when he was angry. Enraged by Adams' refusal to avow or disclaim the charges at issue, Hamilton rashly determined to expose the official shortcomings and neurotic personality of his party chieftain.

As early as July 1, 1800, Hamilton had resolved that it was "essential to inform the most discreet" Federalist notables "of the facts which denote unfitness in Mr. Adams" for the exercise of the presidency.[28] Perhaps some gnawing reservations about the propriety and prudence of such an exercise caused him to delay for a month or so. Once it became clear that the president had no intention of even acknowledging Hamilton's letter demanding a retraction or affirmation of the monarchical proclivities allegedly leveled against him, Hamilton, chagrined by what he viewed as a repudiation of his party standing, decided that the time had come to chop away Adams' presidential pedestal. His critical judgment thus warped, he used an ax far too sharp. Even had he been open to dissuasion, his closest political friends were no help. Contrarily, allies like Fisher Ames, George Cabot, and Oliver Wolcott, Jr., encouraged him, although they admonished him to be prudent and to include no hint that he was driven by political ambition or merely personal antagonism.[29] The warning itself suggested that they thought he might be.

Cabot also wisely advised Hamilton not to sign the proposed partisan polemic, else it would "be converted to a new proof that you are a *dangerous man.*"[30] For his part, Wolcott, who remained on as secretary of the Treasury while also working "assiduously behind Adams' back to bring about his defeat"[31] by elevating Pinckney to the presidency, also urged moderation and refused to cooperate openly with Hamilton's proposed impugnment of Adams' integrity and official ineptness. Were he to do so, Wolcott explained, it would be said (and he should have added "and properly so") "that the President has not injured *me*; that he has borne with my open disapprobation of his measures; and that I ought not to oppose his administration by disclosing what some will term personal or official secrets." Wolcott was nevertheless willing to cooperate covertly, though he was convinced that "the poor old Man is sufficiently successful in undermining his own Credit and influence." "The people," Wolcott explained, "believe that their President is Crazy."[32] The Treasury secretary, as well as the New Yorker's other close political allies, soon cooled to the prospect of Hamilton's publication of his exercise in character assassination.

Hamilton's determination was not at all dampened, however. The fact was that his resolve was neither sudden nor whimsical but the result of long-smoldering, although sometimes suppressed, personal resentment. John Quincy Adams' explanation, written twenty-five years after the event, was not too far off the mark. Hamilton's attack on his father, Adams said, was spawned by disappointment of his military ambition. During Adams' administration, the inspector general "had constantly exercised an influence of personal intrigue and management over a large portion of the party" and "acquired an overruling ascendancy . . . over influential Federalists of New York and New England."[33] Perhaps he was incapable of acknowledging the loss of that ascendancy. Perhaps his true purpose was to enhance the possibility of the election of Pinckney, with whom Hamilton was on cordial terms. Perhaps he had unswervingly convinced himself that Adams had brought the country to the brink of disaster, or perhaps in some convoluted way he believed that in thus securing personal revenge he would also assure rightful public vengeance. One cannot know and can best end the search by repeating Broadus Mitchell's sage conclusion that "no one trait or decision of Adams, no one political event, no single mistake of Hamilton produced the luckless attack."[34]

Mitchell may also be right in saying that Hamilton "had for the nonce lost his grip, his sense of reality."[35] But one must also insist that such behavior was, in fact, not aberrational but consistent. It was Hamilton's exemplification of what Erik Erikson speaks of as "that specific failure that is in each greatness."[36] Obsessed with continued public acceptance of his self-image, Hamilton could not allow it to be besmirched; preoccupied by his repute as a leader of superior talents, he could not tolerate rejection of his claim. The essential sense of self-esteem that he derived from public acclaim of outstanding achievement needed constant reinforcement, even acknowledgment by an avowed antagonist like Adams. "Every day proves to me more and more that this American world was not made for me," Hamilton wrote in 1802.[37] What he perhaps meant was that a new nation that had once offered great scope for his talents and heaped praise upon him now seemed to spurn his advice, to foreclose an opportunity for continued public service, and, above all, to deny him the secure fame that he yearned for. In any event, Hamilton stuck to his resolve to vindicate himself by impugning Adams, to improve the prospects of his own party by revealing that it was torn apart.

According to the generally accepted version of the episode, Hamilton originally intended that his strictures on the character and conduct of Adams be privately printed, shared only with receptive prominent Federalist leaders. Its publication, so the traditional account goes, was due to Aaron Burr, who, hearing of Hamilton's diatribe, properly perceived that its publication would provide powerful ammunition for the Republican campaign. "Arrangements were accordingly made for a copy, as soon as the printing of it was completed," so Burr's contemporary political ally and biographer Matthew L. Davis contended. "The pamphlet was read, and extracts made for the press." The public reaction to these excerpts "compelled Mr. Hamilton to authorize the publication of the entire pamphlet."[38] Recently, the editors of the definitive edition of Hamilton's papers have challenged the traditional interpretation, contending that it is possible that Hamilton himself authorized—or at least implicitly condoned—the public circulation of the pamphlet. The question is worth airing, but as Hamilton's diligent editors concede, we shall never with certainty know the answer, if only "because no account by Hamilton has been found describing his part in the events discussed by Davis" or "his plans concerning the distribution of the pamphlet."[39] One can only say that it would have been singularly in keeping had Hamilton himself contrived the widest possible circulation of his work and that such potent campaign ammunition (whether by his own or Burr's agency) was bound to be seized by the opposing party. As one knowledgeable authority recently observed, "If the printed document did not fall into wrong hands, the indignant or hurt cries of Adams' supporters must advertise it."[40]

Hamilton's philippic, entitled *Letter from Alexander Hamilton, Concerning the Public Conduct and Character of John Adams*,[41] was divided into three sections. The first, and far and away the longest, was a summary of Adams' political career that focused on his ineptitude as president, singling out conspicuous instances of misguided policies and bungling administration. The second part (only three printed pages in the original pamphlet) was an egotistical defense of the propriety of Hamilton's own actions and the purity of his motives. The third (a mere four paragraphs) was a colossal non sequitur in which Hamilton averred that his purpose was not to take away any votes from the president.

The gravamen of Hamilton's complaint was Adams' ineligibility for high public office. There were, the New Yorker explained, "great and intrinsic defects in his character, which unfit him for the office of chief magistrate."[42]

His was "an imagination sublimated and eccentric, propitious neither to the regular display of sound judgment nor to steady perserverance in a systematic plan of conduct."[43] What specific acts demonstrated his unfitness for the presidency, such unsound judgment, and unsystematic performance? A few illustrations from Hamilton's bulky catalog will suffice. The New Englander resented manipulation of the electoral vote in 1788 and 1792 to assure that he would secure fewer votes than Washington. (On this score Hamilton was right, though resentment by one as unabashedly vain and self-centered as Adams was human enough.) Adams was even more offended by the preference that some Federalist notables (Hamilton included) expressed for Adams' running mate, Thomas Pinckney, in the election of 1796, and toward these leaders he bore an ineradicable grudge, the origin, Hamilton believed, of the lamentable schism that bedeviled the party. This split had been unbreachably widened by Adams' misguided foreign policy. On the domestic front, Hamilton lashed out at the president for spitefully dismissing Pickering and McHenry, whose punishment scarcely seemed to fit their alleged misconduct. The New Yorker excoriated Adams for pardoning John Fries, who, as Hamilton saw the issue, should have been made an example of, a sacrifice to the principle of law and order. But such differences between Adams and his inspector general were scarcely sufficient to provoke Hamilton's verbal assault. What really mattered was expressed in the conclusion of his enumeration of the president's offenses: Adams had opposed his appointment as inspector general, "indulged . . . in virulent and indecent abuse" of him and even labeled him the chief of a British faction.[44] In sum, the president, far from admiring Hamilton's preeminent brilliance and public dedication, had not only belittled but also denied them.

On what personal, as distinguished from official, grounds was the president unfit? Hamilton wrote with the vitriol that rage, and maybe envy, inspired. He did not so much discredit as bludgeon his antagonist; the subtlety that his *Letter* lacked was compensated for by shrillness. Adams, this ubiquitous enemy of his country, was obsessed by "vanity without bounds, and a jealousy capable of discoloring every object," one who possessed "disgusting egotism" and an "ungovernable indiscretion of temper."[45] In sum, the president was, in modern parlance, cripplingly neurotic. If one deletes Hamilton's pejorative adjectives and exaggerated language generally, he was unwittingly saying something about himself as well as Adams (though, discounting some distortion, his picture of the president was not an unrecognizable likeness).

Instead of following his line of reasoning to its logical conclusion (Adams' unfitness for the chief magistracy and hence for reelection), Hamilton in the final paragraphs of his *Letter* contradicted what he had expressly striven to prove. What he had written, Hamilton concluded, should not be construed as an effort to wean a single elector from Adams. Loyal party members, supporters of the New Englander and the South Carolinian alike, should "forbear opposition" to either and "acquiesce in the equal support of Mr. ADAMS with Mr. PINCKNEY. . . . Especially, since by doing this, they will increase the probability of excluding a third candidate, of whose unfitness all sincere federalists are convinced. . . . To promote this cooperation [was one of] the inducements for writing this letter."[46]

Not even Hamilton's most steadfast supporters could have swallowed this feebly conciliatory illogicality. Hamilton himself might well have gulped as he penned it. Why, then did he write and publish his philippic? Was it to promote the election of Pinckney as president, as he on one occasion averred? [47] Was it, as a modern biographer insists, "calculated to unseat the Federalist party and usher in what Hamilton professed to dread, a Democratic president"? [48] None of these explanations is altogether convincing. To uncover a more satisfactory solution, one should not view the episode in isolation but as yet another instance of the self-defeating behavior that he had earlier displayed at times of personal crisis, real or imagined.

The incongruousness and particularly the irony of the situation that Hamilton created confounded even the most mindless political observer: the president of the United States, accused by Republicans of being the head of a pro-British conspiracy, damning the most prominent member of his own party as the leader of a faction of British partisans; Hamilton, the "Colossus of Federalism," attacking the president, in Dumas Malone's words, "with a violence entirely comparable to that of the Republican journalists and pamphleteers whom the party in power had sought to silence as dangerous enemies of the government";[49] one purported leader of an alleged monarchical conspiracy denouncing the political philosophy of another.

Such bizarre contrarieties aside, Hamilton's *Letter* alienated many Federalists who had long admired him. "Gen. Hamilton's Letter . . . will not mitigate, but increase the evil" of party disunity, wrote Jedediah Morse. "It will administer *oil* rather than *water* to the fire."[50] "Your ambition, pride and overbearing temper have destined you to be the evil genius of this country," Noah Webster angrily informed Hamilton. "Your conduct on this occasion will be deemed little short of insanity."[51] Even Hamilton's staunchest friends denounced his performance. Robert Troup, Hamilton's longtime friend, reported that in Albany "the general impression among our friends was that it would be injurious" and that in New York City he found even "a much stronger disapprobation of it expressed everywhere."[52] The Republicans, understandably, reacted gleefully to the Federalists' well-publicized internecine squabble, although many of them chose to believe that such infighting was mere blunder, thinly disguising Hamilton's and Adams' common commitment to monarchy. For his part, Hamilton revealed not an iota of regret. The propriety of what his conscience had bade him do was, as usual, unquestioned. Remorse, like conscious self-doubt, was a trait alien to him. He even considered preparing a new edition, revised and amplified, of his *Letter*, indication enough that he attributed to it an efficacy that most others were justifiably too blind to see.[53]

The effects of Hamilton's pamphlet on the outcome of the election remain open to conjecture. Many politicians at the time and historians of a later date believed that the *Letter* deepened the rift among Federalists, diminished

Adams' chances of reelection, and contributed to the eventual demise of the Federalist party. But it is more plausible to conclude that Hamilton, as well as his political allies and foes alike, magnified the political effect of his diatribe. Far from jeopardizing the possibility of a Federalist victory by widening the division among Federalists, one wonders if the *Letter* changed a single vote.[54] Although it appeared in print before most states had formally chosen their electors, the overwhelming majority of the former had already made up their minds, as attested by the remarkably accurate predictions of party leaders.

Far more certain is the effect that the pamphlet had on Hamilton's own political career. His willingness to wreck the party he once had served and defended destroyed his own chance of high political office. Robert Troup wrote what might be construed as Hamilton's political obituary. "The influence . . . of this letter upon Hamilton's character is extremely unfortunate," Troup lamented. "An opinion has grown out of it, which at present obtains almost universally, that his character *is radically deficient in discretion,* and therefore the federalists ask, what avail the most preeminent talents—the most distinguished patriotism—without the all important quality of discretion?" The same question might as appropriately have been asked a decade earlier, but that it would eventually be aired was no doubt inevitable. Similarly, Troup's further comment that Hamilton "is considered as an unfit head of the party" had long been the avowed conviction of many prominent Federalists.[55] For Hamilton, however, it was impossible to concede what he was unconscious of. Nevertheless, some glimmer of the true situation may eventually have broken through the opaqueness by which he preserved the pride so essential to him. If so, the resultant despair may well have led to the fatal encounter on the heights of Weehawken.

For the moment, the results of the presidential election were still in doubt. As results trickled in during December 1800, however, the likelihood of a Republican victory became ever more certain, although the identity of the next president was not. The returns from New England predictably showed the Federalists everywhere victorious; Rhode Island, with four electoral votes, soon joined other New England states in the Federalist column; in New Jersey the Adams-Pinckney ticket got seven Federalist electors; in Maryland, where the elections were by districts, the electors were evenly divided; in North Carolina, the Federalists picked up four electoral votes as against eight for the Republicans. The latter's gravest setback was in Pennsylvania, a key state in which the Republicans expected a sweeping victory; because of complicated election procedures a parliamentary deadlock that pitted the Federalist senate against a Republican-controlled assembly ensued. It was broken by a compromise solution that gave the Jeffersonians eight electors and the Federalists seven. Since the Republicans had made a clean sweep of the other states in the union, thus rendering the votes for the two candidates nearly equal, it was clear that the election would be decided by the eight electors of South Carolina.

"In South Carolina," John Beckley had commented some months earlier,

"great expectations are making on both sides. Our Charles Pinckney is indefatigable."[56] Pinckney, a United States senator and cousin of the Federalist
vice-presidential candidate, was not only tireless but also successful. The
South Carolina political scene was a confusing one, owing largely to the
available options proposed by one or another of the state's prominent political leaders. Some favored the elevation of General Pinckney over Adams,
for example, while others proposed an all-southern ticket joining Jefferson
and Pinckney, a proposal that Pinckney, whose commitment to Adams outweighed his loyalty to the South, squashed. The strategy adopted by Charles
Pinckney, the political renegade but shrewdest campaigner of the Pinckney
clan, was to cultivate assiduously the voters of the state's western counties.
His campaign paid off: the inland counties provided the Republican legislative majority that chose eight electors pledged to Jefferson and Burr.[57] The
Republicans were thus assured of seventy-three electoral votes; the Federalists could count only on sixty-five. "A Republican triumph is now certain,"
a Virginia partisan exulted on December 12.[58]

Uneasy Retirement

But which Republican would be the next president? For the moment, Jefferson, the paladin of his party's crusade, was by no means certain that he rather than his running mate would receive the presidential prize. That would be determined by the House of Representatives, a lame-duck body dominated by the Federalists. What decision would they make? Would they stick by their oft-avowed principle that though the voice of the people might be mistaken, it must nevertheless prevail? Or would they seize the opportunity to deprive the Virginian of the highest office in the land by elevating Aaron Burr to that position? Much depended on Burr himself, whose enigmatical attitude and activities will probably never be satisfactorily understood. Much less (if anything) depended on Hamilton, once the paragon of Federalism, whose standing among his fellow partisans had been irretrievably diminished by his open attack on the Federalists' presidential candidate. Oblivious to his lack of influence, Hamilton tried to determine the outcome of the election in Congress. From mid-December (when it first appeared likely that the election would devolve upon the House) and over the succeeding weeks, as his fellow Federalists appeared increasingly determined to make a president of Aaron Burr, Hamilton's correspondence was dominated by a strenuous effort to elevate Jefferson to the high office for which the voters had chosen him and to consign Burr to the comparative oblivion of the vice-presidency, although Hamilton would have preferred consignment to perdition. It seemed at times as if his detestation of Burr had dispelled his implacable enmity toward the Virginian. So it must have appeared to the few notable Federalists who still heeded the voice of Federalism's fallen titan—steadfast allies like Gouverneur Morris, James Ross, John Rutledge, Jr., James A. Bayard, and Oliver Wolcott, Jr.[1]

It was to Wolcott that Hamilton initially announced the themes that he would play and replay during the congressional contest between Jefferson and Burr. "Jefferson is to be preferred," Hamilton wrote to his successor at the Treasury Department on December 16. "He is by far not so dangerous a man and he has pretensions to character." The same could not be said of Burr. "There is nothing in his favor," Hamilton scornfully wrote. "His private character is not defended by his most partial friends. He is a bankrupt beyond redemption except by the plunder of his country. His public principles have no other spring or aim than his own aggrandisement per *fas* et *nefas*. If he can, he will certainly disturb our institutions to secure himself *permanent power* and with it *wealth*." Pinning on Burr a label that was destined to be endlessly repeated (by Hamilton himself and by historians subsequently), Hamilton asserted that "he is truly the Catiline of America."[2]

As the likelihood of a successful Federalist ploy to make the New York politician the nation's presumably pliable president increased, Hamilton's repetitious excoriation of Burr became increasingly shrill. Although Hamilton's attacks on political rivals, particularly those he also happened to dislike personally, had usually been so, his blistering assault on Burr defies rational explanation. But an attempt to understand is essential if one is to also comprehend the duel that would take place a few years hence. (Had Burr read Hamilton's private correspondence, that fatal encounter might have occurred four years earlier.)

In discussing this puzzling issue of Hamilton's abnormally heightened antagonism, it is tempting to resort to the hackneyed observation that Burr symbolized some of the traits that Hamilton himself revealed but that he could not bring himself to admit to (although awareness of them may have been unconscious). More figuratively expressed, Hamilton's psychic mirror perhaps reflected the image of Aaron Burr. But such an interpretation is not altogether satisfactory. Among Hamilton's political rivals were counted a number who displayed the same qualities that he despised in Burr. Why then single out this one demon for demolition? Perhaps Hamilton was psychically impelled to personify in a single enemy the enmity that he had borne toward so many. He had valiantly tilted with George Clinton, who still remained a power in New York politics. He had fought Jefferson with every weapon at his command, but the Virginian had been chosen to lead the nation that Hamilton believed he had successfully launched. He had fired his heaviest artillery at President John Adams, but Hamilton's countrymen reacted as if he had merely exploded a popgun. Was he now to be bested by a home-state political rival whom Hamilton properly viewed as a far inferior antagonist, deficient in statesmanship, intellect, and character? Not if Hamilton could help it.

Yet another view has some plausibility. It is a psychological commonplace that one sometimes reacts to career frustration by convincing oneself that had one displayed the unconscionable behavior of a successful antagonist, one might also have achieved coveted preeminence. In some convoluted way was Burr, in other words, seen as one who possessed and displayed demagogic, devious, dangerously underhanded behavior of a kind that, had Hamilton himself stooped to employ it, might have guaranteed his own continued political success? Or finally, to put the issue more simply, was Hamilton merely envious? In any event, his strident denigration of Burr illuminates the sources of the animus that led (inexorably one is inclined to believe) to the encounter at Weehawken.

The catalog of Burr's deficiencies and criminality was repeated in letter after letter that the former Treasury secretary wrote to his political allies. Heading the list was his rival's "ambition," not of the laudable kind (as Washington had once described Hamilton's own ambitiousness) but of a pernicious type. Why was Burr's ambition so alarmingly dangerous? Burr's sole "monitor," it would lead him "to use the *worst* part of the community as a ladder to climb to permanent power & an instrument to crush the better part."[3] Here was the crux of Hamilton's charge: Burr's consuming goal was "permanent power in his own hands,"[4] won by "*any* means" and "kept . . . by all means."[5] By what means achieved and retained? "A profligate, a bankrupt," Burr's personal financial exigencies and his inordinate greed for "great wealth"[6] would prevent his satisfaction "with the regular emoluments of any office of our Government. Corrupt expedients will be to him a *necessary* resource,"[7] from which "he will be restrained by no moral scruples."[8] What form would the corruption take? In domestic affairs, "combinations with foreign public agents in projects of gain by means of public monies."[9] In foreign affairs, Burr harbored the scheme of "War with Great Britain as the instrument of Power and Wealth."[10]

Overarching personal ambition was but one of many flaws. Metronome-like, Hamilton ticked off others, among them these: "wicked enough to scruple nothing";[11] "loves nothing but himself";[12] "deficient in *honesty*";[13] "*the most* unfit and dangerous man of the Community";[14] "artful and intriguing";[15] and "a man who despising democracy has chimed in with all its absurdities."[16] Almost unfailingly Hamilton added to these charges the by-now shopworn analogy between Burr and Catiline. "Every step in his career proves that he has formed himself upon the model of *Catiline*," a representative passage read, "and he is too cold-blooded and too determined a conspirator ever to change his plan."[17] In accusations such as these, Hamilton was also indicting a system of government lacking the requisite safeguards to prevent usurpation by a would-be dictator, like Burr. "The truth is that under forms of Government like ours," he wrote, "too much is practicable to men who will without scruple avail themselves of the bad passions of human nature. To a man of this description possessing the requisite talents, the acquisition of permanent power is not a Chimaera."[18]

More interestingly, Hamilton on occasion obliquely attributed to himself qualities that he found lacking in Burr. In one such passage Hamilton commented, "Let it be remembered that Mr. Burr has never appeared solicitous for fame, & that great Ambition unchecked by principle, or the love of

Glory, is an unruly Tyrant.''[19] Hamilton's own covetousness of fame had
long been the wellspring of his public career. His longing for ''glory'' had
been no less so. What is arresting is his presumed belief that his own ''great
ambition'' (of which he had far more than a normal portion) had been successfully curbed by both ''love of glory'' and by steadfast adherence to
''principle.''[20]

It was thus scarcely surprising that Hamilton should have urged his
congressional correspondents to elect Jefferson, the New Yorker's principal
bête noire for a decade.[21] In so doing, he also revealed that beneath the
vilification and scorn he had heaped on his rival, there was a hitherto unavowed awareness that the Virginian had certain redeeming and (by fair
implication) admirable qualities. Even now, Hamilton could not admit as
much (to have done so would have been too patently inconsistent) without
preceding his concession by a halfhearted repetition of stale charges. Having
been the first ''to unfold the true character of Jefferson,'' the New Yorker
wrote James A. Bayard, ''it is too late for me to become his apologist,''
which, in fact, he became in the same letter. The Virginian's ''politics are
tinctured with fanaticism,'' Hamilton, following a familiar script, charged.
''He is too much in earnest in his democracy, . . . he is crafty & preserving
in his objects . . . not scrupulous about the means of success, nor very
mindful of truth,'' and ''a contemptible hypocrite.'' Then, having expressed
opinions whose logical conclusion might have been that Jefferson was eligible for nothing more than the obscurity of retirement at Monticello, he
urged his fellow Federalists to put the Virginian in the White House. In an
assessment of Jefferson that virtually no biographer of Hamilton or student
of the political history of the era has failed to quote, the New Yorker wrote
that

> it is not true as is alleged that he is an enemy to the power of
> the Executive, or that he is for confounding all the powers in the
> House of Rs. . . . Nor is it true that Jefferson is zealot enough
> to do anything in pursuance of his principles which will contra-
> vene his popularity, or his interest. He is as likely as any man
> I know to temporize—to calculate what will be likely to promote
> his own reputation and advantage, and the probable result of
> such a temper is the preservation of systems, though originally
> opposed, which being once established, could not be overturned
> without danger to the person who did it. To my mind a true
> estimate of Mr. J's character warrants the expectation of a tem-
> porizing rather than a violent system.[22]

Thus convinced, Hamilton advised Federalist leaders, who stubbornly insisted that Burr would offer them satisfactory concessions, ''to obtain from
Mr. Jefferson [certain] assurances''—including the preservation of Hamilton's system of finance and public credit, support and increase of the navy,
and neutrality in foreign affairs.[23] In believing that Jefferson would be a
party to such covert bargaining, Hamilton revealed that his insight into the

Virginian's character, although shrewd, was limited. Similarly purblind was Hamilton's assessment of his own role as president-maker. He was politely (and by a few allies, earnestly) listened to and then ignored.

By early January 1801, gossip, both well founded and wild, about Burr's alleged bargaining with Federalist congressional leaders circulated in the corridors of the Capitol and in congressional boardinghouses. Privy to neither Burr's real intentions nor partner to congressional intrigues, Jefferson was resigned but not complacent about the outcome. On the morning of February 11, just as balloting commenced in the House, he wrote to a political lieutenant that whether he or Burr "will be elected and whether either, I deem perfectly problematical: and my mind has long been equally made up for either of the three events."[24] Such resignation was no doubt consoling during succeeding days as roll call after roll call produced no decision. Finally, on February 17 and after thirty-six ballots, his opponents bowed to public opinion and elected him the nation's third and its first Republican president.

The scene of Jefferson's inauguration comported with his ideas of republican simplicity. The new capital "city," located on the Potomac, consisted of a small cleared area dotted by a few scattered buildings, between the surrounding forest and the river. At noon on March 4, 1801, the fifty-seven-year-old statesman, surrounded by well-wishers, walked the short distance from his lodgings at Conrad's boardinghouse to the unfinished Capitol, where the oath of office was to be administered by Chief Justice John Marshall, his cousin and future antagonist. The man who stood before Marshall was, in Henry Adams' description, "very tall . . . sandy-complexioned; shy in manner, seemingly cold; awkward in attitude, and with little in his bearing that suggested command."[25]

Jefferson's inaugural address was delivered in a low mumble, audible only to those immediately around him, but what they heard was characterized by that remarkable grace and felicity of style that make his state papers among the most memorable in American history. Abounding in aphorisms, it was an artful statement of the principles that Jefferson believed "should be the creed of our political faith—the text of our civil instruction": "the diffusion of information and arraignment of all abuses at the bar of the public reason; freedom of religion; freedom of press; freedom of person"; "the support of the State governments in all their rights as the most competent administrations for our domestic concerns and the surest bulwarks against anti-republican tendencies; the preservation of the General Government in its whole constitutional vigor, as the sheet anchor of our peace at home and safety abroad"; "economy in the public expence, that labor may be lightly burdened"; "peace, commerce, and honest friendship with all nations, entangling alliances with none." It was a call for the restoration of harmony and mutual respect and for what is now labeled bipartisanship. "We have called by different names brethren of the same principle," Jefferson said in one of his most captivating sentences. "We are all Republicans; we are all Federalists."[26]

With some of Jefferson's sentiments (particularly his solicitude for the rights of the states), Hamilton surely took exception, but, on balance, he approved of the address. It was, Hamilton averred, "virtually a . . . retraction of past misapprehensions, and a pledge to the community that the new President will not lend himself to dangerous innovations, but in essential points will tread in the steps of his predecessors."[27] Hamilton's perception of the Virginian's essentially pragmatic approach as well as his forecast of the tenor of Jefferson's administration were remarkably accurate. But that emphatically did not mean that he, like some of his fellow partisans, would enlist under the Jeffersonian banner or, for that matter, bestow an apostolic Federalist blessing on his erstwhile foe. He intended instead to retire from public life (presumably because he realized that he had no choice) and to assume a stance of aloofness from affairs of state (of which there was not the remotest possibility). His retirement was in actuality as involuntary as his political powerlessness, although he chose to pretend (and maybe to believe) otherwise.

"To men who have been so much harassed in the base world as myself," Hamilton commented, "it is natural to look forward to complete retirement, in the circle of life as a perfect desideratum."[28] Hamilton's retirement was never complete, but he immersed himself in arrangements for one aspect of this "perfect desideratum": a country estate, befitting a distinguished former statesman and prominent attorney. The site he chose was located in Harlem, some eight miles north of the center of the city. By 1801 he had purchased about thirty acres of land, which extended from a wooded height to the Hudson River. To design an appropriately dignified house he called on John McComb, whose most notable architectural accomplishment was City Hall in lower Manhattan. Hamilton interested himself in every detail of the house, as did Philip Schuyler, who supplied not only advice but material assistance—notably, timber from his Saratoga estate.[29] The two-story house was a square structure with verandas on the north and south sides. It was not, as Hamilton's grandson wrote, "an architectural triumph" but a representative of the "comfortable country house of the period."[30] Hamilton christened it the Grange, the name both of the ancestral Hamilton estate in Ayrshire and the plantation of the Lytton family on St. Croix. The choice was thus a symbolic evocation both of the distinguished Scottish ancestry on which he prided himself and the childhood misfortunes over which he had triumphed.

The Hamilton family moved to the new house in August 1802, although for Hamilton and Eliza's convenience they held onto their house at 58 Partition Street, not far from Hamilton's law office. Although it is difficult to imagine that a man as intense and ambitious as Hamilton could have been at ease without the challenge of public office, he was to all outward appearances contented. Long since suppressed was the familial pain inflicted by the Reynolds affair, and Hamilton and Eliza were apparently deeply devoted to each other and to their house full of children—Philip,* Angelica, Alex-

---

*Philip, the eldest child, had been away at college when the Grange was under construction and was killed in a duel before the family moved there. Another child was born on June 2, 1802, and was named after his late brother.

ander, James Alexander, John Church, William Stephen, and Eliza. Family life was enlivened by the guests, both relatives and friends, who frequently showed up: the Schuylers from Albany, Gouverneur Morris from nearby Morrisania, Rufus King from Jamaica on Long Island, as well as many others.[31]

Such domestic tranquillity was, however, superficial, only thinly veiling the deep sense of grief that had enveloped the household since the death, a year before, of Philip, the eldest child and his father's favorite, in a duel. It was as if fate had written an ominous preview of the encounter that would be staged at Weehawken only a few years later. Philip's death was perhaps not only a prelude to that encounter but also in measure an intangible cause of its tragic outcome.

On the evening of November 20, 1801, Philip, then twenty years old and a recent graduate of Columbia College, attended the Park Theater in New York City, accompanied by a young friend named Price. In the box next to them was George I. Eacker, a lawyer and ardent Jeffersonian who in a partisan oration some four months earlier had (unexceptionably enough) excoriated the Federalists, Hamilton presumably included. Philip and his friend loudly mocked the oration, in a transparent attempt to rile Eacker. They succeeded. The lawyer demanded that the young men join him in the lobby and, following a heated argument, angrily shouted, "I shall expect to hear from you," obviously an invitation to a duel. Both young men accepted. Price's duel took place two days later without harm to either principal. Philip's duel was scheduled for Sunday, and despite attempts of the seconds of the two antagonists to dissuade Eacker, as the senior of the two men, to retract his challenge (promising that if he did so young Hamilton would apologize), the duel took place as scheduled. The site was Powles Hook, New Jersey. Eacker took careful aim, Philip fell, mortally wounded, without having fired a shot. He died the next afternoon.*[32]

Hamilton was distraught. Dr. David Hosack, his family physician, who attended Philip during his final hours, reported that when Hamilton reached his son's bedside, "ascertained the direction of the wound," examined Philip's "countenance and felt the pulse, . . . he instantly turned from the bed, and taking me by the hand with all the agony of grief, he exclaimed in tones and manner that can never be effaced from my memory, 'Doctor, I despair.' "[33] Hamilton's own grief was never effaced from memory, and his words "I despair" were more meaningful than he perhaps realized. His despair over Philip's death deepened his despondency over his early and unwanted retirement, and in the end, despair triumphed in what Erik Erikson has described as one final alternative of man's final stage of life.

---

*According to one of Philip Hamilton's Columbia classmates, "General Hamilton . . . commanded his Son, when on the ground, to reserve his *fire,* 'till after Mr. E. had shot and then to discharge his pistol in the air."[34] There is no substantiating evidence for this assertion, and it is highly unlikely that Hamilton told his son, in effect, to commit suicide.

"Never did I see a man so completely overwhelmed with grief as Hamilton has been," Robert Troup commented shortly after the duel.[35] And it was not soon lightened. The resilience that Hamilton had demonstrated following earlier setbacks and sorrows deserted him. His son had died in defense not of his own behavior but of his father's public career, one that had been brilliant but not untarnished. It is perhaps fanciful to conjecture about the burden of guilt that Hamilton carried and could not manage to suppress. It is less imaginary to surmise that such guilt was heightened by Hamilton's own willingness—demonstrated time and again—to go to virtually any lengths to defend the integrity of his public career, the deep-seated, abiding source of his sense of self-esteem. Did he realize a death too late that Philip had done what he had no doubt been prepared in extremis to do? Whatever the answer, time did not weaken Hamilton's resolve, which may, indeed, have been strengthened by Philip's ultimate sacrifice.

Time did abate the grief that all but incapacitated him during the months following his son's death. Perhaps he sought solace in religion, which would explain a proposal he at this time made, which was, in view of his previous neutral attitude on the subject, oddly out of character. In the spring of 1802 Hamilton, having decided that one prerequisite for good citizenship was religious commitment, recommended the formation of an association to be known as the Christian Constitutional Society, whose purpose (as its name implied) would be to support Christianity and the United States Constitution. For the moment, he presumably believed that the first commitment was the concomitant of adherence to the Constitution, or at least to the Federalist interpretation of that document. The members of the proposed society would pledge themselves to vote for bona fide Federalist candidates, and the organization would afford aid to immigrants and the deserving poor, presumably in the process converting them to the conjoined doctrines of Christianity and Federalism.[36] The plan was stillborn, as perhaps Hamilton preconsciously realized that it would be. It was, in fact, an effort to clutch at any safety line, at a time when personal grief and political frustration threatened to drown him. There were better and more customary ways to rescue himself from such dangerous waters, however. Work helped, and Hamilton sought to dispel despair by energetic absorption in his ever-growing law practice and in affairs of state, although perforce only vicariously.

The latter never ceased to be a major preoccupation. He had closely followed the events that transpired in the nation's capital and continued to comment on them, in private correspondence and in public print.[37] For the latter, he arranged a personal forum. This was the *New York Evening Post,* which he, in cooperation with Troup and other friends, established late in 1801. He persuaded William Coleman to serve as editor, but editorial policy was largely decided by Hamilton. Senator Jeremiah Mason elicited from Coleman the extent and nature of Hamilton's relationship with the *Post.* Coleman explained that "he made no secret of it; that his paper was set up under the auspices of General Hamilton, and that he assisted him." Not that Hamilton was involved in the day-to-day operations of the paper. Instead, his role, as explained by Coleman was this: "Whenever anything occurs on which I feel the want of information, I state the matter to him, sometimes in a note. He appoints a time when I may see him." He then "begins in a deliberate manner to dictate, and I to take down in short hand; when he stops my article is completed."[38] In sum, under Coleman's editorship the *Post* was, in John C. Miller's words, "a mirror of Hamilton's mind."[39] And that mirror pictured a newfound moderateness. It was expressed in the *Post*'s prospectus, which appeared on November 16, 1801. "Though we openly profess our attachment to that system of politics denominated Federal, because we think it most conducive to the welfare of the community . . . yet we . . . believe that honest and virtuous men are to be found in each party." There is an interesting irony in the fact that just as President Jefferson paid Hamilton the unexpected compliment of continuing his policies, so Hamilton came close to endorsing the Virginian's inaugural observation that "we are all Republicans; we are all Federalists."

Hamilton's interests were as broad as the concerns and decisions of the Jefferson administration. As William Coleman remarked, "he always keeps himself minutely informed on all political matters."[40] But the single issue that most engaged his attention was the Louisiana Purchase. It was predictable that it would, in the sense that Hamilton had long coveted American possession of contiguous territory owned by Spain. As inspector general, he had flirted with the idea (perhaps dreamed would be a preferable word) of its military conquest, but having neither the authority nor the requisite forces to do so, he had been obliged to content himself with sharing his aspirations with Francisco de Miranda. By a chain of fortuitous events, this territory fell into Jefferson's outstretched and welcoming hand.

In 1800 Napoleon, preparatory to the reconquest of Santo Domingo, put strong pressure upon the Spanish monarchs to induce them to give up Louisiana and the Floridas. The Spaniards were not reluctant to retrocede Louisiana, which brought them little but large expenses, but were unwilling to relinquish the Floridas. Napoleon settled for Louisiana and that region was returned to France by the Treaty of San Ildefonso of October 1800. Two years later, the Spanish intendant of New Orleans, in preparation for the French takeover, issued a proclamation closing that port to American vessels.

Jefferson's initial reaction was to propose measures that even Hamilton had stopped short of. The United States must, he decided, "marry" itself to the British navy and monarchy[41] (toward which he previously had professed detestation) to abort French imperialism. Hamilton's reaction was different. We must promptly seize both New Orleans and the Floridas, he believed, and negotiate with Napoleon on the basis of our successful military mission. In the event, neither an Anglo-American alliance nor war was the American response. The president decided to send James Monroe to France with instructions to purchase New Orleans from France. The outcome is well-known: Napoleon, having abandoned his grandiose schemes for an American empire, offered to sell not only New Orleans but the entire Louisiana territory. It was the most spectacular acquisition of land in American history, and Jefferson, putting aside his constitutional scruples, readily accepted it.

Hamilton had no misgivings of any kind and, virtually alone among Federalist leaders, applauded the purchase. Although expressing anxiety that the acquisition of such a vast area all at once "threatens the dismemberment of a large portion of our country,"[42] he nevertheless believed that possession of this vast domain must eventually put America on a straight road to national greatness, which was always his overarching concern.

He might also have taken some credit for the successful transaction. Had it not been for his policies that had at the outset solidly established the new nation's solvency and credit, the purchase might not have been possible. As things were, the United States was easily able to absorb the purchase price, and "Republicans—the traditional opponents of government expenditures—were able to speak of a debt of $15 million as 'a triffling sum.' "[43] With the Louisiana Purchase the national debt soared to the highest peak of the period before the Civil War. But most Americans were undisturbed. A national debt, managed by Secretary of the Treasury Albert Gallatin, was something of a national blessing, while under Hamilton it had been considered by the same citizens as a national curse.

To pile paradox on paradox, Hamilton now became the spokesman for civil liberties, which the Republicans only recently had accused him of trying to stifle. He did not, however, receive public acclaim as the champion of individual freedom, an accolade bestowed on his former opponents for their opposition to the Sedition Act of 1798. The Republicans had, in fact, never opposed prosecutions for seditious libel as such but rather the alleged arrogation of that right by national courts, consonant with federal law. Trials for the same offense in state courts were another matter. As Leonard Levy comments, the Jeffersonians, along with their leader, "accepted without question the dominant view of [their] generation that government could be criminally assaulted merely by the expression of critical opinions that allegedly tended to subvert it by lowering it in the public's esteem."[44] And truth was not generally regarded as a defense against the expression of purportedly subversive statements. So it was that state officials and courts unhesitatingly sought to suppress Federalist newspapers, without any sense of inconsistency.

One such notable incident occurred in New York State. Harry Croswell was the printer of a small country newspaper appropriately entitled *The Wasp*. An ardent Federalist, Croswell was indicted in 1802 for "having wickedly disturbed the peace and tranquility" by printing a statement that President Jefferson had paid James T. Callender (the editor who had publicly aired Hamilton's alleged corrupt connection with James Reynolds in 1797) for writing an exercise in character assassination entitled *The Prospect Before Us*. In this pamphlet, Callender had, among other calumnies, characterized Washington as a "traitor, a robber, and a perjurer" and described John Adams as a "hoary headed indendiary."[45] The allegation made against Jefferson was a partial truth, the description of Washington was absurd, and the picture of Adams was not essentially different from that painted by

Hamilton in 1800. Nevertheless, State Attorney General Ambrose Spencer, who was a loyal Jeffersonian, instituted proceedings against Croswell for libel. The *Wasp*'s editor pleaded for a postponement of the trial in order to allow him to bring forth Callender as a material witness to the accuracy of Croswell's charges. The trial judge dismissed the request on the grounds that truth was no defense against libel.

On the advice of the bevy of Federalist lawyers who had defended him, Croswell appealed and the case was put on the docket of the New York Court of Errors. The essential questions before the Court in *People v. Croswell* were whether the defendant had, in fact, printed the alleged libel and the legal proprietary of the lower court's ruling that the truth was no defense against such libel. The case was argued in February 1804 before a full court presided over by Judge Morgan Lewis. Chief counsel for the state was Attorney General Spencer; principal attorney for the defendant was Hamilton, who had readily accepted a case that he considered a particularly challenging and legally consequential one.[46]

Hamilton's summation of his client's cause was described by James Kent, one of the judges who presided at the trial. "This argument and speech of General Hamilton's," Kent wrote in his notes on the case, "was a masterpiece of pathetic, impassioned, and sublime eloquence. It was probably never *surpassed* and made the deepest impression. I never heard him so great."[47]

Consonant with the major legal points at issue, Hamilton centered on the trial judge's adherence to the common-law doctrine that in libel litigation truth was not a defense. Such a doctrine, Hamilton contended, was a departure from ancient common law, originating in repugnant Star Chamber proceedings, and was particularly odious in a republic. Libel, Hamilton argued, was "a slanderous or ridiculous writing, picture or sign, with a malicious or mischievous design or intent, towards government, magistrate or individuals." The critical word in this definition was "intent," and in the ascertainment of intent, Hamilton contended, truth was relevant. "I never did think truth was a crime," he argued. "I am glad the day is come in which it is to be decided; for my soul has ever abhorred the thought, that a free man dare not speak the truth."[48]

Hamilton's theme, in sum, was that "the liberty of the press consists in the right to publish with impunity truth, with good motives, for justifiable ends, though reflecting on government, magistracy, or individuals." Such liberty was at the very base of free government, and its denial would mean that "good men would become silent, corruption and tyranny would go on, step by step, in usurpation, until, at last, nothing that was worth speaking, or writing, or acting for, would be left in our country."[49]

Here was an eloquent argument on behalf of a free press, a free government, and a free people. Hamilton, with audacious legal craftsmanship, turned the case of an obscure country editor into a milestone in the struggle for fundamental and inviolable civil rights. It was his final public testament, and it was an appropriate one, in the sense that he set forth again doctrines that he had embraced during the American Revolution and that he had subsequently deemphasized but never renounced.

Hamilton won the Croswell case before the bar of history but not before the New York Court of Errors. On the last day of the term, Chief Judge Lewis announced that the court was equally split on the case, so the verdict of the trial judge stood. The New York legislature was obviously more responsive to Hamilton's argument than the state's highest court, and in 1805 a libel law incorporating Hamilton's position was enacted. "In time it was embraced throughout the American Republic," one present-day historian observes, "and formed the legal foundation, firmer than the First Amendment, for the idea of a free and responsible press."[50]

XX

Encounter at Weehawken

Hamilton's repute as a lawyer was at its zenith. But his political influence, which was already virtually invisible on the national scene, would soon be in eclipse even in state politics. This was revealed by the New York gubernatorial election of 1804. The backdrop for this political tale was New England, where Federalist extremists, led by Timothy Pickering, pondered the desirability of seceding from a union now governed, as they saw the matter, by southern slaveowners and headed by a Virginian whom they still viewed as an Antichrist. To Pickering and other members of the Essex Junto, the purchase of Louisiana (from which new Republican states would be carved) spelled the doom of New England, its increasing isolation and steadily diminishing influence in national affairs. The successful formation of a separate confederacy depended, it was believed, on the accession of New York. Hamilton, who was approached by the would-be secessionists, indignantly refused to have anything to do with such a scheme. They then pinned their hopes on Burr, whom they knew to be a far more pliable and crafty politician.

Burr was the ideal choice. "Odd man out in the Jefferson Administration," the New Yorker seemingly had no place to go except political oblivion.[1] As vice-president, Burr had been the victim of Jefferson's personal malice. Stung by such malevolence, Burr abandoned his political affiliation as a Republican and identified himself as a Federalist, which in view of that party's shaky status was a measure of the vice-president's desperation. Although Burr was characteristically evasive about joining a northern confederation, he readily accepted the opportunity to run for governor of New York.

Because of the ascendancy of the Jeffersonians in that state, the Federalists did not nominate a candidate for the governorship. The Republican machine chose John Lansing, Jr., as their candidate and, when Lansing unaccountably withdrew, selected Morgan Lewis. Meeting on February 18, 1804, a rump caucus consisting of dissident Republicans and Federalists agreed to support Burr for governor.

Hamilton was in Albany arguing the Croswell case when he heard of Burr's nomination. His opposition was easily foreseeable. In an attempt to detach the Federalists from Burr's candidacy, he once again trotted out his by-now familiar strictures on Burr's character defects and consequent ineligibility for political office. If elected governor, Burr, a man "of irregular and insatiable ambition," would unhesitatingly urge that "a dismemberment of the Union is expedient."[2] To avoid such a disaster, Hamilton pleaded with his fellow Federalists to avoid the fate of the Trojans and to support Lewis, the majority Republican candidate. Lewis was elected by a comfortable majority, but Hamilton's contribution was at best marginal. Five-sixths of the Federalists voted for Burr, but the latter suffered the most decisive defeat of any gubernatorial candidate up to that time. His rout demonstrated the invincibility of the Clinton-Livingston coalition that supported Lewis. Had Hamilton kept in mind this elementary political fact, he might not have bothered to further antagonize Burr. What may in hindsight appear obvious was presumably not so to Hamilton. But the fact remains, as John Quincy put it, that the New York election revealed that the Federalists comprised a minority and "of that minority, only a minority were admirers and partisans of Mr. Hamilton."[3] In sum, short of a miracle, his political career was now over.

How could Hamilton escape awareness of that incontestable fact? The illusion of political power may well have been maintained in the face of the adverse reaction to his attack on Adams four years earlier and his manifestly declining importance in party councils following his retirement from public office. But to have clung to such an illusion following his decisive setback in 1804 would have been delusional, and presumably Hamilton tried to extinguish the fire of political ambition that had so long burned so brightly. Nevertheless, he could not easily (nor perhaps successfully) do so. The altered course of his life imperiled the identity that he had forged as a great statesman, the repute that he cherished above all else. The change may also have brought to the fore doubts and despondency that had hitherto been held in check. Would he win what Erik Erikson has called the titanic "struggle between destructive and constructive forces, . . . between regressive and progressive alternatives"? Blocked in his ambition to continue to assure his fame as a statesman, would Hamilton's "lust for power" turn "into furious anger with himself, [and] with his circumstances"?[4] More specifically, could he settle for his still enviable repute as a distinguished lawyer, the attention of a devoted family, the role of country squire? Hamilton's career would have suggested an affirmative answer. He had, after all, surmounted the many obstacles that had blocked the road of his career and had acquired in the process what few men ever achieve—a place among the heroes of the nation's history. Would he rest content in the awareness of such an accomplishment or would political frustration lead to personal despair? If the latter happened, Burr handed him a way of dealing with it.

Burr's political prospects had been dim before his defeat in the New York gubernatorial race; they now reached the vanishing point. Hitherto he had ostensibly reacted to political preferment or setbacks with an air of insouciance, perhaps because he considered politics a diversion that gentlemen treated with cynical detachment, not as a deadly struggle for power. Whether such a posture had been genuine or sham, he was no longer able to accept political defeat with detachment nor partisan enemies with charity. He had patiently endured too many of both. Heavily in debt, spurned by the leaders of a party whose success in 1800 he had been measurably responsible for, excoriated by political figures he considered his inferiors, Burr sought some kind of tangible revenge. Hamilton, who in private and in public had for years traduced him on every available occasion, was a made-to-order target. (Burr apparently did not dwell on the fact that a more suitable object of vengeance might have been Jefferson, who more than any other person was in fact responsible for the New Yorker's political downfall and disgrace.) Burr chose instead to slay a now-toothless dragon. A good pretext conveniently presented itself.

The excuse was a newspaper report by one Dr. Charles D. Cooper, who wrote that he had heard Hamilton say that he "looked upon Mr. Burr to be a dangerous man, and one who ought not to be trusted with the reins of government." Such a charge was too innocuous and commonplace to serve as the basis of a personal challenge. The sentence that followed was another matter. "I could detail to you," Cooper told his readers, "a still more despicable opinion which General HAMILTON has expressed of Mr. BURR."[5] On June 18, 1804, the latter had his friend William Van Ness (who usually acted as Burr's second in duels) call on Hamilton with a copy of Cooper's newspaper column along with a note from Burr demanding "a prompt and *unqualified* acknowledgment or denial of any expression which would warrant the assertions of Dr. Cooper."[6] In view of the bearer of the letter and its tone there could have been no doubt about its author's intent.

One is entitled to wonder about Hamilton's inner reaction—shock, indignation, apprehension, or resignation—but can only know that he did not seek to escape the trap somewhat clumsily laid for him. He pondered the matter for two days and then turned down Burr's demand. Apropos of the essential allegation at issue, Hamilton wrote, " 'Tis evident that the phrase 'still more despicable' admits of infinite shades, from very light to very dark. How am I to judge of the degree intended?" He was ready to "avow or disavow promptly any precise or definite opinion which I may be charged with." But further than that, he refused to go. If Burr disagreed, "I can only regret the circumstances, and must abide the consequences."[7] It was a fateful commitment.

Burr strongly disagreed, demanded again that Hamilton admit to or disown the offensive comment, and, presumably intent on carrying the dispute to the dueling ground, tersely concluded that "your letter has furnished me with new reasons for requiring a definite reply.'' Hamilton told Van Ness that to this ''rude and offensive'' demand, ''he could make no reply and Mr. Burr must pursue such course as he should deem most proper.'' Although Hamilton did respond, his terse letter to Burr was as unconciliatory as his verbal communication to Van Ness. ''I have no other answer to give than that which has already been given,'' he testily wrote. An impasse between the two antagonists having been reached, correspondence was turned over to their seconds: Van Ness for Burr and Nathaniel Pendleton for Hamilton. Negotiations were futile: Burr refused to budge, and Hamilton yielded only so far as to agree to aver that his comments to Cooper ''turned wholly on political topics, and did not attribute to Col. Burr, any instance of dishonorable conduct, nor relate to his private character.'' Had Burr been willing to let his prey off the hook, such a concession would have been sufficient. He was not and chose instead to enlarge his demands. Hamilton adamantly refused to make any further concession and instead decided that since Burr displayed ''predetermined hostility'' toward him, Van Ness could deliver his principal's ''invitation.'' Burr extended it, and Hamilton, while asking for a short delay to put his affairs in order, accepted. The duel was scheduled for the morning of July 11.[8]

The encounter was not only unnecessary but also inconsistent with the prescribed rules of the *code duello*. According to that code, personal injury, not political enmity, was the only proper basis for a challenge. Nor could it be grounded merely on malice. Before 1804, Hamilton and Burr had contrived to maintain a formally polite personal relationship. During the election of that year, moreover, Hamilton had made no specific or provable charges that, strictly construed, could be considered as personally injurious to Burr. But, as one student of the episode aptly remarks, Burr ''was more eager to get Hamilton within the sights of a pistol than to secure the kind of retraction to which he was entitled.''[9]

But the question remains, Why did Hamilton refuse to give the kind of retraction (an apology would have sufficed) that Burr would have been obliged to accept? Had that proved impossible, why did he not refuse to take part in a practice that he considered abhorrent? Some twenty-five years earlier Hamilton, in explaining why he would not fight a duel, had reminded an overwrought correspondent ''that we do not now live in the days of chivalry. . . . The good sense of the present times has happily found out that to prove your own innocence, or the malice of an accuser, the worst method, you can take is to run him through the body, or shoot him through the head. . . . 'Tis a good old maxim . . . that we ought to do our duty, & leave the rest to the care of Heaven.''[10] In 1804, as in 1779, Hamilton might have left the disposition of his cause to Heaven (or perhaps to posterity). Why did he convince himself that it was imperative to face Burr's pistol? His close friend Oliver Wolcott, Jr., offered a perceptive explanation: Hamilton ''reasoned himself into a belief, that though the custom was the highest degree criminal, yet there were peculiar reasons which rendered it proper for *him* to expose *himself* to Col. Burr in particular.''[11]

What were these unusual circumstances? In a document written shortly before the duel, Hamilton provided his own explanation, presumably for both his family and posterity. He first set forth the "cogent reasons" that made him "desirious of avoiding this interview," among them his strong "religious and moral" objections to dueling and concern for a family, "extremely dear to me," to whom his life was "of the utmost importance." Convincing though such reasons may have been to an impartial observer, they were not sufficient to dissuade Hamilton from meeting Burr at Weehawken. Admitting (and correctly so) that his "animadversions on the political principles, character and views of Col. Burr have been extremely severe," Hamilton nevertheless believed that such strictures had been made "with sincerity" and for "motives and for purposes" that still seemed to him valid. For this reason, "the disavowal required of me by Col. Burr, in a general and indefinite form, was out of my power, if it really had been proper for me to be so questioned."[12] This was obviously a somewhat oblique way of saying that because he had in the past relentlessly maligned Burr, he must be expected to pay the price exacted by his antagonist. But why pay such an exorbitant price? Because "what men of the world denominate honor, impressed on me (as I thought) a peculiar necessity not to decline the call." In what sense was the necessity peculiar for him? Such a decision must be made, Hamilton answered, because on it hinged his "ability to be in future useful, whether in resisting mischief or in effecting good, in those crises of our public affairs, which seem likely to happen" and that "would probably be inseparable from a conformity with public prejudice in this particular." If Hamilton genuinely believed this, he chose a curious way of assuring it. He had resolved, he wrote, "to *reserve* and *throw away* my first fire, and I have *thoughts* even of *reserving* my second fire."[13] As Henry Adams said, Hamilton thus "allowed himself to be drawn into a duel but instead of killing Burr, he invited Burr to kill him."[14]

Hamilton's confidence in his future political usefulness, moreover, was mere whimsy. As he must have perceived, although characteristically he never acknowledged the awareness, a political world dominated by Thomas Jefferson, James Madison, and their stalwart allies was not for him. Perhaps he also experienced "a sense of stagnation," which Erikson maintains is "paradoxically . . . felt by creative people more deeply than by others."[15] He may also have keenly and painfully recalled his son Philip, who in defense of his father's good name had sacrificed his life in a duel with a cold-blooded killer and had himself thus resolved to do likewise. If these surmises are believable, then Hamilton, as Erikson says Martin Luther did, "faced . . . death, nor for the sake of established creed or ties of ancestry and tradition; he did so because of *personal* convictions, derived from inner conflict."[16]

Hamilton outwardly displayed no sign of conflict or apprehension during the days immediately preceding the duel. He calmly attended to his law practice, drew up his will, and wrote two brief farewell letters to his wife. In each of these, he reminded Eliza, as he wrote on July 4, that "the consolations of Religion, my beloved can alone support you. . . . Fly to the bosom of your God and be comforted.''[17] In the second, written on July 10, there was, in addition, one puzzling sentence. Asserting that he had determined ''to expose my own life to any extent rather than subject myself to the guilt of taking another,'' Hamilton added, ''But you had rather I would die innocent than live guilty.''[18] Fawn Brodie, whose writings display an uncommon acute psychological perception, interprets this to mean that Hamilton, ''as suicides often do,'' was putting ''the burden of his coming death squarely on someone else's shoulders.''[19] Was he rather not subliminally recalling Eliza's reaction to the ostensibly long-buried Reynolds affair, as well as to other aspects of his controversial career? Was there in these words a latent reprimand? We cannot, of course, know. We do know that on the night preceding the duel, ''when he was to abandon his family in a fashion far more terrible than that of his own father,'' he slept beside his thirteen-year-old son.[20] Had James Hamilton, on the eve of deserting his family, done the same with his eleven-year-old son, Alexander?

Shortly after dawn on the morning of July 11, Hamilton, Pendleton (his second), and Dr. David Hosack (his personal physician) were rowed across the Hudson to Weehawken. Burr and Van Ness were already there. The formalities of the *code duello* were strictly followed: lots were cast to determine their position and the second who should give commands (Hamilton won both); facing each other, Van Ness and Pendleton loaded the pistols and then measured off the stipulated ten paces; and Pendleton gave the command, ''Present.'' Two shots were fired. Although the precise details of what happened will most likely never be agreed on (the story is so much a part of national folklore and too often reviewed and retold for that to happen), it is likely that Burr took careful aim and that Hamilton, in an involuntary reflex, pulled the trigger of his pistol as he fell. Burr quickly left the field so that Dr. Hosack could not identify him, and the doctor rushed to Hamilton's aid. ''I found him half sitting on the ground, supported in the arms of Mr. Pendleton,'' Hosack recalled. ''His countenance of death I shall never forget. He had at that instant just strength to say, 'This is a mortal wound Doctor'; when he sunk away, and became to all appearances lifeless.''[21]

Hamilton was carried to the waiting barge, and about fifty yards from the Manhattan shore, ''he sighed . . . his eyes, hardly open, wandered, without fixing on any objects: [and he] at length spoke: 'My vision is indistinct,' were his first words,'' and then, ''Let Mrs. Hamilton be immediately sent for—let the event be gradually broken to her; but give her hopes.'' He was taken to the nearby house of his friend William Bayard, where for the next thirty-six hours ''his sufferings [were] almost intolerable.''[22] Eliza, who bore ''with saintlike fortitude this affliction,'' sat by him.[23] When his seven children, the youngest only two years of age, were brought to his bedside ''his utterance forsook him, he opened his eyes, gave them one look, and closed them again, till they were taken away.'' He had, after all, forsaken them. on the altar of his own pride. Eliza remained, and to her Hamilton repeatedly turned, saying, *"Remember, my Eliza, you are a Christian."*[24] How often had she told him that, by way of subtle chiding or rejection? Now the past could be buried, but the gentle rebuke, even as life ebbed, crept out from the dimly recalled crevices of buried momory. But it no longer really mattered. By becoming the martyr, he had acted out her martyrdom.

And, now, religion was a consolation that he wished for himself. Hamilton "has desired to receive the sacrament," Oliver Wolcott wrote on July 11, "but no one of the Clergy who have yet been consulted will administer it."[25] But Episcopal Bishop Benjamin Moore relented. Following Hamilton's confession of "sorrow and contrition" for having engaged in such a "barbarous custom" as dueling and his repentence of "sins past," "lively faith in God's mercy through Christ," and union in "love and charity with all men," Bishop Moore administered the Eucharist. Hamilton's "heart afterwards appeared to be perfectly at rest," according to the bishop, who visited the dying man again on the following day, July 12. Moore remained with Hamilton until two o'clock in the afternoon, "when death closed the awful scene. He expired without a struggle, and almost without a groan."[26] His life had been an awe-inspiring scene, the struggle had ceased, and the ultimate reconciliation achieved. There was nothing to bemoan.

Notes

CHAPTER I

1. This century's most scholarly and meticulous biographer of Hamilton comments that "no documentary evidence for his birthplace has been found," but argues that Nevis is the most likely place. Broadus Mitchell, *Alexander Hamilton*, 2 vols. (New York, 1957, 1962), I, 7, 468 (hereafter cited as Mitchell, *Hamilton*).
2. James Hamilton was the fourth son of a Scottish laird who belonged to the Grange line of the Hamilton family, which dated back to the fourteenth century. His mother, also of a distinguished family, was the daughter of Sir Robert Pollock. Hamilton could thus correctly insist that he had "better pretensions than most of those who in this Country plume themselves on Ancestry." Hamilton to William Jackson, Aug. 26, 1800, in Harold C. Syrett *et al.,* eds., *Papers of Alexander Hamilton*, 26 vols. (New York, 1961–1978), XXV, 89 (hereafter cited as *Hamilton Papers*).
3. Apropos of his father, Hamilton himself wrote as follows: "A Dane a fortune-hunter of the Name of *Lavine* came to Nevis bedizzened with gold, and paid his addresses to my mother then a handsome young woman. . . . In compliance with the wishes of her mother . . . but against her own inclination she married Lavine." *Ibid.*
4. Mitchell, *Hamilton*, I, 7, 473.
5. Although a comparatively unimportant issue, the date of Hamilton's birth has received lavish attention. During the 1950s and 1960s (a period rich in Hamilton scholarship) it was generally agreed that Hamilton was born in the year 1755. The evidence in support of this contention is set forth in Mitchell, *Hamilton*, I, 11–13, and *Hamilton Papers*, I, 1–3. Hamilton's two most recent biographers reject this contention and accept the traditional view that his birthdate was 1757. See Forrest McDonald, *Alexander Hamilton: A Biography* (New York, 1979), 7, 366–367 (hereafter cited as McDonald, *Hamilton*); Robert Hendrickson, *Hamilton*, 2 vols. (New York, 1976), I, 1–3. The arguments of both McDonald and Hendrickson are convincing but based on conjecture. Since the most reliable documentary evidence, the probate court records of Christiansted, St. Croix, gives Hamilton's age as thirteen at the time of his mother's death in February 1768, I have assumed that his birthdate was 1755.
6. H. U. Ramsing, "Alexander Hamilton og hans modrene Slaegt. Tidsbilleder fra Dansk Vest-Indiens Barndom," *Personal-historik Tidsskrift*, 59 de Flargang, 10 Rekke, 6 Bind (1939). Translated by Solvenjg Vahl, 8 (hereafter cited as Ramsing, "Hamilton").
7. Ramsing, "Hamilton," 12.
8. Hamilton to William Hamilton, May 2, 1797, *Hamilton Papers*, XXI, 77.
9. *Ibid.*, I, 3.
10. Mitchell, *Hamilton*, I, 17, without ref.
11. Hamilton to William Hamilton, May 2, 1797; Hamilton to William Jack-

son, Aug. 26, 1800. *Hamilton Papers,* XXI, 77–79; XXV, 88–90.

12. John Church Hamilton, *History of the Republic of the United States . . . As Traced in the Writings of Alexander Hamilton,* 7 vols. (New York, 1857–1864), I, 6 (hereafter cited as John C. Hamilton, *History*).

13. Hamilton to Edward Stevens, Nov. 11, 1769, *Hamilton Papers,* I, 4.

14. The article was published anonymously in the *Royal American Danish Gazette,* Oct. 3, 1772. See *Hamilton Papers,* I, 34–38.

15. *Ibid.,* 6–7; see also 38–39.

16. Knox, who was some thirty years older than Hamilton, had migrated from Northern Ireland to America. After a short time there, he answered a call of the Dutch Reformed church of the tiny West Indian island of Saba. He remained on that small, mountainous island for seventeen years. Then, in May 1772, he moved to Christiansted as minister of its Presbyterian church. Since Hamilton left St. Croix in October 1772, any long association between the two men was impossible. Granted that the effect of a relationship need not depend on its duration, it still seems unlikely that Knox exercised any appreciable influence on Hamilton's intellectual development. The point is aired only because many historians, following the lead of Hamilton's son (John C. Hamilton, *History,* I, 3), have made so much of the association. What the minister did provide Hamilton was an introduction to prominent families in New Jersey.

17. See Mitchell, *Hamilton,* I, 34.

18. Since Hamilton had no acquaintances in Boston nor had been (so far as is known) introduced to anyone, he presumably lodged at a tavern there and promptly left for New York City. Stages left Boston for New York on alternate Mondays and the trip took roughly a week. *Ibid.,* 38.

19. Mulligan's "Narrative of Hercules Mulligan of the City of New York," *William and Mary Quarterly* (hereafter cited as *WMQ*), 3rd ser., 4 (April 1947), 209–211. For information on Mulligan and an assessment of the accuracy of his recollections, see *ibid.*

20. Richard B. Morris, *Seven Who Shaped Our Destiny* (New York, 1973), 227.

21. "Narrative of Hercules Mulligan," 209.

22. Information on the year that Hamilton enrolled at King's College and his activities there are based on the recollections of his friend Robert Troup, recorded more than thirty-six years later. "Narrative of Colonel Robert Troup," *WMQ,* 3rd ser., 4 (April 1947), 212–225. For a thorough account of Hamilton's college years based not only on Troup's "Narrative" but other sources, see Mitchell, *Hamilton,* I, 54–56.

23. "Narrative of Colonel Robert Troup," 212.

24. John C. Hamilton, *History,* I, 22–23.

CHAPTER II

1. *A Full Vindication of the Measures of the Congress, from the Calumnies of their Enemies; In Answer to A Letter, Under the Signature of A. W. Farmer . . .* (New York, 1774). Printed in *Hamilton Papers,* I, 45–78, to which the citations below are made.

2. *The Farmer Refuted: or A more impartial and comprehensive View of the Dispute between Great-Britain and the Colonies, Intended as a Further Vindication of Congress: . . .* (New York, 1775). Printed in *Hamilton*

Papers, I, 81–165, to which the citations below are made.

3. *A Full Vindication,* 47.
4. *Ibid.,* 63.
5. *Ibid.,* 50, 53, 56.
6. *The Farmer Refuted,* 122.
7. *Ibid.,* 96, 126, 136.
8. *Ibid.,* 102, 103.
9. "Narrative of Colonel Robert Troup," 219.
10. *Ibid.* Troup's account, despite its implausibility, has been unquestionably accepted by most Hamilton biographers. So, too, has Hamilton's alleged active role in an episode involving bombardment of the Battery by the British warship *Asia* in August 1775, an uncorroborated incident described in "Narrative of Hercules Mulligan," 210.
11. Hamilton to Jay, Nov. 26, 1775, *Hamilton Papers,* I, 176–178.
12. Hamilton to Jay, Dec. 31, 1775 (acknowledging Jay's unfound letter), *Hamilton Papers,* I, 178–179.
13. Mitchell, *Hamilton,* I, 80, 516, citing Boudinot to Alexander, Mar. 10, 1776, Alexander Papers, New York Historical Society.
14. *Hamilton Papers,* I, 182, n. 2.
15. Morris, *Seven Who Shaped Our Destiny,* 238.
16. The view of most Hamilton biographers is summed up by Mitchell, who approvingly quotes the comment of the Spanish envoy Rendon that Hamilton was the "first Aid . . . of General Washington." Mitchell, *Hamilton,* I, 240–241.
17. James Duane to Hamilton, Sept. 23, 1779, *Hamilton Papers,* II, 185–187.
18. Oswald Tilghman, *Memoir of Lieutenant Colonel Tench Tilghman* (Albany, 1876), 147.
19. Washington to Joseph Reed, Jan. 23, 1776, in John C. Fitzpatrick, ed., *The Writings of George Washington,* 39 vols. (Washington, D.C., 1931–1944), IV, 269 (hereafter cited as Fitzpatrick, *Writings of Washington*).
20. Quoted in Mitchell, *Hamilton,* I, 109.
21. Hamilton to John Jay, July 25, 1779, *Hamilton Papers,* II, 110–111.
22. Hamilton to Gordon, Sept. 5, 1779, *ibid.,* 156.
23. Hamilton to Elias Boudinot, July 5, 1778, *ibid.,* 510.
24. "Publius," *ibid.,* 563.
25. Broadus Mitchell, *Alexander Hamilton: The Revolutionary Years* (New York, 1970), 58.
26. Hamilton to James Duane, Sept. 3, 1780, *Hamilton Papers,* II, 417.
27. For this observation, I am indebted to Mitchell, *Hamilton,* I, 107.
28. Jacob E. Cooke, ed., *The Federalist* (Middletown, Conn., 1961), 223 (hereafter cited as *Federalist*).
29. Hamilton to Nathanael Greene, Oct. 12, 1782, *Hamilton Papers,* II, 183–184.
30. Tilghman, *Memoir of . . . Tench Tilghman,* 131–132.
31. Alexander Grayden, *Memoirs of his Own Time* (Philadelphia, 1846; reprint of 1811 ed.), 275–277.
32. Allan McLane Hamilton, *The Intimate Life of Alexander Hamilton* (New York, 1910), 96, italics added (hereafter cited as Hamilton, *Intimate Life*).

33. Tilghman, *Memoir of . . . Tench Tilghman*, 89.
34. James McHenry to Hamilton, Aug. 11, 1782, *Hamilton Papers*, III, 129–130.
35. Hamilton to Laurens, April 1779, *ibid.*, II, 37.
36. Hamilton to Laurens, Jan. 8, 1780, *ibid.*, 255.
37. See *ibid.*, 522–523.

CHAPTER III

1. See John Laurens to Hamilton, Dec. 18, 1779, *Hamilton Papers*, II, 235.
2. Washington to President of Congress, Apr. 23, 1776, Fitzpatrick, *Writings of Washington*, IV, 506–507.
3. Hamilton to John Laurens, Sept. 11, 1779, *Hamilton Papers*, II, 167.
4. Mitchell, *Hamilton*, I, 102–103.
5. See Hamilton to _____ , December 1779–March 1780, *Hamilton Papers*, II, 236–251. For an inconclusive discussion of possible recipients, see *ibid.*, 234–236.
6. Hamilton to Duane, Sept. 3, 1780, *ibid.*, 400–418.
7. Hamilton to Morris, Apr. 30, 1781, *ibid.*, 604–635.
8. Hamilton to Duane, Sept. 3, 1780, *ibid.*, 401.
9. *Ibid.*
10. *Ibid.*, 402.
11. *Ibid.*, 404.
12. *Ibid.*
13. *Ibid.*, 407.
14. *Ibid.*, 408.
15. Hamilton to _____ , December 1779–March 1780, *ibid.*, 236.
16. *Ibid.*, 236–237.
17. *Ibid.*, 239.
18. *Ibid.*, 242–243.
19. *Ibid.*, 245.
20. *Ibid.*, 245–251.
21. Hamilton to Duane, Sept. 3, 1780, *ibid.*, 403.
22. *Ibid.*, 404.
23. *Ibid.*
24. *Ibid.*, 405.
25. Hamilton to Morris, Apr. 30, 1781, *ibid.*, 617.
26. Hamilton to Duane, Sept. 3, 1780, *ibid.*, 414.
27. Hamilton to _____ , December 1779–March 1780, *ibid.*, 248.
28. *Ibid.*, 242.
29. Hamilton to _____ , December 1779–March 1780, *ibid.*, 242; Hamilton to Duane, Sept. 3, 1780, *ibid.*, 417.
30. Hamilton to Laurens, Jan. 8, 1780, *ibid.*, II, 255.
31. *Ibid.*
32. The principal account of the episode is Hamilton's own version. See Hamilton to Philip Schuyler, Feb. 18, 1781, *ibid.*, 563–568.
33. *Ibid.*, 566.
34. Schuyler to Hamilton, Feb. 25, 1781, *ibid.*, 575–577.
35. Hamilton to Laurens, Sept. 11, 1779, *ibid.*, 165.
36. Hamilton to Gordon, Sept. 5, 1779, *ibid.*, 153–156.

37. Washington to Hamilton, Apr. 27, 1781, *ibid.,* 601–602.
38. This was conferred by general orders dated July 31, 1781, *ibid.,* 658.
39. Schuyler to Hamilton, Feb. 25, May 30, Sept. 16, 1781, *ibid.,* 575–577, 645–646, 676–677.
40. Hamilton to Laurens, Jan. 8, 1780, *ibid.,* 254–255.
41. Hamilton to Morris, June 17, 1782, *ibid.,* III, 93–94.
42. See *ibid.,* 110–113.

CHAPTER IV

1. *Hamilton Papers,* III, 191–193.
2. The first four articles in this series were published on July 12 and 19 and Aug. 9 and 30, 1781. In the following year Hamilton added two articles (dated Apr. 18 and July 4, 1782) to the series. See *Hamilton Papers,* II, 649–652, 654–657, 660–665, 669–674, III, 75–82, 99–106.
3. *Ibid.,* II, 650.
4. *Ibid.,* 651.
5. *Ibid.,* 654.
6. *Ibid.,* 654–655.
7. *Ibid.,* III, 106.
8. *Ibid.*
9. Hamilton to George Clinton, Jan. 21, 1783, *ibid.,* 240.
10. *Journals of the Continental Congress, 1774–1789,* 34 vols. (Washington, D.C., 1904–1937), XXIV, 93–95.
11. Hamilton to Clinton, Feb. 24[–27], 1783, *Hamilton Papers,* III, 268–270.
12. Mitchell, *Hamilton,* I, 298.
13. Hamilton to Clinton, Feb. 24[–27], 1783, *Hamilton Papers,* III, 268–270.
14. Douglas Southall Freeman, *George Washington: A Biography,* 7 vols (New York, 1948–1957), V, 433, 434 (hereafter cited as Freeman, *Washington*).
15. John C. Hamilton, *History,* II, 393.
16. Hamilton to Washington, Feb. 13, 1783, *Hamilton Papers,* III, 253–255.
17. Hamilton to John Dickinson, Sept. 25–30, 1783, *ibid.,* III, 451. For a recent and cogent restatement of the familiar argument that Hamilton, along with like-minded nationalists, was willing to use the army ''in ways totally antithetical to American political tradition and practice,'' see Richard H. Kohn, *Eagle and Sword: The Federalists and the Creation of the Military Establishment in America, 1783–1802* (New York, 1975), 17–39. For the presumed origin of the allegation that Hamilton wished to use the army to force the states to grant funds to the union, see James Madison, ''Notes on Debates,'' in Gaillard Hunt, ed., *Writings of James Madison,* 10 vols. (New York, 1900–1910), I, 335–336 (hereafter cited as Hunt, *Writings of Madison*).
18. Hamilton to Clinton, Feb. 24, 1783, *Hamilton Papers,* III, 268–274.
19. See Mitchell, *Hamilton,* I, 331.
20. Hamilton to John Jay, July 25, 1783, *Hamilton Papers,* III, 416–417.
21. Donald Roper, ''Elite of the New York Bar as Seen from the Bench: James Kent's Necrologies,'' *New York Historical Society Quarterly,* 56 (July 1972), 203.

22. Hamilton, *Intimate Life,* 198.
23. "Narrative of Colonel Robert Troup," *WMQ,* 3rd. ser., 4 (April 1947), 215–216.
24. McDonald, *Hamilton,* 62.
25. Quoted in Nathan Schachner, *Alexander Hamilton* (New York, 1946), 173 (hereafter cited as Schachner, *Hamilton*).
26. Hamilton to Duane, Aug. 5, 1783, *Hamilton Papers,* III, 430.
27. Hamilton to Robert R. Livingston, Aug. 13, 1783, *ibid.,* III, 431–432.
28. For an exhaustively thorough description of the case and documents relating thereto (including its background, proceedings, pleas, Hamilton's brief, and the decision in the case), see Julius Goebel, Jr., *et al.,* eds., *The Law Practice of Alexander Hamilton: Documents and Commentaries,* 4 vols. (New York, 1964–1980), I, 282–419 (hereafter cited as Goebel, *Law Practice*).
29. *Ibid.,* I, 415.
30. "A Letter from Phocion to the Considerate Citizens of New York," *Hamilton Papers,* III, 489–497, 530–558.
31. *Ibid.,* 485.
32. *Ibid.,* 548–549.
33. *Federalist,* p. 93.
34. For the Virginia legislative resolution, see *Hamilton Papers,* III, 666.
35. The "Address of the Annapolis Convention" is printed in *ibid.,* 686–689.
36. See, e.g., Mitchell, *Hamilton,* I, 356–369; John C. Miller, *Alexander Hamilton and the Growth of the New Nation* (New York, 1964; originally published in 1959 with subtitle: *Portraits in Paradox*), 138 (hereafter cited as Miller, *Hamilton*).
37. *Federalist,* 144–145.
38. Andrew C. McLaughlin, *A Constitutional History of the United States* (New York, 1936), 146.
39. Quoted in Mitchell, *Hamilton,* I, 367.
40. *Federalist,* 98.
41. Marcus Cunliffe, *George Washington: Man and Monument* (New York, 1958), 117.
42. Hamilton to John B. Church, Mar. 10, 1784, *Hamilton Papers,* III, 520–522.
43. Hamilton's record in the New York legislature is fully reported in *ibid.,* IV, 1–153.

CHAPTER V

1. *Federalist,* 90.
2. There are several versions of Hamilton's speech: his own notes (on which he presumably relied while addressing the Convention) and four summaries made by James Madison, Robert Yates, John Lansing, Jr., and Rufus King. All of these are printed in *Hamilton Papers,* IV, 178–207. The fullest version (and the one that scholars customarily rely on) is the one made by Madison, from which quotations in my discussion are taken unless otherwise indicated.
3. *Hamilton Papers,* IV, 200 (Yates's version).
4. *Ibid.,* IV, 192.
5. *Federalist,* 62.

6. Miller, *Hamilton*, 51.
7. *Hamilton Papers*, IV, 198 (Yates's version).
8. John P. Roche, "The Founding Fathers: A Reform Caucus in Action," in Leonard W. Levy, ed., *Essays on the Making of the Constitution* (New York, 1969), 180.
9. For the observations in this sentence I am indebted to *ibid.*, 179.
10. Hamilton to Gouverneur Morris, Feb. 29, 1802, *Hamilton Papers*, XXV, 544.
11. For these and other comments on Hamilton's speech, see Mitchell, *Hamilton*, I, 391–392.
12. *Hamilton Papers*, IV, 194.
13. Mitchell, *Hamilton*, I, 380, without ref.
14. "To the Daily Advertiser," July 21, 1787, *Hamilton Papers*, IV, 229–232.
15. *Federalist*, 574.
16. *Hamilton Papers*, IV, 253.
17. For selections from George Clinton's "Cato" essays as well as other representative antifederalist tracts, see Morton Borden, ed., *The Antifederalist Papers* (E. Lansing, Mich., 1965).
18. For an amplification of the remarks in the text, see the introduction to my edition of *Federalist*, xi–xxx.
19. *Ibid.*, 91.
20. *Ibid.*, 97.
21. *Ibid.*, 165.
22. *Ibid.*, 461.
23. *Ibid.*, 471.
24. *Ibid.*, 471–472.
25. *Ibid.*, 96.
26. *Ibid.*, 349.
27. *Ibid.*, 513–514.
28. *Ibid.*, 206.
29. *Ibid.*, 80–81, 103.
30. *Ibid.*, 147.
31. *Ibid.*, 97.

CHAPTER VI

1. James Kent, *Memoirs and Letters*, edited by William Kent (Boston, 1898), 294 (hereafter cited as Kent, *Memoirs*).
2. *Ibid.*, 305–306.
3. *Hamilton Papers*, V, 104.
4. *Ibid.*, 67.
5. *Ibid.*, 43.
6. *Ibid.*, 38–39.
7. *Ibid.*, 68.
8. *Ibid.*
9. George Dangerfield, *Chancellor Robert R. Livingston of New York: 1746–1813* (New York, 1960), 228 (hereafter cited as Dangerfield, *Livingston*). For my assessment of the New York Ratifying Convention, I am greatly indebted to Dangerfield's perceptive analysis in *ibid.*, 220–233.

10. Quoted in *ibid.*, 259.
11. *Hamilton Papers*, V, 41.
12. *Ibid.*, 70.
13. *Ibid.*, 26.
14. *Ibid.*, 96.
15. *Ibid.*, 74–82.
16. *Ibid.*, 94–95.
17. *Ibid.*, 70. For Hamilton's repeated insistence on this point, see, for example, 72, 83, 84.
18. *Ibid.*, 115.
19. *Ibid.*, 57.
20. *Ibid.*, 38, 56.
21. Quoted in *ibid.*, 157.
22. *Ibid.*, 156 n.
23. *Ibid.*, 149.
24. For Hamilton's argument on this score, see *ibid.*, 157–158.
25. *Ibid.*, 177.
26. Madison to Hamilton, July 20, 1788, *ibid.*, 184–185.
27. *Ibid.*, 194.
28. Dangerfield, *Livingston*, 231, quoting *Journal of the Convention*, 67.
29. Mitchell, *Hamilton*, I, 645, n. 69.
30. Miller, *Hamilton*, 213, without ref.
31. James A. Hamilton, *Reminiscences of James A. Hamilton* (New York, 1869), 7.
32. J. P. Brissot de Warville, *New Travels in the United States of America* (New York, 1792), 166.
33. Elected to the Congress on Jan. 22, 1788, Hamilton served as a delegate from Feb. 25 to Oct. 10, 1788. His lackadaisical participation can be followed in *Hamilton Papers*, V, 1–7, 197–200, 203–206, 208–210, 212–217, 224, 229, 331.
34. Nicholas Eveleigh to Tench Coxe, Mar. 24, 1789, quoted in Jacob E. Cooke, *Tench Coxe and the Early Republic* (Chapel Hill, N.C., 1978), 128–129 (hereafter cited as Cooke, *Tench Coxe*).
35. Hamilton to Washington, Sept. 1788, *Hamilton Papers*, V, 220.
36. Washington to Hamilton, Oct. 3, 1788, *ibid.*, 223.
37. *Ibid.*, 222.
38. Hamilton to Madison, Nov. 23, 1788, *ibid.*, 236.
39. Hamilton to Theodore Sedgwick, Oct. 9, 1788, *ibid.*, 225.
40. Hamilton to James Madison, Nov. 23, 1788, *ibid.*, 236.
41. To this end, Hamilton solicited the aid of political friends not only in New York but also in Virginia, Pennsylvania, Connecticut, and New Jersey. See, for example, *ibid.*, 236, 247–249.
42. Hamilton to Supervisors of the City of Albany, Feb. 18, 1789, *ibid.*, 260.
43. *Ibid.*, 256.
44. The "H.G." letters were dated Feb. 20, 21, 22, 24, 25, 26, 27, 28, Mar. 2, 3, 4, 6, 7, 8, 9, and Apr. 9, 1789, and were published in the *New York Daily Advertiser*.
45. *Hamilton Papers*, V, 263, 269.
46. *Ibid.*, 270.

47. The victory in 1789, however, was a narrow one. Clinton defeated Yates by 429 votes in the gubernatorial election. *Ibid.*, 345, n 4.

48. In the selection of presidential electors the senate insisted that it choose four electors and the House four. The assembly, which was numerically superior, demanded that election be by joint ballot. Disagreement of a similar nature took place over the election of U.S. senators. See *ibid.*, 246, n. 3.

49. See, as representative of this viewpoint, Mitchell, *Hamilton*, II, 11–12, and Miller, *Hamilton*, 355. So far as the record reveals, Hamilton's sole effort to intervene on King's behalf was abortive. See Hamilton to King, July 15, 1789, *Hamilton Papers*, V, 362.

50. See Robert Troup to Hamilton, July 12, 1789 (*ibid.*, 359–362), where the complicated legislative maneuvering that resulted in King's election is explained.

51. For this observation I am indebted to Miller, *Hamilton*, 355.

52. Hamilton to Washington, May 5, 1789, *Hamilton Papers*, V, 335–337.

53. Washington to Hamilton, May 5, 1789, *ibid.*, 337.

54. The traditional view that Robert Morris recommended Hamilton's appointment is unsupported by documentary evidence. See Freeman, *Washington*, VI, 234 n. 99.

CHAPTER VII

1. *Federalist*, 105.

2. Hamilton to Edward Carrington, May 26, 1792, *Hamilton Papers*, XI, 442.

3. Leonard D. White, *The Federalists: A Study in Administrative History* (New York, 1948), 117.

4. The description was given by Moreau de Saint-Mery and is quoted in Miller, *Hamilton*, 322, without ref.

5. For a discussion of the provisions of the Treasury Department organic act of Sept. 2, 1789, see White, *The Federalists*.

6. Hamilton to Thomas Willing, Sept. 13, 1789, *Hamilton Papers*, V, 371.

7. The most informative and thorough analysis of the sources (both American and European) of Hamilton's ideas that underpinned his report on public credit is the introductory note to that report in *Hamilton Papers*, VI, 51–65.

8. Although many times reprinted, the definitive version of Hamilton's report is in *ibid.*, 65–168.

9. Miller, *Hamilton*, 122.

10. Louis Hartz, *The Liberal Tradition in America: An Interpretation of American Political Thought Since the Revolution* (New York, 1955), 140.

11. Miller, *Hamilton*, 311.

12. *Hamilton Papers*, V, 85.

13. W. R. Brock, "The Ideas and Influence of Alexander Hamilton," in H. C. Allen and C. P. Hill, eds., *British Essays in American History* (New York, 1957), 42.

14. *Federalist*, 102–103.

15. *Ibid.*, 221–222.

16. Thomas Fitzsimons to Tench Coxe, Feb. 12, 1790, quoted in Cooke, *Tench Coxe*, 147.

17. I have attempted to do so in a detailed analysis of assumption, the removal of the capital, and the famous compromise of 1790, an article on which the account in the text above is based. See Jacob E. Cooke, "The Compromise of 1790," *WMQ*, 3rd ser., 27 (1970), 523–545.
18. Miller, *Hamilton*, 253.

CHAPTER VIII

1. Rush to Tench Coxe, Aug. 15, 1790, quoted in Cooke, *Tench Coxe*, 166.
2. William Sullivan, *Familiar Letters on Public Characters and Public Events . . . 1783–1815* (Boston, 1834), 235, 260.
3. Miller, *Hamilton*, 281.
4. *Ibid.*
5. Merrill D. Peterson, *Thomas Jefferson and the New Nation: A Biography* (New York, 1970), 420 (hereafter cited as Peterson, *Jefferson*).
6. Hamilton's two drafts of this report and his final version are printed in *Hamilton Papers*, VII, 236–342.
7. Hamilton's report is printed in *ibid.*, 570–607. The quotation is on p. 601.
8. For a detailed analysis of Hamilton's reliance on these works and full citations thereto, see the introductory note to Hamilton's report in *ibid.*, 236–256.
9. For an assessment of Coxe's influence on Hamilton's report, see Cooke, *Tench Coxe*, 170–173.
10. *Hamilton Papers*, VII, 323.
11. *Ibid.*, 331.
12. *Ibid.*, 325.
13. Franklin to Tench Coxe, Apr. 7, 1791, quoted in Cooke, *Tench Coxe*, 173.
14. *Hamilton Papers*, VII, 309.
15. Bray Hammond, *Banks and Politics in America from the Revolution to the Civil War* (Princeton, N.J., 1957), 120.
16. Dumas Malone, *Jefferson and His Time*, 6 vols. (Boston, 1948–1981), II, 339 (hereafter cited as Malone, *Jefferson*).
17. Hamilton's draft and final version of his "opinion on the Constitutionality of an Act to Establish a Bank" are printed in *Hamilton Papers*, VII, 64–134.
18. Broadus Mitchell, "Alexander Hamilton as Finance Minister," *Proceedings of the American Philosophical Society*, 102, no. 2 (April 1958), 117–123, reprinted in Jacob E. Cooke, ed., *Alexander Hamilton: A Profile* (New York, 1967), 83–98.
19. Malone, *Jefferson*, II, 345.
20. *Hamilton Papers*, VIII, 97.
21. *Ibid.*, 98.
22. *Ibid.*, 99.
23. *Ibid.*, 107.
24. *Ibid.*, 102, 104.
25. John Marshall, *The Life of George Washington*, 4 vols. (New York, 1930), II, 422; Miller, *Hamilton*, 280.
26. Quoted in Miller, *Hamilton*, 277.
27. Hamilton to William Seton, Aug. 16, 1791, *Hamilton Papers*, IX, 71–72.

28. James Tillery to Hamilton, January 1791, *ibid.*, VII, 614–616.
29. Duer to Hamilton, Jan. 19, 1791, *ibid.*, VII, 442–443.
30. Troup to Hamilton, Jan. 19, 1791, *ibid.*, 445.
31. Kent, *Memoirs,* 39, 78.
32. Dangerfield, *Livingston,* 249.
33. George Dangerfield conjectures that Hamilton, counting on his friendship with the president and the political influence of his father-in-law in New York, "may well have thought that he could be master of the State of New York without any assistance from the Livingstons." *Ibid.*, 245.
34. Duer to Hamilton, Jan. 19, 1791, *Hamilton Papers*, VII, 442–443.
35. Burr was obviously referring to Hamilton when he gloatingly informed Theodore Sedgwick on Jan. 20, 1791, that "I have reason to believe that my election will be unpleasing to several Persons, now in Philada." Quoted in Mitchell, *Hamilton,* II, 137.

CHAPTER IX

1. Frederick S. Oliver, *Alexander Hamilton: An Essay on American Union* (New York, 1906), 247 (hereafter cited as Oliver, *Hamilton*).
2. Miller, *Hamilton,* 289.
3. Mitchell, *Hamilton,* II, 139.
4. *Hamilton Papers*, X, 313.
5. *Ibid.*, 1.
6. The four drafts that Hamilton wrote of this report (plus a preliminary draft by Tench Coxe) are printed in *ibid.*, 15–229. His final version of the report (to which citations below are made) appears on pp. 230–340.
7. *Journal of the House of Representatives of the United States,* I (Washington, D.C., 1826), 141–142.
8. *Federalist,* 73.
9. *Hamilton Papers*, X, 185.
10. This assessment is at odds with other analyses of Hamilton's famous report. A detailed presentation of my thesis is in "Tench Coxe, Alexander Hamilton, and the Encouragement of American Manufactures," *WMQ,* 3rd ser., 32 (1975), 369–392.
11. Hamilton's criterion for protection was the stage of an industry's development. Protection was to be afforded infant industries only. While Hamilton thus recommended some protective duties, he was only a modest— not, as often alleged, an ardent—protectionist. For the encouragement of manufactures, he preferred more direct government aid in the form of bounties and premiums.
12. Hamilton maintained that "it is at least evident, that in a Country situated like the United States, with an infinite fund of resources yet to be unfolded, every farthing of foreign capital, which is laid out in internal ameliorations, and in industrious establishments of a permanent nature, is a precious acquisition." *Hamilton Papers*, X, 276.
13. Hamilton also recommended the labor of young children (*ibid.*, 270). Few of Hamilton's critics comment on this proposal without implying that it was yet another example of Hamilton's callousness toward human rights. Such a judgment is unhistorical. At a time when children were put to work on the farm at a young age and forced to labor long hours in the fields, the suggestion that they also work in factories was neither novel nor callous.

14. *Ibid.*, 267. What should the government do? In addition to utilizing import duties and exemptions, drawbacks, and the like, Hamilton recommended, among other devices, legislative authorization of bounties, in his opinion the most desirable means of encouraging needed new manufactures. Except for this purpose, however, Hamilton eschewed "pecuniary bounties," recommending instead high duties on imported manufactures of materials whose growth the United States wished to encourage and the allocation of the proceeds from these duties to American manufacturers of the same materials. Another way of rewarding pioneers on the introduction of infant industries was to authorize premiums.

15. *Ibid.*, 293.

16. For a discussion of Coxe's "plan" and its antecedents, see Cooke, *Tench Coxe,* 190–192.

17. Hamilton to Duer, Apr. 20, 1791, *Hamilton Papers,* VIII, 300.

18. *Ibid.*, IX, 144–153. The "Prospectus" included, in modified form, Tench Coxe's "Plan for a Manufacturing Society" of April 1791.

19. The authoritative study of the SEUM is Joseph S. Davis, *Essays in the Earlier History of American Corporations,* 2 vols. (Cambridge, Mass., 1918), I, 349–518 (hereafter cited as Davis, *Essays*).

20. James Logan, "Five Letters Addressed to the Yeomanry of the United States . . . ," *American Museum,* 12 (1792), 162.

21. Miller, *Hamilton,* without ref.

22. Davis, *Essays,* I, 307.

23. Dangerfield, *Livingston,* 251, 280.

24. For a comprehensive account of Duer's complicated financial deals, see "William Duer, Entrepreneur, 1747-99," in Davis, *Essays,* I, 111–316.

25. Duer to Hamilton, Mar. 12, 1792, *Hamilton Papers,* XI, 126.

26. Hamilton to William Seton, Apr. 4, 1792, to Philip Livingston, Apr. 2, 1792, *Hamilton Papers,* XI, 225–226, 218–219.

27. Hamilton to Duer, Mar. 14, 1792, *ibid.*, XI, 131.

28. Quoted in Dangerfield, *Livingston,* 251.

29. Quoted in Miller, *Hamilton,* 308.

30. Mitchell, *Hamilton,* II, 179.

31. Thomas Jefferson to T. M. Randolph, Jr., Mar. 16, 1792, Paul Leicester Ford, ed., *The Works of Thomas Jefferson,* 12 vols., Federal ed. (New York, 1904–1905), V, 455 (hereafter cited as Ford, *Works of Jefferson*).

32. Madison made these comments in a communication that appeared in the *National Gazette.* They are quoted in Malone, *Jefferson,* II, 436–437.

33. Henry Lee to Hamilton, June 23, 1792, *Hamilton Papers,* XI, 550.

34. Quoted in Miller, *Hamilton,* 326, a work to which I am indebted for a number of the observations made in the final paragraph of this chapter.

CHAPTER X

1. Peterson, *Jefferson,* 396.

2. Henry T. Ford, "Timothy Pickering," in Samuel F. Bemis *et al.,* eds., *The American Secretaries of State and Their Diplomacy,* 18 vols. (New York, 1927–1970), II, 177.

3. For an amplified treatment of the subject cursorily discussed in the text,

see Gilbert L. Lycam, *Alexander Hamilton and American Foreign Policy: A Design for Greatness* (Norman, Okla., 1970), 121–131.

4. For a detailed discussion of the semiofficial relationship between Hamilton and Beckwith, see Samuel Flagg Bemis, *Jay's Treaty: A Study in Commerce and Diplomacy* (New York, 1924), chapter 4, whose overall interpretation is implicitly rejected in the text above.

5. Julian P. Boyd, *Number 7: Alexander Hamilton's Secret Attempt to Control American Foreign Policy* (Princeton, N.J., 1964), 41, 42, 65.

6. Hamilton to George Washington, July 15, 1790, *Hamilton Papers*, VI, 494. See also Hamilton's earlier letter to Washington on the subject, July 8, 1789, *ibid.*, 484–486. Hamilton's conversations with Beckwith (from which the quotations in the text are taken) are printed in *ibid.*, 484–486, 493–498, 546–549, 550, 550–551.

7. For this observation I am indebted to Broadus Mitchell, *Alexander Hamilton: A Concise Biography* (New York, 1976), 215.

8. Peterson, *Jefferson*, 428.

9. Ford, *Works of Jefferson*, I, 177–179.

10. *Ibid.*, VI, 186.

11. For this paragraph I relied on Miller, *Hamilton*, 314.

12. Hamilton to James A. Bayard, Jan. 16, 1801, *Hamilton Papers*, XXV, 319.

13. Hamilton's composite criticism of Jefferson is drawn from Hamilton to Edward Carrington, May 26, 1792, *ibid.*, XI, 426–445.

14. For this observation I am indebted to Hartz's perceptive analysis of Hamilton in *Liberal Tradition in America*. See especially pp. 12, 15–16, 78–81, 89–90, 93–94, 108–109.

15. *Livingston*, 233. Although Dangerfield applies the phrase only to Hamilton's policy of assumption of state debts, I believe that it aptly describes his fiscal program as a whole.

16. Jefferson lengthily discussed the issue in a letter to George Washington of Sept. 9, 1792, Ford, *Works of Jefferson*, VI, 106.

17. Jefferson to Philip Freneau, Feb. 28, 1791, as paraphrased in Malone, *Jefferson*, II, 423.

18. Peterson, *Jefferson*, 463, without ref.

19. George Gibbs, *Memoirs of the Administrations of Washington and John Adams*, 2 vols. (New York, 1846), I, 73 (hereafter cited as Gibbs, *Memoirs*).

20. Hamilton to Carrington, May 26, 1792, *Hamilton Papers*, XI, 426–445, from which this and the succeeding quotations in this paragraph are taken.

21. Jefferson to George Washington, May 23, 1792, Ford, *Works of Jefferson*, VI, 1–6.

22. Washington's response was relayed in a conversation between himself and Jefferson on July 10, 1792, *ibid.*, I, 198–201.

23. *Gazette of the United States*, July 25, 1792, reprinted in *Hamilton Papers*, XII, 107. This was the first of a series of letters entitled "T.L." Other letters were dated July 28 and Aug. 1792. See *ibid.*, 123–125, 193–194.

24. "An American," *Gazette of the United States*, Aug. 4, 1792. The quotation was from the first of a series of articles under this pseudonym that Hamilton published in the *Gazette*. The other two were dated Aug. 11 and 18, 1792. They are printed in *Hamilton Papers*, XII, 157–164,

188–193, 224.

25. For the representative attacks on Jefferson referred to in the text, see (according to the order in which they are given) *ibid.*, 379–385, 393–401, 498–506, 578–587, 354–357, 361–365, 570–572, 411–412, 613–617.

26. The quotations in order given may be found in *ibid.*, 504, 498–499, 617, 499, 504.

27. Malone, *Jefferson*, II, 455.

CHAPTER XI

1. Washington to Jefferson, Aug. 23, 1792, Fitzpatrick, *Writings of Washington*, XXXII, 130–131; Washington to Hamilton, Aug. 26, 1792, *Hamilton Papers*, XII, 276–277.

2. Washington to Hamilton, Aug. 26, 1792, *Hamilton Papers*, XII, 276.

3. Peterson, *Jefferson*, 472–473.

4. Hamilton to Washington, Sept. 9, 1792, *Hamilton Papers*, XII, 347–350.

5. Jefferson to Washington, Sept. 9, 1792, Ford, *Works of Jefferson*, VI, 101–109.

6. *Ibid.*, 109.

7. Washington to Henry Lee, Jan. 20, 1793, Fitzpatrick, *Writings of Washington*, XXXII, 310.

8. Jefferson's account of conversation between himself and the president on Oct. 1, 1792 is quoted in Freeman, *Washington*, VI, 374.

9. Hamilton to Rufus King, June 28 and July 25, 1792, *Hamilton Papers*, XI, 588–589, and XII, 99–100.

10. King to Hamilton, Sept. 17, 1792, *ibid.*, XII, 387.

11. Hamilton to _____, Sept. 21, 1792, *ibid.*, 408.

12. Hamilton to _____, Sept. 21 and 26, 1792, *ibid.*, 408, 480.

13. The resolutions were presented on Feb. 28, 1793. Jefferson's draft is printed in Ford, *Works of Jefferson*, VII, 220–223.

14. Annals of Congress. *Debates and Proceedings in the Congress of the United States, 1789–1824,* 42 vols. (Washington, D.C., 1834–1856), III (1791–1793), 900 (hereafter cited as *Annals of Congress*).

15. Hamilton's four reports in answer to Giles's resolutions were sent on Feb. 4, 13, 13–14, and 19, 1793. He was also required to answer Senate resolutions dated Jan. 23, 1793, similar to those adopted by the House. Those were answered in three reports on Feb. 5–6, 13–14, and 14, 1793. All of these can be found in *Hamilton Papers*, XIV. The quotations are from *ibid.*, 52.

16. Benjamin Hawkins to Tench Coxe, Apr. 29, 1793, Tench Coxe Papers, Historical Society of Pennsylvania (hereafter cited as Coxe Papers).

17. *Federalist*, 68.

18. Hamilton to _____, May 18, 1793, *Hamilton Papers*, XIV, 476.

19. Hartz, *Liberal Tradition in America,* 73–96, *passim.*

20. Jefferson to James Monroe, June 4, 1793, cited in Mitchell, *Hamilton*, II, 224–225.

21. Washington's Proclamation of Neutrality, issued on Apr. 22, 1793, is printed in *Hamilton Papers*, XIV, 308–310.

22. Jefferson to James Madison, June 29, 1793, Ford, *Works of Jefferson*, VI, 328.

23. See *Hamilton Papers*, XIV, 328–329, 502–507.

24. The series consisted of seven articles dated June 29, July 3, 6, 10, 13–17, 17, and 27, 1793. They are printed in *ibid.*, XV, 33–43, 55–63, 65–69, 82–86, 90–95, 100–106, and 130–135.
25. *Ibid.*, 33–34.
26. *Ibid.*, 85–86.
27. Jefferson to Madison, July 7, 1793, Ford, *Works of Jefferson,* VI, 338.
28. Madison's essays were published between Aug. 24 and Sept. 18, 1793, and are printed in Hunt, *Writings of Madison,* VI, 133–188.
29. *Hamilton Papers,* XV, 66.
30. Mitchell, *Hamilton,* II, 223; Marcus Cunliffe, *The Nation Takes Shape: 1789–1837* (Chicago, 1964), 46.
31. Jefferson to Madison, Aug. 3, 1793, Ford, *Works of Jefferson,* VI, 361.
32. Hamilton's "No Jacobin" series consisted of nine articles, dated July 31, Aug. 5, 8, 10, 14, 16, 23, 26, and 28, and are printed in *Hamilton Papers,* XV, 145–151, 184–191, 203–207, 224–228, 243–246, 249–250, 268–270, 281–284, and 304–306.
33. *Philadelphia General Advertiser,* Aug. 28, 1793.
34. Lyman H. Butterfield, ed., *Letters of Benjamin Rush,* 2 vols. (Princeton, N.J., 1951), II, 746.
35. Mitchell, *Hamilton,* II, 282.
36. *Hamilton Papers,* XV, 344.
37. *Ibid.*, 345.
38. For Hamilton's draft of the president's Fifth Annual Message to Congress, see *ibid.*, 425–432.
39. Report of the Secretary of State on the Privileges and Restrictions on the Commerce of the United States in Foreign Countries, Dec. 16, 1793, Ford, *Works of Jefferson,* II, 470–484.
40. The quoted phrase is from Malone, *Jefferson,* III, 157.
41. Stuart Bruchey, *The Roots of American Economic Growth* (New York, 1968), 122.

CHAPTER XII

1. Quoted in White, *The Federalists,* n.d., citing Madison, *Letters* (Congressional ed.), II, 10.
2. The observation is by Schachner, *Hamilton,* 325.
3. *Annals of Congress,* IV (1793–1795), 155–158.
4. Hamilton wrote two "Americanus" letters, the first dated Jan. 31, 1794; the second, Feb. 7, 1794. They are printed in *Hamilton Papers,* XV, 669–678, and XVI, 12–19. The claim that Smith's speech "was from the pen of Hamilton" was made by John C. Hamilton (*History,* V, 450) and has been almost universally credited by historians. For an analysis of the validity of John C. Hamilton's claim, see *Hamilton Papers,* XIII, 395-447. Smith's speech was delivered on Jan. 13, 1794. See *Annals of Congress,* IV (1793–1795), 174–209.
5. Mitchell, *Hamilton,* II, 291.
6. *Annals of Congress,* IV (1793–1795), 177–192.
7. Jefferson to Madison, Apr. 3, 1794, Ford, *Works of Jefferson,* VIII, 141.
8. *Hamilton Papers,* XXI, 240.
9. The Fraunces episode is thoroughly explored in a long introductory note in *ibid.*, XIV, 460–470. See also *ibid.*, XV, 460–465.

10. Washington to Hamilton, Apr. 8, 1794, *ibid.*, XVI, 249.
11. Hamilton to Washington, Apr. 9, 1794, *ibid.*, 250–253.
12. *Ibid.*
13. Alexander DeConde, *Entangling Alliance: Politics and Diplomacy under George Washington* (Durham, N.C., 1958), 97.
14. Hamilton to George Washington, Apr. 14, 1794, *Hamilton Papers*, XVI, 266–279. The quoted phrase is in *ibid.*, 267.
15. *Ibid.*, 278–279.
16. For information on this controversy and for the most balanced account of Hamilton's role in Jay's Treaty, see Jerald A. Combs, *The Jay Treaty*, especially chapter 8, *passim*.
17. Schachner, *Hamilton*, 331.
18. See Coxe to Jay, May 3, 4, 7 (two letters), and 8, 1794, Coxe Papers.
19. This charge was made by Samuel F. Bemis in *Jay's Treaty: A Study in Commerce and Diplomacy*, published in 1924 and accepted by most historians since that time. An essential corrective to Bemis' interpretation, as I implied earlier, is Combs, *The Jay Treaty*.
20. Morris, *Seven Who Shaped Our Destiny*, 253.
21. Combs, *The Jay Treaty*, 149, 148.
22. This conclusion, as demonstrated in the text above, is in accord with what is now the standard work on Jay's Treaty. Combs writes that "from a survey of the negotiations, it is highly unlikely that Hamilton's injudicious revelation [about America's decision not to join the League of Armed Neutrality] had much effect. . . . Grenville knew that a failure to come to agreement with Jay meant war whether the United States adhered to the Armed Neutrality or not . . . Jay's failures were not the result of the sudden undermining of America's bargaining power" (*The Jay Treaty*, 147). Another recent scholar reinforces Combs's view. Alexander DeConde writes apropos of the charge that "Hamilton sabotaged negotiations on the issue of the armed neutrality"—"that episode probably . . . did little to alter the basic structure of the treaty or even the tenor of the negotiations" (*Entangling Alliance*, 110).
23. For the observation in the final two sentences of this paragraph I am indebted to Miller, *Hamilton*, 418–419.
24. This interpretation is at odds with the opinions of most other historians. To give two illustrations, Alexander DeConde asserts that "Jay's treaty was Hamilton's treaty more than that of any other man" (*Entangling Alliance*, 110) and Broadus Mitchell contends that "the Jay treaty . . . was peculiarly Hamilton's doing" (*Hamilton*, II, 331).
25. Combs, *The Jay Treaty*, 148.
26. *The New Nation Takes Shape*, 148.
27. For an explanation of Hamilton's objections to Jay's Treaty, see Combs, *The Jay Treaty*, 163, and Gerald Stourgh, *Alexander Hamilton and the Idea of Republican Government* (Stanford, Calif., 1970), 199, 266.
28. Jay to Randolph, Nov. 19, 1794, *American State Papers: Documents, Legislative and Executive, of the Congress of the United States*, 38 vols. (Washington, D.C., 1832–1861), *Finance*, I, 503.

CHAPTER XIII

1. *Hamilton Papers*, XII, 316–317.

2. *The Journal of William Maclay: United States Senator from Pennsylvania,* edited by Charles A. Beard (New York, 1927), 387–388.
3. *Federalist,* 75.
4. *Ibid.,* 217.
5. Each supervisor was also inspector of the revenue for one of the surveys in his district.
6. New Hampshire, Rhode Island, Vermont, New York, New Jersey, Delaware, and Maryland were not so divided, and hence there were no inspectors of revenue in those states.
7. For an admirably thorough discussion of the excise law, see White, *The Federalists,* 451.
8. Hamilton had used the phrase many years earlier. Hamilton to Robert Morris, Apr. 30, 1781, *Hamilton Papers,* II, 610.
9. John Neville to George Clymer, Aug. 23, 1792, *ibid.,* XII, 307, n. 5.
10. Pertinent papers describing this episode are in *ibid.,* XII, 305–310.
11. Hamilton to Coxe, Sept. 1, 1792, *ibid.,* 310.
12. Clymer to John Neville, July 20, 1792, Clymer Letterbook, Coxe Papers.
13. Hamilton to John Jay, Sept. 3, 1792, *Hamilton Papers,* XII, 317.
14. Hamilton's draft is printed in *ibid.,* 330–331.
15. Coxe to Hamilton, Oct. 19, 1792, *ibid.,* 596.
16. The most far-reaching modification was made by an act of June 5, 1794. Particularly important was a provision of the act that stipulated that all legal proceedings arising under the excise law be cognizable in state as well as federal courts, which previously had exercised sole jurisdiction.
17. Henry M. Brackenridge, *History of the Western Insurrection in Pennsylvania* (Pittsburgh, 1859), 25.
18. These episodes, plus other recent events in western Pennsylvania, are lengthily described in Hamilton to Washington, Aug. 5, 1794, *Hamilton Papers,* XVII, 24–58.
19. At the end of June 1794, Clymer resigned, but his successor, General Henry Miller, although considerably more objective, was limited by the nature of reports from his on-the-spot agents.
20. *Federalist,* 207.
21. Minutes of the meeting are in *Hamilton Papers,* XVII, 9–14.
22. *Ibid.,* 13.
23. Hamilton submitted two reports, dated Aug. 2 and 5 (*ibid.,* 15–19, 24–58). The opinions of Knox, Bradford, and Randolph are ably summarized in Freeman, *Washington,* VII, 188–190.
24. *American State Papers: Miscellaneous,* I, 97–99. According to the traditional wisdom it was Hamilton who made the decision to intervene militarily. I have contrarily argued that the decision was made by the president in "The Whiskey Insurrection: A Re-Evaluation," *Pennsylvania History,* XXX (1963), 313–346. The present account is largely based on that article.
25. Washington to Hamilton, Aug. 21, 1794, *Hamilton Papers,* XVII, 125–126.
26. The proclamation was dated Aug. 7, 1794, and is printed in Fitzpatrick, *Writings of Washington,* XXXIII, 457–461.
27. U.S. Commissioners to Edmund Randolph, Aug. 30, 1794, quoted in Leland Baldwin, *Whiskey Rebels: The Story of a Frontier Uprising* (Pitts-

burgh, 1939), 198.

28. *Hamilton Papers*, XVII, 136.
29. *Ibid.*, 143, 144, 161–162, 210–211.
30. Hamilton to Washington, Sept. 19, 1794, *ibid.*, 254–255.
31. "Tully No. II," Aug. 26, 1794, *ibid.*, 148.
32. Hamilton to Henry Lee, Aug. 25, 1794, *ibid.*, 142–143. My critical assessment of Hamilton's decision is not intended as an endorsement of the traditional interpretation of his role in the Whiskey Insurrection. This viewpoint was succinctly expressed in these remarks from a recent essay: Hamilton "was bent on forcing the issue against the whiskey remonstrants. . . . *Advocating military suppression,* Hamilton even took the field against the whiskey insurrectionaries" (Morris, *Seven Who Shaped Our Destiny*, 252; italics mine). For my objections to the way in which such scholars (reflecting in this instance the attitude of Jeffersonians at the time) have interpreted Hamilton's role, see my "Whiskey Insurrection: A Re-Evaluation," cited above.
33. *Federalist*, 5,
34. John C. Fitzpatrick, ed., *The Diaries of George Washington 1748–1799*, 4 vols. (Boston, 1925), IV, 209.
35. Freeman, *Washington*, VII, 212.
36. William Findley, *History of the Insurrection in the Four Western Counties of Pennsylvania in the Year MDCCXCIV* . . . (Philadelphia, 1796), 223, 226.
37. Hamilton to Washington, Nov. 11, 1794, *Hamilton Papers*, XVII, 366–367.
38. Hamilton to Washington, Nov. 8, 1794, *ibid.*, 361.
39. Hamilton to Washington, Nov. 11, 1794, *ibid.*, 366.
40. Hamilton to Frederick A. C. Muhlenberg, Dec. 1, 1794, to Washington, Dec. 1, 1794, *ibid.*, 405, 413.
41. The acrimonious dispute between Hamilton and Coxe is described in Cooke, *Tench Coxe*, 265–270.
42. *Hamilton Papers*, XVIII, 46.
43. The phrase was used by Madison in a letter to Jefferson of Jan. 26, 1795, cited in *ibid.*, 47.
44. Hamilton's "Report on a Plan for the Further Support of Public Credit," Jan. 16, 1795, is printed, along with an introductory note in *ibid.*, 46–148.
45. *Ibid.*, 47.
46. Mitchell, *Hamilton*, II, 360.
47. *Hamilton Papers*, XVIII, 59, 51.
48. Seth Ames, ed., *Works of Fisher Ames*, 2 vols. (Boston, 1854), I, 164–165.
49. *Hamilton Papers*, XVIII, 115, 124–125.
50. Quoted in Max Lerner, "John Marshall and the Campaign of History," in Leonard W. Levy, ed., *American Constitutional Law: Historical Essays* (New York, 1966), 57.
51. Oliver, *Hamilton*, 12–13.
52. "Report on a Plan for the Further Support of Public Credit," Jan. 16, 1795, *Hamilton Papers*, XVIII, 126.
53. Hammond, *Banks and Politics in America*, 144.

54. Dangerfield, *Livingston,* 233.
55. Hammond, *Banks and Politics in America,* 120.
56. White, *The Federalists,* 125–126.
57. The phrase is from Miller, *Hamilton,* 326.
58. For these observations I am indebted to *ibid.,* 47.
59. *Federalist,* 488.
60. Mitchell, *Hamilton,* II, 366.
61. Washington to Hamilton, Feb. 2, 1795, *Hamilton Papers,* XVIII, 248.
62. Hamilton to Washington, Nov. 11, 1794, *ibid.,* XVII, 366.

CHAPTER XIV

1. Hamilton to Angelica Church, Dec. 8, 1794, *Hamilton Papers,* XVII, 428–429.
2. Mitchell, *Hamilton,* II, 697, citing *Greenleaf's New York Journal and Patriotic Register,* Dec. 11, 1799.
3. Hamilton to Robert Troup, July 25, 1795, *Hamilton Papers,* XVII, 503.
4. Troup to Hamilton, May 11, 1795, *ibid.,* 340–344.
5. Hamilton to Troup, Apr. 13, 1795, *ibid.,* 328–329.
6. *New York Daily Advertiser,* Feb. 28, 1795.
7. Hamilton to Angelica Church, Mar. 6, 1795, *Hamilton Papers,* XVIII, 287–288.
8. Hamilton, *Intimate Life,* 165.
9. See *ibid.,* 169, n.; Louis Le Guen to Hamilton, May 1, 1800, *Hamilton Papers,* XXIV, 438–439; Goebel, *Law Practice,* II, 48–164.
10. 3 Dallas, *U.S. Reports,* 171–183 (1796).
11. Charles Warren, *The Supreme Court in United States History,* 2 vols. (Boston, 1935, rev. ed.), I, 149.
12. For information on Hamilton's participation in the case, see Oliver Wolcott, Jr., to Hamilton, Jan. 15, 1796, *Hamilton Papers,* XX, 40–41, especially citations and references on 41, n.1. For Hamilton's argument in the case, including a draft of his brief and an introductory note of exemplary scholarly thoroughness, see Goebel, *Law Practice,* IV, 297–355.
13. Bradford to Hamilton, July 2, 1795, *Hamilton Papers,* XVIII, 393–397.
14. George Thatcher to Tench Coxe, May 24, 1795, Coxe Papers. The terms of the treaty were made public by Benjamin Bache, editor of the Philadelphia *Aurora,* who was shown a copy by person or persons unknown. Bache published a brief summary of the treaty on June 29 and the entire text on July 2, 1795.
15. The source of the assertion that Hamilton's defense of the treaty "was replied to by a volley of stones, one of which struck his forehead" is John C. Hamilton, *History,* VI, 225. The most diligent students of the episode conclude that "the story may be apocryphal." *Hamilton Papers,* XVIII, 485, n. 33.
16. *Origins of the American Party System* (New York, 1961), 101–102.
17. *Ibid.,* 116.
18. "The Defense No. I," July 22, 1795, *Hamilton Papers,* XVIII, 481.
19. Cunliffe, *The New Nation Takes Shape,* 47.
20. DeConde, *Entangling Alliance,* 116.
21. King wrote numbers 23–30, 34, 35. Robert Ernst, *Rufus King: American*

Federalist (Chapel Hill, N.C., 1968), 209.

22. *Ibid.*

23. The dates on which the twenty-eight essays written by Hamilton were published are listed in *Hamilton Papers*, XVIII, 476–477. The first three essays appear in *ibid.*, 479–489, 493–501, 513–523; the remaining twenty-five articles that Hamilton wrote are printed in *ibid.*, XIX, *passim.*

24. See, for example, Mitchell, *Hamilton*, II, 344; Schachner, *Hamilton*, 349–351; Miller, *Hamilton*, 427–429; Freeman, *Washington*, VII, 273.

25. Oliver, *Hamilton*, 362–363.

26. *Ibid*, 362.

27. For a representative claim that Hamilton was the one individual most responsible for Washington's decision to sign the treaty, see Frank Monaghan, *John Jay* (New York, 1935), 297–298. Actually, Washington's decision was primarily due to Timothy Pickering and Oliver Wolcott, Jr., who handed over to the president evidence that Secretary of State Edmund Randolph had made remarks to the French minister that were highly indiscreet, perhaps criminally so. Washington, although he considered Randolph's remarks a species of disloyalty to himself rather than a crime, abruptly ended his relationship with the secretary of state, then his closest adviser, and bowed to the importunate demands of his remaining cabinet members that he sign the treaty.

28. Freeman, *Washington*, VII, 350.

29. Washington to Oliver Wolcott, Jr., Mar. 3, 1796, in *Hamilton Papers*, XX, 65–66.

30. Hamilton to Washington, Mar. 7, 1796, *ibid.*, 68–69.

31. Hamilton to Rufus King, Mar. 16, 1796, *ibid.*, 76–77. King almost certainly brought Hamilton's letter to the attention of the president.

32. Washington to Hamilton, Mar. 22, 1796, letter unfound. For the inference in the text above, see Freeman, *Washington*, VII, 353.

33. Hamilton to Washington, Mar. 28, 1796, *Hamilton Papers*, XX, 83–85. See also Hamilton to Washington, Mar. 29, 1796 (*ibid.*, 85–103), in which Hamilton submitted what he believed would be an appropriate reply to the House. The president preferred a more concise message drafted by Timothy Pickering. Freeman, *Washington*, VII, 354.

34. Washington's message, delivered to the House on Mar. 30, 1796, is in Fitzpatrick, *Writings of Washington*, XXXV, 2–5.

35. William Plumer to Jeremiah Smith, Apr. 19, 1796, quoted in Freeman, *Washington*, VII, 356.

36. *Ibid.*, 361.

37. Hamilton to King, *Hamilton Papers*, XX, 112–115.

38. Madison to Jefferson, May 9, 1796, quoted in Freeman, *Washington*, VII, 363.

39. Ames's speech is in Seth Ames, ed., *Works of Fisher Ames*, II, 35–71, and in *Annals of Congress* (4th Congress), I, 1239–1263.

40. *Annals of Congress* (4th Congress), I, 1276.

41. Mitchell, *Hamilton*, II, 350.

42. Hamilton to Rufus King, May 4, 1796, *Hamilton Papers*, XX, 158.

43. Victor H. Paltsits, ed., *Washington's Farewell Address* (New York, 1935), 215, 216.

44. Washington to John Jay, May 8, 1796, in *ibid.*, 239.

45. Washington to Gouverneur Morris, Mar. 4, 1796, Fitzpatrick, *Writings of Washington*, XXXIV, 483.
46. Washington to Hamilton, May 15, 1796, as quoted in introductory note to Washington's Farewell Address, *Hamilton Papers*, XX, 169.
47. Felix Gilbert, *To the Farewell Address: Ideas of Early American Foreign Policy* (Princeton, N.J., 1961), 123.
48. Washington to Hamilton, May 16, 1796, *Hamilton Papers*, XX, 174–178.
49. Hamilton, *Intimate Life*, 111.
50. Hamilton to Washington, *Hamilton Papers*, XX, 264–288.
51. *Ibid.*, 265.
52. *Ibid.*, 293–303.
53. The description is a paraphrase of Thomas Jefferson's assessment. Jefferson to Dr. Walter Jones, Jan. 2, 1814, Ford, *Works of Jefferson*, IX, 448–449.
54. Gilbert, *To the Farewell Address*, 128.
55. *Ibid.*, 134, 136.

CHAPTER XV

1. Ames to Oliver Wolcott, Jr., Sept. 26, 1796, Gibbs, *Memoirs*, I, 384–385.
2. For a discussion of this subject as well as an analysis of Coxe's instrumental role—previously unrecognized—in the Republican campaign of 1796, see Cooke, *Tench Coxe*, 279–292.
3. Jefferson to Thomas Mann Randolph, Nov. 16, 1792, Ford, *Works of Jefferson*, VII, 179.
4. *Letter from Alexander Hamilton, Concerning the Public Conduct and Character of John Adams, Esq. President of the United States* (New York, 1800), printed in *Hamilton Papers*, XXV, 169–234 (hereafter cited as *Letter . . . Concerning . . . John Adams*). Quoted parts are on 194–195.
5. King to Hamilton, May 2, 1796, *Hamilton Papers*, XX, 151.
6. Hamilton to King, May 4, 1796, *ibid.*, 158.
7. *Letter . . . Concerning . . . John Adams*, *ibid.*, XXV, 126.
8. Hamilton to _____ , Nov. 9, 1796, *ibid.*, XX, 376–377.
9. Hamilton to Jeremiah Wadsworth, Dec. 1, 1796, *ibid.*, 418. See also Hamilton to Rufus King, Dec. 16, 1796, *ibid.*, 445.
10. Higginson to Hamilton, Jan. 12, 1797, *ibid.*, 465.
11. *American State Papers: Foreign Relations*, I, 576–577.
12. Washington to Hamilton, Nov. 2, 1796, *Hamilton Papers*, XX, 362–366.
13. Hamilton to Washington, Nov. 4, 1796, *ibid.*, 372–373.
14. On Nov. 3, 1796, Washington ("to rescue my conduct from the imputation of inconsistency") wrote to Hamilton that the request about publication of the secretary of state's letter to Adet had been outdated by the president's acquiescence in Pickering's wishes. *Ibid.*, 366–367.
15. Hamilton to Washington, Nov. 4, 1796, *ibid.*, 372–373.
16. Quoted in Page Smith, *John Adams*, 2 vols. (New York, 1962), II, 908.
17. Hamilton to Rufus King, Dec. 16, 1796, *Hamilton Papers*, XX, 445.
18. Hamilton to Rufus King, Feb. 15, 1797, *ibid.*, 515.
19. Abigail Adams to John Adams, Dec. 31, 1796, quoted in Page Smith,

John Adams, II, 908.

20. John Adams to Abigail Adams, Jan. 9, 1797, quoted in *ibid.*
21. *Observations on Certain Documents Contained in No. V & VI of "The History of the United States for the Year 1796," In Which the Charge of Speculation Against Alexander Hamilton, Late Secretary of the Treasury is Fully Refuted. Written by Himself* (Philadelphia, 1797; hereafter cited as "Reynolds Pamphlet"). The pamphlet is printed in *Hamilton Papers*, XXI, 238–285, to which subsequent citations are made.
22. Maria Reynolds "had what in a more genteel age was called respectable family connections." A native of Dutchess County, she was born in 1768, the daughter of Susanna Van Der Burgh and her second husband, Richard Lewis. Maria's sister, Susannah, married Gilbert Livingston. Maria herself moved far outside the circle of the local squirearchy when she married James Reynolds. "Reynolds Pamphlet," 123, 124.
23. *Ibid.*, 250–251.
24. Reynolds to Hamilton, Dec. 15, 1791, *ibid.*, 376–377.
25. Reynolds to Hamilton, Dec. 19, 1791, *ibid.*, 396.
26. For the exchange of letters between Reynolds and Hamilton in 1791 and 1792, see *ibid.*, XXI, 122–123 n.
27. Charges against both Clingman and Reynolds were dismissed in exchange for their promise to Oliver Wolcott, Jr., to turn over to him a list of U.S. creditors that they had obtained from the Treasury Department. The two had apparently secured the list from Simeon Reynolds, a relative of James. Simeon had been employed for a short time in the office of Joseph Nourse, the register of the Treasury. Julian P. Boyd, ed., *The Papers of Thomas Jefferson*, 19 vols. (Princeton, N.J., 1950–1974), XVIII, 656–657.
28. For a more detailed exploration of the Reynolds affair, see the introductory note on the subject in *Hamilton Papers*, XXI, 121–144.
29. *Ibid.*, 130–131.
30. *Ibid.*, 122.
31. *Ibid.*, 134. For speculation that the friend was Jefferson, see *ibid.*
32. *Ibid.*, 141.
33. Noble E. Cunningham, Jr., "John Beckley: An Early American Party Manager," *WMQ*, 3rd ser., XIII (January 1956), 40–52. Beckley seldom referred to Hamilton without using pejorative words such as "insidious," "contriving," or "contemptible."
34. *The History of the United States for 1796; Including a Variety of Interesting Particulars Relative to the Federal Government Previous to that Period* (Philadelphia, 1797). The charges against Hamilton appeared in chapters 6 and 7 of this work. The complexities surrounding the publication of parts of this book as separate pamphlets or tracts can be followed in *Hamilton Papers*, XXI, 121–122. See also Mitchell, *Hamilton*, 706, n. 24.
35. *Hamilton Papers*, XXI, 132, citing Callender's *History*, 228.
36. The most detailed discussion of the subject and the one on which many other historians have relied is Philip M. Marsh, "John Beckley: Mystery Man of the Early Jeffersonians," *Pennsylvania Magazine of History and Biography*, 57 (January 1948), 54–69.
37. Beckley to Coxe, Oct. 10, 1796, Coxe Papers.

38. *Hamilton Papers,* XXI, 133.
39. For an amplified argument that Coxe furnished Callender with the Reynolds documents, see Cooke, *Tench Coxe,* 248 n.
40. *Hamilton Papers,* XXI, 135.
41. *Ibid.,* 136.
42. See *ibid.,* 135–138.
43. *A Letter to Gen. Hamilton Occasioned by his Letter to . . . Adams,* cited in Mitchell, *Hamilton,* II, 408, 707.
44. Quoted in Miller, *Hamilton,* 523. Abigail Adams agreed, although she was less forthright. "When I have seen that cock sparrow," she wrote to her husband, "I have read his heart in his wicked eyes. . . . They are lasciviousness itself or I have no skill in physiogamy." Quoted in Page Smith, *John Adams,* II, 907.

CHAPTER XVI

1. Quoted in Bradford Perkins, *The First Rapprochement: England and the United States, 1795–1815* (Philadelphia, 1955), 58.
2. Adams to Abigail Adams, Mar. 5, 1797, quoted in Freeman, *Washington,* VII, 437.
3. Quoted in Page Smith, *John Adams,* II, 913, without ref.
4. *American State Papers: Foreign Affairs,* I, 746.
5. Hamilton to Washington, *Hamilton Papers,* XX, 469–470.
6. Hamilton to Smith, Apr. 10, 1797, *ibid.,* XXI, 29–30.
7. Wolcott to Hamilton, Mar. 31, 1797, *ibid.,* XX, 573.
8. Hamilton's letter to Tracy has not been found. (It may be Hamilton's unfound letter of April acknowledged by Tracy on April 6 [*ibid.,* XXI, 8].) The episode related in the text was described some years later by both Hamilton and Adams. Hamilton said that it occurred "immediately after the installment of Mr. Adams as President"; Adams recalled that it took place "at the opening of the special session of Congress in mid May" (Gibbs, *Memoirs,* I, 483).
9. *Ibid.,* citing Adams' *Boston Patriot Letter,* XIII.
10. Charles Francis Adams, ed., *The Works of John Adams,* 10 vols. (Boston, 1850–1856), VII, 522–524 (hereafter cited as Adams, *Works of John Adams*).
11. The one exception to this generalization (depending on what one regards as "serious") was the disagreement between Adams and his cabinet in the summer of 1798 over the relative rank of major generals in the newly augmented army, discussed below.
12. James Richardson, ed., *Compilation of the Messages and Papers of the Presidents, 1789–1897,* 10 vols. (Washington, D.C., 1907), I, 222–229 (hereafter cited as Richardson, *Messages and Papers*).
13. Hamilton to Wolcott, June 6, 1797, *Hamilton Papers,* XXI, 99.
14. Richardson, *Messages and Papers,* I, 253–279.
15. Hamilton to Wolcott, June 5, 1798, *Hamilton Papers,* XXI, 485.
16. There were seven essays in this series, dated Mar. 30, Apr. 4, 7, 12, 16, 19, and 21, and printed in *ibid.,* 381–387, 390–396, 402–408, 412–418, 418–432, 439–440, and 441–447.
17. Mitchell, *Hamilton,* II, 423.
18. See Schachner, *Hamilton,* 375, without specific refs.

19. Hamilton to Timothy Pickering, Mar. 17, 1798, *Hamilton Papers*, XXI, 365.
20. *Ibid.*, 365–366. Hamilton proposed a smiliar program to Oliver Wolcott, Jr., June 5, 1798, *ibid.*, 485–488.
21. Hamilton to Washington, Mar. 8, 1794, *ibid.*, XVI, 134–136.
22. Adams was at this time even willing to enter into an Anglo-American alliance. See Mitchell, *Hamilton*, II, 425.
23. Richardson, *Messages and Papers*, I, 256.
24. For examples of Adams' bellicosity, see his answers to the various addresses that he received from many of the states at this time in Adams, *Works of John Adams*, IX, 194, 196, 198, 203, 204–205, 207, 210, 212. See also Page Smith, *John Adams*, II, 968–969. Only after a reliable report from John Marshall, who returned home on June 18, that the Directory was not so much interested in goading the United States into war as intent on forcing it to follow the lead of France did Adams' war fever subside. He was not even then dissuaded, for, as Page Smith remarks, although Congress before it adjourned in July 1798 "formally abrogated the French treaty of 1778, . . . it disappointed Adams by not going on to a declaration of war." *Ibid.*, 979.
25. A succinct account of the Alien and Sedition Acts is in McLaughlin, *Constitutional History of the United States*, 264–271. Book-length studies are John C. Miller, *Crisis in Freedom: The Alien and Sedition Acts* (Boston, 1951) and James M. Smith, *Freedom's Fetters: The Alien and Sedition Laws and American Civil Liberties* (Ithaca, N.Y., 1956).
26. Hamilton to Pickering, June 7, 1798, *Hamilton Papers*, XXI, 495.
27. Hamilton to Wolcott, June 29, 1798, *ibid.*, 522. Except for the word "body," italics added.
28. *John Adams*, II, 977.
29. See "Introductory Note" to George Washington to Hamilton, July 14, 1798, *Hamilton Papers*, XXII, 4–17.
30. Washington to Hamilton, July 14, 1798, *ibid.*, 18.
31. Adams to McHenry, July 6, 1789, Adams, *Works of John Adams*, VII, 574.
32. The only extant list of Washington's proposals for nominees is found in Washington's letter to Hamilton of July 14, 1799. *Hamilton Papers*, XXII, 19.
33. Freeman, *Washington*, VII, 521.
34. The president stayed in Quincy throughout the dispute over the major generals while his cabinet remained in the capital city. *Hamilton Papers*, XXII, 5.
35. Adams to James McHenry, Aug. 14, 1798, Adams, *Works of John Adams*, VII, 580. Knox believed, as did Adams, that the preference given the principal army officers in 1798 should depend on their relative rank during the American Revolution. This would have put Knox in front, for at the end of the Revolution he outranked both Pinckney and Hamilton. Knox insisted that he still should and implied that he would refuse to serve if his claim were denied. See Knox to James McHenry, Aug. 5, 1798, enclosed in McHenry to Hamilton, Aug. 11, 1798, *Hamilton Papers*, XXII, 69–71.
36. McHenry to Adams, Aug. 22, 1798, in Bernard C. Steiner, *The Life and*

Correspondence of James McHenry . . . (Cleveland, 1907), 325–326.

37. Adams to McHenry, Aug. 29, 1798, Adams, *Works of Adams,* VIII, 588.

38. McHenry to Adams, Sept. 6, 1798, Steiner, *Life . . . of McHenry,* 338.

39. Adams to McHenry, Sept. 13, 1798, Adams, *Works of John Adams,* VIII, 594.

40. McHenry wrote three letters to Washington dated Sept. 7, 10, and 19, 1798; Pickering wrote to the General on Sept. 13. A discussion of these letters and extracts from them are in *Hamilton Papers,* XXII, 14. For Washington's reaction, see his letter to McHenry, Sept. 16, 1798, Fitzpatrick, *Writings of Washington,* XXXVI, 447–448.

41. Wolcott's letter, dated Sept. 17, 1798, is in Gibbs, *Memoirs,* II, 93–99. The secretary of the Treasury reviewed the circumstances surrounding the appointment of the major generals and cautioned the president against a hasty decision to reverse the order in which Washington presumed they were to rank. Wolcott's presentation of the case was a diplomatic reminder of the political implications of Adams' decision. He concluded that ''the least evil will be to suffer Gen. Knox to decline service, if that is his intention. But if he is allowed the rank he claims, and Gen. Hamilton declines . . . the evil will not end with the wound to General Washington's feelings, nor with the public disappointment.'' *Ibid.,* 98.

42. Washington to Adams, Sept. 25, 1798, Fitzpatrick, *Writings of Washington,* XXXVI, 453–462; Adams to Washington, Oct. 9, 1798, Adams, *Works of John Adams,* VIII, 600–601.

43. Adams' *Boston Patriot Letters,* Letter XIV, in Adams, *Works of John Adams,* IX, 294.

CHAPTER XVII

1. These Congressional increments of the nation's military establishment are briefly described in the text above to dispel the confusion that some historians display on the subject. For a succinctly accurate account of the various components of the army, see Richard H. Kohn, *Eagle and Sword,* 229, n.

2. The phrase is from Marshall Smalser's excellent article ''The Federalist Period as an Age of Passion,'' *American Quarterly,* 10 (Winter 1958), 391–419.

3. John F. Hamtramck to Hamilton, Jan. 25, 1799, *Hamilton Papers,* XXII, 437–438.

4. Mitchell, *Hamilton,* II, 466.

5. This situation was rendered worse by the incompetence of Tench Francis, purveyor of public supplies, and Samuel Hodgdon, superintendent of military stores.

6. For an explanation of why recruiting ''was delayed in commencing, and then laggard,'' see Mitchell, *Hamilton,* II, 435–436.

7. For a perceptive explanation of this delay in recruiting, see Kohn, *Eagle and Sword,* 244.

8. *Ibid.,* 243.

9. Somewhat too much emphasis has been placed on Hamilton's record on this issue, however. He was willing to appoint some qualified Republicans as well as aliens with the requisite military experience. For a discussion

of important qualifications to which the traditional view must be subjected, see Mitchell, *Hamilton,* II, 434–435.

10. Washington to Hamilton, Mar. 25, 1799, *Hamilton Papers,* XXII, 586.
11. Hamilton to Washington, July 29, 1798, *ibid.,* 36–39.
12. Washington to Hamilton, Aug. 9, 1798, *ibid.,* 62–64.
13. Hamilton had only one aide, Captain Philip Church, his nephew, who did the requisite copying and as much of the other routine work as he could find time for. A secretary was added to Hamilton's staff in the spring of 1799.
14. For some of the illustrations given in the text, I relied on Mitchell, *Hamilton,* II, 441. Scores of others—too numerous to cite here—may be found in *Hamilton Papers,* XXII. One illustration may suffice. For Hamilton's preoccupation with clothing for the army, see *ibid.,* 54, 245–246, 249, 250, 264, 352, 364, 403, 433, 459–460, 563–564, 581, 587, 591, 593–594, 595–596.
15. For information on Hamilton's role in preparing *Rules and Regulations Respecting the Recruiting Service,* see Hamilton to Jonathan Dayton, Aug. 6, 1798, *Hamilton Papers,* XXII, 50–51, n. 6.
16. Hamilton to John J. U. Rivardi, June 25, 1798; to James McHenry, May 27, 1799; to McHenry, Mar. 21, 1799. *Ibid.,* XXII, 216–222, 151–152, and XXII, 565.
17. Hamilton's proposals are summarized in Mitchell, *Hamilton,* II, 438–439, 450–452. For representative discussions of these subjects by Hamilton, see *Hamilton Papers,* XXII, 29, 392–393, 397, 416–417, 421, 431, 433, 434, 521; XXIII, 103, 247, 596, 603.
18. Gibbs, *Memoirs,* II, 210–211, citing Adams' *Patriot Letter,* XVIII, 85.
19. Mitchell, *Hamilton,* II, 459. That a "war party" existed is undeniable, but it was comparatively small and Hamilton cannot be counted among its members unless his writings are read out of context. A conspicuous example of the latter is a frequently cited letter that the inspector general wrote to Harrison Gray Otis on Jan. 26, 1799. "I should be glad to see, before the close of the Session," Hamilton commented,

> *a law impowering the president, at his discretion, in case a negotiation between the United States and France should not be on foot by the first of August next, or being on foot should terminate without an adjustment of differences, to declare that a state of war exists between the two Countries, and thereupon to employ the Land and Naval forces of the United States in such a manner as shall appear to him most effectual for annoying the Enemy and for preventing and frustrating hostile designs of France, either directly or* indirectly through any of her Allies [Hamilton Papers, *XXII, 440–441*].

This apparent bellicosity is explained in the succeeding sentences of his letter. "This course of proceeding, by postponing the event, and giving time for the intervention of negotiation; would be a further proof of moderation in the Government. . . . If France be really desirous of accommodation, this plan will accelerate her measures to bring it about. If she have not that desire, it is best to anticipate her final vengeance." Hamilton, in other words, was endorsing the policy that the Federalists had followed since the spring of 1798—a program of building up the military strength of the country in order to force France to negotiate and to prepare the United States for war should France remain obdurate. He was not, moreover, making an unequivocal demand for war, but rather asking that the president be authorized to declare it whenever he believed it necessary. For further examples of the manner in which Hamilton's writings have been similarly misinterpreted (particularly his correspondence with Rufus King), see Jacob E. Cooke, "Country Above Party: John Adams and the 1799 Mission to France," in Edmund Willis, ed., *Fame and the Founding Fathers* (Bethlehem, Pa., 1967), especially 59, n. 3 (hereafter cited as Cooke, "Country Above Party").

20. Hamilton to Lafayette, Jan. 6, 1799, *Hamilton Papers*, XXII, 404–405.
21. This contemporary partisan charge has so often received the stamp of scholarly approval as to become almost a historical dogma. See, as virtually random examples, Wilfred E. Binckley, *Political Parties: Their Natural History* (New York, 1958), 82; Gilbert Chinard, *Honest John Adams* (Boston, 1933), 276–279; John S. Bassett, *The Federalist System: 1789–1801* (New York, 1906), 251; Stephen Kurtz, *The Presidency of John Adams: The Collapse of Federalism, 1795–1800* (Philadelphia, 1957), 314–317; Manning Dauer, *The Adams Federalists* (Baltimore, 1933), 209–210.
22. Samuel E. Morison, *The Life and Letters of Harrison Gray Otis, 1765–1848*, 2 vols. (Boston, 1913), I, 102.
23. Gibbs, *Memoirs*, II, 41–42.
24. For succinct bibliographical information on the Kentucky and Virginia resolutions protesting the Alien and Sedition Acts, see *Hamilton Papers*, XXII, 454, n. 1. The debate in the Virginia legislature may be followed in *The Virginia Report of 1799–1800, touching the Alien and Sedition Laws; Together with the Virginia Resolutions of December 21, 1798, The Debate and Proceedings Thereon in the House of Delegates of Virginia, and Several Other Documents . . .* (Richmond, Va., 1850), 108.
25. *Ibid.*, 141. Other southern Federalists concurred with Lee and Taylor. See, for example, James Iredell to Mrs. Iredell, Jan. 24, 1799; William R. Davie to James Iredell, June 17, 1799. Griffith J. McRee, *Life and Correspondence of James Iredell*, 2 vols. (New York, 1857–1858), II, 543, 577.
26. See Philip G. Davidson, "Virginia and the Alien and Sedition Laws," *American Historical Review*, 36 (January 1931), 336–342.
27. Hamilton to Sedgwick, Feb. 2, 1799, *Hamilton Papers*, XXII, 453.
28. It should also be emphasized, however, that Hamilton, as he surely knew, was not empowered to dispatch an army to put down a domestic insurrection. Such power resided in the president. Unless Hamilton was willing to engineer an armed coup d'etat—and there is no reason to believe that he was—the most that he could in this instance have done was to recommend to Adams that the army be employed to suppress domestic opposition to federal laws, a recommendation that Adams certainly would have spurned.
29. Rufus King to Timothy Pickering, Feb. 26, 1798, Charles R. King, ed., *The Life and Correspondence of Rufus King*, 6 vols. (New York, 1894), II, 283–284 (hereafter cited as King, *King*).

30. The bulk of King's correspondence on the subject was, properly, with Secretary of State Timothy Pickering. See, for example, King to Pickering, Feb. 7, 26, Apr. 2, 6, Aug. 17, and Oct. 20, 1798, King, *King*, II, 283–284, 305–306, 393–394, 453–454, 650, and 653.

31. In response to King's importunities, the secretary of state adopted a policy of calculated silence. For his part, the president on Oct. 3, 1798, passed on to Pickering the duplicate of a letter that Miranda had written to the president on Mar. 24, 1798, outlining his plans. "Read it and think of it," Adams instructed Pickering. "It will not be in character for me to answer the letter. Will any notice of it, in any manner, be proper?" (Adams, *Works of John Adams*, VIII, 600). The secretary of state presumably thought not, for he did not answer the letter. See King, *King*, II, 661.

32. Hamilton to Francisco de Miranda, Aug. 22, 1798, *Hamilton Papers*, XXII, 155–156. Despite a renewed plea from Miranda and the insistence of Rufus King (Miranda to Hamilton, Oct. 19, Nov. 10, 1798; King to Hamilton, Oct. 20, 1798, *ibid.*, 205–206, 207), Hamilton did not again write to the Latin American, presumably because he soon realized that Miranda's project was for the time being impracticable. Nevertheless, Hamilton did not relinquish hope that the United States might yet gain possession of Florida and Louisiana. Hamilton to Harrison Gray Otis, Jan. 26, 1799, *ibid.*, 440–441.

33. Arthur Whitaker, *The Mississippi Question, 1795–1803: A Study in Trade, Politics and Diplomacy* (New York, 1934), 117.

34. *Federalist*, 72.

35. This is the contention of my article "Country Above Party," whose thesis is briefly summarized here.

36. *Federalist*, 212.

37. Richardson, *Messages and Papers*, I, 282.

38. Sedgwick to Hamilton. Feb. 22, 1799; Pickering to Hamilton, Feb. 24, 1799. *Hamilton Papers*, XXII, 494, 500.

39. Richardson, *Messages and Papers*, I, 256. Adams had in effect repeated his position a little more than two months earlier. In his annual message of Dec. 8, 1798, Adams had informed Congress that "nothing is discoverable in the conduct of France which ought to change or relax our measures of defense. On the contrary, to extend and invigorate them is our true policy" (*ibid.*, 262). For congressional reaction to Adams' announcement of Feb. 18, see Cooke, "Country Above Party," 55.

40. *John Adams*, II, 1001.

41. The letter to which Adams referred is in *American State Papers: Foreign Relations*, II, 289. For a detailed account of the several sources from which Adams learned of the Directory's altered mood and for the circuitous manner in which Talleyrand conveyed this conciliatoriness to Adams, see Cooke, "Country Above Party," 59–60.

42. *Boston Patriot Letters*, XV, 73.

43. Hamilton to Theodore Sedgwick, Feb. 21, 1799, *Hamilton Papers*, XXII, 493.

44. *Letter . . . Concerning . . . John Adams, Hamilton Papers*, XXV, 218.

45. *Ibid.*, 220.

46. *Correspondence between the Hon. John Adams . . . and . . . Wm. Cun-*

ningham . . . (Boston, 1823), Letter XXX, 93 (hereafter cited as *Cunningham Letters*).

47. Adams to Pickering, Aug. 6, 1799, Adams, *Works of John Adams*, IX, 10–12.
48. Pickering to Adams, Sept. 11, 1799, *ibid.*, 23–25.
49. *Boston Patriot Letters*, XVI, 78–79.
50. Wolcott to Hamilton, Oct. 2, 1800, Gibbs, *Memoirs*, II, 277–278.
51. Adams to Pickering, Oct. 16, 1799, Adams, *Works of John Adams*, IX, 39.
52. Hamilton to Washington, Oct. 21, 1799, *Hamilton Papers*, XXIII, 548–549.
53. Wolcott to George Cabot, Nov. 7, 1799, Gibbs, *Memoirs*, II, 286–287.
54. Hamilton to Sedgwick, Feb. 27, 1800, *Hamilton Papers*, XXIV, 270.
55. *Cunningham Letters*, XXX, 93.
56. For an amplification of this argument, see Cooke, "Country Above Party," 72–77.
57. Hamilton to Martha Washington, Jan. 12, 1800, *Hamilton Papers*, XXIV, 184–185.
58. Hamilton to Tobias Lear, Jan. 2, 1800, *ibid.*, 155.
59. *Ibid.*, 586.

CHAPTER XVIII

1. McHenry to Washington, Nov. 10, 1799, quoted in Fitzpatrick, *Writings of Washington*, XXXVII, 428, n. 74.
2. Hamilton to Jonathan Dayton, October–November 1799, *Hamilton Papers*, XXIV, 599–604. The quotation is on page 600.
3. Gibbs, *Memoirs*, I, 464, citing Adams' *Patriot Letters*, XIII.
4. John Smith to Tench Coxe, May 8, 1800, Coxe Papers.
5. Mitchell, *Hamilton*, II, 467–468.
6. Hamilton to Jay, May 7, 1800, *Hamilton Papers*, XXIV, 464–466.
7. Hamilton to Rufus King, July 25, 1792, *ibid.*, XII, 99–100. For a somewhat strained defense of Hamilton's proposal to Jay in 1800, see McDonald, *Hamilton*, 446, n. 42.
8. See *Hamilton Papers*, XXIV, 467, n. 4.
9. See James McHenry to Hamilton, Mar. 13, 1799, *ibid.*, XXII, 529–532, especially 532, n. 12.
10. See *ibid.*, XXV, 171. The inference that Adams' decision to disband the army was, at least in part, due to his desire to undermine the influence of Hamilton and his supporters is drawn from Page Smith, *John Adams*, II, 1025–1026.
11. *Ibid.*, 1027.
12. For information on McHenry's resignation, see McHenry to Hamilton, May 12, 13, and 20, 1800, *Hamilton Papers*, XXIV, 476–477, 478, and 506–512. The fullest account is in McHenry to James McHenry, Jr., May 20, 1800, enclosed in McHenry to Hamilton, May 20, 1800, *ibid.*, 507–512.
13. Octavius Pickering and Charles W. Upham, *The Life of Timothy Pickering*, 4 vols. (Boston, 1867–1873), III, 488.
14. *Gouverneur Morris* (Boston, 1888), 279–280.
15. Hamilton to Sedgwick, May 4, 1800, *Hamilton Papers*, XXIV, 452–453.

16. Hamilton's stratagems to elevate Pinckney over Adams are described in masterful detail in an introductory note to Hamilton to Benjamin Stoddert, June 6, 1800, *ibid.*, 574–585.

17. Jakob Burckhardt, *Force and Freedom: Reflections on History* (New York, 1943), 313.

18. For information on the role of Coxe and of the *Aurora* (of which Coxe was a frequent contributor and silent partner), see Cooke, *Tench Coxe*, 371–389, *passim*. My account of the election of 1800 above is largely based on the latter work as well as on unpublished research on the subject in the Coxe Papers.

19. See Page Smith, *John Adams*, II, 1038–1041.

20. Quoted in Peterson, *Jefferson*, 637, without ref.

21. Quoted in *ibid.*, 638, without date.

22. Malone, *Jefferson*, III, 482.

23. See Hamilton to John Adams, Aug. 1, 1800; Hamilton to Oliver Wolcott, Jr., July 1, 1800 (especially notes thereto), *Hamilton Papers, XXV,* 51–52, 4–5.

24. For a more damning and detailed explanation of Adams' suspiciousness, see Theodore Sedgwick to Rufus King, Sept. 26, 1800, in Mitchell, *Hamilton*, II, 478, citing King Papers, New-York Historical Society.

25. Hamilton to Adams, Aug. 1, 1800, *Hamilton Papers, XXV,* 51.

26. Page Smith, *John Adams,* II, 1043.

27. Allan Nevins, *The Evening Post: A Century of Journalism* (New York, 1922), 14.

28. Hamilton to Oliver Wolcott, Jr., July 1, 1800, *Hamilton Papers, XXV,* 4–5.

29. For the comments of Hamilton's allies, see George Cabot to Hamilton, Aug. 21, 23, 1800; Fisher Ames to Hamilton, Aug. 26, 1800; Wolcott to Hamilton, Sept. 3, 1800, *ibid.*, 74–75, 77–79, 86–88, 104–111.

30. Cabot to Hamilton, Aug. 21, 1800, *ibid.*, 75.

31. Page Smith, *John Adams,* II, 1043.

32. Wolcott to Hamilton, Sept. 3, 1800, *Hamilton Papers, XXV,* 104–111.

33. John Quincy Adams' comment is in Henry Adams, ed., *Documents Relating to New England Federalism, 1800–1815* (Boston, 1877), 149–151.

34. Mitchell, *Hamilton,* II, 478.

35. *Ibid.*

36. *Young Man Luther: A Study in Psychoanalysis and History* (New York, 1958), 45.

37. Hamilton to Gouverneur Morris, Feb. 29, 1802, *Hamilton Papers, XXV,* 544.

38. *Memoirs of Aaron Burr with . . . Selections from his Correspondence,* 2 vols. (New York, 1857), II, 65–66.

39. *Hamilton Papers, XXV,* 178. The admirable scholarly detective work of Hamilton's editors can be followed in *ibid.*, 173–178.

40. Mitchell, *Hamilton,* II, 474. First published in the Philadelphia *Aurora,* Hamilton's attack on his own party chieftain was given nationwide publicity in the last months of the campaign.

41. For full bibliographical information on Hamilton's *Letter* (previously cited here), see *Hamilton Papers, XXV,* 174–175, n. 27, 28.

42. *Letter . . . Concerning . . . John Adams, Hamilton Papers,* XXV, 186.
43. *Ibid.,* 190.
44. *Ibid.,* 229.
45. *Ibid.,* 190.
46. *Ibid.,* 233–234.
47. Hamilton to Oliver Wolcott, Jr., Sept. 26, 1800, *ibid.,* 122–123.
48. Mitchell, *Hamilton,* II, 474.
49. Malone, *Jefferson,* III, 488.
50. Morse to Wolcott, Oct. 27, 1800, quoted in *Hamilton Papers,* XXV, 178.
51. Page Smith, *John Adams,* 1045, citing Webster's *A Letter to General Hamilton occasioned by his letter to President Adams by a Federalist* (New York, 1800), no p. cited.
52. Troup to King, Nov. 9, 1800, King, *King,* III, 330–332.
53. For information on this issue, see *Hamilton Papers,* XXV, 182.
54. Only in South Carolina could it be argued that Hamilton's *Letter* had any effect. For an explanation of this comment, see *ibid.,* XXV, 185.
55. Troup to King, Dec. 31, 1800, King, *King,* III, 358–359.
56. Beckley to Tench Coxe, Sept. 29, 1800, Coxe Papers.
57. See Ulrich B. Phillips, ed., "South Carolina Federalist Correspondence, 1789–1799," *American Historical Review,* XIV (1909), 529–543, 731–743.
58. John Dawson to Tench Coxe, Dec. 12, 1800, Coxe Papers.

CHAPTER XIX

1. For Hamilton's correspondence with these and other prominent Federalists, see his letters to Oliver Wolcott, Jr., Dec. 16, 1800; to Theodore Sedgwick, Dec. 22, 1800; to Harrison Gray Otis, Dec. 23, 1800; to Gouverneur Morris, Dec. 24, 1800, Jan. 9, 13, 1801; to James Bayard, Dec. 27, 1800, Jan. 16, 1801; to James Ross, Dec. 29, 1800; to James McHenry, Jan. 4, 1801; and to John Rutledge, Jr., Jan. 4, 1801, *Hamilton Papers,* XXV, 257, 286–288, 269–270, 271, 271–273, 304–305, 314–315, 276–277, 319–324, 280–281, 292–293, and 293–298.
2. Hamilton to Wolcott, Dec. 16, 1800, *ibid.,* 257.
3. Hamilton to Morris, Dec. 24, 1800, *ibid.,* 272.
4. Hamilton to Otis, Dec. 23, 1800, *ibid.,* 271. See also Hamilton to Bayard, Dec. 27, 1800, *ibid.,* 276.
5. Hamilton to Ross, Dec. 29, 1800, *ibid.,* 280.
6. Hamilton to McHenry, Jan. 4, 1801, *ibid.,* 292.
7. Hamilton to Bayard, Dec. 27, 1800, *ibid.,* 276.
8. Hamilton to Wolcott, Dec. 1800, *ibid.,* 287.
9. Hamilton to Rutledge, Jan. 4, 1801, *ibid.,* 296.
10. Hamilton to Wolcott, Dec. 1800, *ibid.,* 287.
11. Hamilton to Morris, Dec. 24, 1800, *ibid.,* 272.
12. Hamilton to Otis, Dec. 23, 1800, *ibid.,* 271.
13. Hamilton to Ross, Dec. 29, 1800, *ibid.,* 280.
14. Hamilton to Rutledge, Jan. 4, 1801, *ibid.,* 294; italics added.
15. *Ibid.,* 287.
16. Hamilton to Wolcott, December 1800, *ibid.,* 287.
17. *Ibid.*

18. Hamilton to Bayard, Dec. 27, 1800, *ibid.*, 276.
19. Hamilton to Bayard, Jan. 16, 1801, *ibid.*, 323.
20. Under "principle" Hamilton included a systematic philosophy of government. In commenting that as to Burr's theory "no mortal can tell what it is," Hamilton implied that his own theory had been made clear. In asserting that his rival cared nothing for "institutions that . . . would promise lasting prosperity and glory to the Country," he similarly implied that as secretary of the Treasury his own concern for the country's institutions had been in the service of national "prosperity and glory" (to Ross, Dec. 29, 1800, *ibid.*, 280). For other comments about Burr's lack of any "theory" of government, see Hamilton to Rutledge, Jan. 4, 1801, *ibid.*, 297.
21. Hamilton to Morris, Dec. 24, 1800, *ibid.*, 272–279. For similar recommendations by Hamilton on this score, see also Hamilton to Ross, Dec. 29, 1800, to Wolcott, December 1800, to McHenry, Jan. 4, 1801, to Rutledge, Jan. 4, 1801, *ibid.*, 281, 288, 292, 295.
22. Hamilton to Bayard, Jan. 16, 1801, *ibid.*, 319–320.
23. Hamilton made a similar proposal to most of his congressional correspondents. The one described in the text is from his letter to John Rutledge, Jr., Jan. 4, 1801, *ibid.*, 295.
24. Jefferson to Tench Coxe, Feb. 11, 1801, Jefferson Papers, Library of Congress.
25. Henry Adams, *History of the United States of America During the Administrations of Thomas Jefferson and James Madison*, 9 vols. (New York, 1889–1891; reprinted 1962), I, 185 (hereafter cited as Adams, *History*).
26. Richardson, *Messages and Papers*, I, 309–312.
27. "An Address to the Electors of the State of New York," Mar. 21, 1801, *Hamilton Papers*, XXV, 365.
28. Hamilton, *Intimate Life*, 336, without ref.
29. Schuyler to Hamilton, Aug. 25, 1800, *Hamilton Papers*, XXV, 83–84.
30. Hamilton, *Intimate Life*, 338.
31. *Ibid.*, 348–349.
32. For a detailed recounting of the episode, see *Hamilton Papers*, XXV, 435–438. For contemporary accounts of the duel, see "The Duels between _____ Price and Philip Hamilton, and George L. Eacher," *Historical Magazine*, 2 (October 1867), 193–204.
33. *Hamilton Papers*, XXV, 437.
34. *Ibid.*, 436.
35. Troup to Rufus King, Dec. 5, 1801, King, *King*, IV, 28.
36. Hamilton to Bayard, Apr. 16–21, 1802, and Bayard to Hamilton, Apr. 25, 1802, *Hamilton Papers*, XXV, 605–610, 613.
37. The most conspicuous and ambitious of the latter was a series of eighteen articles entitled "The Examination" and signed "Lucius Crassus" that appeared in the *New York Evening Post* during the winter of 1801–1802. See *ibid.*, 455–457, 458–464, 464–468, 469–475, 476–480, 484–489, 491–495, 495–497, 500–506, 506–511, 514–520, 529–535, 539–544, 546–552, 552–558, 564–569, 569–576, 589–597.
38. G. S. Hillard, ed., *Memoirs and Correspondence of Jeremiah Mason* (Cambridge, Mass., 1873), 32–33.
39. *Hamilton*, 551.

40. *Memoirs . . . of Jeremiah Mason*, 32–33.
41. Quoted in Malone, *Jefferson*, IV, 256; see 251–261 for an excellent analysis of Jefferson's position on the cession of Louisiana.
42. "For the Evening Post," Feb. 8, 1803, *Hamilton Papers*, XXVI, 83.
43. Miller, *Hamilton*, 562, a work to which I am indebted for the observations in the paragraph above.
44. Leonard W. Levy, *Jefferson and Civil Liberties: The Darker Side* (Cambridge, Mass., 1963), 46.
45. The germane paragraph of Callender's calumny that was reprinted in the *Wasp* is quoted in Goebel, *Law Practice*, I, 777. See also McDonald, *Hamilton*, 358, 448 n. 9, where McDonald points out the errors made by other historians in quoting the slanderous remarks.
46. Pertinent documents concerning *People* v. *Croswell*, plus an admirably thorough and informative introductory note, are printed in Goebel, *Law Practice*, I, 775–848.
47. Clinton Rossiter, *Alexander Hamilton and the Constitution* (New York, 1964), 104, 301, citing Kent MS. on Croswell case, New York Public Library, 62–63.
48. Goebel, *Law Practice*, I, 813, 820–821, 822.
49. *Ibid.*, 809. For an excellent amplified discussion of the case that includes memorable quotations from Hamilton's brief in addition to those in the text above, see Miller, *Hamilton*, 553–556.
50. McDonald, *Hamilton*, 359.

CHAPTER XX

1. The quoted phrase is from Milton Lamask, *Aaron Burr . . . , 1756–1805* (New York, 1979), 302.
2. "Speech at a Meeting of Federalists in Albany," Feb. 10, 1804, *Hamilton Papers*, XXVI, 189.
3. Henry Adams, ed., *Documents Relating to New England Federalism*, 167; Adams, *History*, II, 184–185.
4. Erikson, *Young Man Luther* (New York, 1958), 99, 232.
5. Harold C. Syrett and Jean G. Cooke, eds., *Interview at Weehawken* (Middletown, Conn., 1960), 44–45 (hereafter cited as Syrett and Cooke, *Interview*). The factual features of my account of the duel are drawn from this comprehensive collection of documents.
6. *Ibid.*, 43; italics added.
7. *Ibid.*, 53, 54.
8. *Ibid.*, 58, 61, 59, 63, 81, 94–95.
9. Miller, *Hamilton*, 571.
10. Hamilton to William Gordon, Sept. 5, 1779, *Hamilton Papers*, II, 154.
11. Wolcott to Mrs. Oliver Wolcott, Jr., July 11, 1804, in Hamilton, *Intimate Life*, 405.
12. Syrett and Cooke, *Interview*, 100.
13. *Ibid.*, 102.
14. Adams, *History*, II, 189.
15. Erikson, *Young Man Luther*, 260.
16. *Ibid.*, 231.
17. *Hamilton Papers*, XXVI, 293.
18. *Ibid.*, 308.

19. Fawn Brodie, "Discussion" of Jacob E. Cooke, "Alexander Hamilton: Psychoanalysis and History" (with commentaries), *Dialogue: A Journal of Psychoanalytic Perspectives,* 3 (Summer 1979), 17–46. Brodie's remark is on 35.
20. *Ibid.*
21. Dr. David Hosack to William Coleman, Aug. 17, 1804, in Hamilton, *Intimate Life,* 400.
22. *Ibid.,* 402, 403.
23. Angelica Church to Philip Schuyler, [July 11,] 1804, in *ibid.,* 405.
24. Dr. David Hosack to William Coleman, Aug. 17, 1804, in *ibid.,* 403.
25. Wolcott to Mrs. Oliver Wolcott, Jr., July 11, 1804, in *ibid.,* 406.
26. Bishop Benjamin Moore to William Coleman, [July 13?] 1804, in *ibid.,* n. 1.

Index

Note: Alexander Hamilton is abbreviated as AH in this index.